D1601530

DATE DUE

DEMCO 38-296

K

Zhou Enlai and the Foundations of Chinese Foreign Policy

Kuo-kang Shao

St. Martin's Press
New York

ZHOU ENLAI AND THE FOUNDATIONS OF CHINESE FOREIGN POLICY

Copyright © 1996 by Kuo-kang Shao

of America. No part of this book

DS 778 .A2 C467 1996   tsoever without written permission

in critical articles or reviews. For

Shao, Kuo-kang.   ly and Reference Division, 175 Fifth

Zhou Enlai and the
  foundations of Chinese

Library of Congress Cataloging-in-Publication Data

Shao, Kuo-kang.
    Zhou Enlai and the foundations of Chinese foreign policy / Kuo
-kang Shao.
        p. cm.
    Includes bibliographical references and index.
    ISBN 0-312-15892-0
    1. Chou, En-lai, 1898-1976. 2. China—Foreign
relations—1949-1976. I. Title.
DS778.A2C467 1996   96-36088
                                         CIP

Book design by Acme Art, Inc.

First Edition: November 1996
10 9 8 7 6 5 4 3 2 1

I wish to dedicate this work to my wife, Hsi-ping, and to my children, Yai-ping, Yu-ling, and Kan-wen.

CONTENTS

PART 1
The Period of Germination and Preparation: 1910s-1940s

PART 2
Refined Negotiating Skills and the Power Base

PART 3:
The Reality of National Power
and the Foundations of Chinese Foreign Policy

LIST OF ABBREVIATIONS

CQ   China Quarterly

DSB   *Department of State Bulletin*

HSWC   *Hu Shi wen cun* (Selected Essays of Hu Shi) (Shanghai: Ya-dung-shu-quan, 1926)

MZDXJ   *Mao-Zedong-xuan-ji* (Selected Works of Mao Zedong) 4 vols. (Beijing: Ren-min-chu-ban-she, 1951-1960)

NCNA   *New China News Agency*

NYT   *New York Times*

PC   *People's China*

PELZ   *Zhou-Zong-li qing shao-nian shi-dai shi-wen-shu-xin-ji* (Poems, Essays and Letters Composed and Written by Premier Zhou at a Young Age) (Sichuan: Ren-min-chu-ban-she, 1979)

RMRB   *Ren-min ri-bao* (People's Daily), Beijing

SWZEL-1   *Selected Works of Zhou Enlai,* vol. 1 (Beijing: Foreign Languages Press, 1981)

US Relations   U.S. Department of State, *United States Relations with*
with China   *China* (Washington, D.C.: Government Printing Office, 1949)

ZELWJ, 1-2   *Zhou Enlai tong-zhi lu-Ou wen-ji* (The European Correspondence of Comrade Zhou Enlai) 2 vols. (Beijing: Wen-wu chu-ban-she, 1979)

ZELXJ-2   *Zhou Enlai-xuan-ji* (Selected Works of Zhou Enlai) vol. 2 (Beijing: Ren-min-chu-ban-she, 1984)

ACKNOWLEDGMENTS

It is really gratifying for me to have finished this book, with my limited financial resources. In writing this book, I have used primary sources from a number of university libraries and, therefore, wish to express my sincere thanks to Cornell University, Columbia University, the University of Pennsylvania, the University of Wisconsin (Whitewater), Wilkes University, and the University of Central Florida.

The contribution my wife has made to this book is deeper and broader than what can be acknowledged here. She was a constant source of inspiration and strength for me. Every chapter in this book has been improved by her thoughtful comments and criticism.

My thanks to Madeline Gutin Perri and Elizabeth Gratch, who shared the burden of reading and improving the manuscript. I also wish to express thanks to Eileen Stone for the unusual care she exercised in typing the manuscript.

INTRODUCTION

The idea for this book was conceived in the summer of 1986. After some consideration I felt that, despite the vast literature on Chinese foreign relations and diplomacy, there was still no in-depth study of Zhou Enlai's concepts of statecraft available for a general audience, nor was there any focused analysis of Zhou's negotiating skills and his conduct of Chinese foreign policy in the years 1949 to 1976. Thus, I began to pursue this project.

What started as a search for an understanding of the man in relation to his world and his revolutionary and postrevolutionary activities soon became something far more serious. The more I observed, the more interested I became in writing about Zhou's management of China's foreign affairs. The more I studied the books and articles that had already been written about Zhou, the more I recognized the need for a real understanding of the development of Zhou's thinking from his early period of "practical learning" to his later pragmatic approach to China's foreign policy issues. I must emphasize that this is a study of Zhou's views on the practice of China's foreign relations and diplomacy and not a biography of the man.

The search for an explanation of the unique elements and nature of Zhou's conduct of Chinese foreign policy during the years between 1949 and 1976[1] led me from the study of Chinese pragmatism to Zhou's world; the makeup of his personality; his early views on international relations, diplomacy, and foreign policy; and his political role in China. By examining Zhou's thoughts and actions, this book serves as an analytical tool to help the reader comprehend Chinese foreign policy objectives under Zhou's guidance. It is also an attempt to bring scholarship on Zhou up to date as well as to present a close-up view of Zhou as a person. In addition, it provides the reader with greater understanding of the linkage between the characteristics of Chinese philosophical pragmatism and their influence on the formation and conduct of Chinese foreign policy during the most critical period of Communist China.

My approach is to trace Zhou's search for national security and China's diplomatic flexibility and economic growth. Three main objectives, therefore, are embodied in this study: first, to identify the roots and central manifestations of Zhou's pragmatism; second, to examine the influence of Zhou's pragmatic thinking on Chinese foreign policy; and, third, to analyze Zhou's negotiating style and skills. This is a study of how Zhou, the quintessential pragmatist, shaped China's relations with the outside world in lasting ways. It is important to note that Zhou's lifetime spanned the Chinese Communist movement, the Chinese Communist Party's rise to power through civil war, the restoration of China's prestige among Third World nations, the formation of an alliance with the Soviet Union, and diplomatic rapprochement with the United States. As foreign minister of the People's Republic of China (PRC) from 1949 to 1958 and its premier until his death in January 1976, Zhou, among all PRC leaders, had the longest and most direct involvement with diplomacy as an instrument to safeguard China's security interests in response to perceived changes in regional and global distributions of power.

Two explanatory notes are appropriate at the outset of this book, one concerning the terms *foreign policy, diplomacy,* and *pragmatism* as defined and practiced by Zhou, the other having to do with the author's underlying assumptions. It should be pointed out that the influence of Zhou's nondoctrinal approach to Chinese foreign policy in the years between 1949 and 1976 was profound and that diplomacy, as an art of negotiation, had always been in the forefront of his numerous intellectual interests and practical pursuits. The significance of Zhou's approach to China's foreign policy, moreover, lay in his contribution to the development of a pragmatic method as well as to the resolution of many concrete problems with China's neighboring countries and beyond through broad-scale diplomacy and negotiations. For more than two decades Chinese foreign policy under Zhou's guidance amply demonstrated the unusual characteristic of being adaptable to changing conditions, both at home and abroad.

The term *foreign policy,* as used here, refers to the course of action that the Chinese government, under Zhou's guidance, pursued in handling relations with other governments in the first two and a half decades of its existence. It was the substance of China's external relations.[2] To a considerable extent it was the process through which Zhou translated Chinese national objectives into specific courses of diplomatic action. In the final analysis Chinese foreign policy under Zhou's guidance, if it were to succeed, required both timing and flexibility. He had to seize the actual power situation and the opportunity to meet specific contingencies.

Diplomacy, in the strict sense of the term, indicates the methods and techniques used by the agents conducting the foreign affairs of a state.[3] It provides machinery and personnel by which foreign policy is executed. The objective of Chinese diplomacy under Zhou's leadership, and of foreign policy, was to protect China's security by means of negotiation, if possible. Negotiation, meaning the pursuit of an agreement by finding a middle ground through extensive personal interaction, was, in Zhou's view, essentially a bargaining process that could take place either through ordinary diplomatic channels or in international conferences. It could be conducted on a bilateral or multilateral basis, although the classic simplicity of bilateral negotiations always remained the core of Zhou's diplomatic activities.

Zhou's personal negotiations with foreign leaders and governments over a period of thirty years did not consist simply of his prepared speeches delivered at international meetings or pronouncements at state banquets and in press rooms, nor were they purely cold and mechanical discussions. His negotiating skills and methods at the conference table and other personal qualities as a seasoned negotiator played a significant role. In other words, Zhou's skill as a negotiator was as important an element of China's national power as its military capability. The care with which Zhou prepared the ground for discussion was a significant factor in his success.

This book explores extensively the question of how Zhou's concept of pragmatism influenced both the formation and conduct of China's foreign policy. The word *pragmatism* has many connotations. Here, I use it in a very narrow sense. Pragmatism, an antidote to doctrinal rigidity, is a method for the study of problems, both domestic and international. Implicit in the definition of pragmatism used throughout this book is its nature as a practical, less ideology-oriented approach to diplomacy and the development of foreign policy objectives, as taken by China under Zhou's guidance. Zhou stressed China's diplomatic flexibility and fluid state-to-state relations regardless of the differences among political systems. Pragmatism is a mode of thinking that determines an action on the basis of a set of rational and practical criteria rather than the prescriptions of any abstract theory.[4] In Zhou's case, he emphasized practical learning, concrete facts, and tangible national interests such as territorial integrity, economic development, China's pivotal role in the Third World, and its working relationships with the United States and the Soviet Union. In short, the pragmatic approach encouraged Chinese foreign policy to grow out of political rationality as well as necessity.

Zhou's lifelong devotion to pragmatism in the field of interstate relations and foreign policy stemmed from his belief that it was necessary to make proper adjustments to the constraints imposed by a particular time, a specific place, and evolving global realities. His experience of trial and error led him to value highly the "process of development" and "accommodation." Moreover, he considered pragmatic accommodation not only as a justification for diplomatic maneuvering but also an important modus operandi in conducting foreign policy. Thus, he naturally regarded the national and strategic interests of China as the moving force behind Chinese foreign policy. The intricacies of international relations for him were, to some extent, a drama in which one could not be quite sure of what might happen next. The "new China" had no useful precedents to go by and hence had to strike new ground in the sphere of foreign policy strategy. Therefore, the pragmatic principles were essentially statements of what was possible for Zhou to achieve by certain means under certain constraints. As the circumstances of international relations changed, so too would the expectations of what could and should be achieved through the process of adjustment. Change was indeed one of the perennial motifs in the history of international relations, and those who eschewed a deterministic view of history and politics could take advantage of the fluidity created by change to achieve their policy objectives. Zhou tended to deal with China's foreign policy issues and evolving global circumstances through careful experimentation based on rational analysis in his efforts to search for viable foreign policy options.

This book is organized into three parts. Part 1 examines the young Zhou's intellectual development in general and the roots and nature of his early pragmatic thought and actual practice in particular. Part 2 deals with Zhou's negotiating skills and his role in China's foreign policy decision-making process. Part 3 analyzes Sino-Soviet and Sino-American relations as well as the role of the Third World in Zhou's global strategy. In order to understand Zhou's role as a foreign policy leader in China it is essential not only to pay special attention to Zhou's early life as a practitioner of the principle of pragmatism and his initial views on interstate relations, diplomacy, and foreign policy but also to study his role in laying the foundations of Chinese foreign policy in the years from 1949 to 1976.

PART 1

The Period of Germination and Preparation: 1910s-1940s

CHAPTER 1

The Roots of Zhou's Pragmatism

There are a number of valuable biographical studies of Zhou Enlai without which this book could not have been written.[1] There is, however, no comprehensive study of Zhou's intellectual development and his influence on Chinese foreign policy during the period from 1949 to 1976. In this chapter an effort will be made to trace the key strands of ideas that influenced Zhou's approaches to knowledge in general and to political issues in particular. Three elements are identified for this study: (1) the pragmatic ingredients in the philosophy of early Qing scholars, notably Gu Yanwu (1613-82) and Wang Fuzhi (1619-92); (2) the evolutionary theory in Darwinian hypotheses; and (3) John Dewey's experimental method as interpreted and publicized by his student Hu Shi. The purpose of the analysis is to identify the core of Zhou's lifelong pragmatic thought and practice. A systematic analysis of Zhou's early writings reveals that during his formative years he was influenced by a wide range of ideas. He later used these efforts to interpret and conduct international relations.

I will first turn to Zhou's family background and education, with special focus on the influence of Chinese and Western pragmatic philosophy upon Zhou during the early stage of his life.

Zhou Enlai was born at Huaian in Jiangsu Province on March 5, 1898, the son of a Chinese gentry family. His parents, Zhou Yinen (1877-1942) and Wan Donger (1877-1907), maintained close ties with other clan members in both Huaian and Shaoxing in Zhejiang Province. By parental arrangement Zhou was turned over to the household of his second uncle, Yigan (Tiao-chih), for upbringing, and for the next ten years he lived with his foster mother in his grandfather's compound at Bao-you-qiao, a village in the Shaoxing district.[2] There, Zhou received a traditional education in the Chinese classics. His foster mother exhibited a keen interest in his education and engaged a Western missionary to teach him the so-called new knowledge at home, including the English language. In the spring of 1910, at the age of twelve, Zhou left Shaoxing for Shenyang (then called Mukden), the capital of Manchuria. He first lived with another uncle, Yiqian (Tsien-chen), who was a perceptive observer of current sociopolitical and economic problems in China. Later, Zhou stayed with his fourth uncle, Yigang, a police commissioner. Zhou became quite adept at adapting and adjusting to these constant changes in living arrangements and gained considerable composure and flexibility.

During these early years there was a special need for the young Zhou to accommodate his austere, strong-willed, and intelligent second aunt (also his foster mother), who ran her household with an iron hand. Zhou's need to take care of other family members and to survive in the Zhou clan, with all its internal strains, gave him the opportunity to acquire a deft subtlety in dealing with different people under the most difficult circumstances. It is equally true that Zhou was reared in a disciplined household that fostered his strong sense of family duty and loyalty and also a personal sense of humility. This complex family situation, above all, taught the young Zhou to keep calm and to not talk back or take sides in family arguments and disputes.[3] Zhou always retained an affectionate memory of his foster mother, and his extraordinary ability to adapt to the changing realities throughout his life was, undoubtedly, a natural outcome of his unique childhood and early-adolescent experiences.

Zhou finished the initial phase of his formal education in 1912, at the Dongquan primary school, a missionary-sponsored institution near the eastern gate of the city of Shenyang. Manchuria's distinctive atmosphere proved to be a tremendous influence to the young Zhou. In the northeast region of China the "frontier spirit" was still strong and in Manchuria what really mattered was not cultural refinement and racial identity but, rather, one's willpower, vitality, and character. In retrospect, Zhou's dynamic and expansive personality was a result of his experience, one that was isolated from the racial and cultural prejudices of China proper. This personality was nurtured by his subsequent foreign education in Japan and Western Europe. In fact, Zhou always remembered his youth in Manchuria with considerable excitement and gratification. He even attributed his physical strength and endurance in later life to his regular outdoor exercise and the Spartan-like living standards in Manchuria.[4]

In 1913 Zhou went to Tianjin, Hebei, and enrolled at the Nankai middle school, a local boarding school. It was at this unique academic institution that Zhou experienced the first real turning point in his education. At Nankai he learned the fundamentals of a liberal arts education. The greater part of his time was spent in solid study. He impressed his teachers with his literary gifts and from them learned world geography and history as well as natural science. He eventually turned to more serious books and journals and became involved in various student activities. Of these, the one that made him stand out as a person of promise was the role he played in founding the *Respect Work and Enjoy Fellowship Society* (Jing-ye luo-gun she) and in editing its publication at the beginning of 1914. Debate was another field that appealed to Zhou. He practiced frequently to master the art of public speaking. As a result of his labors, the young Zhou became a good speaker, as shown by his performances at the Nankai middle school.

Zhou's personality at the time could be characterized as self-contained and goal oriented. He was, on the one hand, patriotic; on the other hand, he was pragmatic, paying more attention to practical matters than to abstract philosophy. As he went on to meet the intellectual leaders of the Beijing-Tianjin area and his fellow student leaders at Nankai, Zhou tried his best to develop an image of himself as earnest and personable and to cultivate viable relationships with his associates. He apparently won the respect and approval of his classmates, teachers, and, more important, his school principal, Zhang Boling, an eminent educator of the time. By this time Zhou had established himself as a quick thinker who was also physically very active, a young man of endurance and determination.[5] He emphatically embraced the importance of high ethical conduct that was free of duplicity and self-deception.[6]

During this early period it was already clear that Zhou appreciated and cherished the principles of "practicality" and "adaptability." He showed a keen interest in the practical application of knowledge. Alongside the process of learning, he held, there should also be applied activities, concrete actions being part of the essence of knowledge. Unapplied knowledge, for the young Zhou, was devoid of meaning. For this reason he tried his best to pursue *practical learning* (shi-xue) throughout these early years, which in turn nurtured his intellect and his preference for pragmatic knowledge over theoretical speculation.

The Influence of Gu Yanwu and Wang Fuzhi upon Zhou's Formative Years

In attempting to assess the influence of Gu and Wang upon Zhou's early thoughts and actions, it is helpful to situate these men within the intellectual background of their own times and to examine their key ideas and role in promoting *practical learning*, especially during the early Qing period in modern Chinese history (1644-1750).[7] The main purpose of this examination is to identify the major principles of Gu's and Wang's school of thought and to demonstrate how their philosophy became the underpinning of Zhou's basic beliefs, which in turn had a determining and lasting effect on Zhou's lifelong political principles.

In late Ming and early Qing times, under the pressure of social and political changes, new modes of philosophical thought eventually replaced Neo-Confucianism as the core of Chinese culture. The most obvious and dramatic reactions to Sung and Ming Neo-Confucianism were the development of methods of scholarly research as well as debates on the true meaning of knowledge.[8] As the trend in learning shifted from the abstract to the concrete, some outstanding scholars of the early Qing period, notably Gu and Wang, argued for the practical application of knowledge to public affairs as a way to restore Chinese social and political order.[9] They held that the abstract and meditative speculations of the Ming scholars, especially of Wang Yang-ming, were responsible for the decline and collapse of the Ming dynasty (1368-1644).

In their numerous writings the idea of "practicality" (shi) was a central and predominant theme for both Gu and Wang. Both men were proponents of practical thinking and action and systematically and persuasively developed a philosophy that emphasized matters of substance and real use. They were prominent in recommending to their contemporaries explicit measures to initiate a fundamental change in patterns of Chinese thought. Both attempted to shift attention from the abstract to the practical and from individual introspection to engagement in public affairs. They were well-known as strong critics of Sung and Ming Neo-Confucianism, and each in his own way was an advocate of "practical statesmanship" (jing-shi zhi-yong). For both Gu and Wang, however, the Confucian classics contained the principles of practical statesmanship, and such principles could be extracted only by a systematic and extensive study of the classics. They developed a new methodology of learning that stressed research based on extensive evidence and the practical application of knowledge to society. Their major works indeed formed the very core of Chinese pragmatism. In fact, Gu's and Wang's preference for practical studies and serious scholarship itself had a purpose that was grounded in reality: to stimulate the development of Chinese nationalism and to overthrow an alien dynasty, that of the Qing.

Both Gu and Wang used the term *practical learning* to express the values of practicality, solidity, substantiality, and reality. Principles of reality, to them, ought to be verified by real forms and judged by actual things. Therefore, *practical learning* was mainly understood and interpreted by Gu and Wang to refer to learning that was empirical and rational and that was an aid in daily life, both private and public. Truth or reality was the essential meaning of practical learning. For both men it was important to study extensively. What Gu and Wang referred to as practicality and actual results were things that related closely to the tangible improvement and advancement of general welfare in terms of the functioning of government and the contributions of individuals. Moreover, they made a distinction between "learning with a view to one's own cultivation and improvement" and scholarship that was solely concerned with reputation—that is, "learning with a view to the approbation of others." Therefore, both Gu and Wang advocated a commitment to "cultivating the self and governing others," or to "serving the state and pacifying the world," in a correct and positive manner. To this end, they believed, one ought to rectify one's mind, regulate one's family, and govern the state well.

The cornerstone of Gu's contribution to the Qing school of learning rested in his notion of "utility," or practical statesmanship, which brought knowledge and society into a closer relationship, in sharp contrast to the Ming scholars' passion for abstract thinking that was totally separate from any solid knowledge of either Chinese history or social and political reality. Gu's philosophy and activities, it should be noted, are best understood against the background of social and political turmoil in which he lived.[10] As a young man, he had resisted the Manchus and was compelled to live under Qing rule for the next thirty-seven years of his life. The nation's weakness against the Manchu invaders was attributed by Gu to the preceding centuries of empty philosophizing by the followers of the Sung Neo-Confucian school whose teaching, in his opinion, had failed the nation completely in the face of the harsh realities of political decline and foreign invasion. Believing that the failures of the past could be retrieved only by a broad outlook, Gu strongly urged fellow scholars to take into account not just a small set of honored documents, as had been the custom, but all the data necessary to reach an objective conclusion. He stressed the importance of making new hypotheses and testing them by evidence from all relevant sources in the hope of achieving a new generalized knowledge and a new practical view.

Though learning was a means to an end, utility, it was essential to establish the principle of comprehensive and factual scholarship. Without extensive study, Gu believed, it was impossible to verify the various manifestations of a rational principle. In his preoccupation with the methodology of learning, Gu tried to scrutinize every fact thoroughly and to confirm it with extensive evidence. His painstaking research resulted in his major work, *The Record of Daily Knowledge* (Ri-zhi-lu). In spite of his insistence on process, on collecting and examining all relevant evidence to achieve proper understanding and analysis of facts, he nonetheless cautioned: "Recording empty words is not the equivalent of observing action."[11] As he saw it, true pragmatic principles were not fixed concepts but, rather, appropriate responses to each situation. "In view of this," he said, "I decided not to do any writing unless it had a relation to actual affairs of the contemporary world."[12]

Gu's emphasis on the notion of practicality, or the practical application of knowledge to public affairs, had a significant impact on the growth of a new intellectual movement in modern China. The origin of the twin pillars of modern Chinese political philosophy—"seeking truth from facts" (shi-shi qiu-shi) and practical statesmanship—can be directly traced to Gu's teachings. Gu's classical learning was itself a study of rational principles. His rejection of late Ming intellectual trends was based on his observation that the Ming scholars had shifted from the discussion of concrete social, economic, and political issues to the elaboration of "lofty and esoteric doctrines, and the excellence of singlemindedness." Through his efforts a new intellectual trend of "sound learning," or "solid scholarship" (pu-xue), emerged during the early Qing period. According to Chinese classics, Confucius (551-479 B.C.) extolled Shun in *The Mean* (Zhong-yong) because the latter "loved to question others,"[13] and in *The Analects* (Lun-yu) K'ung Wen-tzu was praised because "he was not ashamed to ask and to learn from his inferiors."[14] Seeking to graft his new teaching onto the time-honored classics, Gu summed up his general approach to knowledge in two quotations from *The Analects*: "In your conduct let there be something that you are ashamed to do" (Xing-ji you-chi); and "in your studies make use of the widest range of sources" (Bo-xue yu-wen).

While Gu highly valued empirical research, Wang Fuzhi emphasized logical reasoning. It was Wang who stressed the primacy of the tangible, concrete fact over the abstract, generic classification.[15] Once he said categorically: "Name *[ming]* derives from fact *[shi]*,"[16] or the general formal term derives from specific cognizable examples. The core of Wang's philosophy was his revolt against the abstract in favor of the concrete. Implicit in this theme was the attention given to the proper arrangement of concrete matters. He felt that, inasmuch as concrete things were never isolated but were always related, they changed from time to time and followed certain principles in such relationships and changes. Keeping this basic premise in mind, it was beneficial for people to learn and understand these principles. Concerning how the principle of concreteness was to be obtained, Wang assumed that concrete things had in them the tendency toward concreteness. Since concrete things were different from those in the past, the past simply could not be a pattern of the present.[17]

Since principle was found only in concrete objects, according to Wang, there was no principle of nature that Sung-Ming Neo-Confucianists had employed as the model for Chinese history and society. He advocated an evolutionary and progressive approach to knowledge by suggesting that history would unfold itself continuously in an orderly fashion. This implied that the later period would be better than the earlier one. Consequently, there was no need to revive ancient ideas and institutions for modern application, as each period had its own unique characteristics and specific requirements.

Wang believed that progress could best be achieved under conditions of economic stability and prosperity. "What is not yet completed," wrote Wang, "can be completed; what is already completed can be reformed."[18] He denied that supernatural forces of fate could influence the course of history. Instead, he asserted that the rational principles of nature reside in human desires and that, to use his own words, "without human desires there can be no discovery of the rational principles of nature."[19]

Much of Wang's knowledge came not only from reading but also from observation. The principal cause contributing to the collapse of the Ming dynasty was, in his view, the fact that its intellectual leaders had lost touch with reality. By emphasizing serious scholarship and practical learning, Wang hoped to create a new and dynamic intellectual climate that could be maintained after the overthrow of the Qing dynasty. In retrospect, Wang's unique contribution to Chinese society was his emphasis on the relationship of human desires to the discovery of rational principles. The principles of things in the world were limitless. "What is already excellent," argued Wang, "may become still more excellent. Changes take place with the passage of time, but nothing deviates from the correct path."[20] In the final analysis Wang opposed the restoration of ancient Chinese institutions, and he strongly urged that human nature adapt itself to the constantly changing environment.

During his formative years, roughly from 1910 to 1916, Zhou became acquainted with the works of the Chinese pragmatic philosophers of the early Qing period.[21] When the young Zhou studied the writings of Gu and Wang, he discovered not only teachings of the school of practical learning but also the nature and meaning of Chinese pragmatism. Practical learning stressed the importance of learning both the principles (or substance) of knowledge and the application (or use) of these principles to produce results beneficial to society. In this light practical learning stood out, for the young Zhou, as a necessary and sound form of intellectual inquiry and investigation. It also appealed to him because learning was not confined to the superficial recitation of dogmas for the purpose of pleasing authority or seeking appointment in the government. It was essential, in Zhou's view, to study things *(wu)* and affairs *(shi)* relevant to the needs of life and society. Practical learning was the search for knowledge of things that one could apply in actual life for the advancement of social, economic, and political welfare or at least for the strengthening of one's spirit and body. Therefore, learning must pertain to actual reality and must incorporate practice.

Increasing emphasis, Zhou held, should also be placed on the results of objective and empirical investigation that could have utilitarian value. It was in this specific context that Zhou, in the mid- and late 1910s, began to devote his energy and attention to concrete matters, to dismiss the elements of style and superficiality, and to commit himself mainly to the task of searching for pragmatic scholarship. Zhou believed that a student, as he was at the time, must give first priority to self-cultivation. Upon the foundation of self-cultivation, asserted Zhou, one should also acquire extensive learning in order to cement one's character and give it reality.[22] The logical extension of this learning process placed great value on the notion that knowledge should be of use to society and should focus on political and economic problems and their proper solutions.

When, as a young man, Zhou studied the writing of Gu and Wang, he found a sense of patriotism and nationalism attached to the Ming cause and a concern for reliable interpretation of classical Confucian ideology. More important, he began to appreciate the premise that the application of knowledge to public affairs was the fruit of practical learning. Gu and Wang's criticisms of the danger and futility of an abstract quest for sagehood, together with their undying loyalty to the Ming dynasty, reinforced Zhou's sensitivity to the basic elements of Chinese pragmatic philosophy. It became his conviction that in the process of learning one should inquire, think, and practice; then one could transform one's temperament, cultivate one's character, and become a representative of practical learning. Responding to his primary school teacher's question "Why should we study?" Zhou's answer was distinctly practical: "We should study for China to arise."[23]

The central elements common to both Gu and Wang were the practical interpretation of the nature of political and social activities and a set of empirically-based propositions about the value of learning. Principles of reality ought to be verified by real forms and judged by actual things, with an emphasis on extensive investigation, factual accuracy, broad experience, moral solidity, and rational coherence. Such teachings of Gu and Wang contributed significantly to Zhou's intellectual development. "For meeting heavy responsibilities of the future," Zhou wrote in October 1912, "foundations are laid in the third or fourth years of grade school. Fellow students, we should resolutely begin to confront our duties without regret!"[24] He went on to say, "To reorganize, it is proper to stress practicality; to devote attention to the external aspects of a thing, it is necessary to investigate its reality first."[25] In his early essays Zhou clearly demonstrated his conviction that practical learning was a matter of prime importance. He stressed the value of questioning, sought factual accuracy, and tried his best to understand the relationship between abstract principles and actual situations.

Zhou regarded the education he received at Shenyang very highly. It was in his years at Nankai, as Zhou would later recall, that he was able to lay the foundation for the useful knowledge and habits of mind that he was to possess. During these formative years the writings of Gu, Wang, and others offered him not only intellectual inspiration but also the earliest sources of pragmatism. As a young student, Zhou energetically pursued the practice of investigating things and examining their concrete contexts through study and observation. At this early stage he chose to emphasize the proposition that knowledge was indeed the result of action and that the function of knowledge was to guide action.[26] Knowledge of a principle was genuine if it found expression in action. Consequently, work was knowledge, and without work there was no knowledge. Against this background the young Zhou sought to strike a balance between action and knowledge.

It was also important for Zhou to reconcile the different elements of practical learning. His eager search for the true meaning of the application of knowledge to public affairs was evidenced by his willingness to devote considerable time and energy to the study of concrete issues. He acknowledged that books were full of ideas but felt that the ideas were not worth anything unless one tested their validity by applying them. In pursuing this line of thinking, the young Zhou was undoubtedly under the influence of Chinese pragmatic philosophy, as elaborated and advanced by Gu and Wang. Nowhere was the pervasive influence on the young Zhou of Chinese pragmatic philosophy so apparent as in his adoption of book learning for the purpose of saving his country. The question of the real relationship of knowledge to other activities was examined by Zhou especially in his essays written in 1912 and 1916. It was not so much that he thought about practicality as that he cherished action. For Zhou there was a close relationship between practical learning and positive action.

Zhou's early thought was practical in the sense of being concerned with the utility of knowledge, social interaction, and political activity. What one learned was something that should, as Zhou saw it, satisfy the needs of people and society. Accordingly, he began to emphasize the idea of learning vigorously through practice and for the purpose of practice. Moreover, he felt that one should follow a practical line in acquiring broad knowledge, and in the process one should also restrain oneself with "sincerity" (cheng), or the Confucian concept of "human compassion," so that one could actually apply what one had "learned."[27] Thus, practical learning was not only a matter of utilitarian thinking but also a fundamental principle of social service based on practical action and sincerity. As a young man, Zhou believed that the application of the basic notion of sincerity by policymakers to the world community would certainly lead to peaceful interstate relations, thereby eliminating the use of arms as an instrument of national policy.

Zhou, in seeking the actual practice of learning, considered the preservation of one's mind and the nourishment of one's nature to be the basic principles that would integrate knowledge and practice. "Utter ignorance," claimed Zhou in 1915, "is the shame of a scholar."[28] In addition, he stressed the value of questioning, which, to him, was a matter of urgent necessity. What Zhou referred to as "practical utility" (shi-li) and "talent" (ren-ca) were things that would permit the tangible improvement and advancement of Chinese social and political conditions.[29] These elements, in essence, constituted the substance of Zhou's early concept of utilitarian practicality. Zhou's basic notion of practicality also included training in morality, clear thought, and a deep sense of social responsibility. The principal characteristics of education were for Zhou its moral relevance and usefulness to human life and society.[30]

The Impact of Darwinism on Zhou

Zhou owed the development of his intellectual disposition not only to the pragmatic philosophy of Gu and Wang but also to Charles Darwin (1809-82) and Thomas Henry Huxley (1825-95) through the media of Yan Fu's translations and Liang Qi-chao's works. These works expounded the fundamental elements of competition for survival and adaptability. Zhou's initial interest in Darwinian concepts and theory was reinforced by his commitment to the rise of China as a modern state.

Darwinism was perhaps the first Western *ism* to become widely accepted by Chinese intellectuals and students. Mainly through the books and essays of Liang, Yan's translated Western works, and Chen Duxiu's articles in the journal of the *New Youth* (Xin-qing-nian), Zhou first became aware of the essential tenets of Darwinism. Darwin's key ideas, such as the "struggle for existence" in nature, the adaptation of organisms to their environment, and the "survival of the fittest," had a very substantial influence on Zhou's intellectual development during his formative years.[31]

In the 1910s and 1920s most Chinese intellectuals and students wanted to build a strong and independent China and to win back the respect of the world for their country. The Chinese students of Zhou's generation grew up at a time when China was at the mercy of Western and Japanese imperialism and when crucial social, economic, and political problems in China demanded immediate attention and solutions. Under the influence of Darwinism they believed that citizens or nations had to struggle to survive and that the superior won and the inferior lost. The principle of Darwin's "natural selection" was for them the governing law of the universe. Primarily by struggling to survive and reproduce, each species would manage to adapt exquisitely to its local habitat.[32] Natural selection was not only the driving force but also the key to evolution. Everything was supposed to be evolving; in a given environment members of the same species would compete for survival, and those best adapted to the environment would have the best chance. Whether natural selection was applied to individuals or species, it was still a process of adaptation. Adaptability was indeed the key to survival and success.

This interpretation of the theory of evolution made Darwinism especially pertinent to the Chinese state and society at that time. It supported and sanctified the need for China to compete and adapt for its survival. The highly competitive character of the state system of the modern world required vigilance with regard to power in terms of territory, population, and economic resources. In a world of conflict and competition a state without all the means of political, economic, and military strength would be at the mercy of neighboring countries.

The struggle for survival—the mechanism of evolution—would certainly affect not only the quantity of living organisms but also their quality, and, under these competitive conditions, favorable variations would tend to be preserved and unfavorable ones destroyed. While Darwin himself confined the principle of natural selection to the sphere of biology, his contemporaries eagerly extended it to apply to the field of human affairs. This application of Darwin's biological principles to humans and their efforts, known as social Darwinism, also became a convenient doctrine for justifying various political and economic theories and activities. The social Darwinists, basing their arguments on Darwin's authority, argued that in the struggle for existence the fittest would survive and that struggle, therefore, was essential for the survival of fitness. In foreign affairs this took the form of "political realism," that is, bellicosity and aggressiveness; in domestic affairs it was a defense of the most ruthless competitive practices.

By 1916 Zhou had already studied the translated works of Darwin and Huxley and had made some careful observations and comments on Darwinian doctrines and the social application of the struggle for survival.[33] It was indeed not surprising that Zhou examined China's domestic problems and its international position in light of Darwinian doctrines. Adaptation explained the turns and twists of evolution, and Zhou considered pragmatic adjustment from this time on a mere instrument of successful activity. The key point, however, was that one had to take the initiative and to make continual progress in order to survive. To live in the real world, first, it was essential to know that "things contend; heaven chooses," then to act in accordance with the principle of the survival of the fittest. The logical extension was that China must change in order to turn its weakness to strength. It was in this context that Zhou became increasingly aware of the significance of phrases such as "the strong are victorious" and "the weak perish" (You-sheng lie-bai) as they applied specifically to world politics.[34]

Through the translation of the writings of Darwin and, particularly, through Huxley's classification of the ingredients of social Darwinism, Zhou became familiar with the ideas of evolution and the application to society of the struggle for survival. Darwin's biological hypotheses, as contained in *Origin of Species* (1859), was known to Zhou in the early 1910s as the hypothesis of natural selection. This included the basic notion that it was nature, or the environment, that selected those variants among offspring that were to survive and reproduce. Social Darwinism was a new concept for Zhou, which emphasized not only the progress of human society through fierce competition but also the importance of a given state's power.

The distinguished English biologist Thomas H. Huxley, who had been Darwin's most ardent and articulate defender since the publication of *Origin of Species*, protested in 1893 in *Evolution and Ethics* against social Darwinism, saying it was a distortion of Darwin's original theory. He was against the ethic of ruthless and uncharitable self-interest. In Huxley's view ethical sense enabled man to reject "the ape and tiger methods of the struggle for existence."[35] Huxley was certainly against misusing Darwinian theory to justify unrestricted competition. Instead, he held that within a society selfish assertiveness was bad and that morality was important. He further suggested that human societies had arisen out of the advantages brought by cooperation in the struggle for existence. The survival of individuals depended on the survival of their group, which could survive only if its members were able to restrain themselves and work together. The "ethical process," in Huxley's view, tended "to make any human society more efficient in the struggle for existence with the state of nature or with other societies."[36] His main point was that "in place of ruthless self-assertion it [the ethical process] demands self-restraint; in place of thrusting aside, or treading down all competitors, it requires that the individual shall not merely respect, but shall help his fellows; its influence is directed not so much to the survival of the fittest as to the fitting of as many as possible to survive."[37] Huxley's main concern was thus with "curbing the instincts of savagery in civilized man." He simply wanted people to respect and help one another and to practice self-restraint. He also believed that social morality, the ethical process of human cooperation, was not only a phenomenon produced by evolution; it was humanity's only means toward further evolution.

Zhou applauded Huxley's interpretations of the struggle for survival and evolution. He was obviously impressed by Huxley's attack on fanatical individualism and on the ethic of ruthless, uncharitable self-interest.[38] The doctrines of struggle for existence, natural selection, and survival of the fittest, nevertheless, provided Zhou with a better understanding of the importance of adaptation to one's situation. The ability of an individual or a nation to adjust to ever-changing circumstances, in Zhou's judgment, made the difference between simply existing or flourishing in a new environment. When Zhou looked at the world outside, he urged his fellow students to fulfill their duties and to fight for China's sovereign rights. At the same time, in his numerous articles he urged his countrymen to come together.

Although it was Darwin's theory that provided Zhou with a major source of inspiration, Zhou followed Huxley's clarification of Darwinism. Huxley had been in favor of cooperation and human decency; so was Zhou. Moreover, in his early essays Zhou displayed a strong sense of responsibility and patriotism. His knowledge of the pragmatic tradition of Chinese philosophy was further buttressed by the Darwinian elements of evolution and adaptability. It is misleading, however, to suggest that Zhou was a thorough social Darwinist. Zhou recognized the importance of solidarity and its corollary, self-restraint. In addition, he believed that one of the most important virtues was morality, which alone was the constant force behind all changes. In light of these Darwinian concepts, Zhou examined more thoroughly than before the nature of China's weaknesses, its vulnerable international position, and ways to change this situation.

The Influence of John Dewey's Experimental Method and Hu Shi's Concepts of Pragmatism on Zhou's Intellectual Development

At the time when Zhou came into contact with Western social and political theories and ideas, John Dewey's experimental philosophy gained popularity in China following its interpretation and dissemination by his student Hu Shi. Dewey came to China on a lecture tour that lasted more than two years, from May 1, 1919, to May 21, 1921. With Hu as interpreter, Dewey gave a number of public lectures on his social and political philosophy of pragmatism. His lecture halls were always packed with large crowds, including high school and college students. Thus, it is not surprising that Zhou was well acquainted with Dewey's experimental philosophy.

Dewey's philosophy consisted of three central points: that knowledge was a form of doing, that society had gradually evolved in the course of history, and that theories for solving problems originated in events.[39] Dewey felt that social scientists should pay more attention to evidence and events, maintain an attitude of experimentation, and regard all theories as instruments and hypotheses for remedying specific problems at specific times. Accordingly, he suggested that experimentation, the study of specific events, and the continuous improvement of society should constitute a new social and political philosophy. Dewey's philosophy was concerned with social progress, and it concentrated on the contemporary state of things rather than on any supposedly eternal, fixed conditions. He deliberately attempted to make philosophical investigation relevant to contemporary social problems.

It was Dewey who offered the promise of an evolutionary understanding of human potential, a view that presented boundless possibilities for further development. For Dewey the scientific method of observation and the evaluation of consequences could be applied to human relations and to solving political and social problems. An evolutionary understanding of human beings and society was at the root of Dewey's concept of "growth" as the true measure of social justice. From an evolutionary perspective change signified new possibilities and ends to be attained; it heralded a better future. Moreover, change was "associated with progress" rather than with lapse and decline. Acceptance of the evolutionary perspective permitted Dewey to reject the alleged absolutism and inflexibility of traditional philosophy, especially its postulation of a rigid hierarchy of "fixed ends." It was the concept of growth that guided the philosophical investigation of those contemporary problems that required solution. Therefore, the possibilities for growth served as the capstone of Dewey's philosophical reconstruction.

According to Dewey, all matters of practical action involved an ingredient of uncertainty. The quest for certainty was simply an appeal for an end to the false dichotomy between action and thought. It was also an effort to transcend belief. Moreover, Dewey himself tended to judge a belief by its effects, and he perceived thought as an evolutionary process. Truth, for him, was not immutable but, rather, a workable and practical response to an immediate situation. Dewey, like the Chinese pragmatic philosophers of the early Qing period, emphasized learning by doing and educating the whole person. He directed educational enterprises away from the rigidities of classical instruction and encouraged individuals to experiment with their life experiences, to not be afraid to respond to challenges but to try, instead, to improve each situation by adjustment. He suggested that social, economic, and political ideas and institutions should also be freely altered as required by the needs of the times.

The key element of Dewey's concept of life was that, though the individual was mortal, civilization and society, which embodied the collective lives and cumulative achievements of individuals, would persist from one generation to another into infinity. Individuals, therefore, should constantly strive to improve their society. All human institutions, moreover, were arbitrary constructions designed to preserve society and enhance the individual's enjoyment of life. Dewey's philosophy was thus humanistic, socially oriented, and postulated on ideas of change derived from evolutionary theory. It focused on specific problems instead of abstract principles. It also stressed that experience could give people insight into their own natures and could be turned to creative purposes through an understanding of cause and effect, or, in more typically pragmatic terminology, antecedents and consequences. Truth, therefore, was changeable in proportion to its utility based on experimentation.

On one occasion Dewey told his enthusiastic Chinese audience that "China could not be changed without a social transformation based upon a transformation of ideas. The political revolution was a failure because it was external, formal, touching the mechanism of social action but not affecting conceptions of life, which really control society."[40] Impressed by the eagerness of Chinese youth to listen to his exposition of philosophical and social ideas, Dewey confidently reported, "There is an eager thirst for ideas—beyond anything existing, I am convinced, in the youth of any other country on earth."[41] He also stated that "the most impressive single feature of [his] stay in China was witnessing the sure and rapid growth of an enlightened and progressive public opinion."[42]

Dewey's evolutionary and pragmatic outlook, which advocated change, was fully adopted by Hu. "Not only do the species change," claimed Hu, "but truth also changes."[43] In the revolution of Chinese tradition, Hu insisted, all inferences should be based on evidence, and anything without proof should be held to be doubtful. Historical evolution, or, in Dewey's phrase, the "generic method"—namely, concentrating attention on the origin and evolution of the subject—was proposed as a means of verification. This method stemmed directly from Dewey's pragmatism. Hu openly acknowledged his indebtedness to Dewey by declaring, "Dewey teaches me how to think and teaches me to consider the immediate problems in all cases, to regard theories and ideals as hypotheses which are in need of verification, and to take into account the effect of thoughts."[44]

In his article entitled "Pragmatism," published in *New Youth* on April 1, 1919, Hu wrote, "The knowledge that mankind needs is not the way or principle which has an absolute existence but the particular truths for here and now and for particular individuals."[45] He then went on to state that "absolute truth is imaginary, abstract, without evidence, and cannot be demonstrated."[46] In his clarification of the fundamental concepts of Dewey's philosophy, Hu suggested that experience constituted life, that life meant dealing with the environment, and that, in the act of dealing with the environment, the "function of thought" was the most important element. He asserted that all conscious actions involved the function of thought and that thought was an instrument to be used in dealing with the environment. In his comments on Darwin's theory of evolution, Hu summarized, "When it came to Darwin, he boldly declared that the species were not immutable but all had their origins and developed into the present species only after many changes."[47] He added: "The change of the species is the result of adaptation to environment and truth is but an instrument with which to deal with environment. As the environment changes, so does truth accordingly."[48]

Hu was in favor of gradualism, which he thought was one of Darwin's tenets. "Darwin's theory of biological evolution," said Hu, "has given us one great lesson. It has taught us to understand that biological evolution, whether by natural changes or human choice, all comes from bit-by-bit change."[49] He then went on to assert: "Pragmatism gets its start from Darwinism. Therefore, it can recognize only steady, bit-by-bit improvement as true and reliable evolution."[50] It is fair to suggest that pragmatism was Hu's Darwinism and that his version of pragmatism was grounded in gradualism and its scientific method but was humanized by "its gentleness, tolerance, and compassion."[51]

Hu, an energetic exponent of scientific thinking, followed Dewey in the conviction that truth was an instrument, changing with circumstances. He also strongly advocated "more investigation of the problems and less talk about theories."[52] He contrasted the isms (zhu-yi), by which he meant systems of thought with universal claims, with "real problems" (wen-ti). He appealed to Chinese intellectuals and students to set aside ideological disputes and instead deal with concrete problems. He warned them against the dangers of abstractions and vague generalizations. He felt that the discussion of concrete problems should receive wider attention than windy theoretical disputes and that such effort would allow his fellow countrymen to anticipate the implications of theories as they were applied to specific cases. Drawing on Dewey's experimental philosophy, he stressed a gradual, "bit-by-bit" improvement of Chinese society through the study and solution of specific, practical problems. Therefore, he held that reform, not revolution, was the answer to China's social, economic, and political problems. "Civilization was not created in toto," argued Hu forcefully, "but by inches and drops."[53] To him all-embracing isms were nothing more than "the dreams of self-deceived and deceptive persons, ironclad proof of the bankruptcy of Chinese thought, and the death-knell of Chinese social reform!"[54]

In the final analysis the main element of Hu's thoughts was pragmatism, which became his principal yardstick in evaluating traditional ideas and values. Hu's view on pragmatism and on the study of concrete problems exerted a tremendous impact on the minds and actions of many Chinese intellectuals and students in the years from 1919 to 1921. Zhou was one of these eager and impressionable youths.

In essays and letters published in 1921 and 1922, Zhou expressed his preference for experimental methods and the evolutionary approach to social improvement, and applauded Hu's views and emphases. Yet, Zhou did not entirely agree with Hu in Hu's diagnosis of the real cause of China's problems. For example, in one of his articles published in August 1922, Zhou stated categorically that he greatly admired and respected Hu, the most influential proponent of pragmatism in China, for many of his views and observations.[55] But one of Hu's serious "faults," in Zhou's opinion, was his attributing China's ills to its backwardness in scientific fields and to its own disorder, rather than to "foreign imperialism." Hu's public role in China, moreover, was that of an observer and a political critic instead of a direct participant. Hu was thus strongly criticized by Zhou for being afraid to face reality.[56] Meanwhile, Zhou had enough of a Darwinian faith to believe that it did not matter what had been lost by the Chinese people, for whatever survived would be better for having lasted and "progressed." In the final analysis change and improvement were vital and necessary for China's survival in a competitive world. In the long process of competition and struggle both individuals and countries should turn their weaknesses to strengths and, according to Zhou, China had to change and progress in order to preserve its sovereignty and independence.

It is evident that Zhou's early exposure to the philosophy of pragmatism of Gu and Wang was further infused with Darwin's theories of evolution and adaptability and by Dewey's and Hu's interpretations of "thought" as an instrument to deal with the changing environment. Above all, truth was changeable in proportion to its utility based on experimentation. In the search for truth Zhou tried his best to identify the nexus between the nature of reality and the elements of practicality and workability. The substance of truth, for him, was not something to be judged by absolute, fixed standards. On the contrary, the truth of an idea was essentially a matter of its relevance to the situation in which it might be used. Accordingly, a theory was true if it led people to accurate expectations about the world in which it was applied. In addition, a theory was true if it worked and if it helped an individual in adjusting his or her life to the contingencies encountered in the ongoing process of living. Thus, the utility or practicality against which Zhou wanted to test theories was that which proved useful in an ever-changing, unpredictable human situation.

Learning, according to Zhou, should be practical and concrete. In an essay written on March 20, 1916, Zhou clearly demonstrated his understanding of the relation between knowledge (zhi) and practice (xing).[57] Knowledge and practice were, to him, mutually dependent. He perceived the objective of learning was to be its applicability to life and concrete reality and the results it could yield for society or an individual's self-realization. With his preference for concrete action over theoretical speculation, Zhou suggested an essentially pragmatic approach to meeting the urgent needs of Chinese society. He felt that what was learned should be carried out in action. Moreover, what really mattered was the search for a method of managing prevailing conditions as well as the capacity to make necessary arrangements when changes occurred.

While expounding the importance of purpose and dedication, Zhou asserted that, by advancing simultaneously in knowledge and practice, one could make upward progress.[58] He contended that the interaction of sincerity and knowledge was pivotal in bringing about self-transformation. According to Zhou, sincerity, a sense of duty, and decorum were the three primary virtues. These virtues, however, had important applications and produced concrete effects in the conduct of human affairs, both at home and abroad.[59] He was equally convinced that, without wide learning and extensive investigation, it was impossible for a person to make a proper assessment of key issues. As a result, one would be incapable of making sound judgments on a rational and objective basis.[60]

In the teachings of Gu and Wang, we see a basic type of Chinese pragmatism. The influence of these scholars on Zhou can be traced, to a marked degree, in his attitude toward problems of both experience and thought. As a callow youth, Zhou's evaluation of people and things was based essentially upon practical utility. He was matter-of-fact from the start and he remained pragmatic throughout his life. His faith in personal responsibility and self-cultivation had, from the very beginning, helped shape his understanding of the dimensions of practical utility and his appreciation for pragmatic adaptation. In his view the goal of every student, including himself, should be the pursuit of practical learning, not the acquisition of wealth or career enhancement.[61] The most important duty of a student, therefore, was to study in order to save China from foreign encroachment.

Conclusion

As a young man, Zhou had an unmistakable propensity for practical matters, and it is clear—for example, in his early essays on the aim of education—that the practical philosophy of Gu and Wang exerted considerable influence on Zhou's intellectual development. He accepted their teachings on pragmatism as a means of solving the complex political, social, and economic problems of his time. The roots of Zhou's lifelong pragmatism can be traced to Wang's ideas of practical scholarship and logical reasoning and in Gu's emphasis on practical statesmanship and "seeking truth from facts."[62]

It was extremely important to Zhou to discover truth through practice and through practice to verify and develop truth.[63] When starting with literary knowledge, one was expected to transform it into rational knowledge; then, from rational knowledge, one should actively go through the process of relating one's knowledge to reality. In his mind reality existed in commonplace, ordinary, familiar things. There was nothing real outside experience. But, if one did not study, then one's view was biased. If one did not practice, then one's learning was empty and useless. The term *practical learning* for Zhou implied not merely a name but a concrete reality. It conveyed, at the same time, a sense of utility and cautious investigation. Therefore, practice and knowledge, more practice and more knowledge, and, above all, the unity of knowledge and action reflected Zhou's basic belief in pragmatism. The alternative was a rigid, constraining dogma that stood in the way of continuing growth and adjustment.

Classical Chinese expressions such as "seeking truth from facts" and "doing what is guided by circumstances" (yin-shi-zhi-yi), which had been fundamental to traditional Chinese pragmatism, were fully accepted and frequently quoted by Zhou in his early essays. More important, he maintained these beliefs throughout his life. "Combine study with work and keep them in proper balance," Zhou summarized one of his lifelong guidelines in March 1943, "according to time, place, and circumstances."[64] He never deviated from this conviction. Throughout his life Zhou held that knowledge and action must not be regarded as two separate entities but, instead, should be conceived as functionally unified in their genesis and utility. Second, as a young man, Zhou held the Confucian virtue of sincerity in high esteem and spoke of the intimate relationship between the sincerity of a statesman and the preservation of international peace and order.[65] Zhou also believed in self-discipline and in one's capacity to endure hardship for the attainment of important ends. It was not worthwhile, he felt, to seek out selfish gains; he believed, rather, that one should strengthen one's sense of duty.[66]

In his pursuit of knowledge Zhou displayed calm thought, insatiable inquiry, and great concentration. By temperament he was, perhaps, more interested in action than in study. As he saw it, the more one was concerned with actual circumstances, the less one was preoccupied with style or superficiality. Facts seemed to hold a special attraction to Zhou. Ideological prescription and intuition, basic as they might be, were not substitutes for the labor of gathering facts and studying and attempting to understand them. Such knowledge and understanding, however, were not ends in themselves but constituted the basis for deeper insight into real issues. Zhou's intellectual disposition at this early stage was already conducive to the search for facts and direct, firsthand experiences for the discovery and verification of truth. To get close to the facts was to get close to the realities of the world. An emphasis on actual experience for Zhou meant testing truth in daily life and responding to one's time and place by "drawing on traditional values as relevant to the present" (yin-qu-yi-zhu-jin). With appropriate attention to matters of social welfare, government service, and political participation, knowledge should be conceived of, ultimately, as a means to important and practical ends.

Finally, the Darwinian concept of adaptation, the ability of living organisms to change physically in order to survive a changing natural environment, also made a strong impact upon Zhou's early thought and action.[67] It gave rise to his awareness that the principle of struggle for existence would naturally apply to China's relations with the outside world. The Darwinian concepts of both struggle and progress offered him useful categories with which to view the society and world as he knew them. Evolution proceeded through competition among individuals within a species, which in turn represented the effort of each organism to survive and reproduce in a given environment. Fitness, in this context, was defined as adaptation to an environment. Thus, the extinction of a race could be avoided with deliberate effort—reform or revolution, as the case might be. The ability to adapt, however, was a continuous, flowing process of interrelatedness of what was directly experienced. Human experience, for Zhou, was reality, and reality might be defined and limited by individual experience. A person was, in part, the product of his or her own capacity to adjust, and reality was the interplay of an individual's impartial consciousness and the real world, of which he or she was a part. The logical extension was that the world would have no meaning apart from or outside human consciousness, and human consciousness could flow continuously as long as the organism maintained its vitality and adaptability. Moreover, the experience in which human life and the changing world shared was not fixed, nor was there a pattern to it.

In the final analysis experience did not consist only of an individual's condition, but was also affected by that person's life, a point that confirmed the central role of human will. To be oblivious to the changing environment or to evolutionary growth, and not adapt to it, would certainly cause one to lapse into rigidity and narrow-mindedness. In line with such Darwinian ideas, the international position of China, once a great power, could be improved by conscious and proper efforts. Central to Zhou's thought in the 1910s and early

1920s was his emphasis on the practical, on the useful, on the experience of the individual, and on the very capacity of each individual or nation to adapt to changing circumstances. His thoughts at this stage favored flexibility, as opposed to the rigidity of theoretical formulas, and he made his test of truth an action's workability. Zhou's early approach to knowledge was built on a framework of reality. Rather than envision a world in which relationships were defined by abstract theories, he postulated a world in which reality was the essence of dynamic and immediate interactions. Implicit in this emphasis was the fact that Zhou took human will and choice into account, thus permitting a human role that was in itself creative and constructive. It was a role based mainly on the dimension of human wisdom.

Against the background of Zhou's pragmatic perspectives it is now possible to turn our attention to a more specific examination of Zhou's analyses of diplomatic negotiations in Western Europe as well as his commentaries on the British, French, and American foreign policies of the early 1920s and to his evolving world outlook under the influence of Marxism-Leninism.

CHAPTER 2

Zhou's Early Views on International Relations and Foreign Policy

In tracing the development of Zhou's early pragmatism, it is clear that, in the process of extracting meaning from the practical teachings of Gu and Wang, he combined the basic tenets of Chinese pragmatic philosophy with the Western ideas of biological adaptability and experimental method. These two categories of intellectual inspiration tended to be mutually reinforcing in the development of Zhou's early thinking. By nature and by training, Zhou displayed an inclination, during these formative years, to appreciate the value of moderation, practicality, and the skillful management of concrete problems. What is noteworthy, however, is that on certain issues Zhou's careful observations and realistic assessments of current problems converged enough to make his focus on the nature of knowledge fit with his analysis of the main characteristics of interstate relations. This was especially true in his comments made in the early 1920s on postwar European international relations and foreign policy. For Zhou now viewed pragmatism as an extremely important tool of statecraft in international relations. He also felt that rational analysis of foreign policy issues should be an ongoing process and a way through which a policymaker could develop and formulate policy guidelines.

International relations, in Zhou's view, were conducted by sovereign nation-states. The major powers of Europe during the late nineteenth and early twentieth centuries were not above using their weaker neighbors as pawns in their quest for greatness and benefits.[1] As an observer of European power politics, Zhou had his apprehensions about European interstate relations in the early 1920s, just as he had about the international situation in Asia and the Pacific region. On the question of whether or not the exercise of power was necessary to mitigate the abuses of power, it was Zhou's belief that power should be used to manage power in the world arena.[2] By implication, international law should reinforce the process of diplomacy and strengthen the moral factor in postwar European interstate relations.[3] Zhou's personal interest in European statesmen and in the successful employment of statecraft at this early stage in his life and career was tangential to his primary objective, which was to achieve a better understanding of the art of diplomacy in the West and of the nature and substance of a sound foreign policy.

While studying and working in Paris, London, and Bonn from 1921 to 1924, Zhou made a conscious effort to broaden and enrich his knowledge of foreign affairs. His interest in international events naturally led him to observe systematically and in great depth the modern, competitive, multistate system in action; the efficacy of diplomacy; and the nature of foreign policy in postwar Europe.[4] Zhou's writings during this period have received little attention, yet it was during this early phase that we see the first fruits of his Shenyang and Nankai education and the origins of many of his later interests.

Zhou's main sources of information at this time were Western newspapers, journals, and books, which made up his intellectual diet as a student-observer. The questions that attracted his attention were those concerned with European postwar socioeconomic and diplomatic problems. Pragmatic philosophy clearly influenced Zhou's articles and essays written during this period by serving as a framework into which he fitted the ideas that he had acquired earlier from Gu, Wang, Darwin, Dewey, Hu, and others. He sent his articles on postwar European interstate relations for publication in the *Social Welfare Daily* (Yi-shi-bao), a missionary-sponsored newspaper with its headquarters in Tianjin, China. The essays Zhou wrote in the early and mid-1920s combined a graceful literary style with a perceptive understanding of the individual personalities of particular statesmen and of the consequences of their foreign policies. These writings shed light on Zhou's early views concerning the nature of international relations, the purpose of foreign policy, and the efficacy of diplomacy. From his beginnings as an engaged observer of postwar Europe, Zhou maintained a lifelong interest in the understanding and practice of diplomacy.

In retrospect, his stay in Western Europe proved to be very important to him, serving as a catalyst to his life's work as a statesman. Not only did he observe current European diplomatic events there, but, more important, he developed and nurtured his lifelong interest in foreign affairs. In his early newspaper articles and essays one can identify Zhou's insights into the problems of interstate relations and statecraft, insights he later employed in conducting China's foreign policy from the rise of the Chinese Communist Party (CCP) to national power in 1949 until his death in 1976.

In his numerous articles and essays Zhou expounded four major themes that reflected his early views on interstate relations and foreign policy in Europe as well as in Asia. First, he tried to characterize the European state system.[5] As he saw it, European nation-states engaged in a spectrum of international behavior ranging from cooperation to antagonism. Under evolving international circumstances each major power in postwar Europe must contribute to the stabilization of the new international order based on its perception of its own self-interests and tempered by the need for continental stability. Second, he suggested that in the game of world politics it was essential for policymakers to formulate pragmatic foreign policies in order to maximize their national interests. He recognized that pragmatism was the guiding principle that had traditionally shaped British foreign policies.[6] A conscious effort to mitigate France's fear and Germany's humiliation was seen by Zhou as the necessary prelude to any sound foreign policy of postwar Great Britain. He was fascinated by the operating skills and mesmeric wiles of the British premier David Lloyd George. Third, relations among nation-states were marked by mutual adjustment. Zhou had a clear vision of diplomacy as an instrument for accomplishing national objectives, and he maintained that through diplomacy nation-states were usually able to reconciling differences and to achieve peaceful international change.[7] But the process of reconciling differences between states could be long and difficult. Fourth, in his analysis of Far Eastern international relations Zhou cautioned the Chinese people about the implications of Japan's rising influence in the world arena and the serious consequences of China's diplomatic isolation at the 1921-22 Washington Conference.[8]

Zhou's General View on the European State System and on the Major Trends in Postwar European International Relations

According to Zhou, international relations were conducted among nation-states. Because of the existence of numerous sovereign states, the principal objective of each state was to ensure its security and, ultimately, its independence and survival. The international behavior of states was characterized by the rationalization of an adaptive process. Essentially, relations among nation-states took the form of conflict or cooperation. The conduct of nation-states toward one another was the result not only of their relative power positions but also of the ideas and aspirations that shaped the minds and actions of each nation's decision makers.

Zhou was keenly aware of the power motive operating in interstate relations, as he had observed the constant power confrontations of major nations in nineteenth-century Europe. The possession of power and prestige by some nations in the early twentieth century invariably resulted in some form of encroachment upon the sovereignty and independence of others. International relations thus consisted of the total bilateral relations struck between states at any give time and, consequently, included any subject of mutual interest. These bilateral relations structured multinational relations and defined the expected conduct by which states could carry out joint activities or compete. The existence of weak states might prove irresistible to a strong state and, as a result, the policy of a strong state might seek either to increase power or to demonstrate power at the expense of weaker states. Moreover, the so-called great powers regarded the weaker states as easy prey and were equally content to accommodate one another if a favorable opportunity arose.

Zhou saw conflict between nation-states as a constant factor in European international relations. It was his basic belief that the major European powers were expansionist and ever ready to use force against one another. He described this pattern of European interstate relations as "mutual cheating among the strong and weak states" (jiang-ruo xiang-qi) and "mutual threat among major and small nations" (dai-xiao xiang-he).[9] The major powers manipulated lesser states to increase their own status and international prestige. This tendency was an inherent element of the European state system.

Although conflicts of interest between states were forever present, each state traditionally possessed a wide spectrum of instruments for settling disputes peacefully. These means included the application of economic and diplomatic sanctions, negotiation, arbitration according to international law, and the threat of force designed to make its actual use unnecessary. According to Zhou, in postwar interstate relations the major European governments must accept international law as binding upon all of them. His concepts of international law, international organizations, and peace and war reflected his faith in a community of nations in which the postwar European states could exist side by side, regulating their relations by common legal principles and institutional arrangements. Zhou held that power politics must be tempered by international law and that nation-states must use their power as an instrument of stability and a tool for furthering common interests more vital than their own.[10] Zhou regarded compromise and conciliation as essential factors in postwar European international relations.[11] He also considered the desire of major powers for territorial expansion as an intolerable menace to the interests and security of the weaker states, and he questioned the moral implications of social Darwinism in the realm of foreign policy.[12]

Zhou felt that the sources of stability and uncertainty in postwar European international relations must be sought in the immensity and novelty of problems existing immediately after World War I: the perceived conflicts between Great Britain and France, on one side, and between France and Germany, on the other, and the fiscal restraints on the governments of all the major European states. An incorrigible, long-standing distrust had again seized the policymakers of European states, and this lack of mutual trust, in turn, required vigilance with regard to the possession of territory, population, national resources, and military apparatus. Zhou saw the need for the major European nations to compromise on issues that were vital to the political stability and economic prosperity of the entire continent.[13]

World War I accelerated the breakdown of European equilibrium. To diminish Germany unduly would have defeated Great Britain's fundamental interest, which was the preservation of a balance of power in which Germany was a necessary and essential part. Britain's objective was to restore such a balance of power and return economic stability to Europe. Given the postwar situation, the restoration of German power, within reasonable limits, was desirable for the proper functioning of the European state system.[14] It was only natural that David Lloyd George be wary of the effects of French supremacy upon the balance of power in Europe.[15] The suspicion, distrust, and even antagonism between Great Britain and France, which were key to an understanding of European diplomacy, were most evident in the questions of security, reparations, and the status of Upper Silesia.

For France the basic issues in Europe immediately after the war were primarily political and psychological in nature: namely, how to prevent Germany from becoming once again a dominant power in Europe.[16] For the leading French statesmen, and especially Aristide Briand, the French premier, the security of France meant the strict enforcement of the Treaty of Versailles of 1919, and this prerequisite had to be assured before they could contemplate any leniency toward Germany.[17] Lloyd George, on his part, considered that the basic issues in postwar Europe were economic, not political or military. His concerns were how to restore European economic prosperity and international trade, achieve economic recovery in Great Britain, raise the standard of living, and reduce the burden of unemployment.[18] In the period immediately following World War I, Lloyd George was a staunch defender of Germany's traditional role on the European continent, and he intended to take Germany's side. He was against certain French foreign policies and actions, especially when they seemed to interfere with the British predilection for a "balance of power" in Europe.[19]

Security was, in Zhou's analysis, a basic requirement that France prized to a much greater extent than did other postwar European states. The level of security sought by Briand and other French leaders was closely associated with Germany's industrial and military capabilities. Zhou's analysis of Lloyd George's foreign policy was perhaps the most perceptive among all his elaborations of postwar European international relations and foreign policy, while his examination of Briand's approach to postwar Germany demonstrated a comprehensive appreciation of the complexity of French diplomacy. On both issues Zhou clearly demonstrated his inclination toward pragmatism and a flexible approach to foreign policy issues.[20] It was apparent to Zhou that each major power, while seeking to limit and check others, strove for a supremacy that was difficult to achieve and still more difficult to maintain. Narrow-minded nationalism, Zhou argued, combined with serious diplomatic clashes between Great Britain and France and between France and Germany, had obscured the common interests of postwar Europe as a whole.[21]

Zhou further observed that the key to future European order and stability was close cooperation between France and Great Britain.[22] It was evident to Zhou, however, that this cooperation must be maintained primarily vis-à-vis Germany, whose relations with both France and Great Britain would affect the restoration of European equilibrium. Given the vacuum of power created when Germany was so severely fettered, might not French power loom uncomfortably large if not kept in check? It was obviously in the vital interest of Great Britain to prevent or at least minimize such a possibility. Great Britain was then faced with the task of restoring a balance of power within the European community itself. The main aim of this policy had remained unchanged throughout the modern period, other than its adaptation to the prevailing alignment of forces in postwar Europe. The rationale of preventing any European power or combination of powers from achieving a dominant position remained the same as at the turn of the century, yet the policies based on this rationale were adapted to the evolving European state system during the postwar era.

Zhou's Comments on Pragmatism in Foreign Policy

It is apparent from Zhou's writings that he believed that foreign policy never could, or should, be separated from the realities of the international arena. In his numerous articles published in the *Social Welfare Daily* in 1921 and 1922, Zhou demonstrated his appreciation for the pragmatic approach to the formulation of foreign policy. It was pragmatism that provided the analytical framework within which his analysis of postwar British and French foreign policies and diplomatic maneuvers took shape.[23]

According to Zhou, British foreign policymakers, past and present, always took into account prevailing world conditions in formulating and executing their foreign policy. They carefully compared their own resources with those of other states in order to arrive at a realistic assessment of their own national strength. They fully understood the importance of a stable balance between the changing forces of the international arena and the demands of domestic developments. On several occasions Zhou made the distinction between "rigid foreign policy decisions" and "pragmatic foreign policy" and placed the foreign policy of Great Britain in the latter category.[24] Even so, he admitted that, as long as the world was divided into nation-states, "national interest" was the determining factor in the formation and implementation of a sovereign state's foreign policy.[25] In a world in which states vied for power and influence, the foreign policies of all states must consider security their fundamental requirement. All states were compelled to protect their territorial integrity and political independence. Therefore, national security was inseparably identified with national interest. In Zhou's observations Great Britain's traditional foreign policy tended to aim at maximizing national interests, defined as security, economic prosperity, and maritime superiority.[26] If a foreign policy were based on pragmatism, including compromise and conciliation, its adjustments to world conditions then became dynamic and strategic while still operating within the framework safeguarding national aspirations and interests. If a foreign policy were rigid and dogmatic, it left no room for developing alternative solutions.

Commenting on diplomatic negotiations between Great Britain and France in 1921 and 1922, Zhou suggested that the restoration of a stable Europe depended on several factors. First of all, Great Britain had to act as a reconciling influence, and, to be "impartial," London would have to find a compromise between France and Germany on the issue of war reparations.[27] Lloyd George, as the postwar British prime minister, should articulate the general interests of Paris and Bonn, especially where these were obscured by tensions between the two governments due to the problems of paying war reparations and deciding the future of Upper Silesia.[28] Moreover, Lloyd George should not ignore either legitimate French grievances or the powerful presence of German national pride.

Zhou admired Lloyd George's understanding that excessive French reparation demands could slow down the process of economic and financial reconstruction in postwar Europe; the British government, for strategic and economic reasons, was anxious to have Europe return to stable and prosperous conditions as soon as possible. Lloyd George's readiness to safeguard Great Britain's maritime interests and revive economic relations with the Soviet Union, in Zhou's view, constituted a pragmatic foreign policy that, with its sober recognition of the transient alignments governing relations between states and of their essential interests, was the product of a pragmatic mind. Poise, balance, determination, and flexibility were the hallmarks of Lloyd George's approach to postwar British foreign policy.[29] Zhou observed that elasticity, adroitness, and, above all, "cunning," guided by profound knowledge and an understanding of diplomacy and European affairs, were Lloyd George's main weapons.

What was lasting was the nation, not its accords or alliances. In the competition and struggle for power, Great Britain in postwar Europe had to pursue foreign policy objectives designed to preserve its own interests. This approach was consonant with Zhou's contention that the foreign policymaker of a state should think and act in terms of national interests, defined as security, economic prosperity, and prestige, and in accordance with international circumstances. The fundamental foreign policy objectives of every sovereign state, like those of Great Britain in the postwar years, were the preservation of an optimum degree of national security, the enlargement of its international influence and power, and the realization of a "peaceful era" (xiao-kang), to use Zhou's words. As he saw it, Lloyd George was realistic enough to combine the two strategies—that is, to establish as far as possible London's political and military cooperation with Paris, on the one hand, and to maximize diplomatic contact with Bonn, on the other. While the central aim of British foreign policy under Lloyd George's leadership was to promote national interests, his diplomatic moves and countermoves reflected a high level of flexibility.

In his newspaper articles Zhou frequently described Lloyd George as a shrewd foreign policymaker who took full advantage of diplomacy as an instrument of postwar British foreign policy.[30] Zhou regarded diplomacy as a marketplace in which one was expected to bargain and literally to "purchase" certain commodities at a reasonable price. Major elements in the postwar British diplomatic course of action were, in his view, Lloyd George's visions of "reality," "moderation," and, above all, "practical value."[31] Zhou was conscious of the fact that Lloyd George was treating each diplomatic question, such as war reparations, the security of France, or the status of Upper Silesia, according to its intrinsic merits.

The concept of "maximum diplomatic maneuverability" and its application to Great Britain's foreign affairs made possible Lloyd George's shifts in foreign policy vis-à-vis both France and Germany according to the present circumstances. This implied a proper concern with the balance of power and the economic prosperity of the European continent. Given his practical concern with economy and his sensitivity to the European balance of power, it was natural enough that one of Lloyd George's tasks was to reconcile conflicting interests between France and Germany.[32] The extraordinary national interests corresponded to what the British government had sought and the ordinary ones to what the other European governments had supported, as made necessary by circumstances arising after World War I. Thus, Lloyd George's diplomatic resources ought to have had a very broad area of free play in the European community. Agreement among major European states on the framework of a new order was possible if, in Zhou's analysis, Lloyd George and other European foreign policymakers could calculate the interests of their countries impersonally and rationally.

It should be noted that British foreign trade was seriously injured by the economic chaos that followed the war. If Germany, the most important industrial nation on the European continent, were rehabilitated, all Europe would soon resume a normal economic life, and a revival of British trade would follow. Against this background Lloyd George looked upon both Germany and the Soviet Union as potential customers for his country in international trade.[33] What was more, from Lloyd George's viewpoint Germany represented an indispensable element of the European balance of power, especially set against France or the Soviet Union; hence, its position could not be diminished. He could see in the excessive French demands for reparations a desire to ruin Germany. Recognizing that Great Britain had an interest in the discovery of a "fair" solution to the problem of war reparations, Lloyd George hoped that a well-balanced diplomatic approach, as Zhou put it, would permit a peaceful era to materialize and take root.[34]

Whatever the outcome of the British prime minister's diplomatic approaches might be, it was Zhou's belief that the foreign policy of Great Britain must be judged by its pragmatic value and tangible results and not by preconceived theoretical formulas. In other words, the foreign policy objectives of a state ought to be defined in terms of vital national interest and should be supported with adequate power. He held the pragmatic character of the foreign policy of Great Britain in high esteem and often spoke of proper adjustment or pragmatic adaptation as the instrument that could lead to diplomatic success.[35]

What impressed Zhou about post-World War I British foreign policy was its rational moderation, nondogmatic considerations, and, above all, the subtle balance between the nation's power and aspirations. A key to the British course of action, Zhou informed Chinese readers, was London's vision of "reality."[36] For states, like human beings, the ability to lead and to adjust to the environment was the key to their diplomatic maneuverability and success. The task of defining situations in the context of pragmatic foreign policy required concrete answers to unique questions. Answering these questions correctly demanded, first of all, a thorough and intimate knowledge and understanding of the nation as a whole. Furthermore, it required political and economic judgment of a very high order. It was necessary to adjust ends to means. It was then important to select from a number of possible diplomatic devices the one most appropriate for the situation. These decisions must not be deduced from abstract principles, which might or might not be compatible with the actions of the government, but must be based on the real interests of the nation. Ultimately, the foreign policy of a state must be judged not by its theoretical claim or purity but, rather, by the degree of its pragmatic adaptation. It is not surprising that Zhou used Great Britain on more than one occasion as the classic example of a state that followed a pragmatic approach to foreign policy.

Zhou recognized that it was a real challenge for a foreign policymaker to manage unpredictable events with flexibility. In order to reach the required elasticity of mind, it was important for the foreign policymaker to strike a balance between caution and innovation by developing an awareness of the ubiquity of unpredictability. Zhou seemed to think that it was possible to draw some useful lessons from historical facts, even if such lessons were admittedly narrow in scope and subject to numerous qualifications. The search for international reality was a historical process whose contours were shaped by pragmatism and the particular circumstances in postwar Europe. It displayed continuities, recurrent patterns, and a degree of clarity over time.

In his analysis of postwar British foreign policy under Lloyd George's leadership, Zhou employed the terms *national interests, pragmatic foreign policy,* and *flexible methods and maneuvers* to describe its major characteristics. Fundamentally, foreign policy was based on reality defined by a specific set of international circumstances. The best way for a nation to increase its power and influence abroad was to formulate and execute a well-defined and pragmatic foreign policy. Such a policy, once implemented, would yield very concrete and specific results. Zhou was inclined to place his emphasis on taking concrete actions that would best serve national interests. Careful appraisal of strategic national priorities in the realm of foreign policy, for Zhou, was particularly important. He showed in his articles a preference for proper adjustment and concrete moves, which he believed to be the essence of pragmatic foreign policy.

In his preliminary analysis Zhou found that the traditional British approach to foreign affairs was based on self-examination and the impartial observation of human motives that could not be avoided or resisted. As Lord Palmerston suggested, there was no eternal animosity or friendship between nation-states, and national interest should determine the course of a nation's foreign policy.[37] Zhou carefully distinguished between flexibility and opportunism, yet this distinction did not affect the different approaches of caution and rational moderation that he had stressed in the past.

It was Zhou's strong belief that nation-states must be ready to examine and constantly reexamine their own interests and commitments as international circumstances changed and as new challenges appeared. He had little confidence, however, in the one-sided imposition of views because it tended to crystallize differences and set nation-states in opposition, and, ultimately, it was self-defeating. Not only did Zhou point out the difficulties of establishing order and stability in postwar Europe; he indicated the priority of common interests between the major victorious countries. Moreover, the evidence showed that France in the post-1919 period was placing more emphasis on punishing Germany than on establishing European order and stability.[38] On at least two occasions Zhou stated that British sensitivity to having an "equilibrium" of forces in postwar Europe was of such a nature as to simplify recognition of the advantages of stability.[39] Every development favorable to security and order would be cultivated by the British foreign policymakers.

As a young student and observer, Zhou's analysis was indeed impressive, even though it fell short of the principle of balance of power and its application to British foreign policy in the postwar period. For Zhou, however, a given foreign policy was justified not according to whether or not it was traditional or in accord with abstract doctrine but, rather, whether it would work—namely, by its practicality and its positive results. The need for realistic self-orientation in the complex, changing international environment appeared to be consistent with Zhou's assessment of postwar European international relations and diplomacy. What he referred to as "practicality" and "positive results" were the essential elements that would bear on the actual improvement and advancement of the vital self-interests of a state in terms of the unique contribution of the cautious foreign policymaker and the utilitarian function of diplomacy. Zhou's personal preference for pragmatism over dogmatic, abstract fashion would have been unlikely without prior familiarity with philosophers who emphasized the importance of the concrete and practical. Realistically enough, he reminded his readers of the importance of attaining a peaceful era in interstate relations[40] and held strongly that nations would flourish through hardship.

Zhou's Emphasis on the Reconciliation of Differences among Postwar European States through Diplomacy

Diplomacy was considered by Zhou to be a crucial instrument in the restoration of European stability in the years immediately following World War I. Accommodating differences through diplomacy became possible when the major

European powers realized the importance of their common interests. Therefore, the skillful employment of diplomacy could contribute to economic prosperity and political stability in all of postwar Europe. A precondition for the creation of a stable European order, according to Zhou, was the development of a new consensus among the major European powers, and diplomacy could contribute to peace through mutual accommodations between Great Britain and France and between France and Germany. Given the importance of postwar British-French and German-French relationships, Zhou, in his articles, asserted that diplomacy was the process through which tensions between states were reduced.[41] He further characterized interstate relations as the continuous adjustment of conflicting national interests.

Diplomatic flexibility could be more easily achieved by accommodating fluctuating forces than by pursuing rigidly defined goals. Diplomacy was viewed by Zhou as a nation's capacity for attaining specific ends, although diplomatic flexibility might at times become an end in itself. It was a combination of persuasive influence and the application of various pressures without actually resorting to physical force. Statesmen in Western Europe always attempted to strengthen their ability to pursue political aims beyond their national boundaries in a cautious manner, seeking security, power, and influence through the art of negotiation. In his elaboration of traditional diplomacy as the art of restraining the exercise of power, Zhou suggested that each foreign policymaker expected to enhance his or her national interests through shifting arrangements with the others. The instruments of leverage for international bargaining available to the postwar European governments ranged along a continuum from peaceful solutions to the threat of sanctions. They were determined, in the final analysis, by the relative distribution of power among the major states.

Zhou greatly valued room for diplomatic maneuverability simply because he believed that it provided the most essential element of structuring or cementing the whole process of "compromise" (zhe-zhong). He held the art of "reconciliation" (tiao-ting) in high regard. In his opinion reconciliation was the most crucial element in leading the negotiators toward the discovery of the common ground needed to achieve a stable international order in postwar Europe. More specifically, a country's diplomatic flexibility and international bargaining position, in Zhou's judgment, was contingent on its overall capacity and degree of willingness to reconcile.[42]

The task of negotiators in charge of finding peaceful and equitable solutions to grave conflicts was singularly difficult and complex. In any diplomatic negotiation, asserted Zhou, the more one knew about one's counterpart, the better one's chances for success.[43] Moreover, self-interest, or, to quote Zhou's expression, "self-fattening" (zhi-fei), would always motivate, if not dictate, the minds and actions of a nation's foreign policymakers.[44] In order to acquaint his Chinese readers with the European tradition of settling disputes between states through diplomacy, Zhou urged them to broaden their views about the changing nature of postwar European interstate relations, notably the difficulties in reconciling the basic differences between France and Germany and between Great Britain and France. Such knowledge could provide the observers with the proper perspective to fully appreciate the subtlety of diplomacy as the adjustment of differences through negotiation.[45]

In the years immediately following World War I, France viewed the collective security system of the League of Nations as simply a supplement to the alliance system against Germany. Taken in isolation, the determination to punish Germany was understandable, in Zhou's view, for Germany still constituted a real threat to the sovereignty and territorial integrity of France. According to Briand's original position, Germany was more than capable of bearing the burden of postwar reparations. Germany had suffered no physical damage, and its industrialists were glutted with wealth. The only barrier to reparations payment was the German position of intransigently refusing to pay. Therefore, Briand saw postwar reparations not only in terms of justice, as compensation for his nation's losses, but also as a possible means of keeping Germany in check and delaying its economic recovery. In other words, in Germany's weakness lay France's national security.[46]

Zhou reported in his newspaper articles that Briand's policy of sanctions in 1921 appeared uncompromising and bellicose and that French troops occupied three German towns of the industrial area of the Rühr—Duisburg, Duhrort, and Düsseldorf.[47] The sanctions temporarily increased French flexibility. They could serve as a means to force German capitulation and as levers for the extension of French Rhenish policy. In the event that the German government resisted reparations, now scheduled to be worked out by the Allies, Briand still held the military plan in reserve: full occupation of the Rühr, with or without Great Britain.

In considering French foreign policy in light of these trends and possibilities, it was necessary to recognize the importance of avoiding the danger of isolation at the international conferences held to solve the reparations problem and at the same time restoring the confidence of the French people. To this end the French premier had to exercise delicate and rational statesmanship. Zhou observed that Briand began to shift to a new strategic effort in order to lay the groundwork for a realistic foreign policy suitable for the "conditions in Europe and beyond" (si-zhou-qing-shi), and to bring French foreign policy and objective reality into harmony. To use Zhou's words, the French position on the reparations problem must be "moderate" (he-huan) in nature and should "give way" (rang-bu) to the reality that excessive demands placed on Germany would have negative effects on France's relations with Germany as well as with Great Britain.[48] The main reason underlying Briand's conciliatory position vis-à-vis both Great Britain and Germany in 1922 was, as Zhou observed, his desire to prevent French diplomatic "isolation" (gu-li), which would be a hindrance to further improvement of French international prestige and European stability.

According to Zhou's assessment, Briand was an able and dynamic French statesman, bold in his views but cautious in his efforts to promote "conciliation" (tiao-he) and "compromise" with both Great Britain and Germany.[49] The shift of the "guiding principle" (fang-zhen) of Briand's foreign policy in late 1921 and early 1922 was prompted by the realization that France could not escape dependence on Great Britain and must therefore play a constructive role in strengthening European cooperation and understanding. Such a policy change embodied the recognition of both "self-interest" and mutual interdependence.[50] Zhou went into great detail in identifying and explaining the shift of Briand's conduct of French foreign policy for his Chinese readers. He was very impressed by Briand's evolving positions on the issues of postwar reparations and security in Europe. The importance of any foreign policy should be evaluated, according to Zhou, not on the basis of ideological doctrine but, rather, on its positive results. The need for a constant assessment of the complex, changing international environment was a central theme in Zhou's analysis of Briand's foreign policy.[51]

One major question raised by Zhou was how the defeated Germany was to settle its relations with the major victorious powers of Europe. This, in Zhou's view, required considerable adjustment on the part of the postwar German government. At the very least a commitment to war reparations was necessary to preserve normal relations with Great Britain, France, Italy, and other countries in Europe. On several occasions in his newspaper articles Zhou reported the different approaches of Lloyd George and Briand on the basic issue of the proper amount of reparations to be paid by Germany. The former wished to preserve the economic stability of Germany after the war; his concern for European economic and financial recovery colored his position. Briand was anxious to ensure the security of France, and he was more interested in accomplishing this by weakening Germany's overall national strength through punitive reparations. He believed that France's influence in postwar Europe depended upon its ability to curb the future expansion of Germany. Therefore, he was not committed to improving French-German relations in the spirit of just settlement. Furthermore, according to Zhou, the issue of Poland's claims to Upper Silesia served only to reveal afresh the deepening fissure between the policies of France and Great Britain. France, in its unconcealed appreciation of the fact that Poland now ranked as one of its natural allies, approved of Polish action in absorbing Upper Silesia. The British government, on the other hand, felt strongly obliged to protect Germany against the Polish seizure of its territory as compensation.

In his newspaper articles Zhou observed the failure of French efforts to link a guarantee treaty with Great Britain with a general European security treaty. This failure implied that, as the mainstay of its security, France would have to choose an alliance with Great Britain against Germany, on the one hand, or with its Eastern European allies, on the other. Zhou reported that Lloyd George and Briand tried to reduce tensions between the two countries at the Cannes Conference in early January 1922, but neither expected any far-reaching solutions to emerge from the talks.[52] In his discussions with Lloyd George, Briand's conciliatory attitude toward the British prime minister and his approval of the proposed economic conference of all European states, including the Soviet Union and Germany, were intended to keep the door open for a treaty of French-British alliance. As for Great Britain, Lloyd George announced that his country would promise to assist France if the latter were invaded by Germany but would offer no guarantees of support to Eastern European countries such as Poland and Czechoslovakia.

In Zhou's view Lloyd George was fully aware of the fact that the establishment and preservation of an ordered political scene in postwar Europe would be contingent upon British-French cooperation. Yet, the British prime minister's broad assessment of the European balance of forces, or equilibrium, and of Great Britain's self-interest would compel him to avoid being restricted unilaterally by the British-French agreement manipulated by Briand. The most fundamental fact of postwar European diplomacy, in Zhou's estimate, was that, if international conditions changed, national priorities and commitments would have to be reevaluated. Each great power was a potential aggressor to its neighbor, since it knew this neighbor to be inspired by motives similar to its own. It could not but regard every subtle diplomatic maneuver of its neighbor as a potential challenge. Therefore, Zhou contended, foreign policymakers should think and act in terms of interests defined as "security according to circumstance." In addition, Lloyd George's new emphasis in British foreign policy vis-à-vis France, at the Cannes conference table and his proposed conference at Genoa, for the reconstruction of the European economy was a key manifestation of the British prime minister's "cunning" (jiao-hua). It was but natural that Lloyd George adopted a strategy, to use Zhou's words, of "making a feint to the east, while attacking in the west" (sheng-dong-ji-xi).[53] In other words, there was a strategic shift in the British foreign policy priority from a focus on France to other European nations, but the central theme in postwar British foreign policy remained the same: the inevitable linkage between British-French collaboration, on the one hand, and the maintenance of European order and stability, on the other.

Zhou observed that the conflicting interests between Great Britain and France, and especially between France and Germany, ought to be reconciled through diplomacy.[54] In the same vein the traditional animosity between France and Germany must be restrained for a peace in Europe that would give security and economic prosperity to all its member states, big and small alike. Moreover, the competitive character of the relations among sovereign states made the application of diplomacy to the settlement of international conflicts uniquely indispensable. Despite the appalling waste of energy and human lives caused by incessant rivalries and wars, diplomacy could always exercise a positive and beneficial function. It communicated, Zhou held, a stimulus to intensive negotiations and forced upon European policymakers an ever greater rationalization and justification for their nonmilitary moves and mechanisms. Thus, he regarded diplomacy as an effective technique for managing power and assigned to it a major role in mitigating interstate conflicts in postwar Europe.[55]

Zhou's Analysis of the Washington Conference (1921-1922) and China's Struggle for Survival

As a young man, Zhou was well versed in the modern history of China. At the turn of this century China had been reduced to an object of international relations to be discussed and dispensed with by foreign powers. It had no voice, even on matters affecting its vital political and territorial interests and rights.[56] Moreover, China lacked political unity, developed resources, and strength at home as well as the necessary status abroad to play an independent role in world politics. In his articles written in the years 1916 and 1917 Zhou was very apprehensive about Japan's intentions and its design to exploit the conditions in China in order to obtain special rights and privileges.[57] The underlying force of the May Fourth Movement of 1919 was the powerful drive among Chinese intellectuals and students for the emancipation of their country from its semicolonial status imposed by a series of unequal treaties.

China could not become independent and powerful, in Zhou's view, until it was freed from both the feudal and the imperialist yokes. The warlord government in Beijing had been coerced into granting special economic rights and privileges to foreign powers, obtaining loans on the security of national revenues and economic concessions, and agreeing to foreign capital investment in mines and railways.[58] Zhou was keenly aware of the dangers of Japanese imperialism and militarism. His apprehension was fully borne out of imperial Japan's Twenty-one Demands imposed upon the Chinese government in 1915 and subsequently by unfavorable decisions concerning China at the 1919 Paris Peace Conference. According to Zhou, the whole Asia-Pacific region was controlled by a handful of "imperialist" powers. Japan's imperialist thrust was aimed in the direction of the Asian continent as well as the Pacific region. Great Britain was essentially a status quo power, interested in preserving its superior position in Chinese commerce. On the continent of Asia, Great Britain and Japan had little cause for friction as long as Japanese continental expansion was confined to southern Manchuria.

In the postwar years there was genuine alarm in the United States that Japan might take advantage of the European conflicts to further its special interests in China. The most significant postwar American move to check Japan's military expansion in the Far East was its convening of the Washington Conference in 1921. The Washington Conference grew out of a desire, in the interest of international economy, to reduce naval armament. As far as the United States was concerned, the area of future conflict appeared to be the Far East. Japan was viewed as a potential adversary whose foreign policies apparently conflicted with those of the United States. China had the potential to become the principal field of international tensions due to the weakness and disorganization of the Chinese government.

United States policymakers desired to put an end to the diplomacy of imperialism and secret agreements. They were anxious to halt Japan's policy of territorial expansion in the Far East and attempted to create new conditions for order and stability in China. In order to neutralize the Anglo-Japanese alliance the U.S. secretary of state, Charles E. Hughes, agreed to a more general and consultative pact that also included France. In the Four-Power Treaty of December 13, 1921, the United States, Great Britain, Japan, and France guaranteed one another's rights and possessions in the Pacific and agreed to settle disputes in that region by "peaceful consultation." Should a dispute emerge, however, "out of any Pacific questions . . . involving their said rights which is not satisfactorily settled by diplomacy . . . they shall invite the other High Contracting Parties to a joint conference to which the whole subject will be referred for consideration and adjustment."[59] To guard against a possible Anglo-American military attack, Japan was protected by a pledge of non-intervention in the Far East by the Western powers. According to Zhou, what Japan lost in security in the Anglo-Japanese alliance was regained in the Five-Power Naval Limitation Treaty, which was signed on February 5, 1922. By this treaty the original four powers and Italy agreed to maintain a military status quo in the Far East and refrain from building new fortifications and naval installations. The naval treaty assured Japan of a dominant position in the western Pacific and relative security from British or American attack. The naval ratio of capital ships for the five powers, Zhou reported in his news articles, was fixed at five each for the United States and Great Britain, and three for Japan.[60]

A major question arose here: Could the 1921-22 Washington Conference find a formula that would reconcile the traditional American foreign policy of upholding China's administrative and territorial integrity with Japan's determination to retain its special interests in China? Zhou's answer was that Japan, sensitive to any relative reduction of naval power, would not accept any inferior ratio without corresponding "compensation" (bao-chou).[61] By making three "sacrifices" (xi-sheng)—that is, consent to the naval buildup ratio, the abandonment of the alliance with Great Britain, and the withdrawal of military forces from Siberia—Japan expected compensation from the other major participating states at the Washington Conference. Zhou perceived that the imperialist foreign powers could very well transform their mutually competing aggression into concerted aggression against China in order to preserve their common interests and privileges.[62] It was dangerous, Zhou held, for the Chinese people to overlook the naked power politics of the international arena. Based on this premise, he advocated the principle of "self-determination" (zi-jue) and strongly opposed collective foreign control or foreign spheres of influence in China.[63]

Zhou frequently reminded his Chinese readers about the far-reaching consequences of China's vulnerable position in the world arena and of its diplomatic isolation at the Washington Conference.[64] His strong belief in the struggle for survival and natural selection led him to urge the Chinese people to fight for national independence. He warned that, if the Chinese people did not strive to launch a vigorous resistance to foreign imperialism, the fate of a "divided domination" (hua-fen) or "joint control" (gong-quan) by the major foreign powers would inevitably fall upon their country.[65] As he saw it, the diplomacy of imperialism, once exemplified by the Anglo-Japanese alliance, was now replaced by the Four-Power Treaty, which came to represent the new formula of imperialistic politics, intent upon further exploitation of China.[66]

Zhou thought that the wording of the Four-Power Treaty was vague and general: for instance, "if rights were threatened by the aggressive actions of any other power, the signatories were to communicate with one another fully and frankly in order to arrive at an understanding as to the most efficient measures to be taken, jointly or separately, to meet the exigencies of the particular situation."[67] Zhou's comment on such a provision was that it was nothing but "empty words," or a "gentlemen's agreement."[68] The tripartite understanding

among the United States, Great Britain, and Japan replaced bilateral cooperation between Great Britain and Japan. Such a strategic triangle would serve to
safeguard the participants' respective privileges and special interests in China.
This was still the diplomacy of imperialism, pure and simple. Zhou predicted
that the Washington Conference had only ushered in a period of cooperative
economic exploitation of China.[69] Against this background Zhou called the
attention of his Chinese readers to the various measures of foreign design and,
specifically, expressed his great concern about the presence of a balance of power
among the imperialist states in the Far East,[70] aiming primarily at the exploitation of China. He attempted to rouse the Chinese people to regain their
self-respect and self-confidence and to promote national solidarity.[71]

Conclusion

When Zhou was in his mid-twenties he developed great respect for the
diplomatic skills of David Lloyd George and Aristide Briand. Much of his early
writings were, in fact, devoted to the analysis of their diplomacy. From them
he learned to appreciate pragmatism and flexibility as the cornerstones of
conducting foreign affairs. First, there was a clear tendency in Zhou's articles
to articulate the precise nature of national interests and to connect these vital
interests to the pursuit of foreign policy goals.[72] Second, if any one idea stood
at the center of Zhou's early thought, it was the need for reconciliation in the
process of negotiation between two countries.[73] Third, in responding to dynamic and new global realities, the foreign policymaker must be pragmatic and
must adapt to particular events and forces in conducting diplomacy. In short,
Zhou's preference for concrete and practical solutions, rather than general
principles of a dogmatic nature, was the main reason why he attached great
importance to actions that were appropriate to actual conditions.

It was during his student years in London, Paris, and Bonn that Zhou's
lifelong interest in foreign affairs was first nurtured. Through his writings from
that time one can see how Zhou was seeking to assess the distinctive qualities of
British and French foreign policies. It is obvious, from his analyses, that he fully
recognized the national interests of Great Britain and France that underscored
the diplomacy of both Lloyd George and Briand. At the same time, he understood
and valued their prudence and skill in the use of the devices of statecraft.[74] He
never questioned the fact that the foreign policies of these two major European
countries were designed to foster their respective national interests. Consistently,
he regarded pragmatism in foreign policy as an indispensable regulating factor of

which the foreign policymaker must not lose sight.[75] Zhou's European experience was an important aspect of his intellectual life before 1925.

It is significant that Zhou's synthesis of the postwar European diplomatic experience was perceptive on several levels. He recognized the obligation of the major states to maintain postwar European stability, peace, and prosperity and studied these national goals in terms of British-French, French-German, and German-British relations.[76] Zhou himself could neither predict the emerging order in postwar Europe, nor could he penetrate conceptually into the traditional British policy of balance of power on the European continent. Nevertheless, his overall analyses involved the triangular relations between Great Britain, France, and Germany in the postwar period.

Although his study abroad from 1921 to 1924 did not move him tangibly closer to a successful diplomatic career, it gave the young Zhou an opportunity to observe Western Europe firsthand, aiding him in his early understanding of the basic ingredients of a country's foreign policy and the shifting nature of international relations. Either through his reading, personal observations, or both, Zhou was exposed (at this early age) at least conceptually, to the major diplomatic negotiations and maneuvers in postwar Europe and to the actual conduct of foreign affairs by such competent policymakers as Lloyd George of Great Britain and Briand of France. The flexible practices of Lloyd George in the field of foreign policy attracted Zhou's special attention.[77] Moreover, Great Britain was a country he knew well as a student and for which he had long felt considerable respect due to its political moderation and sophistication. As a critical analyst of foreign affairs and an interpreter of key postwar international events to the readers of the Social Welfare Daily, Zhou had to develop conceptual clarity in dealing with the subject of his special interest.

Zhou believed that in negotiation one should seek not so much to impose as to listen and that compromise was the key to negotiated settlement in postwar Europe. "Diplomatic settlement," in Zhou's view, meant a solution by mutual adjustment and accommodation between states.[78] It followed logically that interstate relations in postwar Europe called for an open mind capable of pragmatic adaptation and a temperament unmoved by emotion or ideological rhetoric. Zhou viewed postwar European diplomacy primarily as complex, shifting coalitions between the major states. He pointed out that both Great Britain and France managed to pursue diversified diplomatic strategies to their respective advantages in the early postwar years and that it was necessary for either Great Britain or France to win over additional supporters or allies to reinforce its international position at any particular time.

These and other preliminary observations may help us understand, at least in part, Zhou's basic views on foreign policy and international relations. The emphasis he placed upon the relationship between a country's foreign policy and its domestic politics and needs, and on its diplomatic initiative and flexibility, fully demonstrated his personal sensitivity to changing international environments and his sense of pragmatism in the delicate process of foreign policy formulation of any given state.[79] In international relations, Zhou reasoned, the policymakers of a nation must understand the foreign policies of other states in order to know best how to conduct their own external affairs. One finds in his analysis of postwar European interstate relations what he perceived to be the essential elements of foreign policy and the traditional function of diplomacy as an art of negotiation.

What was the reality of international relations from Zhou's perspective? It was power politics. States existed, they wished to continue to exist, and they could rely upon power to avoid conquest by their neighbors. Consequently, the struggle of each to be more powerful, on its own or in relation to its allies, than any potential enemy or any combination of enemies was at the heart of the matter.[80] The foreign policy of a given nation might display unique features, but, fundamentally, the struggle for power as the requirement for continued (prosperous) existence was the foreign policy to be expected of all nation-states. As long as the world was made up of sovereign states, possession of power would continue to be essential to their existence. Therefore, means and ends mattered to Zhou. States not only gained their ends simply by possessing armed power; sometimes they actually used it. In addition to armed forces, diplomacy was another important element of power of the state, and negotiation, for Zhou, was the supreme example of its exercise. Whether to avoid a war in postwar Europe by balancing power or to create power relationships in which war could be avoided but with the best prospect of peace in the future, postwar British and French policymakers could, Zhou demonstrated, readily take advantage of their political sophistication and subtle diplomatic style.

Analyzing European interstate relations, Zhou managed to define certain policy prerequisites and patterns and to articulate and rationalize diplomatic maneuvers. From such observations he drew valuable lessons that he later applied to Chinese foreign relations.

CHAPTER 3

The May Fourth
Movement of 1919,
Marxism-Leninism, and
Zhou's Evolving Worldview

What were the historical and cultural factors present in China during and after the May Fourth Movement of 1919 that acted as catalysts for the further development of Zhou's worldview? Were there unique elements that nourished the continuing growth of Zhou's early pragmatism? Why was Marxism-Leninism more meaningful and appealing to him than the many other contemporary schools of political thought in explaining the forces that shape international relations? Can we discern the explanations that would account for Zhou's early emphasis on the attainment of the CCP's international objectives through diplomacy? If so, what was his rationale? These questions are certainly complex, but some suggestions can be advanced.

To begin with, a historical approach is essential, because only by examining the intellectual and political trends that prevailed before, during, and after the 1919 May Fourth Movement are we able to understand the paths along which Zhou's intellect and worldview continued to develop.[1] A careful study of the possible reasons for Zhou's attraction to Marxism-Leninism may also help identify those elements that nurtured his concept of pragmatism and the ways he refined and later applied it when he become the Chinese premier and foreign minister following the CCP's rise to national power in China in 1949.

In retrospect, perhaps the political and intellectual milieu of the May Fourth Movement had as great an impact on the development of Zhou's character and thought as had his family background and early schooling. Therefore, it is impossible to understand fully how Zhou's political orientation was formed without examining the political and intellectual circumstances of the time.

Zhou and His Intellectual Milieu

Upon his graduation from the Nankai middle school in the fall of 1917, Zhou left China for Japan, partly with the idea that it would be instructive to study Japan's modernization and partly to see the outside world. His school days at Nankai had been happy and fruitful. He had been popular and had made many friends. Through his writing and his association with the *Jingyeh Review*, his reputation as a versatile person had become well-known in the Tianjin-Beijing area. He had been on good terms with his school principal, Zhang Boling, and with his teachers. On the eve of his departure for Japan Zhou wrote a poem in which he expressed his expectation that "by ten years of hard study" he would make his "breakthrough."[2]

It is important to note that Zhou's early exposure to Marxism was mainly through reading essays published in *Studies of Social Problems*, a semimonthly Japanese journal edited by Hajimi Kawakami (1879-1946), a socialist professor of economics at Kyoto University. Kawakami elaborated the major tenets of Marxism and became the most ardent academic advocate of Marxist doctrines in modern Japan.[3] In his numerous articles published in *Studies of Social Problems* he strongly criticized the rich for their profit-seeking motives and for their extravagant lifestyles. As Kawakami saw it, poverty was not the fault of poor people; he felt it could be rectified by means of social legislation or through the nationalization of major industries.

At Kyoto Zhou came under the influence of Japanese socialist scholars, especially Kawakami, from whom he learned the major aspects of Marxist theory. Zhou was particularly attracted to the Marxist ideas of dialectical materialism and progress by means of class struggle. Kawakami's interpretations of Marxism, a political philosophy new to Chinese intellectuals and students in the 1920s and 1930s, had a profound influence on Zhou's intellectual development. He studied and utilized its ideas as a philosophical framework within which to analyze Chinese internal conditions as well as contemporary European economies. At the turn of the century China's handful of major cities became centers of commerce and manufacturing spurred by foreign investment capital, railroad construction, and some small-scale domestic industries. In the cities, however, workers could mobilize their discontent, focus their anger, and bring enormous political and economic power to bear simply by refusing to work. The potential for labor unrest grew with industrialization; so did the power of China's burgeoning proletariat. It was but natural for Zhou to consider seriously the workers' revolutionary potential. Within this context he studied the arguments and writings of Marx and found practical meaning in Marxist tenets within the contemporary Chinese scene as well as their useful application.

From 1915 to 1919 Zhou was a regular reader of the *New Youth,* founded and edited by the Japanese- and French-educated Ch'en Duxiu (1879-1942), a professor at Beijing University. From the journal's inception one of its primary purposes was to provide information to its readers to help them fashion an international outlook. In the opening article of the first issue of the *New Youth,* Ch'en suggested that his readers "be progressive in their attitude toward change, utilitarian in their approach to new ideas and new techniques, and cosmopolitan (shi-jie-di) in their view of the world and China's place in it."[4] He attributed special importance to the need for Chinese youth to learn about the contemporary world. "When a people lacks an understanding of the world," Ch'en posed the question, "how can their nation be expected to survive in the world?"[5]

In another article entitled "Differences of Basic Thought between the Eastern and Western Peoples," also published in the *New Youth* in December 1915, Ch'en focused on the negative implications of the traditional values of Confucian ideology.[6] One of the fundamental differences between East and West, in Ch'en's view, was that the former paid more attention to "ceremony," while the latter paid more attention to "practical matters." Confucian scholars, he argued, advocated superfluous ceremonies and stressed the morality of meek compliance and a yielding nature, decrying struggle and competition. Ch'en asserted that this tradition and practice would make the Chinese people too weak and passive to live in the brutal and cynical world of nation-states. In order to rejuvenate the Chinese people, Ch'en strongly urged the adoption of realism as one of the key principles of Chinese education.[7]

The changes advocated by Ch'en were those he perceived as most vital for China to meet the challenge of the West. His emphasis on the Darwinian concept of adaptation and his call for the introduction of science and democracy appealed to the new generation of youth in China, for whom his infusion of moralism into Western ideas held great appeal. Ch'en's student readers, including Zhou, were also attracted to his strong opposition to the existing social and political situation, which they found oppressive.[8] While Zhou was reading and reflecting on Kawakami's interpretations of Marxist economic doctrines in Kyoto, Japan, a society for the study of Marxism—founded in the spring of

1918 by Ch'en and his colleague Li Dachao in Beijing—was also providing an ideological training ground for Chinese youth. After May 4, 1919, the *New Youth* served more and more as a forum for Ch'en and Li's Marxist views.

When the Great Powers attempted to reestablish their colonial policies at the Paris Peace Conference, the vision of hope of Chinese intellectuals and students turned to deep despair, and nationalist feeling ran higher than ever before. On May 4, 1919, students in Beijing organized a demonstration against the Chinese government's acceptance of the terms of the Paris Peace Conference and its humiliating policy toward China. As a result, the May Fourth Movement, an anti-imperialist and antifeudal movement, was propelled forward by the rising fervor of nationalism. The desire of the Chinese people for national independence from foreign intervention and aggression was widespread. The May Fourth Movement directly challenged the unequal treaties dating back to 1842, foreign concessions, naval leaseholds, and, in fact, the entire structure of foreign spheres of influence. The movement helped sanction and widen the scope and intensity of chinese students' and workers' protests against the weak, pro-Japanese, and incompetent warlord government in Beijing that had failed to protect Chinese national interests. In the process demands by Chinese intellectuals and students for an effective government to guarantee China's independence and equality in the family of nations quickly transformed into a revolt against the social, political, and cultural conditions of China and the search for means to rejuvenate the country. In this quest the new generation of Chinese youth fell under the influence of two different Western schools of thought: the Marxist, revolutionary approach, expounded by Li Dachao[9] and Ch'en Duxiu; and the pragmatic, evolutionary approach, championed by Hu Shi.[10]

Back to China from Japan in the autumn of 1919, Zhou enrolled in the Nankai University at Tianjin. He assumed responsibility as the editor of the *Tianjin Students' United League Newspaper* (Tianjin xue-lian-bao), an official newspaper published by the Tianjin Students' Association. He was also instrumental in setting up the "Awakening Society" (Jue-wu-she) on September 16, 1919, organized primarily by students from Nankai and from the First Girls' Normal School in Tianjin. The society began publishing a journal, *Awakening* (Jue-wu), on January 20, 1920. The newly organized society was dedicated to the belief that social progress should be based upon the self-awakening of the individual, and it advocated "a fundamental remaking of man's social institutions." But the ideological goals of this organization were by no means definitive. "We, as students, would never be able, would never dare, to assert that we had reached enlightenment," the manifesto stated. "We have, however, made up our minds to search for enlightenment. We hope that other people in our society will also become determined to march toward enlightenment."[11]

Zhou's friendship with Mao Zedong, who was Zhou's senior by three years, brought him into close touch with a group of patriotic students in the Tianjin-Beijing area. It was through friends of the same progressive bent that Zhou became involved in student government and in organizing student demonstrations.[12] Such activities constituted an important part of Zhou's university experience. His association with radical Chinese intellectuals during his undergraduate years had a great impact on his assessment of China's social, political, and economic problems. Zhou, and his student newspaper, supported the causes of the May Fourth Movement against the incompetency of the disorganized government in Beijing and its appeasement of Japanese aggressive schemes in China and, subsequently, urged his fellow students to take immediate joint actions. At this stage Zhou still had faith in gradualism and did not embrace Marxism unconditionally. He doubted that China needed to follow the Russian example of violent and bloody uprisings in order to establish the new order.[13]

After the May Fourth Movement the *New Youth* became the most influential journal among Chinese students, serving as an important forum for its founder, Ch'en Duxin, Li Dachao, and others to expound their Marxist views. Li's article "My Views on Marxism" appeared in the May 1919 issue.[14] In this controversial essay Li declared that history should not be interpreted forever by Marx's theory of historical materialism, arguing that the theory had been "formulated at a specific time and under specific circumstances." "Nor should Marxist theory," cautioned Li, "be accepted as a whole and applied uncritically to modern society."[15] "On the other hand," he added, "we should not disregard its historical value."[16] In another article, "The Victory of Bolshevism," published in the *New Youth* in November 1918 Li supported the theory of class struggle and emphasized the role of conscious political activity in the making of history.[17]

Hu Shi was also deeply concerned with the urgent social and economic problems in China, but he was not in favor of revolutionary doctrines and radical methods.[18] He won a large following among the Chinese by questioning the validity of Li's views. In a debate with Li in 1919 Hu rejected as impractical the notion of a fundamental solution to the complex problems in China. He had great reservations about the efficacy of using radical methods to improve China's domestic conditions. Instead, he urged the study of specific problems by Chinese intellectuals as the first and most essential step. He held the view that a discussion of concrete problems would attract broader participation than would a windy theoretical dispute. As such, the more focused discussion of real issues and problems would allow people to anticipate the implications of theories as they were applied to specific cases.[19]

Whatever the merits of Hu's argument, it did not seem to have appealed to Zhou. As time went on, Zhou became more convinced of the need for immediate social and political action to resolve China's urgent internal problems, and he began to depart from his earlier faith in gradualism. Now he viewed gradual reform as ineffective in China's struggle for independence, as the great powers were not likely to relinquish the practice of economic exploitation of underdeveloped nations throughout the world and to change their aggressive, expansionist foreign policies. One of Hu's mistakes, in Zhou's opinion, was to attribute China's ills completely to its backwardness in the field of science and to its own disorders rather than to "foreign imperialism."[20] Zhou was obviously disappointed by Hu's reluctance to regard foreign imperialism as a serious threat to China's independence and economic interests, by his distrust of nationalism, and, above all, by his rejection of the value of active political participation by the Chinese people. Zhou criticized Hu for being afraid to face reality.[21]

In an editorial of July 21, 1919, Zhou stressed the need to transform Chinese society and to spread new ideas.[22] He now became more pointed in his analysis of current problems. He criticized Japan's use of the 1919 Paris Peace Conference as a tool for annexing parts of Shandong Province. He urged his fellow students to take immediate action against the pro-Japanese warlords. In another article dated August 6, 1919, he warned the students, "The forces of darkness are forever increasing."[23] He then posed the rhetorical question: "What must we do to defend against them?" His answer was distinctly direct: "There must be preparation; there must be method; and there must be sacrifice."[24] Translating his own words into action, he organized meetings of the Tianjin student groups to demonstrate in conjunction with those in Beijing. "The fundamental solution for Chinese society," declared Zhou on September 6, 1919, "is to uproot and transform all these things which are incompatible with modern evolution: militarism, the capitalist class, powerful cliques, bureaucrats, sexual discrimination, the feudal grading of human relationships."[25]

Zhou's political thinking during and after the May Fourth Movement was shaped by the intellectual milieu of his time. Through Li, Ch'en, and others Zhou was gradually drawn toward the ideology of Marx and Lenin; in them he found an inexhaustible source of political inspiration. The writings in the *New Youth* stimulated Zhou's serious interest in Marxism, and from this point on he began to study in earnest the tenets of Marxism and paid close attention to Lenin's strategies in the Bolshevik Revolution of 1917 and after. It should be noted that in the intellectual disputes between Li and Ch'en, on the one side, and Hu, on the other, Zhou rejected passivity and chose to plunge into political activism. Zhou's activities as a student organizer and as the editor of the *Students'*

United Journal brought him ever closer to socialist ideology.[26] Methods and means became important tools for considerations and actions.

Although at this stage Zhou's ideas were not yet Communist in orientation, they were leaning toward socialism rather than gradualism. Zhou invited Li to come from Beijing to talk to the members of the Awakening Society in late 1919. At the annual meeting of the society in the fall of 1920, Zhou urged that Li direct a joint conference of Tianjin and Beijing student organizations. "Everyone knows," Zhou asserted, "that the road to saving our nation is, from now on, simply to immerse ourselves in the working people, relying on the working class, and get the organizations and unions, big and small, that have sprung up all over the country after the May Fourth Movement, to adopt common activities. Only then will we be able to rescue China."[27] During 1919 and 1920 Zhou also had the opportunity to read translations of Karl Marx and Friedrich Engels' *Communist Manifesto* and Karl Kautsky's *Class Struggle and the October Revolution,*[28] published by the *New Youth.*

During his Tianjin years Zhou was on familiar terms with various small groups of radical intellectuals and political activists. While active in the Awakening Society in Tianjin and in the Society for the Study of Marxism in Beijing, in the winter of 1919-20 Zhou was also in contact with Li. Although Zhou saw some value in Marx's teachings as interpreted by Kawakami and then by Li and Ch'en, he was initially reluctant to accept Marxism unreservedly. Perhaps this was in part because, during this stage, he was more oriented toward action than political ideology. Mass movement, propaganda, self-discipline, and, above all, organization were, in Zhou's mind, indispensable devices for the Chinese people's struggle against domestic warlordism and foreign imperialism. Therefore, he felt that it was urgent for Chinese intellectuals and student leaders to organize and lead the common people if China's national interests were to be defended. He saw mass demonstrations as a useful means of capitalizing on the strong wave of patriotism flowing through China and of bringing tangible pressures to bear upon the Beijing warlord government to curb further foreign encroachments in China.

Zhou believed that great efforts had to be made to gain and preserve China's sovereignty, and even greater efforts were required to deal with China's problems in the international arena, such as tariff autonomy and foreign concessions. He viewed foreign imperialism as essentially responsible for the misery of the Chinese urban working class, because the intrusion of foreign capitalism had ruined native Chinese industrial enterprise and placed the working class in China under worldwide capitalistic exploitation. The British textile factories and Japanese cotton mills in Shanghai were pointed to as concrete examples illustrating the exploitation of cheap Chinese labor by foreign capital.[29] Zhou's concerns with China's position in the world community as well as its deplorable living standards led him to participate actively in the Tianjin-Beijing student demonstrations during and after the May Fourth Movement. Meanwhile, the Bolshevik success in Russia in 1917 had a tangible impact on Zhou. The Marxist-Leninist emphasis on the liberation of the impoverished classes and colonies throughout the world and on proletarian internationalism provided Zhou with an unmatched source of inspiration in the period following the May Fourth Movement.

In March 1920 the Soviets published the *Leo Karakhan Manifesto,* which outlined the new regime's position concerning the concessions of territory and privileges that the previous czarist government had extracted from the Chinese government. The *Karakhan Manifesto* renounced czarist extraterritorial rights in China and repudiated all unequal treaties between the two countries.[30] The news of this manifesto heightened the moral standing of the Bolsheviks for Zhou and many other Chinese students and drew their attention to the Bolshevik Revolution.[31]

Part of Zhou's information about the new Soviet state came from Ch'en's and Li's articles in the *New Youth,* and part of it came from Dewey and, especially, Bertrand Russell, who also lectured in China in early 1920 on the new Soviet state. The assertion by Lenin, the chief architect of the successful Bolshevik Revolution in 1917, that the revolution he led was an international one struck a responsive chord among many Chinese intellectuals.[32] His diagnosis of imperialist oppression as the root cause of the social, economic, and political problems of the world was eagerly accepted as a new gospel of truth.

To understand the reasons for Zhou's ultimate attraction to Marxism-Leninism it is necessary to trace his conversion to communism, and then to examine his belief in the relevance of Marxism-Leninism to contemporary Chinese problems. As late as January 1921, Zhou's mood was still overwhelmingly one of curiosity, probing, and reflection. On January 30, 1921, he wrote a lengthy letter to his cousin Shi-zhou Chen, with whom he frequently discussed China's problems.[33] The letter revealed two facets of Zhou's thoughts: it showed his preference for practical learning and for a happy "mean" (zhong-he) between "conservatism" (bao-shou) and "insurrection" (bao-dong).[34] Practical learning was the constant norm by which Zhou judged the value of learning and scholarship. Therefore, sound learning was to become the core of his own thought and practice throughout his life. As Zhou explained in this letter, the purpose of his planned study in Europe was "to seek practical learning" in order to accomplish his own "independence."[35] It was also his intention to make "an unprejudiced investigation" in order to understand "the social realities of foreign countries and various solutions."[36] What was more important was

Zhou's emphasis on the "future application" of his knowledge to Chinese society. "As to a fixed 'ism,'" Zhou confessed that he was "still uncertain on the basis of his limited study."[37]

In his letter Zhou made thoughtful comments on the relative merits of both "radical changes" and "prudent measures." "It was a difficult task to make a right choice," he wrote, "between the method of making progress in a reckless manner and the way of maintaining a firm, steady attitude."[38] Sound judgment, in Zhou's view, would always depend upon "specific circumstances and needs." To be preoccupied with maximum stability was labeled as "a conservative element." On the other hand, "excessive recklessness would lead to insurrection."[39] In Zhou's discussion he illustrated the dichotomy between radical changes and prudent measures by comparing Great Britain with the Soviet Union. He attributed the success of modern Great Britain to its conservatism and, more precisely, to its "evolutionary reforms."[40] On the other hand, the Soviet Union illustrated "success through insurrection."[41] The accomplishments of Great Britain, to Zhou, were due to "its ability to take precautions at every step, to keep a normal attitude towards problems, and to seek evolutionary reforms."[42] It was the Soviet Union, however, that achieved its goals on the basis of its capacity to solve the problems of an autocratic society "through the device of sudden, proletarian revolution."[43]

According to Zhou, British tradition had the salutary effect of inculcating in the British people a strong love for conservative principles such as political compromise, evolutionary changes, and moderation. Yet, the conservative heritage of British society stood for "gradual, ordered progress," the type that developed as opportunity allowed or as necessity dictated. When Zhou cited the example of the 1917 Bolshevik Revolution, he did not hesitate to point out both the limits and the benefits of the "method of radical change," should the Chinese people prefer it.

In his analysis of possible models of solutions to Chinese problems Zhou demonstrated an awareness of relativity, an appreciation for the value of balance, a distrust of ideological extremes, and a recognition of the wide gulf between social and political abstraction, on the one hand, and practical issues, on the other. Against this background he asserted that it was possible for China to eliminate the ills resulting from the accumulated injurious practices of foreign powers by following the Russian example of revolution. He cautioned, however, that "surrounded by powerful neighbors China's internal moves, especially those along the radical direction, could be restricted" by possible foreign interference.[44] To avoid employing insurrection as a justification for powerful neighbors to interfere in China's domestic affairs, he confessed that a choice between the two types of change, as represented by the Russian method of revolution and British evolutionary reform, was by no means a simple task and that, for himself, he had not yet made up his mind about which course was better for China. To avoid going to either extreme, Zhou indicated balance as a guiding principle for the Chinese people.[45] And he emphasized in his letter, as we might expect, the maximum practical value of relating the means to both the ultimate ends and the specific circumstances. His emphasis, in other words, was placed on the "relativity of method to time and place."[46]

Zhou had a broad interest in European affairs and Western political traditions. As he put it in another letter to his cousin, dated February 23, 1921, "I am convinced that there are two ways of learning a foreign language: one is to read much and the other is to talk much, and my intention is to follow the former."[47] Eager to discover the sources of European influence in the world arena, Zhou wished to observe the British, French, and German political systems, economic development, national characters, and social problems. This broad interest in Western cultural and institutional heritage, rather than just the narrow subject of Marxism-Leninism, substantially enlarged his intellectual horizons. Among the works that he read closely in the early months of his stay in Paris was the English translation of a German book entitled *Life and Teachings of Karl Marx,* written by Max Beer. By 1922 he was looking for a Leninist party and Bolshevik-style revolutionary government and, above all, a flexible strategy.[48] Zhou now placed great value on fundamental change within Chinese society and its institutions and on the importance of improving China's international status. Consequently, he became even more critical of the warlord government in Beijing and of those who refused to consider foreign imperialism as a serious menace to China. His great concern with China's modern transformation and his new preference for revolutionary rather than evolutionary approaches to social reforms convinced him of his personal responsibility to participate in a revolutionary movement against domestic feudalism, warlordism, and foreign imperialism in China. By 1922 he had become a firm believer in the teachings of Marxism-Leninism, and Zhou never departed from this ideological orientation.

In the spring of 1923 Zhou's correspondence with close friends clearly revealed his changed views. Even with his new enthusiasm for Marxism-Leninism, however, he could hardly be described as a die-hard. He had, by nature, a preference for moderation, or, to use his own expression, for "compromise."[49] Equally important was the high intensity of his "search for truth." Basically, he wanted to know how to think and analyze. He believed that the class revolution and the dictatorship of the proletariat should be implemented in China. As for the best methods for achieving these goals, Zhou suggested, characteristically, that they should "be guided by circumstances."[50]

Marxism-Leninism was, for Zhou, fundamentally a practical solution to China's urgent social and economic problems, rather than a pure doctrine. In Marx's and Lenin's teachings and practices Zhou found a real model of flexible means and methods. When his new conviction was buttressed by his strong sense of moral responsibility, he was led naturally toward nationalism. Marxism-Leninism would be a useful tool for achieving the vital national objectives of the Chinese people. Though busy with his task of organizing the Chinese students in Paris, Zhou never lost sight of his eventual goal of returning to China and engaging himself directly in the struggle for socialist reconstruction in China.

Marxism-Leninism and Its Impact on Zhou

Marx's task as historian and sociologist was to catalogue the nature of economic exploitation and analyze the mechanism whereby oppressed social groups could rectify the conditions of their oppression.[51] History, according to Marx, was a conflict between opposing classes—between master and slave, landlord and peasant, and capitalist and worker. With power concentrated in the capitalists' hands, the proletariat would become consolidated and develop a will of its own.[52] After the overthrow of the capitalists, according to Marx, the workers would form a new sociopolitical superstructure more in harmony with the forces of production. This revolutionary change was deemed to be inevitable. When Marx viewed the abysmal working conditions in European societies and the grinding poverty of an increasing percentage of the people in the West, he concluded that the very nature of capitalism produced such conditions. He further contended that only revolution, with its power to raise human beings to a higher level, could remedy the situation. Thus, he strongly asserted that class struggle was bound to produce the final result that would raise the victorious proletariat over the industrial bourgeoisie in an eternal victory.

It should be noted, however, that Marx's primary interest was not in the development of a body of theory. The main objective upon which all his thinking converged was the liberation of the working class from the capitalist system. He insisted that workers and intellectuals should grasp the trend of history and participate in the revolutionary movement. Marx wrote in 1875, "Every step of real movement is worth a dozen programs."[53] His theoretical system was, in essence, a working philosophy, a plan for action, and a weapon for the fight against the existing order.

Marx argued that the issue of "whether objective truth can be attributed to human thinking is not a question of theory, but is a practical question."[54]

He went on to say, "The dispute over the reality or non-reality of a thought which is isolated from practice is a purely scholastic question."[55] The heart of Marx's doctrine was the idea that social life was in perpetual flux, as social conditions were constantly changing, and that the basic factor in social life and social change were the material conditions—that is, a society's economic system and the mode of production and property relations that it entailed. This material factor affected all other forms of social life: the legal, political, religious, cultural, and philosophical. Class struggle constituted the motivating force for historical change. In ancient, medieval, and early modern periods the dominant social class controlled the state's legal and political machinery. The state was an instrument of class domination and law the expression of the will of the dominant class. The essential role of the state was to employ force to guard the interests of the ruling class, which coerced or oppressed the other classes in order to protect its privileges.

The great attraction of Marxism, and especially of Lenin's doctrine of imperialism, to Chinese intellectuals was that it provided them with a means of judging and criticizing the capitalist West from a Western perspective.[56] What impressed Zhou the most was not Marxist economic theory but, rather, the way in which Marx's analysis both explained the fundamental social conditions of China's developing capitalistic order and offered within that explanation the promise of radical social and political change. Marx provided many of the basic tenets of Communist ideology, but it was Lenin who led the 1917 Bolshevik Revolution to success and adapted Marx's approach to international relations. Marx analyzed capitalist society within a national framework and, specifically, in terms of European industrial development. Capitalism, according to Lenin, was a worldwide phenomenon, and imperialism was characterized by its super-abundance of capital in the West, which caused monopoly enterprise to exploit the resources of the underdeveloped areas of the world in order to make profits. Lenin thus extended the Marxist concept of class struggle to the international arena. The quest for exploitable resources, in Lenin's view, was the motivating force behind the penetration by the industrialized countries of the West into the underdeveloped areas of the world.

In his essay entitled "Imperialism, the Last Stage of Capitalism," published in 1916, Lenin outlined new revolutionary possibilities, unforeseen by Marx, by extending his analysis from a focus on the world's industrial centers to colonial and semicolonial countries, which he described as subjected to ruthless exploitation by international capitalism.[57] Proceeding from the fundamental Marxist premise that all political phenomena were the product of economic conditions, Lenin advanced the conclusion that imperialism was the product of Capitalism, the economic system from which it derived its origin and vitality.

The dominant characteristic of this system was its emphasis on growth in the size of the units of production and their association with one another through trusts and cartels.

Monopoly was a natural phenomenon, and in its economic essence, Lenin summarized, imperialism was "the monopoly stage of capitalism," a stage in which competition among many business enterprises would lead ultimately to the control of the economies of most capitalist countries by monopolies.[58] These monopolies would be controlled by a small group of powerful capitalists.

The concept of imperialism in Marxism-Leninism related primarily to the economic relations between the industrialized West and the underdeveloped countries of the world. Lenin favored revolutions whenever possible, even outside industrialized countries of the West, as he perceived that a successful revolution was necessary for the salvation of the oppressed classes of the world. Marx had been the theorist of communism, while Lenin was its strategist and tactician. "Concrete political aims," said Lenin, "must be set in concrete circumstances. All things are relative, all things flow, and all things change."[59] Lenin also instructed his comrades to regard Marxism not as inert dogma but, instead, as an impetus to action. His efforts to accomplish his goals indicate that he believed that the ends justified whatever means were required.

Lenin, the first Communist leader to have the opportunity to apply Marxism, was forced to improvise before and during the Bolshevik Revolution. Even if he did not violate Marx's ideas in the process of implementing them, he certainly modified them to suit his own needs. Revolution was, for Lenin, a science to be studied and applied in a systematic manner. It was chiefly Lenin who developed new revolutionary tactics for attaining socialism in Russia. When the opportunity for the triumph of communism occurred in 1917, Lenin omitted the stage of bourgeois capitalist development and immediately launched the socialist revolution—a major revision of Marx's theory. The institution established to implement this accelerated revolutionary process was called the "Party of the new type," better known as the Communist Party. Lenin and his Bolsheviks contended that this organization would enable the working class to take power "before the time," because organizational planning would compensate for what was lacking in dialectical development. Therefore, he organized the Communist Party as the tightly knit, highly disciplined vanguard of the proletariat. What really mattered in the process of revolution, in Lenin's view, were discipline, method, accuracy, precision, and infinite patience with all facets of the "black art" of revolution.

Indeed, Lenin drew a sharp distinction between fidelity to the core of the Party's aims and the means for their realization, urging the utmost elasticity in the choice of means. After the successful Bolshevik Revolution in 1917

Lenin shifted his attention to problems of leadership, urging that the proletarian movement was doomed without firm leadership and a flexible strategy. It was Lenin who stressed the importance of flexibility in dealing with serious international challenges, such as the signing of the Treaty of Brest-Litovsk in March 1918 and his urging the German Communists not to reject the Treaty of Versailles of 1919. The strictest loyalty to the ideas of communism must be combined with the ability "to effect all the necessary practical compromises, tacks, conciliatory maneuvers, zigzags, retreats, and so on," wrote Lenin in April-May 1920 in an essay that became part of the Communist guide to politics.[60] In addition, Communists must know how to take advantage of the antagonisms and contradictions existing among the imperialists to gain a mass alliance, "even though this ally [alliance] is temporary, vacillating, unstable and conditional."[61]

Although Lenin was a master of the subtleties of Marxist theory, he was interested in such abstractions only when they could be used to further his own plan. His plan was simply to build up in Russia a Marxist party that would be substantially different from the tolerant, legalist socialist parties of the West—namely, a new type of party dedicated solely to revolution. Moreover, Lenin's mind was intensely practical, and he knew that economic conditions in Russia contradicted all Marxist principles. According to orthodox theory, Russia, whose industrialization was just beginning, was not "ripe" for a socialist revolution. But Lenin was convinced that, by organizing around himself a tight core of professional, trained revolutionaries who would look to him alone for guidance, he could eventually succeed. According to Lenin, mastering the Communist doctrine meant assimilating the substance of doctrine and learning to use it in solving of the practical problems underlying the various conditions of the proletariat's class struggle. It meant being able to enrich Communist doctrine with the new experience of postrevolutionary development, with new propositions and conclusions. It meant being able to adjust the theory to harsh realities.

Knowledge, according to Lenin, was always relative because the world's potential was inexhaustible by nature. Therefore, practice was the only test of knowledge. The logical extension was that, if one's perception of an object were incorrect, one's attempt to use it would be unsuccessful. In the dialectical unity of theoretical and practical activities no theory could be true if it could not be verified continuously in action. Theory was inseparable from action, and action taken in the absence of theory was "blind." "Without revolutionary theory," claimed Lenin, "there can be no revolutionary movement."[62] Therefore, spontaneity must be combatted: "The greater the spontaneous upsurge of the masses and the more widespread the movement, the more rapid, incomparably so, the demand for greater consciousness in the theoretical, political, and organizational work."[63]

In the years following the May Fourth Movement of 1919 Marx's philosophy and Lenin's political strategy became important ideological forces in China. Marxism-Leninism, the ideological basis of communism, was the first economic and political philosophy of any consequence in history to promote the power and welfare of the masses. It also emphasized the close relationship that must exist between the Party and the proletariat. Zhou was particularly taken with Marx's economic theory and method of verification and Lenin's political strategy and tactical maneuverability.[64] Their views reinforced his belief in searching for practical methods and solutions to meet China's social, political, and economic problems according to the exigencies of time and place. In Marxism-Leninism Zhou found new meaning in his long-standing opposition to imperialism and the Chinese warlord government. More than just a dogma serving the purpose of a Communist state, Marxism-Leninism was a system of ideas inspiring further thought, reflection, and reinterpretation.

Following the Marxist line of reasoning, Zhou began to write about communism and revolution and to relate them to his concerns about the domestic economy and politics.[65] In January 1921 he stated in a letter to one of his relatives the dangers of radical action and observed that the best way to solve China's problems both at home and abroad was to strike a balance between two extremes: sudden, violent revolution, on the one hand, and excessive conservatism, on the other.[66] It is evident that by then Zhou was already shifting toward a Communist orientation. The achievement of social justice and economic equality in China, Zhou now believed, would require the redistribution of property, transference of the means of production back to the workers themselves, and the nationalization of land. In effect, this meant the radical restructuring of the warlord, bourgeois government in Beijing whose police and other coercive instruments had been organized to defend the property and rights of the most powerful landlords and capitalists. Zhou also suggested that his proposed solution was a careful application of Marx and Lenin's theories and precepts, arguing that anyone applying Marxist-Leninist methods for the purpose of analyzing the Chinese political, social, and economic situation in order to devise successful strategies should expect to "improvise."

Zhou's opposition to capitalistic orders of any type was indicative of his new confidence in Marx's economic theories and the organization of a socialist revolution in China. Given the prevailing social and economic situation, Zhou regarded Marxism-Leninism as a necessary instrument for bringing about China's modern transformation. He accepted the materialistic underpinnings of Marx's outlook while believing that his analysis as a whole was relevant to

China's internal social and economic conditions.[67] In China, for instance, laborers in the factories and foundries worked long hours and were paid low wages. But profit went to those who owned the means of economic production. A realistic understanding of the contemporary world, Zhou suggested, could be possible only by those who were steeped in the study of Marxism. Moreover, in political or socioeconomic reform there remained the question of means. If, according to Zhou, the end that was being sought was correct, the people must choose means that were adequate to its attainment. Therefore, the question of means could not be treated in a vacuum, and a sound decision could only be made on the basis of a systematic investigation of concrete problems. In other words, empirical knowledge was important and applicable to the real world. It was obtained through experiment and observation. Experiment was superior to abstract thought and observation more valuable than speculation. In the final analysis the validity of effective measures must be grounded in practical investigation, experimented with, and further improved.[68]

Lenin's teachings and activities found a kindred spirit in Zhou, as both men placed a high value on pragmatism. What impressed Zhou the most was Lenin's rational and cool calculations of revolutionary opportunity and the Bolshevik leader's emphasis on method, discipline, and accuracy in the process of revolution. Zhou was inspired by Lenin's extraordinary ability to draw up concrete, specific strategies and tactics for implementing the Marxist blueprint. The very core of Lenin's approach, according to Zhou, was the element of a well-disciplined, elite party of revolutionary intellectuals. Zhou's determination to find useful political weapons against the Chinese warlords and foreign imperialists and their collaborators made him keenly aware of the utilitarian value of Lenin's guiding principles on political organization and strategic flexibility.

In addition, Lenin's theses that imperialism was an inevitable stage in the development of capitalism and that foreign imperialism was mainly responsible for China's domestic economic stagnation obviously drew an enthusiastic response from Zhou. To the Awakening Society back in Tianjin, Zhou wrote in March 1923 that the Soviet Union's possible opening to France would be part of Lenin's diplomatic approach. More important, Zhou's personal confidence in "Lenin's strategy" was so great that he even attributed the postrevolutionary successes of the Soviet Union to Lenin. "How admirable Lenin is! He will do everything possible," Zhou proclaimed enthusiastically, "for the benefit of the future development of Communism, at any sacrifice, and with total indifference to public opinion."[69] He also observed admiringly, "The steps of the Communist Party have changed; Lenin himself also recognizes the change."[70] The 1917 Bolshevik Revolution, in Zhou's view, "might have collapsed if Russia had not been under the guidance of Lenin."[71] On the same occasion Zhou exhorted his readers, "We should believe in the theory of Communism and class revolution as well as the dictatorship of the proletariat."[72]

Zhou's brief yet perceptive commentary on Lenin's methods and New Economic Policy (NEP) in the years immediately following the Bolshevik Revolution clearly revealed his appreciation for the element of practicality. At this stage Zhou already began to pronounce unequivocally that the principle of strategic flexibility was the key to foreign policy formulation and its effective execution. As one would expect, his mind was steadily turning to the major debate on means and ends. His concept of a practical design was, as he saw it, a balanced plan. Zhou was not merely impressed by the success of the Russian revolution and Lenin's subsequent policy decisions for the Communist Party of the Soviet Union (CPSU); he also entertained the hope that a similar revolution might take place in China.[73] Zhou saw in Marxism a positive view of progress and the "scientific method" of investigation. He felt that Marxism was relevant to the current situation in China because it might help the Chinese direct the technical powers unleashed by the industrial revolution to remedy its poverty. China's so-called Republican rule, in Zhou's view, was in the hands of militarists who, under conditions of a semifeudal economy, used it to join their own actions with those of foreign imperialists.[74] He could not help but observe that China had become a primary focal point in the rivalries of the major imperialist powers and had declined to the level of semicolonial status.[75]

In his work "Imperialism, the Last Stage of Capitalism" Lenin held that imperialism was a necessary stage in the development of capitalism and an inherent part of it and that imperialism marked the last stage in the growth of capitalism before its final collapse. In modifying Marxist theory, Lenin asserted that, even though competition within a state might be controlled, the struggle between sovereign capitalist states could not be similarly regulated. Imperialism was not a policy, therefore, since that implied an element of selection, but, rather, a matter of compulsion—namely, it was inevitable. Thus, the imperialist stage of capitalism actually denoted the transference of the class struggle from a particular society to the world at large.

In addition, Lenin emphasized the need for party organization as a tool for creating and leading the revolution. The 1918 Treaty of Brest-Litovsk, according to Zhou, was a temporary retreat from domestic consolidation in the Soviet Union, and Lenin's decision to introduce the NEP in March 1921 was clearly political. These were brilliant strategies designed by Lenin for the development of Russia's economy under very unusual circumstances. Zhou saw in the Bolshevik organization the kind of political leadership that he had long felt would be necessary to transform Chinese society and economy. Regardless of the debate on whether or not Marxist-Leninist ideology functioned as "a guide to action" or it was a mere "expedient device," certainly Zhou saw in Marxism-Leninism the potential for a powerful weapon that could be employed against domestic warlordism and capitalism as well as foreign imperialism.

Zhou also turned to Lenin's leadership and methods for guidance when discussing the application of Marxism to reality. Lenin's ideas on the Treaty of Brest-Litovsk and the NEP, for instance, continued to play an important part in Zhou's justification of the practical value of strategic flexibility for decades to come. Zhou's efforts to rationalize Lenin's practices during and after the Bolshevik Revolution were largely related to his own guideline—namely, "to act in accordance with time,"[76] place, and circumstances. It is easy to discern the similarity between this guiding principle of Zhou and Lenin's attempt to make diplomatic or economic adjustment on the basis of existing international situations or economic conditions in postrevolutionary Russia. On the basis of this commonality it is also possible to understand how Marxism-Leninism was perceived by Zhou as a valid guide to strategic maneuvers, more effective and certainly more relevant than any other ideology in strengthening the antifeudal and anti-imperialist movements in China.

Lenin's main attraction to Zhou lay in the former's theory of imperialism, its applicability to China's relations with the West and Japan, and, above all, its utilitarian value. It was within this conceptual framework that methods and means became crucial to Zhou. He agreed with Lenin's basic premise that "a systematic plan of action" was indispensable to preserving "the energy, the stability, and continuity of the political struggle."[77] In line with Marxism-Leninism the primary task of Chinese revolutionaries, Zhou contended, was to obtain the most exact knowledge possible about harsh reality. With reference to the manifold problems of China it was essential to make the Marxist-Leninist theories operational and relevant to Chinese problems, both at home and abroad. Every aspect of Marxism-Leninism, therefore, had to be examined and reinvented on the basis of its relevance to China, so that the Chinese Communists would be able to meet the challenges of a constantly changing domestic and international environment. Zhou was impressed by Lenin's wisdom in drawing a distinction between Marxist aims and the means for their attainment and, especially, by Lenin's urging of the utmost flexibility in the choice of means. Zhou strongly believed that Marxism-Leninism was a guide to action because it constituted not only Communist philosophy but revolutionary strategies as well. In short, Marxism-Leninism contributed to Zhou's continuing grasp of a nationalist and pragmatic mentality, with a strong antifeudal spirit and an intense aversion to foreign imperialism.

The main reason for Zhou, as a young man, to subscribe to Lenin's writings and maxims was his own keen awareness of the importance of having a clear method of operation. He seized Lenin's approach and made it his own, for it was just what he had been groping for: the perfect refinement of his personal preference for the pragmatic accommodation of both reality and doctrine. It was Zhou's early conviction that precepts and practice should be united and that theory and action had to be in balance; knowledge and action should not be regarded as two separate entities, and, in line with this enduring attitude, Zhou focused on the task of integrating doctrine with practice in actual world circumstances.

In retrospect, Zhou's three and a half years in London, Paris, and Bonn not only enabled him to study Marx's works thoroughly; he could also observe the Communist leaders in action. After his return to China from France in the summer of 1924, Zhou commented on the essence of imperialism. "Imperialism, which has appeared only during the past fifty years," Zhou stated, "is the extreme development, or ultimate product, of capitalism. The economic characteristic of capitalism is free competition, which breeds monopoly as the system develops toward imperialism."[78] Proceeding from Lenin's theory of imperialism, Zhou further suggested, "When the economic development of a capitalist country reaches a monopolistic concentration of capital and production, the combined interests of banking and industry will turn to investment abroad and exportation of finished industrial products."[79] In Zhou's analysis it was but natural for the imperialist countries to "exploit the oppressed nations." On this occasion Zhou used his own country as a concrete example: "This is the pattern from which China, a semi-colonial nation jointly controlled by imperialistic powers, cannot expect to escape."[80] He concluded by pointing out that in the period from 1880 to 1900 the Western powers, Japan, and Russia had each established its sphere of influence in China and together virtually deprived China of its sovereign rights. Zhou, by this point, was following an unmistakably Leninist line of thinking.

Lenin and Stalin's Views on International Relations and Zhou's 1930 Report on the CCP's "Foreign Policy toward Imperialism"

According to Lenin, peace under imperialism could only be a temporary lull in the military phase of the revolutionary struggle, because peaceful coalitions and alliances were mere truces between wars. Moreover, it was common practice among the imperialist states to seek markets, new materials, and investment outlets in subjugated areas. As a result, imperialist states were inevitably engaged in devastating periodic conflicts for the redistribution of the world. "[They] prepare the ground for wars," claimed Lenin, "and in their turn grow out of wars."[81] To hope for capitalism without war, Lenin argued, would be sheer "utopia." In his report to the Seventh Congress of the Russian Communist Party on March 7, 1918, Lenin stated: "International imperialism, with its mighty capital, its highly organized military technique, which is a real fortress of international capital, could not under any circumstances, or any condition, live side by side with the Soviet Republic."[82] Speaking to the Fifth Congress of the CPSU on March 18, 1919, Lenin flatly asserted: "We are living not merely in a state but in a system of states, and the existence of the Soviet Republic side by side with imperialist states for a long time is unthinkable."[83] He added: "one or the other must triumph in the end. And before that end supervenes, a series of frightful collisions between the Soviet Republic and the bourgeois states will be inevitable."[84] This central thesis was reiterated by Lenin in his speech on November 26, 1920. "As long as capitalism and socialism exist," said Lenin, "we cannot live in peace; in the end, one or the other will triumph— a funeral dirge will be sung over the Soviet Republic or over world capitalism."[85]

When the Allied military intervention in Russia ended in 1920-21 and the Soviet regime received diplomatic recognition, Lenin managed to modify his earlier views by proclaiming that "peaceful coexistence" between the capitalist states and the Soviet Republic was possible. "Is such a thing possible, that a socialist republic could exist amid capitalist encirclement?" asked Lenin, and his answer was that "this seemed unthinkable in both a political and military sense. Now it is proved, it is a fact, that it is possible in both a political and a military sense."[86]

Following Lenin's death in 1924, Joseph Stalin soon took over party leadership in the Soviet Union; his foreign policy orientation contained the first real foundations of a Communist doctrine of peaceful coexistence vis-à-vis the non-Communist world. In December 1925 Stalin announced that "a temporary balance of power" between communism and capitalism had emerged.[87] "This put an end to the war against socialism," said Stalin, "and gave rise to a period of 'peaceful coexistence.'"[88] In his report to the Fifteen Congress of the CPSU on December 3, 1927, Stalin declared, however, that "the period of peaceful coexistence is receding into the past, giving place to a period of imperialist assaults and preparation for intervention against the U.S.S.R."[89] In making this statement, Stalin had both France and Great Britain in mind. In the final analysis Stalin accepted the tactics of peaceful coexistence only as a necessary expedient in a Soviet foreign policy that would permit Moscow to cooperate with the capitalist states in the West in order to develop the Soviet economy or when Russian national security was in serious jeopardy.

A theoretical formula that was correct for the international exigencies of one epoch might be incorrect and fail to meet the needs of another. The two Soviet formulas, undertaken by Lenin and Stalin, respectively, were relevant to the needs of two different stages in the development of international relations, and, precisely, because of such relevance, the different approaches were therefore correct, each for its own stage.[90] The practical value of Leninism offered a wide scope and an opportunity to justify the revised foreign policy orientation and new diplomatic maneuvers of the Soviet Union. In addition, dialectical method was employed to analyze current international relations. It is important to point out that, although Marx formulated the theory of the formation of the world capitalist system and Lenin developed Marx's thought into the theory of imperialism and of proletarian revolution, neither had articulated a sophisticated theory of international relations. Therefore, both Lenin's and Stalin's interpretations would serve as political rationalizations for revised foreign policies or diplomatic initiatives already in the works.

In late 1920 Zhou organized a branch of the Socialist Youth Group of China in Berlin, and in mid-1921 he participated in the meeting that formally established the Paris branch of the CCP. When he returned to China in 1924 Zhou was appointed secretary of the Guangdong provincial committee of the CCP. In retrospect, the period from 1924 to 1927 was unusual in Zhou's life in that he spent most of his time as an apprentice to the CCP's domestic united front strategy. Zhou always held that a Chinese revolution would have to go through stages from antifeudal and anti-imperialist revolution to socialist construction. Allying with the Guomindang (GMD), he reasoned, would result in a victory of national democratic revolution.

After the 1927 split between the CCP and the GMD, Zhou paid more attention to external affairs. Zhou's consuming interest in the nature of international relations and foreign policy reached a new high point with his 1930 report, known as the *Shao-shan* report, made at the CCP's Third Plenum on September 24, 1930.[91] In the section on "Foreign Policy toward Imperialism" (dui-di-guo-zhu-yi di wai-jiao-zheng-ce) Zhou outlined his proposed approach to Chinese foreign relations and diplomacy in the context of Marxism-Leninism.[92] Lenin's theory of imperialism provided Zhou with a framework of analysis in which he interpreted existing international relations, imperialism, and anti-imperialist forces throughout the world.

First, Zhou held that the sovereignty of China had long been compromised by treaty system politics. The Western powers and Japan had frequently acted together to enter into treaty relations with the late Qing and then the Republican governments to safeguard jointly their special interests in China. As such, the diplomacy of imperialism had been superimposed on China's inequitable relations with the outside world. Zhou strongly advocated in his report the need for the CCP to define its position on China's relations with foreign powers.

Second, Zhou believed that in their domestic power struggle with the GMD government CCP leaders should strive to increase their understanding of international reality along the Marxist-Leninist line. Advanced capitalist states gained control over and exploited underdeveloped areas of economic profit. Therefore, following Lenin's reasoning, the arena of international relations was one in which there were constant confrontations between or among capitalist nations. These confrontations were caused primarily by their highly organized competitions and rivalries over markets and sources of raw materials in the underdeveloped areas of the world.

Third, Zhou argued that there was no basic harmony of interests between capitalist and socialist states. Moreover, the conflicts between these two groups of states were simple conflicts between competing socioeconomic systems and ideologies. The capitalist-imperialist states sought to curb progressive political movements throughout the world. Within this conceptual framework Zhou advocated the adoption of a flexible foreign policy strategy as the fundamental guideline for the CCP's approach to international relations.[93] In his opinion one of the primary functions of the party organization was to outline the long and complicated process of achieving national independence and sovereignty in China. To reject negotiation with the imperialist powers, Zhou held, was to ignore the utility and subtlety of the conventional devices of diplomacy.[94] To illustrate the dynamics of diplomacy, he used the Soviet government in China as an example and pointed out its two main objectives: to consolidate "subjective strength," on the one hand, and to manipulate "objective change," on the other.[95]

Zhou's views, as outlined in the *Shao-shan* report, clearly reflected his notion of foreign policy as an instrument for safeguarding China's interests and for improving its international status vis-à-vis the imperialist powers. His realistic assessment of world affairs substantially contributed to the shaping of the CCP's strategic flexibility in dealing with foreign governments. To promote China's self-interest in a cautious manner, Zhou suggested, CCP leaders would need to adopt a variety of strategies CCP leaders on the basis of changing international conditions. To illustrate the need for compromise in the course of national construction, Zhou cited the classic example of the Brest-Litovsk treaty between the Soviet Union, led by Lenin, and Germany in March 1918. By adopting this strategy, Zhou argued, the Bolsheviks had managed to win the necessary time to strengthen the Soviet regime in Russia, build the Red Army, and rally the revolutionary forces, thereby laying the groundwork for the internal consolidation of power.

In the final analysis, central to Zhou's architecture of diplomacy were the arguments that the CCP's basic foreign policy orientation should be based upon extensive exploitation of the antagonism and contradictions between the imperialist countries and that the strategy of flexibility should concentrate on the restoration of China's national independence and sovereignty.[96] While he urged the Party hierarchy to combat foreign imperialism, he also proposed the use of diplomacy as an instrument of the CCP's policy. He further stressed the need for the Party hierarchy to negotiate with imperialist powers insofar as circumstances permitted based on a realistic appraisal of both domestic requirements and international circumstances. Zhou's concern for China's survival in a world of aggressive imperialist powers and his groping for an instrument with which to regain China's political independence and achieve economic prosperity led him to value highly Lenin's and Stalin's concepts of peaceful coexistence.

Zhou's emphasis in the *Shao-shan* report rested on the general efficacy as well as the complexity of diplomacy and on the employment of foreign policy to improve China's international status as an independent, sovereign state. He advised CCP leaders to be worldly in outlook yet flexible in pursuing the Party's major objectives under changing circumstances in the international arena. He made it absolutely clear that one essential function of government was its skillful use of negotiation not only as a temporary auxiliary tool in the quest for national honor and prestige but, more important, as a medium for long-term adjustment in a world community of nation-states with diverse systems, ideologies, and interests. In this report Zhou forcefully argued for the employment of diplomatic negotiations with foreign leaders and governments as a useful instrument for promoting the vital interests of the Chinese Soviet government.[97] Flexibility in the Party's foreign strategy was, as he saw it, a matter of necessity. He did qualify, however, the preconditions for conducting the CCP's negotiations with foreign imperialists: "the evacuation of the armed forces of the foreign imperialists from Chinese Soviet areas, and the observance of Chinese Soviet ordinances, and non-interference with China's independence."[98] It was necessary to gain an understanding of the nature of foreign affairs through careful observation and analysis, through deliberation and reflection, and, above all, through the assessment of concrete policy alternatives. Equally important, CCP leaders must remain sensitive to the changing international situation and attentive to the particular needs of China; they must be prepared to undertake initiatives on the basis of their assessment of reality, and they should never fall victim to a rigid approach to foreign affairs.

Zhou's concern for the necessary adjustment to shifting realities at home and abroad was highly significant. Obviously, he regarded an evolving foreign strategy as the fundamental element of international relations. He advised CCP leaders that through diplomatic negotiations they would be able to expose to the masses the selfish motives of the foreign imperialists in China. It would then be possible to form a broad anti-imperialist united front and prepare the stage for the struggle of proletarians worldwide against imperialist control. Focusing its "foreign policy" on the restoration of China's sovereign rights, the Chinese Soviet government could demonstrate to the proletariat throughout the world the CCP's primary motives in leading the Chinese Communist revolution and its capacity to mold a mass anti-imperialist revolution.[99] Also, the CCP could convey the message that it was not a proponent of violence and anarchy but, rather, a political force that could lead an orderly process of revolutionary change in China. To claim that the use of diplomacy was restricted unduly by existing conditions both at home and abroad, Zhou further argued, was to ignore the complexity of the revolutionary process. The practice of diplomacy meant the realization of a number of the Party's objectives through nonconventional devices.

Marx believed that Communists should not be motivated by capitalist aspirations. Instead, they ought to seek the rapid spread of proletarian revolution so that the capitalist order could be replaced by worldwide communism. Consequently, it would be extremely important to extend support for revolutionary movements and civil wars that sought to put Communists, or at least noncapitalists, in power. Lenin maintained that it was the duty of the proletariat in the colonial and semicolonial countries of Asia to ally with the bourgeoisie in carrying out the national revolution and expelling imperialism.[100] Basing his argument on Lenin's thesis contained in "Left-Wing Communism, an Infantile Disorder," Zhou held that there were "different paths" to climb the mountain but that "the aim must be climbing the mountain."[101]

In examining the 1930 *Shao-shan* report and its central theme of the CCP's relations with foreign powers, it becomes clear that Zhou's notion of flexible foreign policy and the use of foreign policy as an instrument was to a considerable degree indebted to Marxism-Leninism. Zhou argued that the means to power and the use of power required a strong sense of pragmatism. It was not the pragmatism of the opportunist but, rather, the instrumentalism of the leader that the responsibility of the Communist leaders in China, in Zhou's view, was to adapt the possible range of solutions in the context of current necessities as well as historical circumstances.

At this early stage in his career Zhou was fully aware of the stature of power politics that would justify the employment of force as a legitimate agent of diplomacy. One's knowledge of the precise relationship between a sound foreign policy and an evolving pragmatic practice was not a simple one to him, but, rather, an outgrowth of prudence, experience, and growing sophistication over time. This dynamic policy orientation proved to be a significant element in Zhou's thinking during the 1930s and 1940s. Foreign policy decisions would always be primarily strategic decisions, and these decisions should certainly be correlated with Marxist-Leninist ideology, even if that could only be done by pragmatically reinterpreting the Party's ideological and political position from time to time. Underlying Zhou's concepts and suggestions in his *Shao-shan* report to the Party's Third Plenum was his acceptance of the basic premise that modern states operated on the basis of self-interest. Against this background Zhou favored the flexible conduct of day-to-day diplomacy by government, regardless of intraparty power struggles and competition. By this he meant that it was possible for the CCP and its Soviet government to restore China's sovereignty and independence through skillful negotiations with foreign leaders and governments.[102] This required the formulation of basic national objectives abroad and an overall plan for the use of all means and forces available to the CCP to achieve these objectives.

With confidence in the teachings of Marx and the value of Lenin's analyses and practices, Zhou began to treat foreign policy strategy not as an issue for theoretical speculation but as an area in which improvisation and constant adjustment were required. One could argue that the Marxist-Leninist theory was adopted by Zhou to rationalize and justify the CCP's need to accommodate and compromise as a pragmatic strategy. Zhou, in his 1930 report, laid out one of his lifelong guiding principles: compromise was necessary with foreign imperialist countries in accordance with evolving international realities and urgent domestic needs. Moreover, whatever the ideological prescriptions for formulating a country's foreign policy, the chief determinants were inevitably actual international circumstances and the national perception of realities in the world arena. Changes in practice did not, of course, always mean a departure from the original foreign policy line and, therefore, did not require a reinterpretation of official ideology. Foreign policies were implemented through different instruments and in different forms. But it sometimes happened that changes in foreign policy instruments and practices were so drastic that new foreign policies were indicated, and, in that event, according to Zhou, ideological justification would become necessary.

In his 1930 report Zhou clearly demonstrated his preference for Lenin's strategies and adopted them in the CCP's struggle for power in China. He thought about the urgent problems plaguing China. National sovereignty was his primary concern, but his attention also extended to the nation's social and economic conditions, which were not, to him, separate from and independent of the Marxist-Leninist worldview but, rather, integral to them. He followed in the footsteps of Lenin and Stalin in the early 1930s by adhering faithfully to the basic directives of the Communist International (Comintern), but he adapted them to buttress his unique brand of ideological persuasion. He was a "conciliatory" figure, representing the force of moderation within the Party hierarchy that signaled the emergence of a new policy direction and the practice of more pragmatically oriented methods and goals.

In retrospect, Zhou's discussions of postwar European interstate relations in his numerous essays and articles published in the *Social Welfare Daily* and the *Red Light* (Chi-quang) in the period from 1921 to 1924 and his policy proposals concerning the CCP's approach to China's relations with foreign countries, as contained in his 1930 report, reflected the core of his early approach to international relations and foreign policy. This approach was characterized by pragmatism based on the changing circumstances of international relations. Pragmatism, in turn, became a major component in the subsequent formulation of China's foreign policy strategy.

CHAPTER 4

Zhou and United Front
Politics in China

Not until Zhou reached the age of twenty-seven did he come into notice as a competent organizer. At that time he was in charge of political indoctrination at Whampoa Military Academy, the new base of China's revolutionary army. As deputy director of the political department of the academy, Zhou trained the cadets in the tactics of organizing the masses for class struggle, propaganda, and guerrilla warfare. He also became the confidant to both Michael Borodin and General Galin, the Russian advisors to the Guomindong (GMD) at the military academy. In his writings and speeches to CCP members Zhou took every opportunity to describe the complexity and subtlety of their alliance with the "bourgeois nationalists," as exemplified by the GMD members, in the so-called first united front between the two groups.[1] In his effort to cement cooperation between the parties in the period from 1923 to 1927, Zhou adroitly emphasized their common interests and goals. At the same time, he managed to convert many of the most promising young officers and best troops to communism, turning them into the first cadres of the Red Army in China.

Whatever course of action that could strengthen the CCP's position both at home and abroad was, according to Zhou, the right one to pursue, and whatever move that could weaken its influence and prestige in the Chinese "democratic-bourgeois" revolution was to be avoided. The fundamental guiding principle of CCP policy in the two-stage national revolution, in accordance with Lenin's thesis for colonial and noncolonial countries, was that the end should always justify the means, which were determined by the existing circumstances in China.[2] Zhou's subsequent efforts were constantly guided by this cardinal principle, and, as a result, he could veer, compromise, collaborate, and seek support from various political parties and groups whenever necessary and possible. Thus, the significance of his revolutionary activities from 1924 to 1949 should be judged in relation to how they were treated by the CCP hierarchy.

In spite of his zeal for building a socialist foundation in China, when it became apparent that cooperation with the GMD was needed in order for the survival of the CCP, Zhou, in 1924-27 and again in 1936-45, did not hesitate to follow the line of the united front and the national bourgeois revolution. In the first place Zhou articulated, in ever greater detail over the years, the idea of a united front. As long as the CCP retained its independent identity and revolutionary consciousness, he believed, it would be able to steer a proper course of action regardless of how complex the united front strategy was.[3] Second, he maintained that it was not adequate simply to classify the components of the united front into left, middle, and right. The CCP leaders ought to go a step further and make finer distinctions. "This is necessary when we are dealing with so vast a force," observed Zhou, "which includes not only the proletariat but also the peasantry, the petty bourgeoisie, the liberal bourgeoisie, and sometimes even big landlords and members of the big bourgeoisie."[4] Third, he stressed the importance of "careful analysis" of all social classes in China before making any decisive move.[5] Zhou's vision for the two-staged revolution was not a simple, momentous event but, instead, a process in which the final, violent stage would be preceded by a long period of preparing the common ground, mobilizing all potentially "progressive forces," and winning over the middle forces until Chinese society as a whole was properly organized and the victory of the CCP inevitable.[6] Finally, the first stage of the national revolution, according to Zhou, would complete the "bourgeois-democratic" phase, which involved building a united front with the progressive bourgeoisie, as represented by the GMD. It would bring an end to foreign imperialist oppression and also win complete independence for China.[7] In the countryside it would abolish privileges once enjoyed by the landlord-gentry class and equalize land ownership. In the urban centers it would nationalize the property of reactionary capitalists held to be collaborators with foreign imperialism.

Only with these aims accomplished could the CCP assume the dominant role in the second stage of the national revolution: building socialism in China. Considering all these elements in the long process of national revolution, the CCP must possess the ability to adapt itself immediately to the diverse and rapidly changing conditions of the domestic power struggle. Since different stages of the revolutionary process would bring to the fore different forces to which the CCP might need to attach itself, permanent alliance with any party was deemed unnecessary. The CCP needed to be on constant alert, however, to cope with counterrevolutionary forces.

Zhou's knowledge of the dialectical concept of history, borrowed from Marxism-Leninism, would justify his central theme that any historical period was characterized by a struggle between a dominant but declining economic class and an oppressed but rising class. This dialectical view of history, for Zhou, not only implied that the CCP's united front with the GMD would inevitably collapse at some point but that the GMD, an ally of the CCP in one historical period, could become its principal enemy in another. The CCP's policy of collaborating with the GMD from 1923 to 1927, Zhou believed, should be viewed in the context of both the "stage" of national revolution in China and of the "practical need" for strategic flexibility.[8]

Zhou and His Role in the First United Front between the CCP and the GMD, 1924-1927

In retrospect, the intervening years between Zhou's study in Western Europe in 1920 and his assuming responsibility as deputy director for political affairs at the Whampoa Military Academy from 1924 to 1926 formed one of the most important periods in his political life.[9] During this crucial period Zhou once again demonstrated his ability as a keen observer of both foreign and domestic affairs. In Zhou's early career nothing was more striking than the way in which his growing maturity as a revolutionary corresponded with his competence as a political organizer. Both qualities were evident in his decision to join the first united front of the CCP and the GMD and in his methods of dealing with GMD authorities from 1924 to 1927. United front politics and the presumed common interests between the CCP and the GMD in the Chinese national revolution provided Zhou with the opportunity to test Lenin's theory and to hone his skills in the art of achieving objectives through compromise and coalition.[10]

Zhou's political thought was shaped by what he considered to be practical and possible. Not only was he pragmatic in his analyses of postwar interstate relations; he was also conciliatory in his approach to coalition politics between the CCP and the GMD. He participated directly in the struggle against both domestic warlordism and foreign imperialism in order to establish a unified and independent national government in China. By the end of 1927 Zhou had formulated basic guidelines from which he almost never deviated. These were his preference for practical utility as opposed to ideological desirability and his emphasis on elasticity of mind as opposed to rigidity and narrow-mindness. Zhou's political orientation and activities in the first united front between the CCP and the GMD were illustrated by his undertakings at the Whampoa Military Academy and by his analysis of the nature and immediate goals of the national revolution in China.

Given the political conditions in China in the mid-1920s, it was possible for the CCP, under the leadership of Ch'en Duxiu, to form a united front with nationalist forces, specifically with the GMD, in order to fight against the warlord government in Beijing and against foreign powers.[11] To intellectuals and students the GMD not only offered a vision but also represented a major force for the regeneration of China. The GMD, under Sun Yat-sen, could become a revolutionary alliance of all four major classes in China: peasants, workers, petty bourgeoisie, and national bourgeoisie. The manifesto adopted by the CCP on June 10, 1922,[12] declared, "The CCP takes the initiative in calling a conference to be participated in by the revolutionary elements of the GMD."[13] At this point the Comintern, which was in line with the Leninist thesis, urged the CCP to adopt a policy of cooperation with the bourgeois GMD. Furthermore, the GMD, under the leadership of Sun, would not agree to an alliance in any other form. It appears that the CCP leaders had no choice but to join forces with the GMD. But the question of whether or not the Chinese Communists had to join the GMD as individuals or whether the CCP could simply ally itself with the GMD was still to be decided.

Neither Ch'en nor any of the other CCP leaders had any overwhelming objections to a party alliance with the GMD—a strategy that could serve the CCP's vital interests. The CCP, under Ch'en's guidance, was eventually pressed by the Comintern to build a united front with the GMD in the form of an "inner bloc"—that is, the Chinese Communists were urged to join the GMD in 1923 as individuals and to conduct their activities under the GMD banner but to retain their primary allegiance to the CCP.[14] Cooperation with the GMD also forced the Chinese Communists to abandon, if only temporarily, their revolutionary and socialist programs. In spite of Ch'en's reservations about the feasibility of such CCP-GMD cooperation, he and his colleagues were prepared to explore the possibility of establishing an alliance with the left wing of the GMD, hoping that they could win over the moderates within the organization. It was within this strategic framework that Zhou played the role of trusted liaison officer between the two parties and dealt with the GMD authorities at the Whampoa Military Academy.

It is important to note that, with the approval of Moscow, Michael Borodin was sent to China to be a political advisor of the GMD. Upon arriving in Canton on October 6, 1923, Borodin's immediate task was to establish an independent, non-warlord-controlled military force. Within a month of Borodin's arrival Sun officially appointed him as special advisor to the GMD. As such, Borodin acquired tremendous influence in the GMD, and he personally drafted most of the programs adopted at its First Congress in June 1924.[15] Upon Borodin's suggestion a GMD party organization was formed along the lines of the Soviet Communist Party. Russian influence in Canton was further consolidated when the GMD created a new army at Whampoa Military Academy, with Jiang Jie-shi as its commandant. As deputy director of the political department, Zhou was given the responsibility of providing political training for the cadets. The propaganda machinery at Whampoa was quickly utilized by Zhou and other CCP members as an excellent opportunity for the Left, "one that the CCP and Borodin sought to exploit to the full."[16] It is revealing to note Borodin's observation on the nature of CCP-GMD cooperation. "While working for the stabilization of the GMD," he said, "it must never be forgotten that in reality the work is done for the stabilization of the Communist Party."[17]

In a speech at the inauguration of the Whampoa Military Academy, Sun declared that the GMD did not have a secure base from which to defend the Chinese Republic because the national revolution had the support of the only revolutionary party that did not possess an organized army. "Our aim in opening this academy," stated Sun on June 16, 1924, "is to create the revolutionary task anew from this day, and students of the academy . . . will be the pillars of the future revolutionary army."[18] He also maintained that "in the academy the principles of building the Red Army of the Soviet Union will be followed."[19]

In this initial attempt at cooperation, Zhou's attitude toward the GMD authorities was conciliatory, and he was quite successful in discharging the duties of his department at Whampoa. Zhou was respected by the responsible members of both parties.[20] In his administrative career with the military academy, Zhou learned that the art of achieving political success lay in carefully examining the facts, prudence, perseverance, and, above all, adapting ideas and methods to changing conditions. He tried to reconcile the CCP's interests with those of the GMD and was also prepared to adjust the CCP's doctrinal instruction to political reality. Some of Zhou's efforts clearly revealed his recognition of the complexities and difficulties of cooperating with the more powerful GMD.

At the academy Zhou gave lectures on military campaigns and the peasant movement and trained the cadets in the tactics of organizing the masses for class struggle, propaganda, and guerrilla warfare.[21] The cadets were recruited on the basis of their comprehensive understanding of the political principles of the

GMD. They had to be young, strong, and enthusiastic about the revolutionary task. Cadets were to be imbued with the ideas and ideals of national emancipation for China and of world revolution. The military academy stressed both morale and technical training. The curriculum of the academy was designed by Borodin's Russian specialists on the basis of their own experience with political indoctrination one of its basic curricular components.

As a skillful organizer, Zhou was determined to support any strategy that would unify the CCP and the GMD in their common struggle against warlords and imperialists. CCP leaders, by and large, had little sympathy with the Moscow- and Comintern-imposed pro-GMD policy line. Ch'en, for instance, had great misgivings about the united front strategy from the beginning, although, as the secretary-general of the CCP, he felt duty-bound to carry out faithfully the Comintern directives. His misgivings were probably shared by most leading Chinese Communists. Nevertheless, it was Ch'en who first recognized Zhou's organizing expertise and winning personality, and it was with Ch'en's support that Zhou had his first opportunity to play an important role in united front politics.[22] Although the immediate task was essentially military, both GMD and CCP leaders agreed on the need to broaden popular mobilization against warlord control. Before it could become a secure base for further military operations, Quandong Province and its capital, Canton, had to be solidly organized for the forthcoming national revolution. Ch'en personally had tremendous confidence in Zhou's ability to act prudently, in line with instructions from the CCP hierarchy.

The "bloc within" policy was directly under the guidance of top party leadership. As the liaison officer between the two parties, Zhou was drawn deeply into the daily activities of cooperation. His responsibility in the political department at Whampoa was one for which he was well qualified by virtue of his personality, experience, and training. His appointment as the highest Communist staff member at the military academy placed him in a position of prestige and influence, and he now had a unique opportunity to put into practice the strategy of the united front.

Zhou was in favor of the alliance with the GMD for more practical reasons.[23] First, during the first several years of its existence, the CCP had represented and regarded itself as the party of the working class. It had attempted to advance the national revolution by using the proletariat as its base and strikes as it weapons. Zhou felt, however, it was important for the CCP to broaden its national appeal by focusing its energy on cooperation with all revolutionary classes and groups against foreign imperialism and warlordism in China.[24] Second, a related question that had arisen out of the alliance with the GMD was whether or not the CCP's acceptance of the postponement of Chinese proletarian expectations might contribute to the devitalization of both Marxist ideology and the Communist movement itself in China. According to Zhou, the CCP had no army, and the alliance with the GMD would provide CCP members with the opportunity to convert some of the promising young officers at Whampoa and well-trained cadets of the GMD to communism, thereby turning them into the backbone of the Red Army.[25] Third, warlord armies controlled every province, and in each province local military leaders vied for power and influence. Through its alliance with the GMD the CCP would be better equipped to mobilize the masses. This point was especially important in view of the fact that during its early stage of growth the CCP was by no means a working-class party but, rather, it was primarily a party of revolutionary intellectuals. Therefore, it was imperative for the CCP to participate in the joint armed struggle with the GMD against the warlords throughout the country to widen its power base. At the same time, Zhou coolly assessed the nature of the CCP-GMD alliance and came to the conclusion that a workable alliance was contingent upon the CCP's capacity and willingness to adjust. This adjustment required at least a muting of the "class struggle," one of the distinctive and critical elements of Marxist doctrine.

It is evident that this guiding principle of necessary adaptation had a tremendous influence on Zhou's analysis and evaluation of the CCP's relations with various sections of the GMD. Against this background Zhou saw the united front approach essentially as a "strategic maneuver" and held that CCP leaders had to cooperate with the bourgeois forces if they were seeking ultimate revolutionary success.[26] He also believed that the "national revolution," which would be both difficult and long-lasting, would go through different phases. Moreover, the Chinese Communist movement, which was weak and unorganized at the moment, must first be strengthened and then expanded.[27] The united front strategy was not an end in itself, according to Zhou, but merely a way for the CCP to attain its major objectives. Zhou, whose mind and heart were set with great clarity on a distant goal—building socialism in China—now threw himself into the urgent, immediate task of serving not only as a strong advocate but also as a genuine practitioner of the united front strategy.

The years from 1924 to 1927, in retrospect, provided Zhou with a unique opportunity to test his own pragmatic principle against the evolving conditions of CCP-GMD cooperation and competition. The CCP, based solely on the small Chinese proletariat, seemed to him to be a party that needed allies, and at that time the GMD offered the best prospect for an alliance. Zhou's role in this phase of domestic united front politics was shaped not only by his personal convictions but also by circumstances. From the beginning he took a deep interest in the coordination of CCP-GMD revolutionary activities. To further the CCP's causes Zhou tried earnestly to cooperate with GMD authorities at all levels. His responsibility in the political department at Whampoa Military Academy helped the young deputy director to develop and crystallize his political strategy.

The alliance with the GMD, for Zhou, was to aid in unifying the nation and carrying out the national democratic revolution.[28] Immediately after this political revolution China could begin the task of socialist construction without going through extensive capitalist development. This task of socialist revolution would be carried out by the proletariat. Zhou considered the GMD a four-class party and not simply the party of the bourgeoisie. It was his conviction, however, that the proletariat was still the key to carrying out China's social and economic development.[29] While Zhou believed that China would eventually have to undergo a proletarian revolution, he did not believe that, under existing circumstances in China, this had to be the first step in the long revolutionary process. When Zhou participated in the CCP-GMD united front movement in 1924, he went along with the Comintern line, which, in essence, reaffirmed his own analysis of the nature of Chinese society and his belief in the need for a transitional bourgeois stage of the revolution.[30]

Meanwhile, the CCP as a party was radical, middle-class, and weak both in numbers and discipline. Zhou, as a trusted liaison between the two parties, had to persuade the CCP members to understand the practical value of the Party's temporary alliance with the GMD. Both conceptually and for pragmatic reasons, Zhou had to reconcile the class struggle with the national revolution. In his view the national revolution, or the revolution of the GMD's Three Principles of the People, which was based on cooperation between the proletariat and property-owning classes, was intended to overthrow the governing class of feudal elements. China's urgent problems and economic conditions required broad cooperation among revolutionaries of all persuasions. The Chinese Communist revolution must go through a number of "steps" before the proletariat could reach the road of survival. China was in a process of great transformation, ready but as yet unable to break through into a new revolutionary stage. Not only must the Chinese Communists recognize the strategic advantage of their alliance with bourgeois revolutionaries; they must also support the goals of national revolution. As Zhou perceived it, the CCP members had two main political aims. The first was to increase the importance and influence of the Party. The second was to transform the national revolution from its bourgeois stage to the proletarian phase.[31]

The common objectives of the CCP and the GMD and the military and political supremacy of the GMD government in Canton had rendered the pragmatic reinterpretation of Marxism-Leninism more and more desirable. It was Zhou who was obliged to define and refine class struggle and revolutionary aims. In general, he placed the element of flexibility squarely in the center of the CCP's overall approach to national revolution. Faithful to Marxism-Leninism, Zhou contended that it was advantageous to establish a workable relationship with the bourgeois nationalists in China; it was equally important to win over the moderate and left-wing factions of the GMD. Not only did he value the practical considerations of united front politics, but he also stressed the importance of attracting the middle and petty bourgeoisie to the side of national revolution. According to Zhou, the application of the united front principle to the CCP-GMD cooperation demanded at least mutual understanding and restraint.[32] Therefore, Zhou urged his compatriots to adopt the course of moderation and adjustment. Even so, his support for the program of national revolution to be carried out in alliance with the GMD was conditional, as he continued to maintain that, ultimately, the national revolution was to be followed by the class revolution, which would pit the proletarian class against the property classes. Nonetheless, to win the confidence of the GMD, Zhou assured its members that "a Communist Party, serving the workers and peasants and guiding them into the path of national revolution, will in no way hinder the GMD in its leadership of the various classes working for the revolution."[33] "On the contrary," he added, "both parties will benefit by complementing and supporting each other in their practical work."[34] Under GMD leadership Zhou asserted that the CCP's political views and criticisms were nothing other than "well intentioned."[35] Underscoring the common objectives between the two parties, Zhou concluded, "We hope that it [the GMD] will accept them, for they are fundamentally different from the hostile criticisms and disruptive propaganda of the imperialists, warlords, and semi-feudal forces."[36]

During his assignment at the Whampoa Military Academy, Zhou was already in favor of avoiding direct confrontation with the GMD authorities. He held that conditions within China were not ripe for a proletarian class struggle and that the national revolution could best be accomplished if CCP members closely followed the united front approach in cooperating with the GMD. Zhou's support of the united front strategy had as much to do with his realistic assessment of the revolutionary strength of the Chinese urban workers as with his desire to maintain international Communist discipline. Most important of all, Zhou wanted to underscore as forcefully as possible his personal conviction that the united front strategy was a necessary but temporary expedient that allowed the CCP to establish an alliance with the GMD to promote "shared interests" and that the CCP must always uphold its own position in the national revolution. "While we agree that the revolutionary GMD is the leading force in the national revolution and the members of the

CCP must join the GMD to carry on common struggle," observed Zhou, "it does not follow that the CCP has lost its identity and should no longer have any independent views."[37] On the other hand, Zhou perceptively pointed out that, "in the course of the revolution, each class has its own aims and, particularly when democracy is in the process of being realized, each has its own interests to pursue."[38] It was the priority of the CCP to press the GMD government to fulfill "the political and economic demands of the workers and peasants."[39]

Satisfying the just demands of both workers and peasants without driving the patriotic landlords, anti-warlord army officers, and anti-imperialist businessmen into the arms of warlords was by no means a simple task. To avoid alienating any constituent group, Zhou, with characteristic flexibility, devised a subtle strategy, adapting alternate methods of cooperation and competition with the GMD in the national revolution. He extended the scope of the united front far beyond cooperation with the center and the left wings of the GMD, and he courted political alliance with all groups across the entire political spectrum, pragmatically obliterating, for the time being, any consideration of classes or class struggle. He was clearly convinced that the CCP could not attain power through a rigid course of action.[40]

When the CCP was directed by the Comintern to put aside, temporarily, the objective of attaining political power and to strive, instead, to influence the policy orientation of the GMD government in accordance with the requirements of the united front strategy, its leaders had to come to terms with the bourgeois elements in China. Zhou, as one of the Party's young organizers, not only followed the Comintern line but, more important, fully recognized the practical value of cooperating closely with the bourgeoisie during this specific stage and under these unique political conditions. Close cooperation between the two parties, in Zhou's view, made it possible for the CCP to overcome its political isolation. In addition, Zhou believed that "the middle-of-the-roaders" must be won over to the side of the CCP.[41] As a corollary, any success in winning over the moderates could substantially strengthen the CCP's overall ability to reach other nonproletarian groups and forces throughout China.

Zhou believed that the CCP must recognize that there were a variety of bourgeois classes and that the degree of each group's revolutionary potential and determination could not be taken for granted. Furthermore, the degree to which they were inclined toward revolution would not be immutable, and it could be influenced. To take full advantage of this potential it was imperative for the CCP to analyze each political group thoroughly in terms of its self-interest and likelihood to fashion an optimal relationship with the CCP.[42] In addition, the CCP must adopt appropriate policies that minimized any possible negative effects that such political alliances might have upon its main objectives.

Zhou articulated his position on and strategy for united front politics in a series of articles published in *Red Light* and *Guide* (Xiang-dao), two major official publications of the CCP. "The GMD right wing," Zhou argued as early as October 1924, "always remained opposed to the revolution, and was always predisposed to seek collusion with warlords and imperialists."[43] It was also his guess, however, that the members of the GMD's left wing—that is, the masses of workers, peasants, and students—were in favor of the revolution.[44] In order to carry out the national revolution more effectively, Zhou urged the moderates within the GMD "to break resolutely with their psychology to compromise, dissociate from the right wing, and ally themselves with the left wing."[45] If the right (or conservative) wing of the GMD could be held in check, the left wing progressively strengthened, and the middle group won over, the CCP, as Zhou observed later, would then have sufficient reason to look forward to a growing influence in a broad-based party whose aims were essentially consonant with its own.

On the other hand, in pursuing united front politics, the CCP leaders would have to address some fundamental questions. How would the Chinese Communists be able to relate to the GMD, mainly a revolutionary bourgeois party? What might be the dangers of cooperating with bourgeois groups? Would cooperative efforts between the CCP and the GMD necessarily lead to a consolidation of the CCP's power base and influence in China? Or would such cooperation indeed be necessary for the national revolution? The core of the strategic alliance, Zhou asserted, was the proletariat-peasantry, which was not hostile to the nonproletarian classes.[46] Built upon this core of proletarian-peasant unity, united front policy could be used to draw additional strength from other classes in Chinese society by emphasizing "common interests." To this end the CCP's political and economic programs must be broader than the original objectives of the Party. Within this conceptual framework CCP leaders agreed that the GMD was the leading force in the national revolution and that the CCP fought in alliance with the GMD against their common enemies. The CCP, however, should be prepared to seize the appropriate moment to break away from the GMD and begin to pursue its own objectives.

Before the break occurred, the CCP leaders should do everything possible to strengthen proletarian organizations. Zhou worked relentlessly to further the CCP's objectives at the Whampoa Military Academy. He was successful in winning over to his position many of the instructors and cadets at the academy. In fact, his influence over many of the cadets greatly alarmed the GMD authorities at Whampoa. In the spring of 1926 Zhou was arrested by GMD authorities but was not detained for long.[47] Some of his comrades in the

Communist Party maintained that he bore considerable responsibility for the March 20 incident. Others suggested that this episode tested Zhou's endurance and revealed his extraordinary ability to handle delicate situations.

Meanwhile, Zhou was torn between his official duties at the military academy and his allegiance to the CCP. The need to maintain a working relationship with GMD leaders further complicated matters. Besides, the deteriorating relationship between the CCP and the GMD had to be improved. After his release Zhou searched for measures of compromise to preserve at least some degree of CCP-GMD cooperation. He was deeply distressed by the GMD purge of CCP members at the academy. At this stage he still believed that the split between the two parties could be averted through cooperative measures, in spite of the fact that he was disturbed by the GMD's actions against members of the CCP and of the local trade unions.

Zhou continued to view the GMD as a natural ally of the CCP and spoke of the national revolution as part of the process of the proletarian revolution, which was the main objective of the CCP. He still maintained that there should be no serious obstacle to close cooperation between the CCP and the GMD.[48] On the contrary, of all the anti-imperialist and antifeudal forces in China, the CCP's relations with the revolutionary bourgeois party should be the least complicated, despite their differences in political ideology and economic interests. Zhou even tried to capitalize on the residual spirit of cooperation before the real split between the two parties. Not until December 1926 did Zhou begin to acknowledge publicly the strained relations between the two groups and the class-based conflict of interests. "Though the national revolution is the common aim of all the oppressed classes," said Zhou, "the proletariat is the most uncompromising revolutionary class in the prolonged struggle, while the national bourgeoisie is inclined to compromise and the petty bourgeoisie often vacillates."[49] The atmosphere of mistrust engendered by interparty confrontations prompted Zhou to remark that, "if there were conflicts, they would be conflicts between the masses of revolutionary workers and peasants and a bourgeoisie that was compromising with the imperialist enemies."[50] Referring to the possible split between the two parties, he added: "If there were a split, it would be a split between an alliance of the revolutionary left wing of the GMD and the Communists on the one hand and the right wing that was abandoning the revolution on the other."[51] It is clear that at this point Zhou had not yet completely given up on the CCP-GMD alliance, except that he accepted the inevitable split with the right wing of the GMD.

When the Northern Military Campaign was under way in the summer of 1926, Zhou was assigned to organize the members of trade unions in Shanghai against the warlord Sun Chuan-fang. By March 1927 Zhou had succeeded in mobilizing a force of 800,000 workers in Shanghai. The power of the labor movement organized and inspired by Zhou was demonstrated by the working-class uprising in the city of Shanghai on March 21, 1927. The workers liberated the city even before Jiang's solders arrived on March 22. Once the split between the two parties became a fact in April 1927, Zhou strongly urged the CCP leadership to be decisive in its struggle against Jiang and his right-wing GMD. "If, despite all his acts of betrayal, we continue to be indecisive, seeking to relax the tension by postponing struggle," warned Zhou, "Jiang will consolidate his regime in southeastern China and form even closer ties with the imperialists."[52] He went on to say: "In view of the overall situation, there should be no further political relaxation or compromise. A gross error has already been committed in Shanghai following the uprising. If we again fail to go forward, our power will be shaken in proportion as the enemy advances and we retreat, and political leadership will fall entirely into the hands of the right wing [of the GMD]."[53] It should be noted that the April 1927 split between the right and left wings of the GMD created a situation of competing authority: with one power center at Nanjing, over which Jiang resided, and another power center at Wuhan, headed by Wang Jing-wei and supported by the CCP under Comintern directives. The CCP leaders issued a manifesto on July 13, 1927, announcing that they had withdrawn their representatives from the GMD government but would continue to collaborate with the "true revolutionary members" of the GMD.

As time went on, Zhou no longer entertained any illusions about what the CCP was likely to achieve. He became keenly aware of the fragility of revolutionary achievement through political alliance and the CCP's vulnerability due to its lack of military force. Yet the united front experience remained crucial to Zhou's understanding of the nature of interparty cooperation and competition and to his recognition of the importance of timing in making decisive moves. Zhou reflected on the CCP's first united front strategy in an address delivered at a study session of the cadres of the Southern Bureau of the Central Committee of the CCP in Chongqing in the spring of 1943. "It was our Party that drew the revolutionary youth into the GMD," asserted Zhou, "and it was our Party that enabled it to establish ties with the workers and peasants."[54] He also elaborated on his assessment of the makeup of the GMD. "In the GMD in Guangdong at that time [in mid-1925], the centrists were in the minority while the left-wingers constituted the overwhelming majority."[55] The influence of the GMD right wing was substantial, in Zhou's estimation, therefore, CCP policy was "to strike at the right wing, isolate the center, and expand the left wing."[56]

On March 3 and 4, 1944, Zhou made a report to the Sixth Congress of the CCP in which he further remarked on the CCP's first united front with the

GMD in the period from 1923 to 1927. "There was much controversy at the time," said Zhou, "over the question of joining the GMD. But it was wrong to think that the sole purpose of joining was to help the GMD."[57] He then declared that the decision to cooperate with the GMD was not unanimous within with CCP. "In the beginning Zhang Guotao was against joining the GMD, and later he held that at least the industrial workers should remain outside. He did not understand that when the masses of workers and peasants entered the GMD, they could help reform it and win leadership in it."[58] He also revealed the complacency of some CCP leaders at the time. Zhou recalled: "At the Fourth National Congress of the Party, Peng Shuzhi held that leadership automatically fell to the proletariat, that it was an 'automatic leadership,' so there was no point in the proletariat's striving for it."[59] He added: "This shows that he didn't see that the bourgeoisie was fighting to seize leadership. So when Jiang Jie-shi launched an anti-Communist attack on March 20, 1926, after the Second National Congress of the GMD, we were totally unprepared."[60]

Accounts of the reasons for the split between the CCP and the GMD in 1927 differ, but it appears that Jiang and the GMD leaders were afraid of the rising strength of radical agrarianism and were concerned lest they be cut off from access to the capital and the commerce of the West and from the Chinese big bourgeoisie. As Zhou saw it, Jiang was "oppressing the workers, wooing the bourgeoisie, consolidating his political power, and getting control of sources of revenue in order to be able to undermine the allegiance of impoverished left-leaning troops."[61] Three decades later Zhou commented on the 1927 Shanghai revolts and on his own weaknesses: "I was responsible for leading the armed revolts, but I lacked experience and was weak in understanding political dynamics. I am an intellectual with a feudalistic family background. I had had little contact with the peasant-worker masses because I had taken no part in the economic process of production. My revolutionary career started abroad, with very limited knowledge about it, obtained from books only."[62]

The 1936 Xi'an Incident and Zhou's Role in Its Peaceful Settlement

The Xi'an Incident of December 12, 1936, was staged by two GMD generals, Zhang Xueliang and Yang Hucheng, who demanded cessation of the Chinese civil war in the interests of united resistance against Japan's territorial expansion in China. With Jiang under house arrest, Generals Zhang and Yang immediately announced to the nation their eight-point proposal. Jiang was asked by the two generals to promise "the abandonment of civil war and the cooperation between the GMD and the CCP" and "a defined policy of armed resistance against any further Japanese aggression."[63] Zhang and Yang also cabled the Central Committee of the CCP in Yenan to send a delegation to Xi'an to discuss plans for resistance against Japan and for resolving the major problems arising from their action. When Zhou, chief of the CCP delegation, arrived at Xi'an on December 14, 1936, he found that Zhang and Yang had unilaterally announced an eight-point proposal but had no overall plan for the immediate future. At this time, however, Zhou believed that there were no conflicting interests that could not be harmonized between the CCP and the GMD through negotiations. He was in favor of a strategy aimed at forming a nationwide anti-Japanese coalition. He perceived his role in the incident as that of an arbiter. He conveyed the CCP's position to both generals in practical terms[64] and indicated that it would be critical to reach a peaceful settlement of the Xi'an Incident so as to unify China's forces of resistance against the Japanese aggressors.

Zhou's immediate objective at Xi'an was to avoid a national crisis by proposing a rational solution to the complicated problem. In his preliminary discussions with Zhang, Zhou reviewed the proper measures for dealing with Jiang and the GMD government in Nanjing. He also made a careful analysis of the current situation both at home and abroad as well as of the potential impact of the Xi'an Incident. The implications of the incident, in Zhou's view, were far-reaching, and, unlike mass uprising, the demands were backed by military force. Although Jiang was taken by surprise, his power and prestige remained intact. At this initial stage of negotiations the problem lay not with Jiang but with Zhang and Yang, who suddenly found themselves at the center of public attention without having thought out a careful plan prior to Jiang's kidnapping.

From the very beginning Zhou employed a tactful and moderate persuasive style in his discussions with both Zhang and Yang, viewing the incident in terms of political realities. Should the CCP adopt a more conciliatory position on this episode, Zhou reasoned, it would then be possible for the Party to establish a more normal relationship with Jiang and his GMD government in Nanjing. In his talks with Zhang on the evening of December 14, Zhou suggested that any peaceful settlement of the incident must be based on Jiang's willingness to end the civil war in China and to lead a nationwide united front against the Japanese invaders.[65] At the same time, he hinted to Zhang that the Soviet Union might decide not to support their actions. He praised Zhang for his courage and intelligence but also reminded him of his lack of experience and knowledge in dealing with such a national crisis. Zhou sought to persuade Zhang of the need for a quick, peaceful settlement and a guarantee by Jiang to resist Japan.

In his conversation with Yang the following day Zhou followed the same strategy.[66] In order to persuade Yang to support the CCP's approach to the incident fully and also to alleviate Yang's fear that Jiang would seek revenge, Zhou proposed the formation of a triangular alliance of Yang's Northwestern and Zhang's Northeastern Armies with the Communist forces as a counterweight to Jiang's possible reprisal against the Xi'an insurgents in the future.[67] He was able to convince both Zhang and Yang that Jiang's life should be spared, as Jiang was a popular political figure capable of rallying all the anti-Japanese forces throughout China.

Zhou's initial success afforded him greater leverage and maneuverability when he began direct negotiations with GMD representatives on December 23. At the first meeting with Song Ziwen, Jiang's brother-in-law and chief delegate, Zhou formally put forward the CCP's six-point proposal for a peaceful settlement of the Xi'an Incident.[68] He offered the CCP's promise to support Jiang in "unifying China to fight Japan."[69] With special reference to the future status of Zhang and Yang, he proposed that, "during the period of the transitional government, a Northwestern Joint Army should be formed" and that "the Northeastern Army . . . and the Red Army should establish a joint committee under the leadership of Zhang Xue-liang."[70] Song agreed with Zhou in principle and promised to forward these proposals to Jiang. After two days of intensive discussions between Zhou and Song Ziwen and between Zhou and Song Meiling, Jaing's wife, an agreement was finally reached regarding the issues of the Chinese civil war and the anti-Japanese united front. On the basis of Jiang's prior personal agreement with the CCP's six-point proposal, on the evening of December 24 Zhou finally met with Jiang alone to hold a direct discussion and reassured Jiang of the CCP's willingness to support his leadership in a wartime coalition of anti-Japanese forces throughout China. Zhou carefully conveyed the CCP's spirit of reconciliation and respect for Jiang's leadership and authority and the desire of the CCP to remove all past prejudices and to forge a new working relationship between the CCP and the GMD.[71]

In dealing with Jiang, his wife, and his brother-in-law, Zhou employed the most effective moves and counter-moves and knew how to assess the strengths and weaknesses of the negotiating parties realistically. At no time did he overlook Jiang's pride nor the influence of the pro-Japanese faction within the GMD government in Nanjing. At the core of Zhou's negotiations was his personal conviction that the Chinese people preferred a war against the Japanese invaders to a continuous power and ideological struggle between the CCP and the GMD. The prospect of agreement between the two sides increased perceptibly by the following day when Ziwen Song told Zhou that he himself was "to take full responsibility for forming a government satisfactory to the people and for ridding it of the pro-Japanese faction"[72] within the GMD government in Nanjing and for "the withdrawal of troops and the removal of the government armies . . . from the Northwest."[73] The immediate problem was how to find a common ground between Zhou and Song. While Zhou wanted the GMD government to stop its suppression of the Chinese Communists, Song expressed the hope that the CCP should "back him in his advocacy of resistance to Japan and in his struggle against the pro-Japanese faction"[74] within the GMD government. Furthermore, Jiang was not prepared, at this crucial juncture, to go much further than his initial offer to negotiate directly with Zhou when he got back to Nanjing, nor was he willing to sign a political document confirming his personal commitment before his departure from Xi'an.

An end to the Chinese civil war and the formation of a united front with the GMD government against Japanese aggression were the immediate objectives of Zhou's negotiations at Xi'an. In a telegram sent to Yenan on December 29, 1936, Zhou justified his position by pointing out that the peaceful settlement of the Xi'an Incident represented a "new stage in China's political life."[75] It meant "a halt in the attacks on the Red Army," "an end to the policy of concession in external affairs," and "the formation of a preliminary national united front."[76] The Xi'an Incident and the nature of its settlement signified, in Zhou's own words, "a division and realignment of class forces and, in particular, a process of definitive division in the bourgeois camp. They are significant because they have rallied and consolidated the left wing in the bourgeois camp and discredited the notion that a middle course is possible."[77] He cautioned, however, that "the process of division is not yet complete, and, generally speaking, there are still three groups—the anti-Japanese, the capitulationist, and the middle."[78] In his analysis of the new political realities Zhou indicated that "the anti-Japanese forces have been strengthened and at least partially legalized," that "a fatal blow has been dealt to the pro-Japanese faction," and that "the middle-of-the-roaders are beginning to draw closer to the left wing."[79] To further clarify the meaning of his observations on the issue of division and realignment of class forces in China, Zhou added, "Our policy should be to combat the pro-Japanese faction, strengthen the left wing with the Northwest as the center, and influence and draw in the middle-of-the-roaders."[80]

The maintenance of normal relations with the proposed "transitional government" headed by Kong Xiangxi and Song Ziwen was Zhou's top priority in his negotiations with GMD representatives at Xi'an. "While not in the least relaxing our criticism of its [the provisional government's] weakness," asserted Zhou, "we should encourage and support its anti-Japanese tendencies and try to bring about gradual, even if not major, democratic reforms."[81] Then he went on: "Like all transitional governments, it is bound to vacillate, and there are various possibilities as to its future."[82] In line with his assessment Zhou strongly suggested: "We should combat every instance of vacillation and push it to become an anti-Japanese government."[83] Zhou felt that the CCP must work actively in the formation of a "nationwide movement of unity for resistance against Japan."[84] This nationwide coalition should include the GMD government and, in Zhou's words, "various groups outside Nanjing [the GMD government], but with the Northwest as our [the CCP's] center and resistance to Japan as our precondition and objective."[85] On the same occasion Zhou reiterated the need for the CCP to adjust pragmatically to the changing political environment. "We should transform all Party work," he urged in his telegram communication with Yenan head-quarters, "adapting it to the new circumstances, so that the Party becomes the leader in the political life of the country."[86]

Throughout the difficult negotiations with both Zhang and Yang as well as with Jiang, Zhou conducted himself with extreme caution, courtesy, and self-control. Upon discovering both Zhang and Yang's uncertainties about their future course of action, Zhou immediately acted as an arbitrator, performing a challenging but necessary duty. He did what he believed had to be done with as much flexibility as the task required. He knew the men with whom he was dealing, and he had sufficient insight into the feelings and grievances of those who were involved in the Xi'an Incident to know the importance of give-and-take. Throughout the negotiations Zhou was trou-bled by the possibility that the GMD government in Nanjing might initiate a punitive campaign against the Xi'an insurgent leaders. His proposal for establishing a triangular alliance of the Northeastern, Northwestern, and Communist forces was a masterful strategy. Not only could it provide Zhang and Yang with the military security that they needed for countering Jiang's retaliation, but, more important, it would significantly increase the military strength of the CCP.

The fact that Zhou was negotiating from a position of weakness made his accomplishments in handling the Xi'an Incident even more remarkable. It was through his persistence and persuasive power that Zhou was able to negotiate successfully with Zhang and Yang for the preconditions of Jiang's eventual release. Although Jiang insisted that he would not sign any agreement pertaining to the conditions of his release, he did promise that the CCP could participate in the future war against Japan if the Chinese Communists pledged their support for Sun's Three Principles of the People. "Judging from what has happened," declared Zhou in his December 25 telegram to Yenan, "there was a real change in Jiang Jie-shi's attitude while he was here. He is sincere in delegating matters to Song Ziwen, and Song is really determined to resist Japan."[87] Out of the chaos at Xi'an, Zhou hoped to bring better order, which could heal longtime animosities between the CCP and the GMD and channel Chinese patriotism into action. It was by no means a simple task. "We didn't sleep for a week," Zhou told his close associate Wang Bingnan, "trying to decide what was possibly the most difficult decision of our entire lives."[88]

Initially, the CCP Political Bureau (Politburo) intended to exploit the Xi'an Incident as a justification for setting up a national antigovernment in Xi'an, isolating if not totally discrediting Jiang.[89] In the meantime, however, it was crucial to the Soviet Union that the government of Jiang be induced to resist Japan rather than reach a compromise that could possibly free Japan to turn against the Soviet Union.[90] This consideration dictated, once again, a policy of CCP coalition with the GMD. In his negotiations Zhou aimed at optimum cooperation with Jiang and his GMD government in Nanjing, and tried to integrate the activities of the peasants, workers, students, petty bourgeoisie, and national bourgeoisie of the whole country into a nationwide united front against Japanese aggression. Only after Zhou had reached an understanding with Jiang did the CCP begin to modify its original plan of organizing a "Northwest anti-Japanese government" to "cooperate with the GMD."[91] From a historical point of view the peaceful settlement of the Xi'an Incident in late December 1936 was certainly the key to the formation of the second united front between the CCP and the GMD.

Viewed in hindsight, it is clear that Jiang never truly intended to cooperate with the CCP. In his book *Soviet Russia in China,* published in 1951, Jiang formally denied that he entered into any political negotiations with the Chinese Communists in Xi'an and maintained that he never "bargained" for the peace that was achieved.[92] Zhou was not entirely oblivious to this possibility. In his reminiscence nine years after the Xi'an Incident he recalled: "During the Xi'an Incident, I once asked Jiang Jie-shi, 'We called for an end to the civil war; why wouldn't you stop it?' He answered, 'I was waiting for you to come to the Northwest.' I said, 'We've been in the Northwest for more than a year.' He had nothing to say to that."[93] Zhou concluded by suggesting that "it is quite clear he [Jiang] was thinking of exterminating us in the Northwest."[94] Nevertheless, from a historical perspective Zhou was instrumental in the peaceful settlement of the Xi'an Incident. Through his efforts it was possible to bring about temporary compromises and accommodations between the CCP and the GMD and the resulting cessation of armed hostility, which in turn led to the formation of a nationwide anti-Japanese united front throughout China.

Zhou and His Role in the Second United Front, 1937-1945

During and after the Xi'an Incident Zhou was one of the strongest advocates within the CCP hierarchy of continuing to search for ways of collaborating with the GMD government. But such collaboration was only a useful means to an end—namely, to enhance the national influence of CCP during the second united front with the GMD. It was, therefore, important for the CCP to adopt and maintain the correct position. As long as Yenan was willing to adjust its ideological interests to prevailing national aspirations, Zhou held, the Chinese Communist movement would certainly gain a stronghold in China. The current need was to adapt the CCP's positions on both domestic conditions and international circumstances. The CCP's credibility would depend, to a large extent, on its working relationship with the GMD government. At this stage in its growth the CCP once again needed a flexible policy vis-à-vis the GMD.[95] Being clear about the purpose of another united front approach to domestic politics would, in Zhou's view, enable CCP leaders to avoid "capitulationism," on the one hand, and "adventurism," on the other.

The CCP's self-interest was absolutely central to all considerations.[96] Throughout the early years of the second united front between the CCP and the GMD, Zhou tried in his interviews with foreign journalists, his essays for Party publications, and his lectures and reports at public meetings to clarify the main purpose of the united front approach. The goal of the CCP's strategy, Zhou maintained, was to move the GMD government to a policy of total resistance to Japanese aggression in China. It was important to convince the GMD leaders that without mass mobilization there was no hope of successfully resisting the Japanese invaders.

American journalist Edgar Snow, in an interview held on July 9, 1936, asked Zhou the reasons for the success of the "counter-revolution of 1927" and about the "chief mistakes of the Chinese Communists."[97] Zhou's answers were explicit. The first mistake, Zhou held, was "in not deepening the revolution among the peasants in Guangdong and Guangxi Provinces."[98] The second mistake was that the CCP "failed to develop the necessary revolutionary leadership among cadres of the GMD army."[99] The third mistake was that the Chinese Communists "threw away" their "chance to hold hegemony of the GMD, then still a revolutionary party."[100] On the issue of democracy and communism, Zhou stated in his interview with Nym Wales (Mrs. Snow) on June 22, 1937, that preparations for the war of resistance to Japanese aggression and democracy were "like the two wheels of a bicycle, one before the other."[101] He also indicated that in his fourteen years of political life he had been striving for democracy and not for proletarian dictatorship. "We want to give up the

Soviet system," Zhou told Snow's wife, "in order to change into the national democratic system along the road of the Three Principles" of Sun Yat-sen.[102] By its very nature this national democracy would include "the landowners, bourgeoisie and petty bourgeoisie with the workers and peasants."[103] On another occasion, in a conversation with Wales, Zhou made further qualifications about the final goal of the CCP and the importance of its independent course of action. "Our ultimate goal," said Zhou, "is Communist collectivism."[104] He added emphatically, "But China cannot develop along the same route as the USSR."[105] In order to substantiate his argument Zhou listed five points to verify that the new democracy advocated by the CCP was in conformity with the Three Principles of the People: nationalism, democracy, and people's livelihood.[106]

In his extensive interview with another American journalist, James Bisson, on June 23, 1937, Zhou said: "On our side we also have good reason to conclude a united front agreement. We can push ahead with the anti-Japanese struggle and extend it to all parts of China. The mere existence of the united front negotiations is a stimulus to mass anti-Japanese sentiment. It thus offers a base on which to organize the whole Chinese people."[107] He added, however, "On the other hand, if the Sian [Xi'an] Incident had been handled provocatively, the civil war would have spread and grown sharper. Only the Japanese would have gained, not Nanking [Nanjing] and not us."[108] Zhou further justified the change in Yenan's policy and action by pointing out: "For ten years we used revolutionary means, an armed struggle, to build up the worker-peasant democratic system. Now we want to use the political struggle, peaceful struggle, to create the national democratic republic."[109] It was Zhou's view that the CCP in the second period of cooperation with the GMD should not repeat the experience of the first united front. The operation, this time, must be stable and sustained, and it called for mutual understanding and mutual concessions.[110] As the CCP was taking the initiative in the rapprochement with the GMD, its leaders must forget the enmity between the two parties in the past. What really mattered most, in Zhou's opinion, was that CCP leaders keep their word.[111] He also stressed that the CCP should take an active role in the national crisis so as to bolster its political status throughout the nation.[112]

Zhou was convinced, however, that the will for victory in the domestic power competition was not enough and that real results must be sought within the framework of adjustment and adaptation.[113] Nonetheless, he was realistic enough to believe that genuine cooperation with the GMD could only be achieved "little by little."[114] He told Bisson his line of thinking in a straightforward manner: "First, it comes in the anti-Japanese struggle. With this, the advances needed in the political field become possible."[115] He went on to qualify: "Both must go together, but one before the other, like the wheels of a bicycle, not in parallel like the wheels of a rickshaw. Preparation for the defensive war against Japan comes first, then the movement for a democratic republic. Of course, each affects the other."[116] It was Zhou's central theme that "the wheels move together, but the anti-Japanese movement is the front wheel."[117] In the long process of a "socialist revolution" in China it was essential to carry out the bourgeois revolutionary task first. This primary task, Zhou held, sought "to uproot foreign imperialism and Chinese feudalism."[118] This new emphasis reflected a subtle change in the CCP's original policy. It really meant, to use Zhou's own words, "changing the worker-peasant democratic system into a national democratic system," one that would include "the bourgeoisie, the petty bourgeoisie, and the landowners along with the workers and peasants."[119] It also meant "a change in method"—that is, the transformation from a "revolutionary means, an armed struggle, to build up a worker-peasant democratic system to the skillful use of political struggle, peaceful struggle" in order to build a "democratic republic in China."[120]

Independence of the CCP within the framework of the united front, according to Zhou, was a matter of relativity. But this relative independence must be held by the Party hierarchy in Yenan. Moreover, Yenan's cooperation with the GMD government in the war of resistance against the Japanese aggressors should focus on specific tasks. This strategy would allow the CCP enormous flexibility and reinforce its adaptation to shifting political forces and circumstances. So, politically, organizationally, and ideologically, the CCP must have its relative independence—that is, "relative maneuverability."

Obviously, Zhou's negotiations with GMD authorities were not based on an equal footing. The indignities that he encountered in the course of negotiating with GMD officials in 1937 sorely tested his patience and ability. He frequently heard remarks such as the "unconditional surrender of the CCP" or "its total annihilation." Nonetheless, he carried on. In his interview with Bisson he said: "Negotiations are continuing," but he remarked frankly, "It is hard to learn to cooperate after ten years of conflict."[121]

Immediately after the outbreak of the Sino-Japanese War on July 7, 1937, Zhou intensified his contacts with the GMD government and managed to develop a plan of compromise, as stated clearly in an open letter of December 22, 1937, addressed to the Chinese people. In this letter the CCP leaders offered the GMD authorities four specific concessions, including their decisions to abolish all Chinese soviet governments and to accept the reorganization of the Red Armies into a national revolutionary army.[122] The actual terms of the united front represented a compromise between what the GMD government wanted the most and the maximum concessions the CCP would make. The

Red Army was to be renamed the Eighth Route Army and would function in cooperation with the GMD military forces against the Japanese invaders. Both the land revolution and the armed insurrection against the GMD government were to come to an end. In return, the GMD government promised an end to the civil war and the blockade of Soviet areas. In addition, it promised subsidies to the Eighth Route and the reformed New Fourth Armies. But the route to cooperation proved to be rocky. On November 16, 1937, speaking at a joint rally in Linfen, Shanxi, on the issue of the war of resistance and the administrative system in North China, Zhou revealed the limited efforts made by the GMD government: "Over the last three to four months, the GMD has not loosened its control either over the government or over the mobilization of the people. To this day the GMD party headquarters is sticking to the policy of control over the mobilization work. Control without mobilization is a universal phenomenon."[123] He felt that the national government should include "representatives of all political parties or groups and all military forces to join in the government and in the task of saving the country."[124] Japan's invasion and its territorial expansion in China generated a strong response among the Chinese people, whose nationalism now became focused on imperialist Japan. Nationalism, in Zhou's opinion, could be a powerful weapon in defending China's independence and sovereignty. It is not surprising that he viewed the problems of nationalism and Communist revolution in these specifically Chinese terms. Because of China's semifeudal and semicolonial status, Zhou was convinced that the Chinese proletariat should form a united front with the bourgeoisie. On January 4, 1938, Jiang announced his approval of the GMD plan for reorganizing the National Military Council on the basis of equal participation, thereby making the Southwest Military Group and the CCP equally responsible for the continued resistance to Japan.[125] Meanwhile, Zhou was appointed deputy director of the Political Training Department of the Council. "The GMD," Zhou wrote in an editorial in the *New China Daily* on October 8, 1938, "is now playing the leading role both politically and militarily. Its progress has a decisive effect on China's war of resistance and our final victory."[126]

The anti-Japanese united front, according to Zhou's analysis, consisted of "the proletariat, the peasantry, the petty bourgeoisie, and the liberal bourgeoisie, and at times even included some big landlords and members of the big bourgeoisie."[127] Since the components covered a broad spectrum and were both complex and uneven in strength, Zhou acknowledged the difficulties in uniting all these classes. For this reason he pointed out the need for CCP leaders to recognize these actual and potential anti-Japanese united front forces and, especially, to know "how to win over the vast majority and oppose those few persons who contend with us for leadership."[128] He cautioned, "If we don't understand this, we will commit errors."[129] Zhou expected that the urban petty bourgeoisie, as represented by the intellectuals, was likely to play an active role in the nationwide anti-Japanese united front. As he put it, "we are strong only when the workers, peasants, and urban petty bourgeoisie stand united."[130] He categorized the liberal bourgeoisie as an intermediate force and believed that the CCP should "win it over, unite with it, or at least neutralize it, but should not rely on it."[131] With reference to the big landlords and the big bourgeoisie, Zhou was more conscious and realistic. "Some big landlords and some members of the big bourgeoisie," said Zhou, "may sometimes join the united front, but with obvious ambivalence."[132] His analysis of this situation was strictly dialectic: "The bourgeoisie has two sides to its character; so does the petty bourgeoisie. But the dual character of the big landlords and the big bourgeoisie is more apparent; reaction is deeply ingrained in them."[133] In order to compete with them, Zhou cautioned the CCP, "we must be constantly on our guard, oppose their reactionary tendencies, and never rely on them."[134] Based on historical experience, Zhou thought that it was possible for the CCP to lead the big landlords and the big bourgeoisie only "temporarily."[135] These groups might accept the CCP's leadership only when they had to and only "on a specific question" or for "a certain period."[136] Once they had the strength or the necessary foreign aid, Zhou conceded, they would split with the CCP. By and large they could accept the CCP's leadership only when they were "weak."[137]

In the years from 1937 to 1945 Zhou became the key voice speaking for the CCP in the united front movement and was able to devote his efforts to working with the non-Communist minor parties and groups. Even though he faced tremendous handicaps, he succeeded in winning over the "neutral forces." Almost single-handedly, he held all the anti-GMD forces together during the crucial period from 1945 to 1949. His ability to negotiate with GMD authorities and his success in winning over the third forces in China provided a classic example of his application of the pragmatic principle to the domestic power competition between the CCP and the GMD.

Within the CCP there was considerable resistance to the very concept of a united front with the GMD. The task of making the united front work required not only the cooperation with the GMD, but also the clearest possible understanding by CCP leaders of precisely what was at stake. Throughout the early years of the united front Zhou tried to instruct CCP members on the opportunities, dangers, and practical value of united front politics. Zhou's reflections on the united front, published on April 30, 1945, became a CCP classic.[138] Together with two other documents—namely, his report at a meeting of welcome in Yenan, given on August 2, 1943, and his statements on the Sixth

Congress of the CCP, delivered at the Central Party School in Yenan on March 3 and 4, 1944—it formed the core documentation of Zhou's overall approach to the united front movement in China.[139] Central to his strategy, Zhou considered the winning over of the third forces a prerequisite to the ultimate victory of the Chinese Communist movement.

Sometimes it is nearly impossible to distinguish Zhou's political and strategic views from those of Mao Zedong.[140] Zhou, like Mao, was essentially an advocate of "coalition government" based on the participation of all political parties and groups in China. Unlike Mao, he actually brought a large segment of the "third forces" into the Communist front as an antidote to the overwhelming GMD power and influence. In his own way he managed to maintain close personal relations with the leaders of the third forces. His attempt to achieve a coalition of the non-GMD elements, with the CCP as a bridge or unifying factor between them, was rather successful. Projecting power and influence into the field of third forces must be based, according to Zhou, on a clear and persuasive explanation of the CCP's position on the future political system of China. He took every opportunity to persuade the leaders of the third parties and groups that the coalition government could strengthen Chinese democracy. By stressing the importance of the political rights of individuals and groups, he was successful in winning over various political and cultural leaders to support the coalition government.

Zhou realized it was possible to establish better relations with the neutral forces between the CCP and the GMD. His success in achieving this end was all the more remarkable given the fact that, at that time, some CCP leaders completely overlooked the importance of winning over the "third parties and groups." Zhou insisted: "It is necessary to clarify forces into left, middle, and right. It is correct to make such distinctions and wrong not to."[141] At the December conference in 1937, according to Zhou, some CCP leaders had wanted "to classify the political forces not into left, middle, and right" but, instead, into "anti-Japanese, and pro-Japanese."[142] "With the exception of forces that were pro-Japanese," Zhou summarized their position, "they believed that all classes were as solid as iron in their opposition to Japan."[143] "This kind of thinking," argued Zhou, "reflected the influence of the landlords and the big bourgeoisie," and the logical result was that "the warlord and fascist character of Jiang Jie-shi's GMD was obliterated."[144] Zhou's criticism was obviously directed against the view expounded by Wang Ming in his report delivered at the meeting of the Politburo of the Central Committee of the CCP on December 9, 1937.

Zhou also criticized the errors made by the leftist elements in the CCP. Zhou stated, "Those with the 'left' viewpoint believe only in the proletariat, only in the vanguard of the proletariat. They alienate themselves from the masses and don't ally themselves even with those in their own ranks. This is also wrong."[145] Zhou believed that is was crucial to follow Mao's theoretical analysis of the left, middle, and right forces and of the ways to win over the middle force, develop the progressive forces, and isolate the die-hards and reactionaries. Otherwise, the CCP could actually "isolate" itself in a so-called united front movement.

Zhou was disposed to initiate many actions but was conscious of the limits imposed upon him by the Party and by national sentiments. His personal role in the formulation of the CCP's policy toward the third forces was the most important one. His contributions, therefore, should be placed in the context of the changing relations between the CCP and the non-GMD and non-Communist elements and parties in China throughout the 1940s. What were the new opportunities during the second united front, if the CCP leaders were ready to take advantage of them? During this period the relationship between the CCP and the GMD was a tenuous one. Although they were proclaiming the theme of national salvation and pretending to be tolerant of each other, these two enemies-turned-partners were really harboring deep mutual suspicions and dreaming very different political dreams while in the same bed.

The period from 1940 to 1946 was a significant one in Zhou's political life. He was an advocate, defender, and practitioner of the united front strategy, and he was, more than anyone else in the CCP, keenly aware of both the dangers and potentials of such a strategy. Zhou himself voiced the sentiment that "the changes in the united front" were so frequent and so complicated that the CCP members "must be clear-headed and be able to investigate problems and study them analytically."[146] In retrospect, Zhou's united-front experience was fundamental to his political attitude toward the third forces. It explained his understanding of and appreciation for their value. No one who had participated in the united front of 1937-45 and witnessed its aftermath as Zhou did could ignore the impact of the third forces on the politics of a divided nation. He had seen firsthand how much political pressure the third parties and groups had exerted on the GMD government during and after the Sino-Japanese War. He had seen what the third forces meant to the CCP in the long process of a domestic power struggle. From this experience Zhou was to carry over to the new regime of the CCP the practice of strategic flexibility not to mention the fact that his success in winning over the third forces had greatly contributed to the dramatic increase of his prestige and influence in Party circles.

In retrospect, Zhou placed heavy emphasis on analyzing and studying the political groups in the united front movement so that the CCP could fully capitalize on their political potential. Zhou observed that the various "left" and "right" opportunists within the CCP hierarchy were not clear about the problems associated with different political groups and their self-interests. As a result, they made many unnecessary mistakes; while the CCP rightists often mistook enemies for friends, the leftists always mistook friends for enemies. "Under certain conditions," said Zhou in 1945, "some enemies have two sides to their nature."[147] Zhou, after examining the errors made by the rightists within the Party, stated, "When forming a united front with them, Comrades with the right deviationist viewpoint think only of the possibility of uniting with them and forget their reactionary nature. . . . Those who made the right deviationist mistake tried to whitewash them, covering up their reactionary nature."[148] In order to benefit from the divisions in the camp of the ruling classes, Zhou stressed the possibility of working relationships between the CCP and other groups. His criticism of the CCP leftist elements was equally strong: "Comrades with the left deviationist viewpoint fail to see the changes taking place at a turning point."[149] He went on: "They think only of the reactionary nature of their enemies and forget the possibility of uniting with them."[150] Accordingly, they talked constantly about "drawing distinctions and refuse to take part in common action with others. They are in a hurry to achieve socialism."[151]

In order to formulate a correct strategy for the Chinese Communist revolution, it was important to understand the complexity of the changes in China's class relations and the key issues in the Chinese Communist revolution and to focus the CCP's strategy on winning over the "middle forces." For Zhou the contradiction between Jiang Jie-shi and regional power groups was simply "a contradiction within the camp of the ruling classes."[152] Zhou reminded CCP members, however, that "people with the left deviationist viewpoint don't recognize this contradiction, believing all enemies should be overthrown at the same time. But the result of trying to overthrow everybody is that nobody is overthrown."[153] Those with the left viewpoint, in Zhou's opinion, would consider "an enemy anyone who was an enemy yesterday, though he may be a friend today."[154] He then suggested that the leftists believed only in "the vanguard of the proletariat" and alienated themselves from the masses, refusing to ally themselves even with those in their own ranks.[155] The result was political isolation. According to Zhou, the policy of the CCP should be designed to develop the progressive forces, win over the middle forces, and isolate, split, and attack the die-hards. "Only in this way," Zhou reasoned, "will we avoid left or right mistakes."[156] Zhou was equally blunt in his assessment of the CCP Right: "The enemy camp can change."[157] He then added, "Those with the right deviationist viewpoint take all who were friends yesterday to be friends today, even if they have in fact become enemies."[158] In attempting to win over the third forces, however, Zhou maintained that the CCP must retain its own identity, aims, independence, and initiatives and also must vigilantly guard the other components of the united front.

Central to domestic united-front politics was the maintenance of Party independence. According to Zhou, independence within the united front was a matter of relativity, and it must be retained politically, ideologically, and organizationally. From the CCP's point of view independence was to be defined as "independence of the proletariat, which has its own policy and ideology."[159] Zhou further clarified: "It allies itself with others, but is not to be assimilated by others. Wherever there are distinctions, there is struggle."[160] The proletariat was for solidarity in the united front on the condition that its independence and initiative be maintained. Moreover, it felt it should not allow itself to be influenced by the other classes. Without making distinctions between the proletariat and other classes in Chinese society, Zhou argued, the CCP would "merge with the others and certainly be influenced by them."[161] The great advantage of the united front to the CCP was that it once more opened the cities of China to its propaganda.

At the same time, Zhou strongly opposed direct military confrontation with the GMD under any guise. He realized that, if the CCP decided to challenge the united front strategy rather than gradually becoming an integral part of it, a renewed contest for power in China would occur, thereby making China vulnerable to Japanese conquest. He also realized, more keenly than his colleagues, that the achievement of a united and independent China, free to choose its own destiny, could become a nationwide commitment shared by the Chinese people of various classes and one that the CCP could honor.

Fundamental to the development of Zhou's political outlook was his united front experience. It was through the united front movement that his preference for pragmatism over rigidity was reaffirmed; he learned the complexities of political motivations that defied the simple categorization of political groups and of the importance for the CCP of asserting its independence. "In the course of the revolution, owing to frequent changes in the relations between the enemy and ourselves and in the conflicting camps as well as to constant change in the overall situation," Zhou remarked, "the problems of the united front have been very complicated."[162] He added: "With the enemy sometimes collaborating, sometimes splitting, the situation became even more complicated, especially since people representing each class were themselves changing in their allegiance. When they changed allegiance, those who had not previously been our enemies sometimes turned against us, and this was confusing."[163] The only things that "remained unchanged throughout the period of the revolution," according to Zhou, were the enemies of the new democratic revolution, which were "imperialism and feudalism."[164] Even in this instance, Zhou observed, "the imperialists sometimes collaborated with each other and sometimes split—and the splits lasted a long time."[165]

Such shifts in alliance invariably created opportunities in which the CCP could maneuver. Therefore, Zhou firmly believed in the need for mutual accommodation, not merely as a method of reconciling conflicting interests but as a political environment that could make the united front strategy viable. Zhou's pragmatism was reinforced by his firsthand experience in the united front movement. He subsequently extended this approach from domestic politics to the broader issues of international relations. Pragmatism, as Zhou observed, was a necessary response to political problems, one based on the acceptance of reality and on the use of flexible methods in finding solutions. This pragmatism became the hallmark of Zhou's political style and the foundation of his many achievements.

PART 2

Refined Negotiating Skills and the Power Base

CHAPTER 5

Zhou's Negotiating Skills and Strategy prior to the CCP's Rise to National Power in 1949

A special chapter of Zhou's negotiating skills and style can be justified on two grounds. First, as a member of the CCP's Politburo since 1927, Zhou had successfully played the role of mediator in the Xi'an Incident of 1936; he then continued to sharpen his bargaining skills as a negotiator while heading Yenan's delegation to the 1944-46 talks with GMD representatives at Chongqing, the wartime capital of the GMD government, and at Nanjing, after the GMD government's return to the prewar capital. Second, from his routine contacts with foreign correspondents through the CCP's news agency in Chongqing during the war, and particularly from his subsequent direct negotiations with U.S. emissaries, notably General Patrick J. Hurley, General George C. Marshall, and Ambassador John Leighton Stuart, Zhou broadened the scope of his diplomatic negotiations to include an international perspective. This chapter, accordingly, summarizes and evaluates Zhou's approaches to negotiations with both GMD authorities from 1937 to 1946 and with U.S. emissaries from 1944 to 1946 in order fully to understand the evolution of his negotiating skills and style. The narrative will cover an analysis of the negotiating processes, the climate in which Zhou's negotiations with GMD representatives and U.S. envoys took place, the issues discussed, and the results of the protracted and difficult negotiations.

During this period Zhou was negotiating under strict instructions from the CCP hierarchy in Yenan, and any deviation from their plans required their approval. He stayed at Chongqing, acting as liaison officer between the CCP and the GMD. In addition to his negotiations with the GMD authorities, he maintained direct dialogues with Hurley and Marshall and kept extensive contacts with the "third" political parties and groups in China. Through subtle moves and his characteristic discretion he was able to modify the CCP's rigid responses to existing circumstances both at home and abroad.

Zhou's negotiations with the GMD government after the Xi'an Incident can be divided into three phases. In the initial phase, up to 1943, the main question at issue between Zhou and his GMD counterpart was whether or not there was "real preparation" for "armed resistance" to the Japanese aggression. The main points of this phase included the establishment of the CCP's legal status, the status of the armed forces and "border areas," and the formation of a "united front" among all political parties in China. The second phase lasted from November 1944 to October 1945, and it was characterized by Zhou's insistence upon the establishment of a coalition government in China immediately after the Sino-Japanese War. The beginning of this phase was marked by Hurley's direct talks with Mao and Zhou in Yenan on November 8, 1944, resulting in a five-point proposal designed specifically to resolve the impasse between Chongqing and Yenan. The final phase, from January to December 1946, was identified by the establishment of a truce agreement for the Northeast and of the "line of the Political Consultative Conference [PCC]." It was during the last two phases that Zhou entered into direct and extensive negotiations with Hurley, Marshall, and Stuart.

The Initial Phase of Zhou's
Negotiations with the GMD Government: 1937-1943

After the 1936 Xi'an Incident and the cessation of Chinese civil war negotiations between the CCP and the GMD began at Wuhan for the formation of an anti-Japanese united front. Zhou, in his official capacity as vice-chairman of the Red Army Military Committee, was appointed by the CCP as chief delegate to the united front negotiations. In mid-January 1937 Jiang's intention was communicated to Zhou through General Zhang Qun, the GMD representative: if the Chinese Communists and the Red Army were sincere enough to obey the GMD government, they would be granted an opportunity to cooperate with it. During the negotiations in Wuhan, Zhou's basic position was to call for "an alliance of all parties,"[1] which meant "a united front organization, a common program, and reform of the existing political apparatus."[2] From the beginning he rejected Jiang's proposition that there could be no party "outside the GMD."[3] Instead, he demanded the GMD's support for the formation of "an alliance in which we would each have a share but would maintain independent organizations" as a precondition to any negotiated settlements.[4] Zhou's negotiating position was based on the premise that the Chinese Communists "could join the GMD," but they "would have to preserve" their own "party organization."[5] This was in line with the position of the Chinese Communists during the first period of cooperation with the GMD, at the time of the Great Revolution from 1923 to 1927.

Zhou occupied himself with the immediate task of establishing a "wartime coalition" against the Japanese aggressors while attempting to convince Jiang to negotiate with Yenan in "good faith."[6] Zhou believed that the GMD authorities were bent on "physically abolishing" the CCP's "armed forces and political power."[7] Therefore, Zhou proceeded in his negotiations with tremendous caution. He warily noted, "beneath the calm waters, there was a reef."[8] Despite his reservations about the reliability of the GMD authorities, Zhou was neither anti-GMD nor insensitive to the prevailing national mood. To overcome the obstacles to an agreement between the two parties, Zhou felt the need to work out a temporary arrangement to stabilize the relationship and to permit the two parties to focus on the war against the Japanese.

Early in 1943, when Yenan had not yet recovered from the Japanese attacks of the two previous years and the GMD government had adopted a policy of combining the use of military force with negotiation in dealing with the CCP, Jiang treated Zhou with disdain and decided not to grant legal status to the CCP nor to allow the expansion of its troops to four armies of twelve divisions. The best Zhou could do under the circumstances was to keep a close watch on domestic developments and learn how to manipulate them to the CCP's advantage. His efforts to safeguard his party's interests and to advance policies of conciliation in the hope of cementing the anti-Japanese united front were influenced by his sense of what was politically possible. He developed a negotiating strategy that combined conciliation with firmness. Negotiation with the GMD authorities, he recognized, could not be refused if offered. In addition, he held that, if he could keep the negotiations with the GMD government alive, the Chinese people would eventually pressure Jiang to make concessions to the CCP. Therefore, Yenan had much to gain from the negotiations with the GMD representatives at Chongqing.

Speaking in Yenan on August 2, 1943, Zhou stated publicly that, in order to uphold national unity, the Chinese Communists were "prepared to continue consultations with the GMD and work together with them to eliminate the grave danger of civil war and solve existing problems."[9] He added that, "such consultations, however, must be held in a spirit of sincerity, on an equal footing, and on the basis of mutual concessions. There must be no heightening of friction while negotiations are going on, no maneuvering of troops while messengers are going back and forth, no demands for the abolition and dissolution of our Party while there is talk of unity. And let no one in the GMD conceive of GMD-Communist cooperation as GMD-Communist integration and hope to achieve it through coercion; that would lead not to unity but to civil war."[10] Zhou offered a rather pessimistic appraisal of the GMD's attitude toward the CCP. He remarked on August 16, 1943: "As for their attitude towards us, everything is aimed at eliminating us, though their tactics may vary from soft to tough. But the soft tactics are only a temporary expediency and never mean a change for the better; at the very same time they are preparing for the next tough move. At times when toughness doesn't work, they can temporarily soften up a bit."[11]

Jiang became even "more demanding" in the second round of negotiations between the CCP and the GMD. He insisted, for instance, that the CCP "couldn't have more than eight divisions of troops" and could become legal "only after the troops were reorganized."[12] In addition, the border areas had "to be changed to administrative areas," and the CCP's war zone "had to be moved even farther north."[13] Yet, throughout his negotiations with GMD representatives, Zhou constantly stressed the absolute necessity of not reaching any agreement that was contrary to the vital interests of the CCP. He was careful not to promise that the CCP's armies could be immediately reduced or integrated into the national army. The same reservation was present in his reaction to the proposed change of the border areas into administrative regions. At the same time, he was groping for a solution that would counteract the GMD's position of superiority. The participation of the third parties in these discussions offered him the counterweight he was searching for. By winning over the moderates, the CCP could broaden its bases of potential alliance and also gain the sympathy and support of the Chinese people. Zhou maintained that his future negotiations with the GMD authorities would have to be conducted in a systematic and open fashion, in the presence of the third parties. Zhou's definition of *third party* was "democratic personages and foreigners."[14]

Zhou, Hurley, and the Second Phase of CCP-GMD Negotiations: November 1944-October 1945

With the recall of General Stilwell, President Franklin D. Roosevelt sent Hurley to China as his special envoy. In line with official instructions, Hurley undertook the task of bringing the GMD and the CCP together to organize a coalition government. Hurley himself was confident about having Soviet support for China's unification under GMD leadership. He also felt that the United States government should continue to deal with Jiang's regime as the sole representative of China. He was convinced that the Soviet Union and the United States could cooperate to help China establish a free, united, democratic state. In his scheme of priorities, political unification of China was subordinate to the overall objective of sustaining the GMD government in China. Therefore, he decided not to aid the Chinese Communists directly by supplying U.S. arms and advisors, continuing, instead, to treat Jiang's GMD government as the only recognized government of wartime China. One of the top priorities of U.S. policy was, to use Hurley's own words, "to unify all the military forces of China" under the guidance of Jiang Jie-shi "for the purpose of destroying Japan."[15] In order to sustain Jiang's leadership in China, Hurley strongly held that he would supply the Chinese Communists forces only after the conclusion of an agreement between the GMD and the CCP and that any aid to the CCP from the United States must go through the GMD government.

With this definite purpose in mind Hurley flew to Yenan on November 7, 1944, for two days of face-to-face talks with Mao and Zhou. Extensive discussions between them produced, on November 10, a five-point draft agreement, officially known as the "Agreement between the National Government in China, the Guomindang of China, and the Communist Party of China."[16] This unique document, signed jointly by Mao, as chairman of the Central Executive Committee of the CCP, and Hurley, as the "personal representative of United States President Roosevelt," formally put relations between the GMD and the CCP on an equal footing. Moreover, the five points of the agreement, including the formation of a coalition government, were sufficient to form the basis for further negotiations between the two parties.

On November 10, Hurley, accompanied by Zhou, flew back to Chongqing and took part in the ongoing negotiations between Zhou and the GMD's representatives. After Hurley submitted the draft agreement to the GMD government, Jiang debated him about the serious implications of accepting the proposal for a coalition government. To accept the proposal would, for Jiang, be tantamount to acknowledging total defeat of his party by the Chinese Communists.[17] Nevertheless, Hurley urged Jiang to keep the channels of communications with Yenan open.

The GMD government, through Hurley, counteroffered on November 21, 1944, with a three-point proposal. The outstanding feature of the counterproposal was rejection of the idea of a coalition government. Nevertheless, it promised "to pursue policies designed to promote the progress and development of democratic process in government."[18] Should the CCP accept the Three People's Principles, turn over its military forces, and have confidence in the GMD government's sincerity regarding the future redistribution of political power, the GMD government would grant the CCP legal status, a place on the National Military Council, and some political and civil liberties.

On November 22 the GMD government's three-point counterproposal was officially handed to Zhou, whose initial reaction to this unexpected move was guarded. He expressed only qualified acceptance and stated that such an important decision would have to be referred to the CCP hierarchy in Yenan. As was to be expected, Zhou was disappointed by the GMD's reply. Even more disturbing were his discussions with Hurley and General Wedemyer, in which the U.S. officials insisted that there were some positive elements in the GMD government's counterproposal. Zhou made every effort to appear conciliatory and willing to make proper adjustments—a posture calculated to influence political opinion in China and abroad.

Zhou was confident that, whatever accord might result from his direct negotiations with the GMD authorities, Yenan would gain the support of the third political parties and popularity among the Chinese people. He insisted on first reaching agreements on concrete issues, however, including legal recognition of the CCP as a political party. It was not the first time that Zhou found himself in disagreement with the GMD authorities. More specifically, he saw in Jiang a major stumbling block to a satisfactory agreement between the two parties. To make matters worse, Hurley now reversed his endorsement of the five-point proposal, which he had signed on November 10 in Yenan, and began to press Zhou to accept the GMD's three-point counterproposal. He made it clear that the CCP would receive no U.S. aid, military cooperation, or political support until it had reached a political compromise acceptable to Jiang.[19] President Roosevelt, acting on Hurley's recommendation, ordered all U.S. military officers not to aid any elements in China that Jiang did not specifically approve.[20] Despite his conciliatory appearance, Zhou would not yield on the principle of coalition government. On the other hand, the GMD government, negotiating from a position of strength, refused to yield its privileged status. Further talks between Zhou and GMD officials thus produced no fruitful results.

Following his arrival in Yenan, Zhou wrote to Hurley indicating that the GMD government's refusal of the CCP's five-point proposal clearly showed "disagreement with our suggestions for a coalition government."[21] The GMD's three-point counterproposal definitely precluded the possibility of his returning to Chongqing "for further negotiations."[22] He told Hurley of Yenan's decision to publish the five-point proposal "in order to inform the public."[23] In his reply to Zhou, Hurley took the position that he was against publication of the five-point proposal on the grounds that the GMD-CCP negotiations were pending. He also indicated that it was his understanding that the five-point offer of settlement proposed by Mao and Zhou was not a "'take it or leave it' proposition."[24] Nor was the GMD's three-point offer the GMD's "final word."[25] He regarded both documents as "steps" in the GMD-CCP negotiations. On December 16, 1944, Zhou wrote Hurley another letter, this time stating that negotiations with the GMD government could not be resumed until Jiang agreed to form a coalition government. "The one fundamental difficulty with respect to these negotiations was," in Zhou's own words, "the unwillingness of the GMD to forsake one-party rule and accept the proposal for a 'democratic coalition government.'"[26]

After further exchanges between Hurley and Zhou in early January 1945, Zhou returned to Chongqing on January 24. It was Zhou's understanding that his trip to Chongqing was for the purpose of proposing to the national government, the GMD, and the Chinese Democratic League that "a meeting of all parties" should be held.[27] He further suggested that this would prepare the way for a coalition government.[28] He also expressed his wish that the GMD government would quickly accept this proposal because it represented the only way to overcome the present crisis. Zhou insisted, however, that the five-point proposal of November 10, 1944, must remain the guiding principle for political coalition in China. Moreover, the CCP would not submit the command of its troops to the GMD government as long as the one-party rule of the GMD was not abolished. In short, the new government ought to be reconstructed on the basis of "a coalition administration representing all parties."[29] Zhou favored the establishment, at that time, of a military commission to reorganize the Chinese armed forces, but he would not agree that such a commission should be permitted to reorganize the Communist troops. China's entire military establishment should be reorganized, and he would be glad to see an American serve on such a commission.[30]

Though still insistent on the formation of a coalition government as the prerequisite for transferring the armies from party to state control, Zhou made the constitution of a national affairs conference the main task of his visit. He hoped that such a conference would serve as a forum to publicize Yenan's causes and pave the way for a coalition government. He openly declared the CCP's position on further negotiations with the GMD by stating unequivocally that, unless a genuine coalition government were established, the CCP would not give up its armed forces. The convocation of the national affairs conference was eventually accepted by both parties, and Zhou left for Yenan on February 16. Prior to his departure Zhou informed Hurley that "one-party rule should be immediately ended"[31] and that a democratic government based on a "democratic constitution" should be adopted by a people's convention.[32] The establishment of a coalition government in China remained an immediate goal of Zhou's negotiations with the GMD.

The stalled negotiations between the CCP and the GMD took a new turn after the signing of the Sino-Soviet Treaty on August 14, 1945, and the Japanese defeat. Jiang invited Mao to Chongqing to discuss matters of national interest. Mao's meeting with Jiang on August 28 was only a "formal gesture," and "substantial talks" were conducted by Zhou and GMD representatives Wang Shi-jie and Zhang Qun. The intensive talks conducted between Zhou and his GMD counterparts during the following forty-one days covered a variety of subjects ranging from reorganization of the government on the basis of democracy to nationalization of the armed forces. Zhou took the initiative in offering concrete proposals and in making concessions, while the GMD side played the passive role by either rejecting or adopting Zhou's recommendations in the tentative agreement. It was now agreed that the transitional period of national government under GMD tutelage should be brought to an early end and that a constitutional government should be inaugurated. The preliminary step toward the establishment of a constitutional government would be the convocation of a political consultative conference to which all parties and nonpartisan leaders should be invited. The PCC would serve as a forum for all parties to exchange views and discuss questions relating to peaceful national reconstruction and convocation of the National Assembly.

Yet there were still major issues to be resolved—namely the question of the incorporation of Communist forces into the national army and the problem of political control in the "liberated areas" dominated by the Chinese Communists. Both sides understood that the political power of the CCP rested on its armed forces and the territory under its control. On the question of Communist troops Zhou insisted on the CCP's retaining direct control of a minimum of twenty divisions.[33] The two sides reached a general agreement on this issue, but many difficulties still awaited real solution. On the question of the territory under CCP control the negotiating parties were so far apart that they could not even reach a verbal agreement. Zhou at first demanded what was, in effect, recognition by the GMD government of the current status of the CCP's eighteen "liberated areas."[34] Upon the GMD's rejection of this demand Zhou asked, instead, for exclusive control of the five provinces in North China and Inner Mongolia and a share in the control of six other provinces and four major cities in China. Subsequently, Zhou modified his demands slightly, now asking for exclusive control of the border region of Shanxi-Gansu-Ningxia, the four provinces in North China and Inner Mongolia, and a share in the control of two other provinces and three major cities. Zhou further proposed that all the "liberated areas" should temporarily retain their present status until constitutional provisions for the election of provincial government officials were adopted and put into effect.[35]

A joint communiqué was finally drawn up, and its three main headings were democratization, local administration, and nationalization of troops. Both sides agreed to accept its basic principles, though they withheld all decisions on how the agreement was to be implemented. Yenan dropped the demand for a coalition government in favor of a modus vivendi under which the GMD government would recognize the local authority of the Communist liberated areas. The abandonment of the demand for a coalition government and of the insistence of gaining control over "liberated areas" reflected Zhou's weak negotiating position; he had to be content with preserving the CCP's regional influence. At least, such de facto regional control could provide the CCP with a real power base so as to maintain intact its political and military organizations and from which it could possibly at some future date expand its political power. Most significant was the fact that Zhou's prolonged negotiations with the GMD representatives in Chongqing provided the Communist forces with badly needed time to cross over the Great Wall to Manchuria.

Unlike in the early days of the negotiations, Zhou was no longer interested in asking the GMD government to grant legal recognition to the CCP. The Chinese Communists now were fighting to secure control of their own territory and troops, and, hence, their independence. By mid-1946 Zhou followed a new two-pronged strategy of negotiations and warfare. The CCP-GMD negotiations had, for Zhou, already become a smokescreen covering up the extensive fighting between the Red Army and GMD military forces. The CCP was attempting to expand its area of military control. In Zhou's own words, this period was "characterized by heavy fighting behind a facade of negotiations. That is, heavy fighting went on while the talks were being dragged out."[36] Furthermore, he also realized the propaganda value of continuing to negotiate with the GMD, and he turned the process of negotiation into "a means of educating the people."[37] Zhou was very successful in bringing certain facts and issues before the public to generate a more broad-based discussion of matters of national importance. In the process he also garnered considerable popular support for some of the causes that the CCP was espousing, such as the formation of a PCC and the formation of a democratic coalition government. The turning tide of public opinion, in retrospect, proved to be the beginning of the end of the GMD government.

Zhou and Marshall's Mediation:
The Final Phase of CCP-GMD Negotiations: 1946

After Ambassador Hurley's resignation on November 27, 1945, President Harry Truman appointed General Marshall as his special envoy to China, giving him the rank of ambassador. In his instructions to Marshall on December 15 Truman asked him to use U.S. influence to bring about the "unification of China by peaceful, democratic methods . . . as soon as possible."[38] Marshall was also instructed by Truman to find a fair and reasonable basis for the settlement of military and political differences between the GMD and the CCP. On the same day the U.S. president issued a formal statement of United States foreign policy toward China in connection with Marshall's departure for the mission. In short, the United States recognized the GMD government as "the only legal government in China" and "the proper instrument to achieve the objective of a united China."[39] It was Truman's intention that, "with the institution of a broadly representative government, autonomous armies should be eliminated as such and all armed forces in China integrated effectively into the Chinese National Army."[40] Based on this guiding principle, Marshall was expected to help liquidate the Communist-led army by giving the CCP representation in the GMD government. In his memorandum for the War Department dated December 9, 1945, Marshall stated, "To the extent that our influence is a factor, success will depend upon our capacity to exercise that influence in the light of shifting conditions in such a way as to encourage concessions by the Central Government, by the so-called Communists, and by the other factions."[41] Meanwhile, Marshall's main task was to bring about a reasonable settlement between the GMD and the CCP that would result in the formation of a coalition government in postwar China.

Soon after his arrival in Chongqing on December 23, 1945, Marshall told Zhou that the American people had brought World War II to an end "by generous expenditures of men, air power and sea power and atomic power, of which they are very conscious."[42] Having made that expenditure, the U.S. government and people were intensely concerned about anything that "might start a war again."[43] During his preliminary discussions with the new U.S. envoy Zhou indicated the CCP's willingness to make necessary political compromises so long as the arrangements made for a coalition government would protect its military and political base. From Zhou's point of view a truce was necessary merely because it would stabilize the intense military confrontations between the CCP and the GMD government. This did not mean, however, that the CCP's vital interests were to be ignored. On the contrary, it was quite appropriate to use every possible means short of military operations to curb the GMD government's further expansion throughout China.

On January 4, 1946, Marshall informed Zhou that the U.S. government was "committed to the movement of National Government troops to Manchuria."[44] In response, Zhou concurred with "the inclusion of an exception in the cessation of hostilities agreement," which would permit the movement of the GMD movement into Manchuria.[45] It should be pointed out that, prior to the convening of the PCC, it was agreed that a Committee of Three, composed of a representative of each party with Marshall as chairman, was to be formed to discuss questions arising out of the cessation of hostilities. Zhou and Zhang Qun, representing the CCP and the GMD government, respectively, held their first meeting on January 7 in Marshall's presence. The negotiation reached its height on January 10, when the Committee of Three secured a cease-fire. With reference to Manchuria it was stipulated in the minutes of the meetings published in the Joint Statement that the relevant provision of the Order for Cessation of Hostilities "does not prejudice military movements of forces of the National Army into or within Manchuria which are for the purpose of restoring Chinese sovereignty."[46] According to this agreement, both Jiang and Mao were to issue orders to their respective armed forces to cease hostilities and halt all movements of troops. The cease-fire agreement of January 10 granted the GMD government the right to move its troops into Manchuria as the Soviet armies were leaving. Marshall also urged that an Executive Headquarters field team in Manchuria be organized to prevent possible clashes between the two opposing forces. The GMD government, however, was not willing to accept Marshall's proposal, though Zhou endorsed it. It appeared that the GMD government was determined to occupy Manchuria entirely, despite the fact that it was not in a strong position to do so militarily.

It became evident that Zhou was prepared to take on both general and specific issues in his resumed negotiations with the GMD government through the Committee of Three and the Three-Man Military Subcommittee, with Marshall as the third member for each.[47] He viewed the cessation of hostilities between the CCP and the GMD government as the first constructive step toward an agreement on military reorganization and even on reorganization of the national government. The crux of the urgent task at hand was how to bring hostilities to an end when the cease-fire order became effective on January 13. The solution seemed to revolve around army reorganization and demobilization. It was agreed that the CCP's army was to be reduced to ten divisions and the GMD forces to sixty divisions. Zhou concurred in principle, hoping the proportional strength of the various forces could be maintained and that separate localities for garrisons could be arranged. It was later agreed that these questions would be discussed thoroughly by a Three-Man Military Subcommittee, to which Zhou and Zhang Zhizhong were appointed representatives for their respective parties, with Marshall as the advisor. After a series of deliberations and exchanges of views, an agreement was reached on February 25, 1946, on a basic plan for the reduction of the GMD's and the CCP's armed forces as well as integration of the two into a national army.

In spite of the cease-fire order both sides continued military actions in the field. Meanwhile, the Committee of Three and the Three-Man Military Subcommittee conducted more negotiations on unresolved and new issues. The question of Manchuria was one of great complexity, and it remained the bone of contention between the GMD government and CCP leadership. At the press conference in Chongqing on March 18, Zhou formally stated: "We would like to tell our GMD friends that since they demand that others abide by the agreements and yet write into the resolutions of the Second Plenary Session provisions that run counter to the resolutions of the PCC, one cannot but think that some deception is involved. Just what are they trying to do? They are trying to blur the issues."[48] Zhou indeed had great reservations about the willingness of "a considerable number of die-hards within the GMD" to carry out the truce agreement, the resolutions of the PCC, and the reorganization of troops agreed upon by both sides.[49] There was no evidence to suggest that Zhou did not negotiate in good faith in January and February 1946. Subsequent events also suggested that he continued to advocate a flexible and realistic posture in dealing with the GMD government, in sharp contrast to Jiang's practice of raising his demands and stepping up military operations in both Manchuria and North China after every temporary military victory won by GMD generals.

On the issue of Manchuria Zhou made his position clear. "As to the situation in the Northeast," he said, "two months ago General Marshall suggested sending a field team there to mediate military clashes. We agreed immediately."[50] He added, however: "We have made two suggestions on how to resolve this problem. One is to send the field team without preconditions, put an immediate end to all military clashes, investigate on the spot, and then bring back the findings so that problems can be settled by the Committee of Three. The other method, which is better, is to hold negotiations in Chongqing on general principles for the settlement of military and political issues and then send the field team to attend to matters at issue, in accordance with the agreed principles."[51] Zhou felt that there could be no guarantee of peace unless military clashes between the two sides ceased throughout the country. "Domestic issues are matters for which everyone shares responsibility," declared Zhou at the press conference, "and they should be settled peacefully and by political means."[52] He went on to say: "This is the view not only of the

Communist Party, but of the other democratic parties and the people in the Northeast as well."[53]

Moreover, it was now a matter of primary importance to bring the phase of political tutelage under the GMD to an end and to move toward an interim government "by setting up during this transition period a government of national solidarity" that was to be based on "cooperation among the various parties."[54] Zhou made a dramatic appeal for support by calling on "the people of the whole country and on our friends in the allied countries and in the various parties to support and supervise the implementation of all the resolutions of the PCC."[55] On April 4 he made another public plea for the GMD government to agree to a peaceful settlement: "The Manchurian question," said Zhou, "must be settled through negotiation with all democratic political parties participating."[56] The GMD government's troops, however, now equipped with U.S. supplies, continued to move into Manchuria in full force. This caused Zhou to protest to Marshall that the CCP might have to reconsider its position if the U.S. government continued to support a particular party in the Chinese civil war.

The Chinese Communist forces occupied Changchun on April 18, after the withdrawal of Soviet troops from Manchuria. This military move was a direct violation of the cessation of hostilities order. Zhou informed Marshall at this time that the CCP wished to revise the ration of one Communist division to fourteen government divisions in Manchuria as previously agreed upon in the military reorganization plan. Further, he was strongly opposed to the movement of any additional government troops in Manchuria.[57] Marshall responded by suggesting that the total number of national government troops moved by U.S. facilities into Manchuria was less than what was authorized for Manchuria in the military reorganization agreement.[58] At this crucial moment Marshall suddenly decided to withdraw from his mediating role between the two parties as they negotiated a settlement of the Manchurian problem. Nevertheless, he continued to hold separate meetings with Zhou and GMD representatives and to act simply "as a channel of communication" between them.[59] In the meantime each side pressed on with full force to bring more cities and regions under its military control in order to be in a more advantageous position when the next round of negotiations started.

Marshall suggested to both Jiang and Zhou that a high-level echelon of the Executive Headquarters at Changchun function as an agent to terminate the fighting prior to entering into new negotiations.[60] This proposal was based on the anticipation that GMD troops could possibly occupy the city in less than six months. Zhou's response was that he had to transmit the proposal to Yenan for further instructions.[61] As was to be expected, the CCP's reply to Marshall's proposal was distinctly cool. The CCP had every reason to fear that the GMD government might likewise raise the status of other cities in Manchuria, such as Harbin, already controlled by the Communist forces, after its occupation of Changchun. On May 23 Marshall informed Zhou that the proposal suggested by Jiang was the basic requirement for any general agreement. It included the following conditions: (1) the CCP must make every effort to facilitate the restoration of communications; (2) in any agreement regarding Manchurian issues provisions must be made for carrying out the military demobilization and reorganization plan within specified dates; and (3) the generalissimo would not commit himself to further agreements without an understanding that, when field teams or high-level staff groups reached an impasse, the final decision would be left to the U.S. member.[62] Zhou's reply was that he would try to solve the problem of communications with his GMD counterpart and that he had no objection to the second point. As for point 3—that is, the binding authority of the U.S. member in making the final decision—Zhou indicated that he had to consult the CCP hierarchy in Yenan for further instructions.[63]

The GMD military position was substantially improved, at this point, when Jiang ordered his reinforcements to move into Manchuria. Changchun fell to government troops on May 23, the same day on which Zhou was informed by Marshall that the three points set forth by Jiang were prerequisites for any general agreement. The successful military moves of the GMD government had a far-reaching psychological impact on both sides. The GMD leaders, notably Jiang and his generals, thought that they could settle the problem of Manchuria once and for all by military force. The subsequent military operations of the GMD government clearly indicated that at this time it had decided to use military campaigns rather than negotiations to achieve its objectives. On the other hand, the CCP asserted that it had shown reasonableness in responding to Jiang's three preconditions, but Jiang once again proved to be an unreliable negotiator. The net result of the GMD's breach of faith was intensified suspicion within the CCP of Jiang's double-dealing—of his using negotiations as a shield for his military campaign in Manchuria. On May 24 Jiang once again demanded the execution of the cessation of hostilities agreement and of the agreement for military reorganization as agreed upon by both sides on January 10 and February 25, respectively. He also told Marshall that this would be his last effort at negotiating with the CCP and that his terms for truce had to be accepted by the CCP within ten days.[64] When Marshall presented Zhou the truce terms set forth by Jiang, Zhou asked for an extension of the ten-day period to fifteen days on the grounds that there were many complicated plans to be agreed to and that he had to fly to Yenan at least once for consultations with the CCP leadership.[65]

Unable to think of any other course of action and convinced that a resumption of talks with the GMD government was necessary to provide time badly needed to restore its military position in Manchuria, the CCP leaders were obliged to comply with Jiang's truce terms. Zhou then returned to Nanjing and reached an agreement for the resumption of communications with his GMD counterpart. Several days of negotiations followed, and Zhou confined himself to one specific demand: the preservation of the status quo in civil administration in northern Jiangsu. Zhou gave the highest priority to the cessation of hostilities and an extension of the Manchurian truce due to the military superiority of the GMD government at the moment. On June 17 Jiang indicated to Marshall, for transmission to Zhou, the nature of his demands, with time limits attached. The GMD government's proposal required the evacuation of Chinese Communist forces from Rehe and Chahar Provinces before September 1 and the evacuation by the Chinese Communists before July 1 from all localities in Shandong Province, which had been occupied by the Communist troops as of June 7.[66] With respect to Manchuria the GMD demanded its occupation of various cities then held by Communist forces, including Harbin, Andong, and others. Zhou's initial response to these stringent terms was that, "except for the restoration of the status quo in Shandong Province prior to June 7, none of the points could be considered"[67] and that "the date of June 7 should be applied to Manchuria only, in accordance with the orders issued by both sides halting advances, attacks, or pursuits by their troops in Manchuria, beginning on that date, while the restoration of original positions in China proper should be based on January 13, in accordance with the cessation of hostilities order of January 10."[68]

After his preliminary talks with officials of the GMD government, Zhou informed Marshall that nothing new had emerged "to justify" his return to Yenan to consult with the CCP hierarchy, as recommended earlier by Marshall.[69] At Marshall's suggestion Jiang agreed to extend the truce period until June 30 for the purpose of permitting further time to negotiate matters referred to in his original fifteen-day truce order. Meanwhile, Jiang presented two additional terms: (1) the Communists were to withdraw from Jinan-Qingdao Railway before August 1, 1946; and (2) the procedure for demanding a unanimous vote in the Committee of Three and the Executive Headquarters was to be revised before June 30, 1946.[70]

In the resumed meetings of the Committee of Three Zhou made concessions in granting the deciding vote to Americans on the field teams and in Executive Headquarters regarding issues related to cessation of hostilities procedures, interpretations of agreements, and their execution.[71] On June 21, however, he formally proposed on June 21 that (1) the Committee of Three should immediately stop the fighting in Manchuria and China proper and a new order for the termination of hostilities should be issued, with the additional stipulation that U.S. members of field teams should have the power to execute this order and to decide upon investigations to be made by the teams; (2) after the cessation of fighting the Committee of Three should work out a plan for the restoration of communications, and the Chinese Communists pledged that the repair of railways would have first priority; (3) following the cessation of hostilities the Committee should work out arrangements for the reorganization and demobilization of armies throughout China, including Manchuria, and the staff of both parties under U.S. leadership should work out a plan for the Committee of Three's approval; and (4) a second session of the Committee of Three should be convened to discuss reorganization of the government and protection of the people's rights.[72] Zhou further proposed that "during the period of army reorganization the Communist troops be reorganized in Communist areas and government troops in government territory, and that training be carried out by U.S. officials who were trusted by both sides, the two forces to be brought together and integrated after this interim period."[73]

Marshall responded to Zhou's proposals by reiterating the original preconditions of Jiang's announcement of the truce on June 5. A "definite understanding of the CCP's demands regarding the redistribution of troops in North China," in Marshall's view, must be substantiated. According to Marshall, this should have been decided upon in March and April, when the CCP was to have submitted a list of its troops for demobilization.[74] On June 26 Zhou explained to Marshall that the CCP had found it difficult to reach any meaningful agreement with the GMD government. "While it was entering into agreements on military matters, it did not know what the Government attitude would be later in regard to political questions,"[75] said Zhou. He further observed that under the GMD government proposals, the government troops would in many cases move into Communist areas and thus change the civil administration there. Therefore, "the movement of Government armies into Communist-held areas for the purpose of demobilization," in Zhou's own words, "would mean occupation of Communist territory through negotiation as a substitute for occupation by force."[76] In order to ease the GMD government's fear of a nationwide Communist presence, Zhou expressed Yenan's willingness to withdraw from some areas, but, he qualified, "Such areas should be left ungarrisoned."[77] At the conclusion of the meeting, Zhou pointed out to Marshall, "both Rehe [Jehol] and Shandong [Shantung] Provinces were largely under Communist control and it was more logical to expect the government to evacuate these provinces than to demand the Communists to do so."[78]

Marshall's prestige, his apparent sincerity, his professional goal of helping China achieve peace, unity, and democracy, and, above all, the enormous power of his country might have been sufficient to encourage fruitful negotiations between the GMD and the CCP. The United States, according to Marshall's original instructions, was not prepared to give massive military support to Jiang with a view to unifying China. But military means were available to Marshall in carrying out his mission. The emphasis was on preventing Soviet penetration of China by promoting China's unification and independence.

As time went on, Marshall encountered increasing difficulties in bringing the GMD and the CCP together to agree on a set of terms before the situation changed, usually as a natural consequence of what he categorized as lack of good faith on one side or the other, and a new set of proposals based on the changed situation became the basis of a new round of negotiations.[79] Marshall's early success was largely a result of his persuasion and political stature. It was also true that the two contending parties found it unwise not to accommodate him. The fact that both GMD and CCP leaders turned to Marshall for support against the other party indicated their assumption that the United States was likely to remain a crucial factor in China's domestic politics. Each side knew that, once the U.S. government committed itself unequivocally to one side, that side would be assured of success in the struggle for power in China. For this reason the GMD and the CCP readily accepted both Hurley's and Marshall's mediation efforts in order not to alienate the United States. Yet Marshall himself acknowledged that U.S. aid to Jiang and his GMD government created difficulty and embarrassment in his efforts at mediation. He also admitted that it encouraged GMD leaders to push forward with determination against the Communists.[80] Jiang's confidence in his ultimate military success was so complete that he told Marshall that he "could control the situation in Manchuria and that fighting in North China would be local" and that, if General Marshall were patient, "the Communists would appeal for a settlement and would be willing to make compromises necessary for such a settlement."[81] On another occasion Jiang indicated to Marshall that "it was first necessary to deal harshly with the Communists, and later, after two or three months, to adopt a generous attitude."[82]

With the changing military situation in Manchuria now favoring the GMD government, Zhou suggested an indefinite cease-fire in lieu of Jiang's stringent proposal of a ten-day truce before the PCC. He also urged a complete cessation of all military activities, both in Manchuria and to the south of the Great Wall, pending resolutions to be formulated through mutual compromise. "During the past twenty years," Zhou argued, "we have fought almost without stop, but also without any final settlement."[83] He added, however: "I can declare without hesitation that even if we kept on fighting for twenty more years we still would not reach any solution. The fighting must stop!"[84] It was his basic position that political democratization must proceed along with the nationalization of the armed forces. "We must recognize," Zhou reported to the PCC, "that many political and historical factors were involved in the development of the personal and partisan armies that are still fighting each other today. The troops led by the Communists were forced to take up arms."[85] He then went on to say: "We agree completely with the motion of the Young China Party delegates that the armed forces must not belong to any individual or party, but must be controlled by a democratic government that can truly represent the nation."[86] With special reference to the issue of military reorganization, Zhou urged the inclusion of neutral, objective personnel in all agencies and offices.

On August 10, Marshall and John Leighton Stuart, the new U.S. ambassador to China, issued a joint public statement in an effort to make both sides and the Chinese public focus on urgent national issues and to arouse public pressure for ending hostilities.[87] Responding to this event, Jiang issued his own public statement on August 13, blaming the Chinese Communists for the breakdown in negotiations.[88] He claimed that government policy had always been that political means were to be used to settle political differences, provided the Chinese Communists gave assurance and evidence that they would carry out the various agreements reached. The government's implementation of the agreement on the cessation of hostilities reached on January 10 was contingent upon the withdrawal of the Chinese Communists from areas in which they threatened peace and obstructed communications. When Jiang gave his blessing to the formation of a Committee of Five to pave the way for the organization of the State Council, he demanded the acceptance of the five preliminary conditions by the Chinese Communists, with specific time limits varying from a month to six weeks.[89] These stringent terms included the withdrawal of Chinese Communist forces from important cities or areas in Jiangsu, Shandong, and Rehe Provinces.

On September 15 Zhou sent Marshall a memorandum from Shanghai requesting the convening of the Committee of Three to discuss the issuance of an order to end hostilities.[90] All previous events, including the meeting of the Committee of Five in early July, the participation of Ambassador Stuart in the mediation since mid-July, the Marshall-Stuart joint statement of August 10, and Stuart's subsequent proposal for an informal Group of Five, in Zhou's words, "were all exploited by the government authorities for dovetailing the talks into the fighting with a view to camouflaging the large-scale war which they had waged."[91] He concluded that, "since the June armistice, all intricate ways to solve the issue have proved futile and non-instrumental in breaking the deadlock."[92] Against this background Zhou asked that the Committee of Three be convened "to discuss the question of cease-fire."[93] Zhou followed up with another letter to Marshall on the next day, stating that he would return to Nanjing as soon as a meeting of the Committee of Three was convened.[94] On September 19 Marshall communicated to Zhou the GMD government's negative response to Zhou's request. According to Marshall, Jiang "would not authorize the attendance of the government member of the Committee of Three at such a meeting" before the Committee of Five could meet and make some progress toward "an agreement for the organization of the State Council."[95]

In another memorandum, dated September 21 from Shanghai, Zhou again repeated his request for a meeting of the Committee of Three on the grounds that the committee was "the sole legal agency handling cease-fire matters."[96] It was Marshall's obligation as committee chairman, according to Zhou, "to hold joint discussions with the two Chinese parties" on the most urgent problem of the prompt cessation of hostilities.[97] "There is no precedent in the record of the Committee of Three," argued Zhou, "that any Chinese party has ever rejected your invitation to its meeting."[98] "Nor is it conceivable," he added, "that anybody would ever boycott such a meeting."[99] Zhou maintained, therefore, that any insistence on placing the informal Committee of Five before the Committee of Three was not only unwarranted but "merely a pretext for the purpose of obstruction."[100] "Should the Committee of Three nevertheless fail to meet," concluded Zhou, "I can hardly convince myself that there is still a second way leading to cessation of hostilities."[101] He threatened "to make public all the important documents since the armistice in June, in order to clarify the responsibility and appeal to the general public for judgment."[102]

Zhou later recalled the events of July 1946: "Marshall said that, since negotiations between the political parties yielded no result, the GMD and the Communist Party should hold direct talks. We said, very well. And so a five-man meeting was held, but still nothing came of it. The third time, Marshall and Stuart suggested negotiating the reorganization of the government first. I agreed, but I said the cease-fire would have to be guaranteed. Neither Jiang nor Marshall nor Stuart could guarantee this, so there was nothing that could be discussed. We took the initiative and proposed a resumption of the sessions of the Committee of Three and a return to the positions of January 13. Marshall wouldn't call the meeting."[103] Under these circumstances Zhou left for Shanghai.

On September 26 Marshall and Stuart addressed a joint letter to Zhou, urging him to return to Nanjing without further delay in order that "we may together explore all conceivable ways and means" of achieving a peaceful arrangement.[104] On September 27, in response to Marshall and Stuart, Zhou again reiterated his request for a meeting of the Committee of Three. He indicated that he was willing to return to Nanjing "for a discussion of the ways and means to stop the civil war," since the GMD government "not only gives no signs for the cessation of hostilities" but, in actuality, was "increasing its efforts by many folds in the active offensive upon Kalgan, Harbin, North Jiangsu and other areas."[105] Zhou held firmly to his initial position on the extension of a truce in Manchuria and demanded that the GMD government discuss with him the organization of the State Council. Once again Zhou wanted the Committee of Three to handle these arrangements. His position was that he would support the discussion of political problems provided that an unconditional cease-fire order was issued or that the Committee of Three could meet immediately to discuss the question.[106] Obviously, Zhou continued to rely on Marshall's mediation to modify Jiang's demands so that there would be room for further negotiations between the two parties.

It was also fairly clear that a major consideration for Zhou regarding the negotiations in the early fall of 1946 was how best to sway public opinion by adopting a conciliatory and reasonable posture in dealing with the GMD. Zhou was quick to perceive the potential advantage of using public opinion as leverage to exert pressure on Jiang and the GMD. The superior military strength of the GMD government certainly put Zhou at a considerable disadvantage in his negotiations with GMD representatives. The sale of U.S. surplus arms to Jiang posed a major threat to the CCP, and the supposed impartiality of Marshall and Stuart was called into question. Zhou reportedly said to Marshall, "Isn't there an element of hypocrisy when you know—and everybody knows—that anything you turn over to the National Government goes to the front facing the Communist troops?"[107]

The advance against Kalgan, a center of Chinese Communist power in Inner Mongolia, by the GMD troops led Zhou to inform Marshall on September 30 that, if the GMD government did not cease its military operations against Kalgan and nearby areas, the CCP would lay the blame on the GMD government for causing a "total national split" and the abandonment of "its pronounced policy of peaceful settlement."[108] The GMD government's military campaign against Kalgan led Marshall to question Jiang's policy. He also felt he could no longer continue in the role of mediator if military operations continued. Finally, Marshall warned Jiang on October 1 that, unless the fighting stopped, he would terminate his mediation between the two parties. "I disagree with the evident government policy of settling the fundamental differences involved by force," explained Marshall, "that is, by utilizing a general offensive campaign to force compliance with the Government point of view or demands."[109] He then added, "I recognize the vital necessity of safeguarding the security of the government, but I think the present procedure has passed well beyond that point."[110] He concluded that, unless a basis for agreement were found to end the fighting without further delays, in the form of proposals and counterproposals, he would recommend to the U.S. government that it terminate his efforts of mediation.[111]

On the following day Jiang agreed to declare a conditional truce of a few days in the Kalgan area. The issuance of the cease-fire order was to be based on two prerequisites: first, the CCP should submit without delay the lists of its members on the State Council and of its delegates to the National Assembly; and, second, the location of Communist troops under the military reorganization plan should be determined immediately, and Communist forces should enter such locations according to agreed dates, which were to be decided upon by the Committee of Three and carried out under the supervision of Executive Headquarters.[112] This conditional truce was unacceptable to CCP leaders on the grounds that "there should be no time limit to the truce period" and that "they would not negotiate under military coercion."[113] Instead, the CCP wanted a complete cessation of the attack on Kalgan. The only way for the GMD government to show its sincerity was to withdraw its troops to their original position.

In order to clarify the terms of the truce proposal Marshall went to Shanghai to resume direct talks with Zhou. On October 9 Zhou presented Marshall with a three-point military proposal and an eight-point political proposal that, in Zhou's words, "represented the Communist stand on military and political issues."[114] The military proposal required that "all troops resume the positions held in China proper as of January 13 and Manchuria as of June 7, that the location of all troops until the time of army reorganization should be fixed, and that Government troops moved after January 13 should be returned to their original locations."[115] The political proposal contained specific points for discussion by the Committee of Five and the PCC Steering Committee, which were all related to the PCC resolutions. On the same occasion Zhou also responded to Jiang's truce proposal in a memorandum addressed to Marshall, in which he stressed the CCP's willingness to participate in meetings of the Committee of Three or the Committee of Five to have "simultaneous discussion" about ending hostilities and "the implementation of the PCC resolutions," provided that the GMD government "permanently call off its attack on Kalgan."[116] On October 10 GMD government troops entered Kalgan, and the GMD government announced the resumption of nationwide conscription. On October 11 the GMD government issued an edict announcing that the National Assembly would be convened on November 12. Five days later Jiang made a public statement in which he presented an eight-point proposal.[117] The GMD government was prepared to arrange for the immediate cessation of hostilities upon the CCP's acceptance of the proposal.

On October 24 Zhou informed Stuart that Yenan could not accept the
GMD government's eight-point proposal.[118] In discussing the situation with
Marshall on October 26, Zhou said that, if GMD military advances continued,
there would be no need for further negotiations, and perhaps it was the
Committee of Three's turn to hold a meeting to decide what action should be
undertaken.[119] Zhou's deep suspicion of any terms presented by the GMD
government was evident throughout the conversation. He indicated, however,
that if the "Third Party Group" could produce a well-conceived compromise
proposal, he would be willing to discuss it with the "third force."[120] He had
made two points perfectly clear: the CCP would not negotiate with Jiang under
military coercion, and the Third Party Group should be urged to take an active
and impartial role in seeking common ground for the resumption of CCP-
GMD negotiations. At this point Zhou no longer expected his negotiations
with the GMD authorities and the Marshall-Stuart mediation to lead to any
meaningful results. Marshall also admitted his inability to end hostilities
between the GMD and the CCP military forces.

Given the prolonged impasse, the potential role of the Third Party Group
loomed large. In October the Third Party Group offered its three-point
proposal for a settlement of differences.[121] It called upon both sides to issue
an immediate cease-fire order and for all troops to remain in their present
positions. Local administrations throughout the nation were to be organized
by the restructured State Council according to PCC and "Peaceful Reconstruction" resolutions. The Steering Committee of the PCC was to be convened in
order to plan for the reorganization of the government. Moreover, all parties
were expected to participate in the discussion of convening a national assembly.
Zhou unofficially accepted practically the entire proposal, but the GMD
government's continuing military operations against Andong forced him to
wait for instructions from Yenan before proceeding further. On his part Jiang
completely rejected the proposal and insisted that his eight-point proposal of
October 16 should be adopted by the Third Party Group.[122] As a result, the
efforts of the Third Party Group also proved to be fruitless.

At the scheduled meeting on November 4, which the GMD government
representative did not attend, the Third Party Group simply asked Zhou to
present the CCP's views. Zhou reiterated Yenan's positions on both military
and political issues. His presentation, to use the words of the U.S. *White Paper,*
was outlined "very completely, covering every issue."[123] In his later account
Zhou observed candidly: "The last act of the play was mediation by a third
force. The third force people had not yet acted as the mediator all by themselves.
In order to enable them to learn something, to realize that mediation would be
fruitless, we agreed to let them try. Jiang put forward eight conditions; we put

forward two. The third force people wanted to make an attempt at mediation and asked us to return to Nanjing. We agreed and returned to Nanjing together with them. They suggested a compromise."[124] As a result of his meeting with the Third Party Group, Zhou sent Marshall a letter, dated November 8, stating that, since his return to Nanjing, "all negotiations were conducted through the Third Party."[125] "Through their good offices," wrote Zhou, "there is some possibility for the reconvening of the Committee of Three."[126] Zhou's letter was noncommittal in nature and referred only casually to Jiang's statement of October 16, but it did hold open the door for continued negotiations with the GMD government.[127] On November 10 the GMD government requested a meeting of the Committee of Three, and Zhou agreed to attend an informal meeting to be held on November 11. At this point Zhou told Marshall that the unilateral action of the GMD government in convening the National Assembly contrary to PCC resolutions made it futile to proceed with arrangements for the termination of hostilities.[128] After the GMD government representative presented the official proposal in detail, Zhou agreed to transmit the proposal to Yenan for prompt reply.[129]

In spite of Zhou's constant warnings, a "National Assembly" met at Nanjing on November 15, 1946. The following day Zhou held a press conference and issued a written statement on the GMD's convening of the assembly in which he stated that this action was contrary to PCC resolutions. He maintained that a legitimate National Assembly could be convened "only under the auspices of a reorganized government and only after the resolutions adopted by the PCC have been put into effect one by one."[130] Moreover, GMD authorities had guaranteed not to hold a National Assembly controlled exclusively by one party. Therefore, such an assembly could gather only after the civil war was truly ended, the resolutions of the PCC carried out, the people's rights and freedoms protected, and the government reorganized. "Only then," in Zhou's own words, "will a National Assembly be an assembly of unity in which various parties participate."[131] With the convening of the National Assembly, Zhou stated flatly, "it [the GMD] has definitely broken all the resolutions adopted by the PCC as well as the Truce Agreement and the program for the reorganization of troops, and has blocked the road to peace talks."[132] He indicated that the CCP categorically refused to recognize the legality of this so-called National Assembly. Zhou called this body a "one party" assembly summoned by the GMD government authorities "to white-wash their dictatorship."[133] He declared that the door to negotiation had been slammed shut by the single hand of the GMD. Zhou called on Marshall on November 16 and indicated his intention to return to Yenan. On this occasion Zhou also expressed his fear that the GMD government "would undertake offensive operations" against Yenan.[134] He also told Marshall that, if this occurred, it would mean "the end of all hope for a negotiated peace."[135] He departed for Yenan on November 19 aboard Marshall's private airplane.

In his exchange of views with Jiang held on December 1, 1946, Marshall indicated that, in his opinion, the complete distrust of the national government by the Communist Party during the past spring had been succeeded by an overwhelming distrust on the part of the CCP of the good intent of any proposal advanced by the government toward a peaceful settlement of differences.[136] He pointed out specifically that the rather reasonable approach of the GMD government, as represented by Jiang's eight-point proposal of October 16, had been compromised by its military attack on CCP-controlled Andong and Chefoo at the time the proposal was announced.[137] Marshall suggested that the Chinese Communists were too large a "military and civil force" to be ignored by GMD authorities and that the power and influence of the CCP "could not be eliminated by military campaigning."[138] Instead, efforts must be made by the GMD to bring the CCP into a coalition government to avoid having military action disrupt the process of negotiation. Jiang's response to Marshall's observations and suggestions was that the CCP never intended to cooperate with the GMD government. Therefore, it was imperative that the CCP's military forces be liquidated once and for all.[139]

A message from Zhou, dated December 4, was forwarded to Marshall in Nanjing by Dong Biwu for transmission to Jiang. It set forth the CCP's terms for reopening negotiations, which Jiang could not be expected to accept. "With a view to complying with the aspiration of the entire Chinese people for peace and democracy," stated Zhou, "our Party takes the stand that if the GMD would immediately dissolve the illegal National Assembly now in session, and restore the troop positions as of January 13 in accord with the cease-fire order, negotiation between the two parties may still make a fresh start."[140] Zhou's message, however, did not directly respond to Marshall's previous request for clarification by CCP leaders on whether or not they wished him to continue in his role as mediator. U.S. mediation between the GMD and the CCP and Zhou's direct talks with Marshall came to an end when Marshall was recalled on January 6, 1947. In his farewell message to the Chinese people Marshall blamed the GMD's "irreconcilable groups" for their "feudal control of China"[141] and their lack of interest in implementing the PCC resolutions. He also criticized the Chinese Communists for their "unwillingness to make a fair compromise."[142] The greatest obstacle to peace in China, in Marshall's view, was the almost overwhelming suspicion with which the GMD and the CCP regarded each other.[143]

Conclusion

Civil war in China might have been avoided had Zhou and the GMD government negotiated in good faith, with Marshall as the mediator. In retrospect, agreements worked out between the CCP and the GMD in January and February 1946, with Marshall's help, represented only a deceptive facade behind which each side tried to maneuver for a better political and military position. In practical terms the real value of Marshall's mediation was regarded by Zhou as a rare opportunity to extricate the CCP from its military vulnerability.[144] Using his astute negotiating skills, Zhou attempted to win Marshall's support. His proposals and counterproposals during negotiations with GMD authorities in 1946 were framed with a view to avoiding any obvious offense to Marshall and Stuart.

Basically, Zhou's main objective was to obtain a settlement on the CCP's terms, if possible. Otherwise, he attempted to use the negotiations to publicize the CCP's official views and legitimate grievances and to influence the political opinions of both the U.S. government and the Chinese people. He knew the power that language and oratory had on the minds of the Chinese. In his talks with GMD representatives and with Hurley, Marshall, and Stuart, Zhou himself recognized fully that public opinion and influence, both at home and abroad, would be valuable in putting pressure on Jiang and his government to make concessions to the CCP's demands.

Zhou's negotiating style was both systematic and thorough. Throughout the CCP-GMD negotiations, especially from 1944 to 1946, he kept himself constantly attuned to reactions at home and abroad and formulated his proposals and counterproposals on the basis of expected domestic and foreign responses. As a man of remarkable negotiating skills, Zhou had both the toughness of mind to handle confrontation and the skills and judgment to be conciliatory. Flexibility was a hallmark of Zhou's negotiating style; his patience, attention to detail, and extraordinary talent for making adjustments as circumstances changed, distinguished him as a national spokesman.

Throughout the negotiations Zhou tried to balance a concern for the legitimate aspirations and rights of the CCP with a realistic assessment of the political and military ascendancy of the GMD apparatus. He was one of the first CCP leaders to recognize the uncomfortable but incontestable fact that the CCP, without the backing of its military forces, was certainly at the mercy of the GMD government and that meaningful negotiation was impossible on such a basis. During Marshall's mediation in 1946 Zhou frequently found himself on the defensive. He was compelled by necessity to expose as well as to challenge the GMD government's self-serving maneuvers. Overshadowed by the GMD's military strength, Zhou found public opinion and the Third Party Group his own party's best available means to counterbalance this situation. His conduct of negotiations and well-timed press conferences illustrate his adroitness in turning a position of weakness to his advantage. Even though his negotiations did not succeed in obtaining all concessions desired by the CCP from the GMD government, nonetheless, he single-handedly managed to win the sympathy and even support of the public. This phenomenon eventually was critical in shifting the power equation between the GMD and the CCP.

CHAPTER 6

The Structure and Process of Foreign Policymaking in China from 1949 to 1976 and Zhou's Role

This chapter examines the foreign policymaking process in the People's Republic of China (PRC), in general, and Zhou's role in the formulation of Chinese foreign policy during the years 1949 to 1976, in particular. The study of foreign policy in this institutional context provides an indispensable background for a wide range of foreign policy issues with which a number of decision making entities were involved. It also provides valuable insight into the relative importance of various participants in the development, formulation, and implementation of specific foreign policy decisions.[1] The present case study examines Zhou's role in foreign policy deliberations, from his active participation in the decision making and implementation phases. As a retrospective analysis, grounded in the context of process and situation, it seeks to shed light on Zhou's perceptions about the foundations of Chinese foreign policy. Examining Zhou's role in the Chinese foreign policymaking process helps clarify how specific decisions were made and under what circumstances. The process of foreign policymaking in China around the mid-twentieth century involved the selection of a particular course of action, from among several alternatives, to create a desired outcome. In order to know the identity and lines of authority within the Party hierarchy that directed diplomatic actions during and after major international events, it is necessary to gain a proper understanding of the process whereby foreign policies were debated, formulated, and executed in China.[2]

The fundamental element in the foreign policymaking process in China from 1949 to 1976 was the identification of national interests under specific circumstances. The issue of national interest was always a challenging one for the CCP. The support of the masses had to be won for the Party's chosen course of action, and a consensus on the national interest was necessary in key matters relating to the independence, security, and economic growth of the country and on the assessment of significant resources, both human and material, required for the implementation of a chosen foreign policy. Unless the CCP leaders could clearly define their national interests and were prepared to safeguard them through policy and action, their direction of foreign affairs might be determined more by the actions of the leaders of other nations than by their own choices.

In attempting to understand the structure and process of foreign policymaking during the first two and a half decades of Communist rule in China, the first section of this chapter focuses on the institutional context in which Zhou and the other CCP leaders dealt with critical issues and problems in terms of China's basic foreign policy considerations. It includes research on the patterns of influence within the Party and government hierarchies, such as who held "power," membership in the Party's Politburo and its Standing Committee, and other factors associated with personalities and roles from 1949 to 1976. Certain fundamental questions are relevant here, including: (1) How and where were foreign policy decisions made in China during the period under discussion? (2) Who really took the initiative in raising a foreign affairs issue for official consideration and suggesting a solution or strategy? and (3) What role did Zhou play in the formulation of Chinese foreign policy?

The Role of the Party in China's Foreign Policymaking Process

Foreign policy decision making in China during the period from 1949 to 1976 was the prerogative of the CCP, and, in fact, ultimate power was vested in a narrow ruling group of the Party.[3] Only the top Party leaders were principal decision makers in the realm of foreign policy. The process of foreign policymaking process involved defining the issues to be addressed and the national objectives to be achieved and identifying the best ways to deal with foreign affairs issues once they had been articulated. It included developing alternative courses of action and weighing their relative merits, limits, and risks. Within the Party, however, the authority to conduct foreign policy was set on a hierarchical basis according to the principle of "democratic centralism."[4] This principle was characterized by a web of organizations with vertical chains of command that ultimately merged at the apex. Consequently, orders and decisions moved downward, and information and suggestions moved upward, each along vertical lines. Foreign policies were formulated by top Party leaders and implemented through established institutional channels.

Decision making on major foreign policy issues was highly concentrated within the PRC. The hierarchical pyramid had the triennial meetings of the National Party Congress at its base, the semiannual meeting of the Central Committee of some fifty to one hundred members at its intermediate stratum, and almost daily meetings of the Politburo at the top. But even this top level had yet another, even smaller executive group, the Standing Committee, which consisted of the Party chairman and six high-ranking Party leaders; Mao, as Party chairman, was the highest-ranking member of the Politburo and its Standing Committee. Under normal conditions the Party chairman presided over the Standing Committee. The Standing Committee controlled the Politburo, which in turn controlled the Central Committee. The exercise of power by the top leaders required, among other things, the loyalty of all Party members and functionaries. The principle of Party unity and discipline and the restrictions of views contrary to the Party line were vigorously maintained, and ultimate authority continued to rest with the small ruling group at the top. Therefore, the central apparatus headed by the Party chairman, the Standing Committee, and the Politburo formed the institutional structure for making China's foreign policy decisions. In the final analysis, in the period from 1949 to 1976 major foreign policy decisions were made by the leading members of the Politburo and, especially, by its Standing Committee.[5] The important role of group deliberation was not only a necessary mechanism for soliciting opinions to form sound foreign policy choices but also a device to build consensual support for those decisions.

In Communist theory a sharp line marked the dichotomy of functions between the Party as the policymaking organ and the government as the administrative agency. On the other hand, one of the unique aspects of Communist government administration was the "leading role" of the Party. Formally outside of, and separated from, the state structure, the Party in actuality arrogated to itself complete power to "supervise" government administration in order to ensure that policies were correctly implemented. Within a few years of achieving power, CCP leaders fashioned a centralized administrative machinery in which top government officials were also Party leaders. The distinctive element of this system was that the Party and the government were interlocked through influential members of the Party, who were found at all intersecting points. This functional system of authority, both within the Party organization and between the Party and the government, was the basis both for generating policy discussions (tao-lun) and for reaching resolutions (jue-yi).

These dual roles were best described by Dong Biwu, a senior member of the Politburo. "The Party," Dong said as early as 1951, "should issue proper directives to the state administrative organs on the nature of the tasks to be carried out. Through the state administrative organs and their subsidiary departments, the policy of the Party should be enforced, while the operations of those organs should be supervised."[6] Deng Xiaoping, a Politburo member since 1954, articulated the same theme. In his report on the revision of the Party constitution to the Eighth National Congress of the CCP on September 16, 1956, Deng said: "First, Party members in the state organs and in particular the leading Party members' groups formed by those in responsible positions in such departments should follow the unified leadership of the Party. Second, the Party must regularly discuss and decide on questions with regard to the guiding principles, policies . . . and the leading Party members' group in the state organs must see to it that these decisions are put into effect. . . . Third, the party must . . . exercise constant supervision over the work of the state organs."[7] This interlocking mechanism, whereby members of the Politburo and its Standing Committee were also high-ranking administrators, was intended to institutionalize the primacy of the Party and its highest instrument of power, the Standing Committee. It also effectively eliminated any possible gap between decision making and the implementation of adopted decisions, as the distinction between the Party and the government was more theoretical than real.

According to the principle of democratic centralism, members of all high Party organs were elected from below and were periodically accountable to the organizations that had elected them.[8] The smaller Party organs at the pinnacle, the Politburo and its Standing Committee, were formed by the Central Committee. Although the Central Committee and the Party Congress alike met regularly, in reality they became little more than sounding boards for outlining and publicizing foreign policy decisions already reached in secret in the central Party organs, and thus they lacked any substantial influence in the foreign policymaking process. The lion's share, indeed a monopoly, of foreign policy decision making had passed to the Politburo and especially to the seven top Party leaders, who constituted its Standing Committee and in effect delegated to themselves the most important role in the foreign policymaking process of China.

The Politburo and its Standing Committee were the key bodies in which fundamental issues of foreign policy were discussed;[9] the degree to which the final decisions of these bodies were based on real participation, however, or whether or not they were taken by majority vote is impossible to determine.

Likely, there was an inner core of three or four persons who were Mao's most intimate and trusted colleagues and who played the most significant roles in shaping China's foreign policy decisions. No doubt, too, there were individual members within the Politburo and its Standing Committee who carried greater weight in the field of foreign affairs than others. The Constitution adopted by the First Session of the Party's Eighth Congress in September 1956, however, institutionalized collective leadership. As foreign affairs issues were examined, proposals recommended, and decisions made by the members of the Politburo and its Standing Committee, these bodies, with their overlapping and inter-locking memberships, constituted the ultimate source of authority in incorpo-rating security and economic development into national policy.

But the pattern of "collective leadership" in China's foreign policy formulation must not be accepted without further qualifications. First of all, the internal working processes and operations of the Politburo, and especially its Standing Committee, during the period under discussion were kept secret; no authentic records of its deliberations are available. Second, this concentra-tion of authority and the actual power relationships among the members of this small ruling group suggest that the foreign policy decision making power in China was both institutional and personal. Between 1949 and 1976 the Politburo and its Standing Committee included not only persons with high Party standing but also top government officials, including the premier. In this way the Politburo or its Standing Committee might be regarded as a forum for the discussion and reconciliation of the interests of Party and government. Third, the personal experiences and personalities of those who were in control of the levers of real power played a major part in foreign policy formulation. It is reasonable to conclude that foreign policy decisions were made by a small circle of powerful men occupying strategic posts at the top of the Party and state hierarchies.

Apart from the institutional component of decision making there was a key personal element: a tendency to follow the guidance of certain individuals in matters of foreign policy and to accept their proposals. As chairman of the Party and a prominent theoretician of Communist theories and precepts, Mao was normally the "first among equals" within the Politburo and its Standing Committee.[10] He was the supreme leader, and his personal role in foreign policy decisions was both symbolic and real. His decision making power was not simply the official authority invested in the office of the Party chairman. The supreme authority and influence that he enjoyed resulted from the fact that he had organized and led the Party through the long struggle for power. Mao's impressive ability to present a synthesis to include points of views was well-known.[11] By keeping opposition inside the Party hierarchy rather than forcing it outside, Mao demonstrated his remarkable capacity to bridge most differences and maintain an outer front of unity. Mao himself demonstrated his ability to mold the top leaders of the Party into a tightly knit team that worked well together. He was able to provide the CCP with a comprehensive theoretical foundation upon which to structure the direction and course of China's foreign policy.

Mao, however, always emphasized the need for reaching consensus. By and large he was remarkably successful in maintaining a spectacular facade of unity among Party leaders with regard to Party lines and decisions. As the top ideologue and fountainhead of legitimacy of China's political system, Mao remained the sole authority figure for the Party and state and was in a position to define both the parameters and issues of China's foreign policy. His real influence was asserted through his leading role in the Politburo and its Standing Committee, both of which had decisive power in the policies of the Party and the government. His ability to assert his leadership was reinforced by his capacity as a preeminent theorist in assessing China's relations with the outside world. Mao did not dictate foreign policy measures, but his overall theoretical analysis had the effect of establishing the parameters within which foreign affairs issues were defined and discussed.

Zhou's Role in China's Foreign Policymaking Process

From 1945 to 1956 the Party operated under the constitution adopted at the Seventh Congress. This constitution stressed, among other things, the "thought of Mao Zedong." The first Party Central Committee plenum met on September 28, 1956, and elected Mao as chairman of the Central Committee and of the Politburo. The constitution adopted by the First Session of the Eighth Congress in 1956 contained a significant shift. It made no reference to the "thought of Mao" but, instead, underscored the role of collective leadership. The reorganization of the top Party structure in 1956 meant that China would be governed by a collegium over which Mao no longer ruled supreme. Four other top leaders—Liu Shaoqi, Zhou, Zhu De, and Ch'en Yun—were elected vice chairmen of the Politburo and its Standing Committee. As first vice chairman, Liu was delegated to share part of Mao's power to conduct certain important conference proceedings.[12] Moreover, Mao was deprived of the Central Secretariat, which controlled the Party's day-to-day operations. Henceforth this vital Party organ was supervised by the secretary-general, Deng Xiaoping.

Membership in the Politburo was determined, in actuality, not by the Central Committee but by the Politburo itself; therefore, in practice it was a self-perpetuating body. Under the circumstances the personal experiences, ideological preferences, and personalities of those in control of the levers of real power played a major part in formulating China's foreign policy. The terms *power* and *influence* describe critical elements in this decision making process. *Power* meant direct participation in forging foreign policies, and *influence* was a person's ability to affect outcomes in the foreign policymaking process.

Zhou, the Politburo, and Its Standing Committee

The Politburo met regularly; among other things it dealt with important foreign policy issues and had the power to make major foreign policy decisions.[13] The Politburo was small, consisting of seven to thirteen members during the period from 1949 to 1955. It was enlarged to seventeen members in 1956 and to twenty in 1958. Politburo members occupied leadership positions in all important Party and government institutions, and, as individuals, they wielded great influence, derived from their status as Politburo members and from their other prestigious positions. Furthermore, the Politburo was charged specifically with the responsibility for deliberating all major foreign policy questions; hence, from the outset it was the top foreign policy decision making organ of the Party. Third, in the early years the method of reaching key foreign policy decisions within the Politburo still followed the pattern established by the CCP during its Yenan period from 1936 to 1949. Basically, it was a process of decision making by general consensus among the leading Politburo members; thus, it was a collective rather than an individual enterprise.[14]

Meetings of the Politburo were held to discuss and approve foreign policy matters initiated by individual members. General guidelines and the overall framework for specific foreign policy decisions, however, were defined and evaluated by Mao and Zhou. During the deliberation, if disagreement emerged, attempts would be made to reach a majority decision among Politburo members in the name of Party unity. Majority decisions within the Politburo were binding on minority members, and the strictest obedience of all members was required. Indeed, the Party Politburo was composed of a highly disciplined elite, and it was the key foreign policy decision making power in China. The Party delegated to the Politburo the exclusive role of leading the nation in its search for security and for establishing regional as well as global influence. Members of the

Politburo held their prestigious positions partly because of their long-standing connections with the Party through the revolutionary movement and civil war and partly because of their close association with Mao. They had worked together as revolutionaries for more than two decades and formed a tightly knit group—united, above all, in their respect for Mao. As chairman of both the Central Committee of the CCP and its Politburo, Mao occupied a dominant position in the formulation of Chinese foreign policy.[15]

A Standing Committee of the Politburo was created at the Eighth Party Congress in 1956. The Standing Committee began to share and in many respects eclipsed the Politburo's authority in China's foreign affairs. Although the Politburo debated major issues relating to external affairs, it usually deferred the leadership role in this area to the Standing Committee. The Politburo's Standing Committee thus functioned as the highest Party organ of foreign policymaking and had full authority on diplomatic strategies and international negotiations.

The Standing Committee of the Politburo included the chairman, the four vice chairmen, and the secretary-general of the CCP. The four vice chairmen were all top Party leaders, and their elevation to vice chairmanship indicated their rising political influence vis-à-vis Mao. In retrospect the creation of the Standing Committee marked not only the transfer of power from the Politburo to the Standing Committee but also the gradual devolution of power from Mao to other high-ranking Party members. At the second session of the Eighth Party Congress, held in May 1958, Mao, as a result of the purge of provincial Party organizations, was able to enlarge the Politburo and its Standing Committee. Lin Biao was added to the latter group; this gave Mao at least a four-to-three voting edge in that body, assuming that Mao, Zhou, Lin, and either Ch'en or Zhu voted together. All members of the Standing Committee were directly involved in formulating China's foreign policies, and they represented the pinnacle of power in the Chinese political system. It was, therefore, at the Standing Committee level that the final decisions of foreign policy were collectively made.[16]

It was the Party's practice, however, to assign individuals within the Standing Committee to oversee certain sectors of Party and government operations and to report on policy problems pertaining to them. Each member of the Standing Committee, while participating in the collective discussions of the group, was also delegated specific responsibilities. This division of functions among the members of the Standing Committee served to reinforce the Party's control of as well as its links to the government. Indications of the division of responsibilities within the Standing Committee can be gleaned from the official positions that its members occupied and the reports and pronouncements they made. Among the leading members of the Standing Committee Zhou assumed jurisdiction over key aspects of foreign policy and administrative activities related to it.

Zhou's institutional role in dealing with foreign representatives both at home and abroad made him a key participant in the conduct of China's foreign relations. Moreover, because Zhou had been a Politburo member since 1927 and a member of the Standing Committee since its creation in 1956, his views carried considerable weight on all major foreign policy issues. His expertise and control over vital information no doubt enhanced the importance of his role in China's foreign policymaking process. His influence, however, ultimately rested on his Party position, and his Party position was, in turn, strengthened by his close personal relationship with Mao. Siding with Mao in every round of the intra-Party power struggle since the late 1930s, Zhou demonstrated his consistent loyalty. His ability to take other CCP leaders into his confidence made him extremely popular and influential, and his political strength was directly related to his skill at mediating between contending groups and his special rapport with competing leaders. Zhou was a reputed "tide watcher," well-known for his ability to sense and move with the political tide. Also, he was a consummate practitioner of persuasion. He was known for his ability to win over detractors and opponents to his point of view.

With the establishment of the PRC Zhou believed that the conduct of Chinese foreign policy should become more concerned with diplomatic methods and less with revolutionary rhetoric. In China's relations with other nations diplomacy should, by necessity, take precedence. He pointed out that foreign policy should not be developed in a vacuum and that domestic and external conditions should constitute the foundation of a realistic approach to foreign affairs. Zhou participated regularly in the foreign policy deliberations of the Politburo and of its Standing Committee. As previously noted, he was also responsible for overseeing government administration and the conduct of China's foreign relations.

Of the members who were on both the Politburo and its Standing Committee Mao and Zhou were the two most influential by virtue of their positions as chairman of the Party and premier of the State Council, respectively. It was Zhou who had the constitutional responsibility for providing leadership in integrating various aspects of national security and other interests into a realistic and well-coordinated foreign policy. When members of the Politburo and its Standing Committee were faced with pressing matters on foreign policy, they were generally inclined to follow Zhou's lead, leaving day-to-day operational decisions to his discretion. Furthermore, the expertise in foreign relations of most members of the Politburo and its Standing Committee was limited. Naturally, when dealing with China's foreign policy issues, they tended to rely heavily on information, preliminary analyses, and judgments provided by Zhou. Therefore, his expertise in foreign affairs and his ability to provide the Party hierarchy with unified, coherent foreign policy proposals ensured the increasing importance of his role in the foreign policymaking process. His close alliance with Mao as a source of political backing within the Party enabled Zhou to enjoy unprecedented latitude in initiating and implementing foreign policy decisions.

Within the Politburo and its Standing Committee Zhou was undoubtedly the principal voice on external affairs. Between them Zhou and Mao monopolized decision making on China's foreign policies. The reasons for Zhou's decision to support Mao's foreign policy orientation as opposed to that of Liu Shaoqi during the Cultural Revolution from 1966 to 1968 and Lin Biao in the post-Cultural Revolution years were numerous, but the history of Zhou's relations with Mao and their shared realistic appraisal of global forces provide part of the answer. In Lin's case, Zhou tried to confine the debate on China's foreign policy to the Party center. Lin, seeking to strengthen his position, maneuvered to include top military leaders in deliberations on China's foreign policies so as to challenge Zhou's dominant influence in the Politburo and its Standing Committee.[17]

As the Party apparatus and its operation continued to evolve, an increasingly difficult problem was to ensure that all top-level leaders within the CCP maintained support for those foreign policies deemed important by the Politburo or by its Standing Committee, advocated by Zhou, and sanctioned personally by Mao. From the early 1960s on the roles of both the Politburo and its Standing Committee went through a significant change, and both of these Party organs began to lose their decision making power in some respects. One of the factors that brought about this change was the increasing tendency of Mao and other CCP leaders to rely heavily on Central Committee work conferences to deliberate important issues. Second, Mao more vigorously asserted his personal control over policy decisions. Especially during the years of the Cultural Revolution the entire political system in China ceased to perform its routine functions. Mao and such special ad hoc bodies as the Cultural Revolution Group assumed overall control of the multiple functions previously exercised by the Politburo and its Standing Committee. After the Cultural Revolution these political entities were reconstituted, and in the early 1970s both organs once again became top-level Party institutions in which important foreign policy decisions were made.

Zhou's Functions as Premier and Foreign Minister

Under the "Organic Law" enacted by the PCC of 1949 the highest official decision making organ was the Central People's Government Council, of which Mao was chairman. It met twice a month to deliberate issues regarding major policies of state. When not in session, its powers were delegated to the State Administrative Council, headed by a premier (Zong-li). On September 30, 1949, the Central People's Government Council appointed Zhou as premier and, concurrently, minister of the Ministry of Foreign Affairs (Wai-jiao bu-chang). The Organic Law remained in force for five years while steps were undertaken to introduce a new constitution.[18] The First National People's Congress (NPC) was convened in Beijing from September 15 to 28, 1954. Its most important task was the adoption of the Constitution, which formally terminated the transitional period of the New Democracy (1949-54). Under the Constitution the highest administrative organ was the State Council (Guo-wu-yuan).[19] Zhou was again appointed premier, to preside over the State Council. He also held the post of foreign affairs portfolio from 1949 until early 1958.

As premier and foreign minister, Zhou was in a pivotal position to handle China's relations with foreign countries. According to the 1954 Constitution, the State Council was the "highest executive and administrative organ of state power."[20] In line with Article 4 of the Organic Law of the State Council, a plenary session composed of the premier, the vice premiers, the ministers, the chairmen of the commissions, and the secretary-general, was to meet once a month, and the premier might call special meetings when necessary. The premier was specifically bidden by the Constitution to attend meetings of the Supreme State Council to discuss important state affairs. The Party issued general directives to the government administrative apparatus but did not directly conduct affairs of state. In his 1957 *Report on the Work of the Government* Zhou clarified the distinction between Party leadership and state administration. "Some people," said Zhou, "have criticized the lack of clear division of function between the Party and the government."[21] He went on: "In directly issuing political calls and announcing policymaking decisions to the masses, the Party, far from hampering the work of the government, renders great help."[22]

The State Council,[23] headed by Zhou from 1954 to 1976, consisted of those ministers who were the most senior members of the Party. It represented a strong concentration of political power and was marked to a considerable extent by its personnel's constancy, even during the tumultuous period of the Cultural Revolution. Foreign relations were handled by the premier and the minister of foreign affairs. Zhou held both positions concurrently from 1949 until early 1958, when he handed over the Ministry of Foreign Affairs to Ch'en Yi. Although Zhou relinquished his official duties as foreign minister, as premier of the State Council he continued to play a major role in supervising and coordinating China's foreign relations and diplomacy.[24] Because the Party had always exercised substantial political power, Zhou's foreign policy initiatives might have been limited to choices sanctioned by the Party.

The functional relationships between the State Council, the Standing Committee of the NPC, and the chairman of the PRC were primarily determined by the relative Party standing of those who held these positions at any given time. Zhou, for instance, added to his power and prestige by being a leading member of the Party's Politburo and its Standing Committee. As an individual, he could almost monopolize the foreign policymaking process, from actual negotiations with foreign countries to the adoption and implementation of his foreign policy decisions. Yet the government was not the locus of foreign policy decision making. It was merely an administrative body designed to carry out the foreign policy decisions made by top party organs such as the Politburo and its Standing Committee. Its function, however, was more important than that of the Party in terms of the day-to-day administration of policy, particularly for the management of China's foreign affairs, economy, foreign trade, and defense. This dual system helped the government, under Zhou's guidance, to maintain its institutional integrity.

The administration was supported by experts in foreign affairs, economic planning, and national defense, and thus Zhou's position in coordinating the activities of top Party and government organs related to Chinese foreign affairs was unique. His position of power and numerous personal connections gave him free access to leading members of the Party center and government apparatus. He alone in the Ministry of Foreign Affairs had an expert staff that could make systematic and continuous studies of the foreign situation. Under Zhou's personal guidance the foreign service officers of the Ministry gained experience and credibility, and, as a result, its recommendations carried considerable weight with the Politburo. Even though the Party played a dominant role in formulating and executing foreign policies, the Ministry of Foreign Affairs was nonetheless instrumental in enforcing the foreign policy decisions of both the government and the Party.[25] In addition, the Ministry participated actively in the initial stage of the foreign policy decision making process when problems were stated, analyses outlined, and solutions suggested.

As premier of the State Council, Zhou regularly dealt with a broad range of political, diplomatic, and economic issues, sometimes making preliminary decisions and sometimes preparing positions and recommendations that went to the Politburo and its Standing Committee for consideration.[26] Whenever the

State Council under Zhou's leadership decided that a particular foreign policy issue was of great importance, it would refer the matter for discussion to the Politburo and its Standing Committee. Once the foreign policy was decided on by those groups, directives flowed back down the line to the State Council. If the top leadership considered an official sanction necessary, a meeting of the Party Central Committee or of the Supreme State Council might be convened. Under extraordinary circumstances the Party Congress might meet to listen to Party and government leaders and vote on recommendations.

Zhou's effort to place professional specialists in responsible positions on the State Council and its Ministry of Foreign Affairs made it possible for him to formulate policy recommendations on the basis of the careful analysis of internal and external conditions. Under Zhou's guidance both administrative organizations managed to achieve a high degree of stability and competence. There is ample evidence to suggest that Zhou entrusted the principal staff members of the Ministry of Foreign Affairs with weighty matters and that he highly regarded their reports, position papers, and opinions.

Ch'en Yi served as head of the Ministry of Foreign Affairs from 1958 until his death in January 1972. The routine administrative affairs of the Ministry were carried out by vice foreign minister Qiao Guanhua and later by Ji Pengfei, another vice foreign minister. After Ch'en's death, Ji led the Foreign Ministry until he was replaced by Qiao in November 1974. Both Ji and Qiao worked under Zhou's direct supervision. Some of the key members of the Ministry of Foreign Affairs represented Zhou at different international gatherings—for instance, Ch'en at Geneva in 1961-62 and Wang Bingnan at Warsaw and at meetings of the U.S.-China talks—but all conferences and negotiations of primary importance Zhou attended and conducted himself.

The experts in the Foreign Ministry advised Zhou on the political, economic, military, and other aspects of a given foreign affair situation, and the diplomats in the field provided him with *in loco* assessments and intelligence. On the more technical aspects of defense, armament, and military strategy Zhou relied on the National Defense Council and the Ministry of Defense. The tasks of collecting and analyzing political intelligence were critical. Lack of reliable intelligence could greatly increase the risk of foreign policy failure. On the other hand, large quantities of materials had to be consolidated and analyzed to manageable proportions before Zhou could bring them to the attention of the Party hierarchy. In this regard Zhou developed his own method of safeguarding the integrity of his sources of information. By encouraging different individuals and groups to provide him with information, Zhou managed to free himself from exclusive dependence on any single individual or agency for fact gathering. Instead, Zhou mobilized competing groups of administration, Party, and intelligence agencies to generate the information and data that he needed.

The State Council, the most important center for "executive decision making in the government," consisted of the top Party leaders. Its routine functions included those "to formulate administrative measures, issue decisions and orders and verify their execution, and to direct the conduct of external affairs."[27] It was too large in size for effective decision making. A small Standing Committee, composed of Premier Zhou, the vice ministers and the secretary-general, was created, meeting frequently thereafter. The State Council under Zhou's leadership was the nerve center that guided China's foreign policy, even if it did not make final foreign policy decisions. In 1962 Premier Zhou and twelve of the sixteen vice premiers were all regular or alternate Politburo members. By changing their titles of office, this group could, in effect, be regarded as the top political group of either the Party or the government, as the occasion required. Yet, despite the impressive array of political heavyweights on the State Council and its Standing Committee, power appeared to be a function of Party membership rather than state position.

The actual day-to-day conduct of China's foreign relations was largely in the hands of various ministries under the State Council, of which the Ministry of Foreign Affairs was the most important one. The Ministry of Foreign Affairs was not a decision making body, but its analyses and recommendations directly affected final foreign policy decisions. The Foreign Ministry not only provided a vital official channel through which the views of foreign affairs experts could reach the top Party organs, such as the Politburo and its Standing Committee, but, more important, it was a key link between the Party hierarchy and the principal government officials responsible for conducting foreign affairs. It also had a distinctive role in carrying out foreign policy decisions. In the final analysis the influence of the State Council and its Foreign Ministry under Zhou's personal supervision was exercised through the high-ranking Party members who occupied pivotal positions in both Party and administrative organizations.

It is reasonable to conclude that there were several ways in which China's foreign affairs decisions were made. One important distinction was between policy and administrative decisions. Party leaders generally took matters into their own hands. As a consequence, policy decision making power remained in the hands of the powerful leaders of the CCP. The other category of decisions dealt with operational and administrative situations, which required more practical and technical considerations. Zhou, as a leading member of the Party and as premier, not only made foreign policy recommendations to the Party inner circle but also participated directly in decision making on foreign policy issues at the highest level. At the same time, he presided over the administrative bodies that were responsible for the implementation of China's foreign policy decisions. With his membership in both the Party and the administrative organs he was the vital link between the two spheres of institutional structure; most important was the fact that this setup afforded him the unique opportunity practically to monopolize Chinese foreign policy from beginning to end.

Zhou's Relationship with Mao and Its Impact on Foreign Affairs

Zhou's role in China's foreign policy decision making process was undoubtedly strengthened by his close relationship with Mao. He enjoyed Mao's confidence in both his knowledge and judgment on foreign policy matters. Given that no important steps in China's foreign policy were taken without Mao's final approval, this close relationship enabled Zhou to exercise great latitude in shaping the direction of China's foreign relations. Throughout the periods of united front and civil war Mao and Zhou had cooperated for survival and collaborated on the quest for national power. Their mutual reliance and close working relationship was forged in hard times and withstood the most severe tests imposed on both men. "Mao Zedong (Mao Tse-tung) and Zhou Enlai (Chou En-lai) both cooperated very well," wrote former CCP leader Zhang Guotao, "one making plans inside, and the other negotiating outside."[28]

The close personal bond between Mao and Zhou continued to grow during the postrevolutionary period. They maintained regular and direct communications with each other, generally meeting several times a week. When he was on diplomatic missions, Zhou constantly sent Mao reports. He discussed foreign policy issues with Mao, listened to his views and analyses, and then systematically laid out his proposed course of action and alternatives. Zhou's ability to translate Mao's ideas into concrete policies while skillfully grappling with political problems and bureaucratic interests enabled him to play a unique part in China's foreign policy decision making process. His skills at negotiating, persuading, and moderating were vital to the realization of China's major foreign policy goals. He became Mao's most trusted collaborator and emerged in the early years of their postrevolutionary partnership as the Party's most highly regarded policy maker and negotiator.

Zhou respected Mao's knowledge of Chinese history and society as well as his determination to "seek truth from facts."[29] Mao believed in plain dealing, plain speaking, and, always, "hard struggle."[30] More important still, he placed emphasis upon the ability of dedicated men to solve China's difficult problems and upon the need to overcome arrogance and complacency. Mao had risen to national power declaring his determination to restore China's international status and influence. Both Mao and Zhou were devoted to the quest for improving China's relations with the outside world. Mao was at times a man of action and at other times a thinker. Zhou, on the other hand, did not separate the two but, rather, epitomized unity of the two forces. Zhou shared with Mao the compelling desire to see China once again become a great country commanding the respect of the world community. Zhou's greater patience and willingness to be conciliatory was evident in his choice of means, as compared with Mao's more blunt approach to the same issues.

As an ideologue, Mao usually provided the Party with an authoritative assessment of the international situation and pointed to the future diplomatic course of action. Mao's influence on China's foreign policymaking process after the rise of the CCP to national power was paramount. In the winter months of 1958-59, however, Mao anticipated opposition to his leadership as a result of his Great Leap Forward programs. Therefore, he decided to step down as head of state, handing the title to Liu Shaoqi in the hope that, with Liu's support, he would deflate the opposition and strengthen his position.[31] In stepping down, Mao was probably also trying to concentrate his attention upon "questions of the direction, policy, and line of the Party and the State,"[32] as indicated in the official statement. Another reason, perhaps, for Mao to give up chairmanship of the government was his desire to avoid the kind of successional struggle that occurred in the Soviet Union after Stalin's death in 1953. Therefore, Mao's resignation as chairman of the PRC can be viewed as part of a planned program of transition. In the spring of 1959 the PRC elected Liu to succeed Mao as head of state.

Although Mao relinquished his government post, he continued to hold the chairmanship of the Party, the real locus of power in the regime. In early July 1959 an enlarged Politburo conference was convened at Lushan, Jiangxi. Attending the conference were regular members and alternates of the Politburo and important officials of the Party, the government, and the People's Liberation Army (PLA). Defense Minister Peng Dehuai's challenge to Mao's Great Leap Forward economic policies and commune programs received support from only one of the seven members of the Politburo's Standing Committee, Zhu De, and was opposed by four other members (excluding Ch'en Yun and Deng, who were not present). Peng received support primarily from the military officers but failed to recruit to his camp more civilian Party officials, particularly those in charge of the economy.[33]

With Mao's reduced role in initiating the policy, there was a corresponding growth in the power to initiate by other top Party leaders, particularly Liu, Deng, Ch'en, and Zhou. Mao was kept informed of major domestic developments, and his approval was still sought for important decisions. It is not entirely clear, however, what kinds of foreign policy issues were considered important enough to require his direct, personal involvement. Broad issues that were "strategic," including those related to China's policies of a united front with Third World nations and of delicate triangular relations with the two superpowers, obviously fell into this category, as did problems that related to China's national security.

After the Lushan confrontation with Peng and in the wake of disastrous failures of the Great Leap Forward and commune programs in the late 1950s and early 1960s, Mao, for a variety of reasons, no longer played an active part in China's foreign policy decision making process. From this point on, as Mao remarked wryly on one occasion, Liu and Deng began to treat him as if he were already dead. During the same period Zhou appeared to have lost most of his influence in the sphere of foreign affairs, with special reference to the Sino-Indian boundary dispute. The approach Zhou advocated at this time emphasized the "three peaceful principles—that is, peaceful coexistence, peaceful competition, and peaceful transition. This conciliatory and yet pragmatic foreign policy orientation suddenly changed after 1958, when Liu began to exert more influence on Beijing's foreign policy formulation. By 1962 Zhou's leadership in the field of foreign affairs, which was virtually undisputed since 1949, was challenged within the Party hierarchy. Even though Zhou's authority was still great, he could no longer hold the sway. There is evidence that Zhou and Ch'en Yi tried to dissuade Mao and others from resorting to armed conflict with India in 1961 and 1962. But Liu sided with Mao, and they overrode Zhou and Ch'en.

Even Mao's role in foreign policy formulation was restricted between 1958 and 1965. During this period Liu, as chairman of the PRC and as a senior member of the Politburo and its Standing Committee, exerted tremendous influence on China's foreign relations and diplomacy.[34] It was Liu's design to revive the Sino-Soviet alliance to counter United States military activities in Vietnam. In the early 1960s the International Liaison Department discussed the possibility of adopting a new foreign policy line based on "three reconciliations and one reduction." The so-called three reconciliations were with "reactionaries," "revisionists," and "imperialists,"[35] and the one "reduction" referred to aid to revolutionary struggles abroad. Zhou's policy of three peaceful principles was discussed but not adopted.

By 1965 Mao was prepared to launch another revolution that would dramatically defy the power holders taking the capitalist road within the Party. This effort was the Great Proletarian Cultural Revolution. In September 1965 Lin Biao came on strong, both as a defender of Mao's doctrines and as a global strategist. In the Eleventh Central Committee Plenum, held in August 1966, Mao and his supporters managed to discredit the leadership of Liu and Deng and censored them for having produced and enforced an erroneous "bourgeois reactionary line." The final communiqué of the plenum was adopted on August 12 and reflected the decisive triumph of Mao and his supporters.[36] Lin replaced Liu as the second in command under Mao. During the Cultural Revolution, from 1966 to 1968, CCP leaders were preoccupied with the nation's internal struggles, and foreign relations became a secondary concern.

Although the Cultural Revolution resulted from differences over domestic problems, the hidden strains in the central leadership over foreign affairs were among the issues that divided Party leaders. The dispute in foreign affairs was essentially one in which Mao's opponents tried to challenge his residual power so as to control China's policy decision making process. As expected, the internal power struggle had an immediate impact on foreign relations, as the dominant leaders in China adopted a revolutionary line of intense militancy and turned inward toward inescapable isolation.

During the Cultural Revolution period Zhou tried to confine the power struggle to nonadministrative units. For this reason he prevented a wholesale purge of the Ministry of Foreign Affairs, the Ministry of Finance, and PLA units in strategic locations. Instead of taking an ideological stance, Zhou chose to explain his overall position in practical terms. He managed to maintain his pragmatic attitude even during the radical upheavals of the Cultural Revolution. In fact, his position was more consistent than that of any other leaders, in the sense that he did not swing from one extreme to another but persistently upheld a moderate and flexible line. His practical strategy of seizing power selectively, at the crucial stage, served Mao's goal of revolutionizing the ruling structure while maintaining the continuity and stability of the government apparatus. By keeping close relations with both Mao and Lin, Zhou maximized his maneuverability in foreign policy decision making while shielding himself from criticism by the radicals when any foreign policy line worked less favorably than expected. Zhou also clarified the term *power holders* by distinguishing between power holders and the "power holders taking the capitalist road." Moreover, Zhou's personality, skills, and ability to protect his subordinates made him extremely popular and influential.

Zhou's role during the Cultural Revolution, as far as Mao and Lin were concerned, was that of negotiator and organizer.[37] His importance went far beyond what his governmental position warranted. The success of Zhou's political activities during the Cultural Revolution depended on both his personal influence and institutional authority. His power in the arena of foreign policy and diplomacy during this crucial stage was exerted through the Politburo and its Standing Committee, among other channels. In the long process of power struggle and ideological conflict the Mao-Lin-Zhou alliance managed to defeat Liu's Party apparatus.[38]

In the post-Cultural Revolution period Zhou's prestigious position was once again confirmed when the Ninth Party Congress, held in Beijing in April 1969, named him again as a member of the Politburo's Standing Committee. He also served as secretary-general of the Ninth Party Congress. The Party leadership immediately after the Cultural Revolution presented itself as a combination of the Maoist Left, the moderates of the old Party and state apparatus around Zhou, and Lin's central military machine and the regional commanders. The position of the Left within this new power structure became steadily weaker soon after the Ninth Congress because it was deprived of its organizational basis through the Red Guard movement. The major burdens of political and economic reconstruction then fell upon Zhou, whose purpose was to create a viable collective leadership within the Party.

Although Zhou ranked third in the Party hierarchy behind Mao and Lin during and after the 1966-68 Cultural Revolution, he was at the center of every important decision in the field of China's foreign policy.[39] Following the Ninth Party Congress, and particularly after the Second Plenum of the new Central Committee in August 1970, the State Council, under Zhou's leadership and with the backing of the moderates within the top hierarchy, began to implement the new foreign policy of the Five Principles of Peaceful Coexistence in its dealings with almost all nations. There was a renewed emphasis by Zhou on government-to-government relations in Chinese diplomacy. Zhou calculated that there were certain assets upon which Chinese foreign policy could draw during this crucial period: the U.S.-Soviet global conflict, the gradual withdrawal of U.S. military forces from Vietnam, and the antihegemonic trends among the small- and medium-sized nations of the Third World and beyond.[40] Since both China's regional and international positions depended upon a viable foreign policy, it was important to develop one that would promote Chinese interests and maintain national security.

After the Ninth Party Congress Mao and Lin began to struggle against each other. Lin supported Ch'en Bode in an attempt to seize the premiership. The issues that divided Mao and Lin were strategy for rebuilding the Party and foreign policy. Their conflicts resulted in an open confrontation when the Central Committee of the Ninth Congress convened its second plenum at Lushan in late August 1970. Zhou supported Mao in his struggle against Lin.[41] The official communiqué issued from the two-week closed-door meeting declared that the nation's foreign policy was "on the basis of adhering to the five principles" and that China "strive[s] for peaceful coexistence with countries having different social systems."[42] It was the first time in more than five years that this phrase had been heard in public. Once again the foreign policy line designed by Zhou was endorsed by the Party. Zhou was again the principal voice of China's external affairs. Mao and Zhou together wielded the most power in the newly structured foreign policy decision making process in the early 1970s. The reasons for Zhou's decision to support Mao's foreign policy line—first against Liu during the Cultural Revolution and then against Lin in the post-Cultural Revolution years—were numerous, but the history of Zhou's personal relations with Mao and their shared views in assessing the global situation provide a major part of the answer.

Conclusion

Zhou occupied one of the highest official positions in the government and was also a leading member of the Politburo and its Standing Committee. He kept in close touch with other members of the Party hierarchy, especially with Mao, who remained, by and large, the ultimate source of Party authority for making foreign policy decisions from 1946 to 1976. All major foreign policy decisions must be acceptable to him as Party chairman. Zhou, as a high-ranking Party and government leader, had considerable influence on foreign policy decisions and even more on the implementation of foreign policies sanctioned by the Politburo and its Standing Committee. He regarded Mao as an outstanding national figure who had led the Chinese Communist movement to its final victory. Zhou viewed Mao both as the symbol and source of Party unity and as a leading ideologue for the Party.

Mao, for his part, shared the general respect for Zhou's negotiating talents and organizational achievements. He delegated many responsibilities to Zhou, because the premier was an expert on external affairs, and also shared his basic outlook on international relations. Given the two men's complementary qualities and the fact that Zhou had, as early as 1935, adjusted his political career to Mao's leadership within the Party hierarchy, a close relationship between Zhou and Mao was developed and maintained for more than two decades. This relationship had the beneficial effect of bringing together the two distinct approaches of Zhou and Mao, which were described as "pragmatic" and "doctrinaire," respectively. "Of all the men who had been senior to Mao in the Party hierarchy," Dick Wilson has suggested, "only Zhou survived as a continuous member of Mao's team. It would be going too far to say that Mao trusted Zhou, but over the years the two did grow to need each other more and more."[43] Wilson concludes: "He [Zhou] had the reforming fecundity of a Napoleon, combined with the political tenacity of a Metternich."[44]

In what manner did Zhou exert his influence upon China's foreign policymaking process? Among members of the Politburo and its Standing Committee Zhou was very active both in providing policy alternatives and in making final decisions. Within the Party, leadership was theoretically exercised according to the principle of democratic centralism. In fact, the important decisions on foreign policy were made by a small group of top leaders. There were occasional conflicts over power and, above all, over foreign policy lines within the Party hierarchy. A constant struggle for supremacy at the very top testified to the need for redistribution of political power among the top leaders. Accordingly, the CCP leaders devoted considerable time to attempting to legitimatize their authority in the policy decision making process. When the legitimacy of these leaders was seriously questioned, their continued authoritative role became tenuous. Realignment of political forces within the Party hierarchy, whatever the outcome, testified to the proper formation of the necessary link between authority and legitimacy.

The replacement of one top leader for another within the CCP could result from various factors and circumstances. Serious diplomatic and economic dislocations arising in the aftermath of misjudgment by a policy maker might contribute to his ouster. A rigid stance on certain foreign policy issues, when there was a need for flexibility and acquiescence, could eventually force a complete change in leadership. At any rate, political leaders—whether competent, misjudged, or merely too weak to survive in government—were replaced as a matter of course.

Ways of establishing new political authority and influence included, among others, reorganization of the high-level Party organs and their members. Persistent challenges by other CCP leaders, according to Zhou, could result in weakness in foreign policy, blunders in administration, and lack of adequate attention to vital foreign policy issues. The others could also undermine Zhou's leadership and prestige within both the Party and the government. As such, Zhou had to maintain his political resiliency at all times, and he was extremely successful in achieving this end. His political longevity, in turn, contributed substantially to the stability of China's foreign policy.

PART 3

The Reality of National Power and the Foundations of Chinese Foreign Policy

CHAPTER 7

Zhou and Sino-Soviet Relations

Its failure to come to terms with the United States in late 1949 left the newly established Chinese Communist government in a precarious diplomatic and military position. Defense against possible U.S. military attack without substantial outside help was at best a tenuous proposition, and, under the circumstances, China's alliance with the Soviet Union, engineered by Zhou, was the most realistic alternative. Zhou would have attempted to maintain a delicate balance between the two superpowers as the cornerstone of Chinese foreign policy, if it were at all possible. Yet, considering the uncompromising, hostile attitude of the United States, he judged that China simply could not afford to lose the military and economic support of the Soviet Union.[1]

By 1949 the antifascist alliance of World War II had broken apart, and the Cold War between the United States and the Soviet Union was well under way. The two superpowers and their respective allies faced off across Europe and, in Asia, established governments, some colonial and others newly independent, battled Communist-led wars of national liberation. In a matter of months postwar international politics had taken on a bipolar power configuration, with the United States and the Soviet Union at sword's point around the world. The United States' emergence as the chief rival of both China and the Soviet Union was significant because of the decisive U.S. military superiority in East Asia and the Pacific region generally, the Americans' growing influence in Korea and Japan, and their bilateral relations with the GMD government in Taiwan. Zhou knew that the CCP would not have enough leverage after its rise to national power to play the two superpowers off against each other; therefore, he reasoned, China's global strategy and its immediate self-interest in Asia could be much better served by an alliance with the Soviet Union. At the same time, he was apprehensive that China might become submerged in the Soviet power orbit and, thus, initially, he tried to persuade the United States to quit supporting the GMD government under Jiang and also sought to maintain a distance from Moscow. Zhou seemed to believe that, unless state-to-state relations with the United States were established, China's policy of inclining toward the Soviet Union was the only available means of counterbalancing the threat posed by the United States.

While the United States remained the dominant power in the Pacific region and exercised significant control over Japan after World War II, the Soviet Union reestablished its controlling position in northeastern Asia, and both countries raced to expand their power and influence in postwar China. Zhou, who envisaged China as an independent entity beholden to neither of the two superpowers, was to be a vital part of the new structure of international relations in postwar East Asia.[2] In his efforts to promote genuine national independence Zhou embarked on a successful bid for coleadership of the Communist world. At the same time, he tried to conserve China's resources for internal reconstruction by avoiding large-scale military confrontation with the United States. Given the tremendous disparity in both military and economic capabilities between China and the United States, it was essential for Zhou to focus first and foremost on the problem of national security. Zhou's foreign policy orientation, aimed at improving of national security, stressed the strategic value of carving out an important role for China in Asia and increasing its influence in the Communist bloc. Indispensable to these objectives was the formation of an alliance with the Soviet Union. China's international status as coleader of world communism would be reinforced by such a military alliance, and direct Soviet military and economic support could accelerate China's internal reconstruction.

Even though Zhou regarded alliance with the Soviet Union as his country's main security device against the United States, he was equally determined that China should not become a Soviet satellite. For thirty years Zhou had devoted his life to Communist revolution for the purpose of achieving China's independence and equality with the other major powers in the world community.[3] Ideology aside, the national interest of China overrode all other considerations. His attitude toward the Soviet Union, while publicly one of cordial and mutual cooperation, was essentially ambivalent. From the last years of World War II to the conclusion of the Sino-Soviet alliance in 1950, Zhou vacillated between viewing the Soviet Union as the key element in curbing U.S. expansion in the Far East and as an obstacle to his desire for reconciliation with the United States. The underlying reasons for this dilemma were related to his attitude toward the system of alliance, which was in turn linked to his perception of China's self-interest.

A treaty, in Zhou's opinion, was a useful instrument through which China's national strength and influence could be enhanced. It was his responsibility as premier and foreign minister of the PRC to formulate a coherent foreign policy that would integrate the nation's military, economic, and diplomatic strategies. For Zhou all alignments, whether formalized in alliance or tacitly struck, were conditional. Each arrangement was but one more means at China's disposal, and no single alignment could satisfy China's overall interests. Chinese vital interests alone, not those of other states, were the ultimate measure of the utility of an alignment or alliance.

In weighing the power balance in the winter of 1949-50, two aspects were central to Zhou's strategy for safeguarding China's national interest: the balance of military power between the United States and the Soviet Union to ensure China's national security and the question of China's independent status in the world community. National security, more than anything else, was Zhou's primary objective. His endeavor to achieve this end also had two other aspects, territorial and military. It is clear that China and the Soviet Union were in the same defensive position vis-à-vis U.S. expansion in Asia. In the three-cornered Chinese-American-Soviet competition, curbing excessive U.S. expansion in postwar Asia was a common Chinese-Soviet interest. Zhou wished, above all, to prevent a clash between China and either of the two superpowers.

An essential aspect of Zhou's view of the international situation at the end of 1949 was his stress on China's independent status in the world community.[4] At the end of the Chinese civil war the Communist government in Beijing was left with a devastated economy and the formidable task of protecting China's national security against U.S. military supremacy in the Far East. At this stage Zhou seemed to entertain no illusion that reconciliation with the United States would be achieved quickly. He recognized that an alliance with Moscow against Washington could inherently restrict China's foreign policy options as well as the latitude of its diplomatic maneuverability. Since the close relations of the United States with Taiwan constituted a serious threat to the Beijing government, Zhou felt that an alliance with Moscow was urgently needed to overcome this vulnerability. The United States, instead of withdrawing from Asia after World War II, as expected, was now deeply involved both militarily and economically in Japan, South Korea, Taiwan, and the Philippines. China must, in Zhou's view, adapt itself to the emerging constellations of forces in the Communist bloc and in the world at large.[5] An alliance with the Soviet Union at this crucial phase meant that China could play the Soviet Union off against the United States and its clients, Japan and Taiwan.

These were Zhou's major considerations when he entered into direct negotiations with the Soviet government in Moscow in the winter of 1949-50.

Zhou's pragmatic moves, directed at reinforcing Sino-Soviet relations, were central to the task of promoting China's national security. It was also important for Zhou to adjust China's foreign policy to suit the changing international situation so that it would reflect new power realities in the world arena. Immediate and long-term interests, Zhou argued, required China to bridge the gap between international power relations and its search for complete independence.

Zhou was summoned by Mao to Moscow on January 20, 1950, when the Mao's initial talks with Stalin entered a more serious phase. Zhou took part in extensive discussions with Stalin and A. Y. Vyshinsky from January 21 to February 14. He tried his best to resolve problems such as the terms of a treaty of alliance between China and the Soviet Union, the status of the Chinese Changchun Railway and of Ports Arthur and Dairen, Soviet credits to China, and trade relations between the two countries.

Zhou wanted to prevent U.S.-Soviet cooperation at all costs and to keep the Soviet Union as close an ally as possible in order to ensure China's territorial security and Asian peace. One of his assumptions from the outset of the negotiations was that Japan would eventually recover from its defeat and would then develop an expansionist role in postwar Asia with the economic and military support of the United States. While in Moscow, Zhou proceeded to negotiate for a military alliance and an economic agreement between China and the Soviet Union. He wanted, above all, to have a carefully crafted elaboration of China's bilateral relations with the Soviet Union so as to establish such relations on a firm and clear basis—not one of dependence but, rather, of cooperation.[6] Furthermore, the military, economic, and technical agreements between the two countries would give substance to the new alliance. The Soviet alliance could provide CCP leaders with two distinct advantages: (1) the opportunity to reconstruct China's economy through Soviet economic assistance; and (2) the reinforced military strength vis-à-vis the United States and its clients.

It is clear that the quest for national security was the basis of Zhou's approach to the Sino-Soviet relationship. Although Beijing and Moscow shared the ideology of communism, it was Chinese interests that in the final analysis determined Zhou's diplomatic negotiations with his Soviet counterpart. Two specific elements must be pointed out. First, most of the CCP leaders, including Zhou, were also military men; therefore, their realistic appraisal of the importance of joint Sino-Soviet military forces was fundamental to their sanction of this policy orientation. Second, the Chinese negotiators, Zhou in particular, insisted from the beginning of the Sino-Soviet negotiations on the principle of equality between the two countries as a prerequisite of any formal agreement.

He pushed this principle one step further to the concept of equal but different partners. Zhou was successful in incorporating the principle of equality in the Sino-Soviet Treaty of Friendship, Alliance, and Mutual Assistance, as both parties agreed "in conformity with the principles of equality, mutual benefit, mutual respect for national sovereignty and territorial integrity, and noninterference in the internal affairs of the other contracting party, to develop and consolidate economic and cultural ties between China and the Soviet Union, to render each other all possible economic assistance and to carry out the necessary economic cooperation."[7]

An excellent example of Zhou's emphasis on the practicality of an alliance can be seen in his proposal for joint military action in the case of a clash with the United States. This approach exemplified his intention to address the issue of power imbalance in postwar East Asia as quickly as possible. It also reflected Zhou's genuine belief that military considerations were an integral part of diplomatic maneuvers.

During the course of the negotiations, which lasted three weeks, Zhou discussed concrete issues in detail with the Soviet side; it soon became apparent that an agreement was possible, because by early February Zhou had managed to convince his Soviet counterpart of the practical value of a military alliance between the two countries. The precise military arrangements were then worked out. Zhou seized upon the success of his negotiations with Moscow as an opportunity for renewed emphasis on the central theme of promoting "mutual benefit." In the treaty both parties agreed "to adopt all necessary measures at their disposal for the purpose of preventing the resumption of aggression and violation of peace on the part of Japan or any other state that may collaborate with Japan directly or indirectly in acts of aggression."[8] In case one party was attacked by Japan or any state allied with it, thus becoming involved in a state of war, the other party would "immediately render military and other assistance by all means at its disposal."[9]

The treaty confined China's freedom of action within narrow limits, especially for making diplomatic initiatives. By the treaty both parties were bound "not to conclude any alliance directed against the other contracting party" and "not to take part in any coalition or in any actions or measures directed against the other contracting party."[10] On the other hand, it provided China with a measure of security. In addition, the Soviet government agreed to grant long-term credits amounting to 300 million U.S. dollars at 1 percent interest over a period of five years for the purchase of machinery and equipment from the Soviet Union.[11] The Chinese government agreed to redeem the credits, as well as the interest on them, in actual goods and hard currency in the course of ten years, the first payment to be effected not later than December 31, 1954.

More specifically, the Chinese Changchun Railway and the military installations at the Manchurian naval base of Port Arthur would be returned to China
immediately upon the conclusion of a peace treaty with Japan or not later than
the end of 1952. Soviet troops would then be withdrawn from Port Arthur. The
question of Port Dairen would "be further considered"; the agreement stipulated, however, that the administration of Dairen fully belonged to the Chinese
government.[12] Technically, joint Sino-Soviet administration was to continue in
Manchuria, as both the Chinese Changchun Railway and Port Arthur were still
to be used by both countries. The agreement also called for Chinese recognition
of Mongolia's independence. These provisions, undoubtedly, represented
Zhou's "concessions" in return for economic aid.

The Treaty of Friendship, Alliance, and Mutual Assistance, signed on
February 14, 1950, became the cornerstone of the new China's foreign policy
for a greater part of its first decade. The signing of the treaty represented an
important first step in the long and complex process of restoring China to major
power status. It came into existence at a time when China was under the shadow
of U.S. military supremacy, there was a threat that Japanese militarism would
be revived, and the United States backed Taiwan. It was perhaps a short-term
coalition for specific purposes, but its practical value was amply demonstrated
with the outbreak of the Korean War;[13] the Sino-Soviet treaty effectively
prevented the United States from attacking Chinese military targets for fear of
escalating the localized conflict in Korea into a full-fledged atomic war with the
Soviet Union. Given the problems and circumstances of the time, Zhou
achieved what was possible after five weeks in Moscow. Soviet power offered
China protection against a resurgent Japan and also against the United States.
In conformity with Zhou's line of reasoning at the conference table, the phrase
"by all means at its disposal" was added after "the other contracting party shall
immediately render military and other assistance."[14] The new Sino-Soviet
relationship was not simply an ideological coalition but also a union of parallel
interests in which the Chinese government, under Zhou's guidance, intended
to maintain its independence.

Zhou's search for China's national security was accomplished in several
ways during the years 1949 to 1954. First, through alliance with the Soviet
Union Zhou sought to inhibit the United States from taking advantage of its
nuclear capability. Second, an active role for China in the Communist bloc
could substantially enhance its bargaining position vis-à-vis the capitalist West.
Third, China should have the means for decisively responding to foreign
aggression on a selective basis; it must not put itself in a position in which the
only choice open to it was a general war. Less disruptive forms of confrontation
should replace large-scale, violent conflict. To deter foreign aggression it was

important to have flexibility and the resources to make immediate response possible.[15] Nevertheless, Zhou's approach was essentially a defensive, strategic outlook in response to the adverse trend in global power developments in the postwar era combined with an anticipated shift in the balance of power within the coming decade.

The period from 1949 to 1950 witnessed considerable Sino-Soviet cooperation. The Korean War, which started in June 1950, served to strengthen the Sino-Soviet alliance. It forced the Chinese and Russian Communists into extensive political and military cooperation. Before China's direct involvement in the Korean War, Zhou met Stalin in Sochi and posed the question of whether or not "Chinese troops ought to be moved into the North Korean territory in order to block the path of the Americans and South Koreans."[16] According to Nikita Khrushchev, Zhou's and Stalin's initial conclusion was that it would be "fruitless for the Chinese to intervene."[17] Khrushchev added, however, "Just before Zhou Enlai (Chou En-lai) was to return home, one of them—either Zhou Enlai on Mao Zedong's (Mao Tse-tung's) instructions or else Stalin himself—reopened the whole matter."[18] The outcome was that Zhou and Stalin "agreed that China should give active support to North Korea."[19] Both believed that the Chinese troops that had already been stationed along the border "could manage the situation completely" and "would beat back the American and South Korean troops and save the situation from disaster."[20]

During August and September 1952 Zhou was again in Moscow for negotiations on issues left unresolved by the 1950 treaty of friendship and alliance. According to an auxiliary agreement in the treaty, control of the Chinese Changchun Railway and the naval base at Port Arthur were to have passed to the Chinese government upon the conclusion of a peace treaty with Japan or, in any case, not later than the end of 1952. Zhou was accompanied by economic experts Ch'en Yun, a Politburo member, and Li Fuchun, a key member of the State Planning Commission. Both Ch'en and Li took part in negotiations with the Soviets concerning the extent and types of Soviet technical and economic assistance during the period of China's first Five-Year Plan, from 1953 to 1957. Zhou's extensive negotiations with the Soviet government secured the return of all rights and property of the Chinese Changchun Railway to China without compensation. Soviet troops, however, would continue to remain in Port Arthur for the time being on the basis of "joint use" of the facilities.[21] The reason given for the extension of the Soviet military presence at Port Arthur was the Chinese concern over the Japanese treaty with the United States and the potential danger of war in the Pacific area. An increase in Soviet assistance and a long-term loan to China were also formalized.

The mutual profession of friendship between China and the Soviet Union was expressed in many ways. For instance, Zhou tried to promote China's vital interests by collaborating with the Soviet Union in the international sphere. At the 1954 Geneva Conference he played a major role in championing the causes of Ho Chih-ming and the neutralization of Indochina. On their part the Soviet leaders accepted China's position as associate leader in the international Communist movement. During Khrushchev's state visit to Beijing in September and October 1954, a joint declaration was signed by the two governments to reiterate that the relationship between China and the Soviet Union was based on "the principles of equality, mutual advantage, mutual respect of state sovereignty, and territorial integrity."[22] There was no specific reference to China's acceptance of the Soviet Union as the leader of the Communist bloc, nor was proletarian internationalism mentioned. In his address to the Soviet Council of Ministers, Soviet Foreign Minister V. M. Molotov referred to China as "coleader" of the Communist bloc. "The most important result of the Second World War," said Molotov, "was the organization, side by side with the world capitalist camp, of the world camp of socialism and democracy headed by the Soviet Union and the PRC."[23]

Zhou's initial efforts in foreign affairs seemed to be confined to countries bordering China and to the Communist bloc. His strategies and policies in the international arena were influenced by the CCP's ideological orientation. At the core of Communist ideology was the basic theme that the world was divided into two opposing camps, capitalist and socialist. It was asserted that conflicts between these two camps were inevitable because the capitalist forces were inherently expansionist and unwilling to accommodate the rise of the socialists. The workable formula, in Zhou's estimation, was somewhere between ideological prescriptions and political realities. Accordingly, his attention was focused on the issue of national security. The formation and maintenance of a "united" socialist camp led by the Soviet Union and China could be the cornerstone of a broader strategy.

A discernable trend toward achieving a delicate balance between Communist ideology and political realism was to emerge, against this background, in Zhou's handling of China's relations with the Soviet Union and the Communist states in Eastern Europe. This approach was reflected in his position on the Polish and Hungarian uprisings in 1956. Despite his previous focus on Asian affairs, Zhou was quick to sense the unique situation in Eastern Europe in 1956 and took the initiative to pacify the Polish and Hungarian leaders, on the one hand, and to promote the unity of the socialist camp, on the other. The way in which the Soviet Union had conducted its de-Stalinization campaign left the impression that the Soviets viewed the problem of the international

Communist movement as only their concern. Zhou viewed their failure to consult with leaders of other Communist parties and states as a very serious issue. In retrospect, Khrushchev's de-Stalinization, which resulted in political disorders among various Communist states in Eastern Europe during 1956, provided Zhou with an opportunity to articulate the official Chinese views on Communist interstate relations and to help define the desired new intra-Communist bloc relationship.

On December 24, 1956, the Chinese government announced that Zhou, who was then touring Southeast Asia, would visit the Soviet Union, Poland, and Hungary in January 1957. On his visit to Moscow in early January to discuss the Eastern European situation with Soviet leaders, Zhou criticized them for interfering in Poland's internal affairs and brandishing the big stick to thwart any policy or action that ran counter to the Kremlin's decision. Nevertheless, he endorsed the Soviets' "determination to eliminate abnormal features that existed in its relations with other socialist states."[24] It was his intention to bring the norms of "genuine discussion," "amicable consultation," "the Five Principles of Peaceful Coexistence," and "proletarian internationalism" into the discussion.[25]

From Moscow he journeyed to Poland and Hungary. In his speeches at Warsaw and Budapest in mid-January Zhou pointed to the "mistakes" in the mutual relations of Communist countries and suggested that "these mistakes should be corrected."[26] In Warsaw Zhou complimented Wladyslaw Gomulka and other Polish leaders for "improving" and "strengthening" Poland's relations with the Soviet Union and indicated that China would oppose Moscow's undue interference in their domestic affairs.[27] The joint communiqué issued at Warsaw also took account of the "concrete conditions" that existed in individual socialist countries and emphasized China's support for Poland's efforts to strengthen "socialism based on Lenin's principles."[28] It also supported the Polish desire for respect of its sovereignty and for noninterference in its domestic affairs by other socialist countries.

In Budapest Zhou criticized the Soviet leadership for not observing the principles of equality of nations and proletarian internationalism. Nevertheless, he promised China's support to János Kádár, leader of the Soviet-backed Hungarian government. He said that China supported the Soviet Union's effort "to smash the counterrevolution" in Hungary and assured Kádár that the Chinese government would support the program of the Hungarian Communist Party and the Hungarian government as long as it did not impair "the unity of the socialist bloc" and the cohesion of the Warsaw Treaty Organization, or Warsaw Pact.[29]

After returning to Moscow from Budapest on January 18, 1957, Zhou and Bulganin issued a joint communiqué concerning the Soviet handling of relations between Communist states,[30] in which China's "Five Principles of

Peaceful Coexistence" were endorsed as the proper basis for Communist interstate relations. The communiqué reaffirmed that "the socialist countries are independent and sovereign states and relations between them are based upon the Leninist principle of national equality."[31] Problems arising between Communist states should be worked out through genuine exchanges of views and solved "through frank consultations and comradely discussion."[32] "In the mutual relations between the socialist states," it asserted, "there are no essential contradictions and conflicting interests. Even if in the past there were some mistakes and shortcomings in these relations, at the present time they are being overcome and eliminated."[33] It was Zhou's conviction that "these mistakes and shortcomings can by no means eclipse the fundamental and principal aspect of the relations between socialist countries—that of mutual assistance and cooperation. . . . It is fully possible to combine the unity of socialist countries and the independence of each individual country in their mutual relations."[34]

Back in Beijing Zhou reiterated the principle for the resolution of differences among Communist states. In his report to the NPC on June 26, 1957, he summed up the Chinese approach to the developing pattern of Communist interstate relations. "International socialist solidarity," said Zhou, "based on proletarian internationalism and the principle of equality among nations is unbreakable."[35] In Zhou's view differences between socialist states were to be expected, and, as a result, they would be resolved through comradely discussion and consultation. If these differences could not be worked out, they should at least be minimized; otherwise, the solidarity of the Communist bloc simply could not be maintained. Moreover, to uphold the principle of national equality required a commitment to the practice of open discussion and mutual consultation through intra-Party channels. Zhou felt that genuine unity of the Communist bloc could be achieved only if each Communist state respected the independence and equal rights of the other. Consequently, any issue with reference to common interests should be discussed directly by all parties concerned.

In retrospect, the Polish and Hungarian crises in the autumn of 1956 provided Zhou with his first major opportunity to play a mediating role in the affairs of the Communist world. On the whole, he wanted to preserve China's close relations with the Soviet Union while offering the Polish and Hungarian governments support as an incentive to move away from Moscow's total control. During his tour of Warsaw, Budapest, and Moscow he chose to stress the need to maintain the unity of the Communist bloc under the leadership of the Soviet Union, but at the same time he reiterated the importance of satisfying the legitimate aspirations of Communist governments throughout Eastern Europe to attain greater internal autonomy.[36] One of Zhou's main themes was that the leadership of the Soviet Union could not be accepted without qualification. He also wanted to seize the opportunity to form a new pattern of intrabloc relations. According to Zhou, the basic formula should allow the Communist countries in Eastern Europe to enjoy a substantial degree of independence in managing their internal affairs, and at the same time they should strive to maintain the unity of the socialist camp. This new pattern of relations among socialist countries should restrain the tendency toward both "great-nation" chauvinism and excessive small-state nationalism.

The Communist bloc, as a collective entity in contemporary international relations, ought to be guided and united by the common interests of its member states and by their common ideology. It was important, therefore, to work out a viable formula for intrabloc relations. If the leaders of the Communist countries failed to achieve this basic objective, the weakening and even the eventual collapse of the Communist bloc could be anticipated. This was one of the major issues repeatedly raised by Zhou during his discussions with Soviet leaders in Moscow.[37] In his talks with Gomulka and Kádár, Zhou also indicated China's concern about the weakening condition of the Warsaw Pact alliance. He suggested that this weakening would create a real threat to the countries in the socialist camp of being overtaken by Western imperialism.[38] Zhou felt that unity among the socialist countries of Eastern Europe, headed by the Soviet Union, was the most powerful guarantee of peace as a whole.[39] The aggressive forces of imperialism were not afraid of one Poland or one China; what they feared was unity among the socialist countries.

A close examination of Zhou's speeches and statements at Budapest, Warsaw, and Moscow clearly reveal his intention to establish Communist interstate relations on a new footing of national independence and group identity. The approach also reflected his desire to create a new paradigm for the relationship between China and the Soviet Union. Zhou was fully aware of the reality of Soviet predominance in Eastern Europe. His support for the greater independence of the Communist countries in Eastern Europe from the Soviet Union provided him with an inroad to the socialist camp and earned him enormous prestige among those countries. More important, independence for the Eastern European countries would be the best insurance of China's independence vis-à-vis the Soviet Union.

The Soviet policy of détente with the West, especially with the United States, created considerable anxiety for CCP leaders, as they began to doubt the prospect of recovering Taiwan. In deciding to renew military pressure on the Chinese offshore islands, Zhou and other CCP leaders hoped to force Moscow to give China greater support. On August 28, 1958, Beijing provoked the Taiwan Strait crisis by heavy bombardment of Quemoy. Ostensibly, this military action was taken to discourage the acceptance of the "two China" policy by international organizations and conferences.[40] In effect, it preempted the military attack by the GMD forces of the Chinese mainland, and it also made it necessary for the Soviet Union to shed its ambiguity in the realm of diplomacy.

Moscow watched the developments for a week before promising Beijing, on August 31, "more and material aid" and issuing a warning against the assumption that U.S. hostilities against China could be prevented from spreading to other regions.[41] It is important to point out, however, that the Soviet Pacific fleet played no role at all throughout the crisis, nor was there a suggestion of any other related Soviet military activities. Moscow specifically committed itself to responding only to a U.S. attack on China itself. In fact, Moscow did not commit itself to any involvement if the United States responded militarily to a Chinese air or sea attack in a way that avoided a direct attack on the mainland. It was only when Soviet leaders were certain that there was no danger of nuclear war that they pledged their support for China in its military confrontation with the United States.[42]

Zhou and other CCP leaders believed that in order for China to achieve its national objectives, including the recovery of Taiwan, China and the Soviet Union had to apply increasing pressure on the United States. Thus, Zhou was greatly disturbed by Khrushchev's growing "revisionism" and search for accommodation with the West. While Zhou did not completely abandon the premise of bloc solidarity, he became increasingly concerned about the likelihood that such solidarity might compromise the vital security interests of China. From his point of view the crisis of the Chinese offshore islands and the Sino-Indian border dispute of 1959 fully demonstrated that the Soviet Union was not prepared to offer China the desired support, both military and diplomatic.

On June 20, 1959, the Soviet government dealt China another blow. It unilaterally rescinded the agreement of October 15, 1957, to provide China with nuclear assistance.[43] The Soviet refusal to provide China with a prototype of an atomic bomb and technical data on its construction, in Zhou's view, was ample proof that Soviet leaders were determined to keep China dependent. As a result, Zhou began to see Soviet foreign policy aims as an obstacle to the further growth of China's influence in the international arena. These events reinforced Zhou's belief that China should develop its own nuclear capability. He and other CCP leaders now became convinced that China could not depend on the Soviet Union to build its nuclear arsenal and that the Chinese government had no alternative but to rely on its own resources to develop nuclear weapons.

Zhou still sought to avoid open disagreement with Soviet leaders, even though significant differences had emerged between the two countries. At the Twenty-first Congress of the CPSU, held in Moscow in January 1958 Zhou cautiously recognized the historic role of the CPSU and the fact that the Soviet Union stood at the head of the socialist camp. The consolidation of the countries of the socialist camp, which was led by the Soviet Union and the consolidation of the unity of the ranks of the international Communist movement, of which the CPSU was the center, were, in Zhou's view, still the sacred duty of Communists everywhere.[44]

In his interview with Edgar Snow in October 1960 Zhou indicated that the Communist governments of China and the Soviet Union were expected to "formulate their policies by integrating the principles of Marxism-Leninism with the specific conditions of their respective countries."[45] Therefore, the two governments would certainly have differences in the way they looked at certain questions. "To have no differences whatsoever," said Zhou, "is impossible in the realm of thinking. Even in the thinking of a single person, one sometimes looks at a question in one way and at another time in another way."[46] Thus, Zhou believed that "differences in emphasis in the policies of the two countries" were bound to occur.[47] He added: "In a specified period of time, it is a natural thing that there are some differences between two parties on theoretical questions and on ways of looking at things. To be exactly identical would indeed be something strange and incomprehensible."[48] What is significant in this interview is the fact that Zhou openly acknowledged the policy differences between China and the Soviet Union. The basic issue between the two major Communist countries, according to Zhou, was whether the combined resources of the Communist bloc should be used to serve separate national interests or to support anti-imperialist forces throughout the world.

At the Twenty-second Congress of the CPSU, held in Moscow in October 1961, Khrushchev publicly attacked the Albanians. Khrushchev's charge was based on his contention that Albanian leaders had failed to comply with the de-Stalinization policy adopted by the Congress of the CPSU in 1956.[49] Thus, the Albanians had violated the general lines of the international Communist movement. The real issue was: What motivated Khrushchev to initiate a frontal attack on Albania at this point in time? The attack was the first step on the part of the Soviet leadership to curb the steadily growing dissident voices in the international Communist movement. Khruschchev's attitude toward Albania illustrated his attempt to reimpose Soviet control over the Communist camp. Therefore, Albania's defiance of the Soviet Union in 1960 and 1961 was a refusal to subordinate national perspectives to the primacy of Soviet policy. In fact, one major political objective of Albanian leaders was to acquire national autonomy in both domestic affairs and foreign policy. As Khrushchev intended, his frontal attack required every Communist party to take a public position on the Albanian question.

This development boded ill for CCP leaders. First, it clearly demonstrated that inside the Communist bloc the Soviet Union was reasserting its dominant role, thus excluding China from sharing the leadership. The close tie between Albania and China made Khrushchev's attack on Albania a thinly veiled assault on China. Second, Chinese leaders suspected Moscow of holding private talks with the United States at their expense.

Recognizing the true nature of the attack, Zhou rose to Albania's defense and strongly criticized such unfraternal behavior. He challenged the Soviet leaders by declaring that such a public and unilateral attack on a ruling Communist party would neither contribute to the unity of world communism nor help resolve the problem at hand.[50] In a speech delivered in October 1961 concerning the Albanian issue, Zhou considered Khrushchev's accusation as anything but a "serious Marxist-Leninist attitude" and felt it threatened to play into the hands of the enemy.[51] It was Zhou's central theme that all fraternal parties and states were equal and that the Soviet leadership had extended Communist intraparty conflicts into Communist interstate relations. According to Zhou, the Soviet-Albanian controversy invalidated the Moscow Declaration of 1957 and the Moscow Statement of 1960, both of which had confirmed the principles of equality and independence for all Communist states.[52]

Relations between the Soviet Union and Albania were by no means unique, for the pattern between them raised, in principle, the issue of relations among all the Communist states. The Soviet attitude toward Albania, if not basically changed, would constitute a serious impediment to developing relations among the Communist states along the line agreed to in the Moscow Declaration and the Moscow Statement. In Zhou's view the one-sided Soviet criticism of Albania demonstrated that the Soviets were not interested in working with other Communist countries to arrive at intermediate measures. These measures would include the gradual development of certain rules and principles, acceptable to all Communist states, regarding their mutual relations. They would be employed to formulate a guiding principle of consensus without fear of Soviet dominance in relations between the Soviet Union and other Communist states, upon which Zhou felt that the Soviet Union had no legal power to impose its own decisions. Furthermore, Soviet leaders had no right to expect the leaders of other Communist states to accept their policy decisions. Therefore, no resolution of any congress of any Communist Party could be taken as the common line of the international Communist movement or as binding on other fraternal parties.

To CCP leaders the Soviet attitude toward Albania once again manifested the great-nation chauvinist tendency in Moscow's relations with other Communist parties and countries.[53] Zhou's unusually sharp response in October

1961 to the Soviet condemnation of Albania was a warning to Moscow to refrain from similar treatment of other Eastern European states and of China itself. When Khrushchev denounced Stalin at the congress of the CPSU, Zhou registered his defiance by leading the Chinese Communist delegation to Lenin's and Stalin's graves to pay their respects on October 21, 1961.

The second de-Stalinization at the Twenty-Second Congress of the CPSU convinced Zhou and other CCP leaders that the Soviet Union was embarking on a "revisionist" course of international development—that is, détente with the United States—and that Soviet foreign policy would endanger China's national interests. To break away from Soviet dominance Zhou offered economic, scientific, and technical assistance to Albania and declared that the Chinese people were proud of their friendship with the Albanians and admired their relentless struggle against revisionism. On December 31, 1963, Zhou arrived in Albania for a ten-day visit to reinforce China's close association with the Albanian leader, Enver Hoxha.

In 1963 and 1964 the historic border problem between China and the Soviet Union escalated into a dispute over conflicting territorial claims.[54] Before the 1960s no major border tensions, disputes, or crises emerged between the two countries. Yet, as political relations between them deteriorated, frictions in their border regions increased. The once placid boundary became a long line of hostile confrontations, and each side feared that the other would exploit the situation. Both sides took measures to tighten border controls, strengthen local defense, and reinforce their regular military forces near the border. Zhou indicated that the Chinese government wanted to examine the old treaties signed by imperial China during the age of European imperialism and to renegotiate those unequal treaties in order to settle the Sino-Soviet boundary disputes peacefully. Pending a negotiated settlement, he suggested, both countries should maintain the status quo along the common borders.

In his report to the Fourth National People's Congress on January 21, 1964, Zhou stressed China's need to stand on its own. He also warned that ultrachauvinism was a detriment to world revolution. "Regarding our relationship with Russia," said Zhou, "we have been, through no fault of our own, confronted with extreme difficulties, and we have suffered from them."[55] He went on to explain: "However, we would continue to stress the importance of solidarity and do our best to maintain a normal relationship."[56] The first open reference to the proposed Sino-Soviet negotiations came when Zhou told Snow on January 23, 1964, "We have reached an agreement with the Soviet Union that negotiations be held on Sino-Soviet boundary questions."[57]

On February 25 the two sides finally met in Beijing to discuss border and territorial problems. These talks proved to be fruitless, and they were broken off before the end of the year. After Khrushchev stepped down as leader of the Soviet Union, in October 1964, Zhou again led a Chinese delegation to Moscow. He attended the celebration of the forty-seventh anniversary of the CPSU; the new Soviet leaders, headed by Leonid Brezhnev, greeted Zhou cordially on November 5 and involved him in high-level discussions. Although these talks did not bring about satisfactory results, Zhou's immediate positive response to the new Soviet leadership at least showed the CCP's hope of reconciling with the Soviet Union. Back in Beijing on November 14, however, the CCP leadership cautioned the Chinese people against the danger of "Khrushchevism without Khrushchev in person."[58]

During 1965 Soviet leaders seemed to be conciliatory toward China, and, for a while, the Sino-Soviet frontier appeared to be quiet. But tensions began to mount as Mao's antirevisionist Cultural Revolution went into full swing in 1966. Border incidents broke out again, particularly along the Amur and Ussuri Rivers between Manchuria and the Soviet Far East and in the northwestern section between Xinjiang and Soviet Central Asia. The Soviet leaders' position on their territorial dispute with China was unmistakably clear: they were prepared to uphold the Sino-Soviet boundary demarcation at all costs.

In mid-June 1966 Zhou paid a state visit to Rumania with a specific mission: to persuade the Rumanians to join the Chinese in their common struggle against the Soviet Union. The Rumanian leaders, for their part, wanted to use the occasion of Zhou's visit to demonstrate their stance of independence from the Soviet Union. At a state banquet held on June 17 Zhou praised Rumania's resistance to undue interference from outside and its continuous struggle "to defend its independence and sovereignty and the principle guiding the relations between fraternal parties and fraternal countries."[59] He promised that in their joint struggle the Rumanian people could always count on the support of the Chinese.

After eighteen months of intensive debate among top CCP leaders Zhou prevailed in his position that China must continue to practice a low-risk strategy by avoiding direct confrontation with the Soviet Union. He still maintained the hope that, by following a cautious strategy, it might be possible to improve relations between the two countries. The invasion of Czechoslovakia by Soviet troops occurred on August 21, 1968, and it dashed Zhou's illusion. Though he had little sympathy for Alexander Dubcek's experiment in democratic socialism in Czechoslovakia, Zhou viewed the right to national sovereignty both as a matter of principle and as an issue directly linked to China's own national interest. In a speech delivered at the Rumanian embassy in Beijing on August 23 he condemned the Soviet Union, saying it had become a "social imperialist" power. The Soviet invasion of Czechoslovakia was, he said, identical to Hitler's "aggression" against that country in 1938.[60] He further charged that a socialist country such as the Soviet Union in which a revisionist leadership took power would become something else. As the revisionists restored capitalism, the government would begin to behave in both domestic and foreign affairs like a capitalist rather than a socialist state. The Soviet maneuver in Czechoslovakia was "the inevitable result of the great-power chauvinism and national egoism practiced by the Soviet revisionist leading clique."[61] Zhou denounced the Soviet military invasion of Czechoslovakia as "the most barefaced and most typical specimen of fascist power politics played by the Soviet revisionist clique of renegades and scabs against its so-called allies. It marks the total bankruptcy of Soviet modern revisionism."[62]

After the Czechoslovakian incident Zhou introduced the term *social imperialism* to describe the conduct of Soviet foreign policy. Brezhnev's new doctrine of limited sovereignty sanctioned the right of Soviet military intervention in countries of the Communist camp.[63] At this point the Soviet threat to China was both ominous and immediate, for the Russians were already making thinly veiled warnings about a "preemptive" attack, preferably in concert with the United States, against Chinese nuclear installations. More than a million Russian troops were developed along the five thousand-mile Sino-Soviet border, hundreds of Soviet nuclear missiles were targeted at Chinese cities, and border clashes were growing in both frequency and intensity. The danger of a Sino-Soviet military confrontation reached a peak in early 1969, when two serious clashes took place on March 2 and 15 at Chenbao (Damansky) Island in the Ussuri River.[64] The border clashes confirmed Zhou's apprehension of Soviet expansion. He was now convinced that Soviet expansion was a fixed policy and an immediate threat to China's national security. He also came to the conclusion that the strategy of alliance with the Soviet Union was no longer relevant to the political and military realities in East Asia.

Both the Sino-Soviet border clashes in March and Brezhnev's proposal, in June 1969, of an Asian system of collective security, with all its anti-Chinese implications, served only to exacerbate Zhou's fears about Soviet intentions. Before 1969 the conflict between the two countries had been essentially ideological and political; now it developed into a direct military showdown. Each side saw in the other a growing threat to its own security, and both were prepared for large-scale military confrontations. Moreover, Moscow intensified its efforts to muster forces inside the Communist bloc against the Chinese. The border clashes occurred on the eve of the CCP's Ninth Party Congress in March 1969, dramatizing the Soviet threat and helping to mobilize domestic support for Zhou's new foreign policy strategy. To retain the necessary diplomatic flexibility in East Asia in the face of Soviet military hostilities, it now became imperative to improve China's relations with the West. The only effective alternative, under the circumstances, was actively to seek dialogue with the United States, with the hope of gaining support, diplomatic or otherwise, to counter Soviet expansion in East Asia and beyond. Furthermore, Zhou saw Soviet expansionism as a destabilizing factor that could upset the current international equilibrium. In this threat Zhou found it possible to identify China's goals and interests with those of the West. They now shared some basic foreign policy orientations and parallel interests. Under the changed circumstances Zhou envisioned a new strategic policy based on China's security interests—namely, a closer relationship with the West and, particularly, with the United States—feeling this could ward off the Soviet threat and hence safeguard China's national security.

Initially, Zhou's attempts at rapprochement with the United States encountered serious opposition from his radical colleagues, and his efforts were further hampered by the U.S. intervention in Cambodia in 1969 and 1970. Meanwhile, the Soviet Union increased its military moves along its common borders with China. As the danger to the Chinese government grew, some CCP leaders urged reconciliation with Moscow at almost any price. Zhou was opposed to such a course, but his diplomatic flexibility was limited insofar as the United States was still an opposing superpower. Therefore, avoiding of a large-scale war between China and the Soviet Union was still the major objective of Zhou's foreign policy orientation, and his willingness to negotiate on the boundary problem was still evident. In June 1969 the Sino-Soviet Joint Commission on Border Rivers met, holding its first talks in several years.

Soviet Premier Aleksey Kosygin attempted to meet Zhou at Ho Chih-ming's funeral, held in Hanoi on September 9, 1969, but Zhou left for Beijing before Kosygin was due to arrive. On his way back to the Soviet Union Kosygin stopped over in Soviet Central Asia; he there received word from Moscow that Zhou had agreed to meet with him. He changed his plans and flew to Beijing instead. Zhou met Kosygin at the Beijing Airport on September 11.[65] During their three-hour talk Zhou maintained the position that, as long as the Soviet Union recognized in principle the "unequal" nature of the nineteenth-century boundary treaties between czarist Russia and Qing China, a new agreement could be reached between the two nations.[66] He also proposed that both countries should try not only to avoid overt military conflict but also to resolve long-standing problems and to achieve a degree of mutual accommodation.[67]

Following the Zhou-Kosygin meeting frontier incidents on the Sino-Soviet border, which occurred almost daily during the spring and summer of 1969, virtually ceased. On October 7, 1969, the Chinese government announced that negotiations for resolving the border conflict would be held in Beijing at the deputy foreign minister level at a date still to be decided. It expressed the hope that the Soviet government would take a truly "serious and responsible attitude" toward border negotiations.[68] The border issue should be "settled peacefully," the statement went on, "even if it cannot be settled for the time being, the *status quo* of the border should be maintained and there should definitely be no resort to the use of force."[69] The announcement reiterated the official Chinese position that China did not demand the outright return of territory that czarist Russia had annexed in Siberia and Central Asia during the nineteenth century under what the Chinese contended were unequal treaties. New talks between deputy ministers finally began in Beijing on October 20, 1969, and diplomatic representation at the ambassadorial level was restored in 1970.

In the years from 1968 to 1970 Zhou's preoccupation with Soviet conflicts perceptibly shifted to a balance-of-power strategy designed to strengthen China's position vis-à-vis the Soviet Union. In 1969 the Zhou-Kosygin meeting at the Beijing airport, the official Chinese statement of October 7, and the opening of new negotiations gave the two nations a pause long enough to step out of their drift toward war. Despite each one's effort not to provoke new border incidents, however, an atmosphere of military confrontation continued. Buildups along the Soviet border rose from fifteen divisions in 1968 to twenty-one divisions in 1969, thirty in 1970, and more than forty in 1973. The border talks between the two countries eventually proved fruitless.

In addition, the Soviet policy of containing China was evident in new diplomatic initiatives with nations on China's periphery, such as Podgorny's visit to North Korea and Mongolia and Kosygin's visit to India, Pakistan, and Afghanistan in 1969; M. S. Kapist, head of the South Asian Division of the Soviet Foreign Office, visited Burma, Laos, Cambodia, and Japan in the same year. The visit of the Mongolian deputy foreign minister to Burma, Cambodia, Nepal, India, and Afghanistan in April 1969 was perceived as part of the Soviet-Mongolian campaign against China.

Another indicator was the advent of the Soviet-sponsored Asian collective security system in June 1969. The Chinese government regarded this as an attempt by the Soviet Union to step up its competition with the United States in Asia, particularly in the southeast, by taking advantage of the recent American defeat and U.S. resignation to its military limitations, implicit in the Nixon Doctrine. In strategic terms the Chinese government also regarded the collective security system as an anti-Chinese alliance. With some justification CCP leaders interpreted Soviet diplomatic moves—such as Brezhnev's Asian collective security plan and Kosygin's plan for a regional economic group consisting of Afghanistan, India, Iran, Pakistan, and the Soviet Union—as devices to encircle China with hostile and unfriendly neighbors. The Indo-Soviet entente, closer

Hanoi-Moscow links, and Moscow's strong opposition to a treaty of friendship between China and Japan were also regarded by CCP leaders as strategic actions by the Soviets against China.

Just as problems with China had been an important stimulus to the Soviet Union to reach agreements in the West, China's Soviet problem compelled Zhou to move in the same direction. Soviet expansionism in Asia thus set in motion patterns of realignment that would have long-range implications. Zhou, like Mao, was always mindful of the danger of China being encircled by the United States and the Soviet Union. For all his preoccupation with diplomacy Zhou never entirely departed from his belief in the use and threat of force as instruments of national policy. In retrospect, the Sino-Soviet military conflict along the Ussuri River in early 1969 achieved the immediate effect of warning the Chinese of their government's determination to use force; it was also instrumental in persuading the Chinese people to mend their fences with the United States.

Zhou was forced to reassess the foreign policy strategy in use since the early 1960s. Were the original policy goals still relevant in the changed international arena? How should China respond to growing Soviet power and influence in Asia? With the support of Mao, Zhou began to advocate a new global strategy that would enhance China's diplomatic imperatives as well as its economic and political aspirations. It was a strategy in which the Soviet Union was cast as the principal enemy; accordingly, it dictated diplomatic accommodation of the United States. Subtle changes could be detected in Zhou's new emphasis on diplomatic diversification and the greater attention devoted to détente policy with the United States. His overall military-security strategy was designed to develop a limited alignment with both the United States and Japan in order to curb the expansion of Soviet influence in Asia. To avoid diplomatic isolation and also to find a counterweight to Soviet hegemonism, the United States offered China the best possible option. Third World nations, though they could hold the key to creating a new world order in the future, were of secondary importance in relation to China's military security.

Despite his denunciation of "power politics," Zhou began to pursue an energetic balance-of-power strategy to maximize China's diplomatic flexibility and thus counteract Soviet expansion in Asia. At the same time, he thoroughly comprehended the gravity of the situation between China and the Soviet Union. A slight misstep could plunge China into a more extensive border war—a war that could increase China's diplomatic vulnerability and further delay its economic buildup. Therefore, despite border clashes between China and the Soviet Union, diplomacy still had a role to play in order to sustain a modicum of normalcy in their relationship. The forty Soviet divisions on the Chinese border were a constant threat, and Soviet leaders were planning a preemptive attack on the nuclear facilities in Xinjiang Province. Zhou knew the importance of preventing the Soviet use of force against China under all circumstances. The U.S. invasion of Cambodia at the end of April 1970 led Zhou to evaluate the relative threats posed to Chinese security interests by the Soviet Union and by the United States. Within the Party hierarchy there was a pro-Soviet and anti-U.S. tilt as a result of the U.S. invasion of Cambodia.[70] Internal debates among top CCP leaders focused on the question of whether the Soviet Union or the United States was China's main "enemy." The pro-Soviet faction had its base in the military and was led by Lin Biao. Zhou formed a coalition in late 1970 with many regional military leaders who neither liked nor trusted Lin, and this coalition of pragmatists and moderates within the Party was prepared to advocate a policy of détente with the United States and to adopt an economic policy of modernization. Top CCP leaders themselves remained sharply divided about whether China should improve its relations with the Soviet Union or reach an understanding with the United States.

Meanwhile, Zhou was ready to take advantage of existing antagonisms between the Soviet Union and the United States in his efforts to maximize China's national security. "If China sought détente," the American journalist Snow asked Zhou in an interview in Beijing on August 18, 1970, "would the possibilities be better for negotiating with Russia or with the United States?"[71] The premier's answer was, "I have been asking myself the same question."[72] Zhou's ambiguity regarding his intentions could confuse his opponents. Ensuing events proved that Soviet leaders had underestimated Zhou's determination to establish working relations with the United States, nor did they expect Zhou to be able to form a coalition to oppose the hegemony of the Soviet Union in Eastern Europe and beyond.

On the whole Zhou wanted to expand China's diplomatic maneuverability by normalizing its relations with the Soviet Union while establishing preliminary negotiations with the United States. China was vulnerable to nuclear devastation from both directions, and, therefore, Zhou was inclined to define the problem in terms of taking advantage of the future triangular relationship among all three nations. There were factions and influential individuals within the Party hierarchy who favored some sort of reconciliation with Moscow in preference to rapprochement with the United States. Zhou preferred to reduce tensions with both the United States and the Soviet Union, but he realized that, as long as Mao was alive and remained in power, a Sino-Soviet reconciliation was not likely. The United States' military presence in Vietnam and its invasion of Cambodia, however, made it difficult to persuade many CCP leaders to accept détente with the United States. Zhou thus had to cast his policy orientation as a strategy to check Soviet expansion in Asia. The United States was identified as the key to reordering international power realities. Cooperation with the United States was now promoted as very much in China's self-interest.

Zhou recognized that China's leverage with the Soviet Union against the United States was diminishing noticeably. Furthermore, he was convinced that, with U.S. power now retreating from Asia and Soviet power expanding, a Soviet embrace might be more perilous than continued hostility. Both Mao and Zhou were determined to affirm a foreign policy position within the Party hierarchy whereby China would never again play second fiddle to the Soviet Union within the Communist movement. Yet, since the Soviet Union was clearly unwilling to accept "parity" with China, and China did not possess sufficient capability to assert equality with the Soviet Union in the Communist bloc unilaterally, the conditions for a limited Sino-American reconciliation appeared to be present.

In his report to the Ninth Party Congress on August 24, 1973, Zhou observed that the Soviet Union appeared to be obsessed with China.[73] On November 7, 1974, Zhou asked Soviet leaders for a nonaggression pact meeting. He linked the idea to a pullback of forces along the disputed frontier. He disclosed that the idea of signing a nonaggression pact was part of an understanding he had reached with Kosygin on September 11, 1969. "The mutual understanding achieved in September 1969 at the meeting of the premiers of the two states," said Zhou, "that an agreement should be signed on nonaggression, non-use of force, maintenance of the *status quo* on the frontier, the prevention of military conflict and clashes, the separation of forces in disputed regions, and the solution of all frontier questions through talks—should be adhered to."[74] This proposal was rejected by Soviet leader Brezhnev as "absolutely unacceptable." In his report to the Fourth NPC on January 13, 1975, less than a year before his death, Zhou reiterated China's official position on the nature and conditions of Sino-Soviet boundary negotiations. He once again urged Soviet leaders to recognize the existence of boundary disputes between the two countries, to avoid military conflict, and to make the separation of forces in disputed regions. In addition, he asked Soviet leaders to engage in boundary negotiations with the Chinese government in order to solve the boundary disputes peacefully.[75]

As his health deteriorated after the signing of the Shanghai Communiqué in February 1972, Zhou continued to advocate a flexible foreign strategy. He saw it as an instrument for implementing his domestic policy of "Four Modernizations." Over a period of more than five years, from his meeting with Kosygin at the Beijing Airport in September 1969 to his last report to the NPC in January 1975, Zhou made repeated attempts to improve China's relations with the Soviet Union.[76] In this final report he did not close the door to the possibility of future boundary negotiations with the Soviet Union. As a major advocate of restraint and a balanced approach in diplomacy among CCP leaders, Zhou consistently practiced the principle of mutual adjustment insofar as circumstances permitted. Thus, it is reasonable to assume that he never completely abandoned his hope of reconciliation with the Soviet Union.

CHAPTER 8

Zhou and the Evolution of Sino-U.S. Relations

After World War II Zhou, as the CCP's chief negotiator, was prepared to develop a modus vivendi with the United States government as much because of the dominant U.S. power position in postwar Asia as because of the need for a flexible policy to strengthen China as an independent state. His exploratory endeavor was short-lived, however, in the face of Washington's negative response to his diplomatic overtures. The study of Beijing's relations with the United States from 1949 to 1976 provides a useful illustration of the interaction of policy, ideology, and practice in the context of Zhou's search for China's national security and opportunities for economic development.

Toward the last stage of World War II, the United States attempted to use China as a counterweight to Japan, thus restoring the Asian balance of power. Anticipating this postwar power realignment, the United States accorded China both legal and political status as a "great power." During the crucial phase of the Chinese civil war U.S. Secretary of State George C. Marshall sought to clarify Washington's official position by cautioning the U.S. embassy in China as early as August 13, 1948, that "developments in China are obviously entering into a period of extreme flux and confusion in which it will be impossible with surety to perceive clearly in advance the pattern of things to come."[1] He made it clear that the United States government must preserve "a maximum freedom of action";[2] he later warned that the United States "must not become directly involved in the Chinese civil war" and that the United States "must not assume responsibility for underwriting the Chinese government militarily and economically."³ It is obvious that at this point the U.S. government was reluctant to assume additional military and diplomatic responsibilities, with the accompanying commitment to maintain considerable forces for achieving "the objective of reducing the Chinese Communists to a completely negligible factor in China in the immediate future."⁴

With the founding of the People's Republic of China, the U.S. government was understandably concerned about the balance of power in Asia. In a speech to the San Francisco Commonwealth Club on March 15, 1950, Secretary of State Dean Acheson warned the Chinese people that, "whatever happens within their own country, they can only bring grave trouble on themselves and their friends, both in Asia and beyond, if they are led by their new rulers into aggressive or subversive adventures beyond their borders."⁵ Zhou rejected Acheson's assertion that the Sino-Soviet treaty was "hostile to the interests of the U.S." as well as to those of China, and he ridiculed it as the vain attempt of a "mosquito trying to shatter the fortress of world peace" (namely, the Sino-Soviet alliance).⁶ He advised the U.S. government "to cool down and look at the map! The affairs of the Asian people must never be interfered with by such American imperialists as Acheson and company on the other side of the Pacific Ocean!"⁷ Zhou also underscored Chinese suspicions about U.S. intentions when he noted that the United States "seized control over Japan and South Korea after World War II" and that it was also attempting "to control China, Indonesia, Vietnam, Thailand, Burma, and India."⁸

From the outset Zhou looked at the U.S. actions in the Taiwan Straits not only in the narrow context of U.S. intervention in the Chinese civil war but also in the broad framework of what he considered the aggression of U.S. imperialism against the Asian people. He viewed U.S. policy in Taiwan as the major obstacle to China's emergence as a major power. The U.S. military presence in Taiwan was regarded by Zhou as a symbol of continuing U.S. hostility toward China, part of the design of U.S. imperialists to once again dominate the Asian-Pacific region. The Korean War further eroded Sino-American relations. After the outbreak of the Korean War U.S. President Harry Truman announced, on June 27, 1950, that "the occupation of Formosa [Taiwan] by Communist forces would be a direct threat to the peace and security of the Pacific area and to United States forces performing their lawful and necessary functions in that area."⁹

Zhou's response to Truman's June 27 order placing the U.S. Seventh Fleet in the Taiwan Straits was both swift and unequivocal, revealing China's surprise and anger both at the abrupt change in U.S. operational policy and at the extent of the new American commitment. On June 28, at a meeting of the Central People's Government, Zhou described the intervention of the U.S. Seventh

Fleet in China's unfinished civil war as an "armed aggression against the territory of China" and a "total violation of the United Nations Charter,"[10] which Zhou viewed as one more step in the "conspiratorial schemes of American imperialism for aggression against China and to grab Asia by force."[11] Zhou charged not only that the Korean War was caused by the attack on North Korea by South Korea, with the backing of the United States, but also that this attack was part of a premeditated conspiracy designed to encircle China. He evoked the UN Charter to support his case against the action of the United States in Taiwan and announced China's determination to liberate the island regardless of any "obstructive action the imperialists may take."[12]

From Zhou's perspective Taiwan was part of China, and to deny the island's unification with the Chinese mainland was simply an act of aggression against China. "All the people of our country will certainly fight to the end single-mindedly," said Zhou, "to liberate Taiwan from the grasp of the American aggressors."[13] He then went on to predict that "the Chinese people who defeated Japanese imperialism and Jiang Jieshi, the hireling of American imperialism, will surely be victorious in driving off the American aggressors and in recovering Taiwan and all other territories belonging to China."[14] Yet, the most action-oriented part of Zhou's June 28 statement contained no threat of immediate action; rather, he had to content himself with a Last Judgment vision of the ultimate collapse of the United States, in which "all the oppressed nations and peoples of the East are undoubtedly capable of burying the vicious and hated American imperialist warmakers once and for all in the flames of the great struggle for national independence."[15] According to Zhou, "All that Truman's statement does is merely to expose his premeditated plan and put it into practice."[16] American interference in Taiwan was seen as part of an aggressive design to extend its imperialistic control over the whole of Asia, including Taiwan, Vietnam, and the Philippines.

In his cable to UN headquarters at Lake Success on August 20, 1950, Zhou expressed China's serious concern over the Korean issue. "Korea," noted Zhou, "is China's neighbor. The Chinese people cannot but be concerned about the solution of the Korean question."[17] He added, however, that "it must and can be settled peacefully."[18] On September 24, Zhou cabled UN headquarters to protest against the U.S. air intrusion over Andong, China. His wording went well beyond the accusation of "criminal action" contained in his August protests: "The case is even more serious than the strafings by the United States airplanes which occurred formerly . . . [and] exposes more clearly than ever the determination of the United States of America to extend the aggressive war against Korea, to carry out armed aggression on Taiwan, and to extend her aggression against China."[19]

Zhou also warned United Nations member states of their collective responsibility for curbing the enlargement of the Korean War. "The flames of war being extended by the United States in the East," stated Zhou, "are burning more fiercely. If the representatives of the majority of states attending the United Nations General Assembly should still be pliant to the manipulation of the United States and continue to play deaf and dumb to these aggressive crimes of the United States, they shall not escape a share in the responsibility for lighting up the war-flames in the East."[20] In view of the forthcoming General Assembly debate on the crossing of the 38th parallel in Korea, Zhou's references to "the manipulation of the United States" and "lighting up the war-flames" appear as thinly veiled pressure designed to swing the wavering delegations against continuing the conflict. In addition, Zhou indicated that the peace-loving peoples throughout the world "definitely will not stand in face of this with folded arms."[21] This was meant to be a hint about China's intention to intervene in the Korean War.

In his report to the Council of the Central People's Government on September 30, 1950, Zhou stated that, in spite of the Chinese people's desire for peace, they "never have been and never will be afraid to oppose aggressive war," adding that "the Chinese people absolutely will not tolerate foreign aggression, nor will they supinely tolerate seeing their neighbors being savagely invaded by the imperialists."[22] This was Zhou's strongest and clearest warning so far about the impending Chinese intervention in the Korean War. It is important to note that Zhou focused upon the UN command's crossing of the 38th Parallel as a possible casus belli.

U.S. military forces had, according to Zhou, invaded China's borders and might at any time expand military operations in Korea. On October 1 South Korean forces crossed the 38th Parallel. The next night Zhou summoned K. M. Panikkar to the Chinese Ministry of Foreign Affairs, and in the course of the meeting he told the Indian ambassador that "no country's need for peace was greater than that of China, but there were occasions when peace could be defended only by the determination to resist aggression."[23] Should U.S. troops cross the 38th Parallel, "they would encounter Chinese resistance."[24] On October 11 Beijing radio repeated the warning, and on October 18 Zhou sent a protest about the violation of the Manchurian border by U.S. aircraft.[25] The United States government did not attach too much importance to the information received from New Delhi. In fact, President Truman wrote about the episode later: "The problem that arose in connection with these reports was that Mr. Panikkar had in the past played the game of the Chinese Communists fairly regularly, so that his statement would not be taken as that of an impartial observer."[26] Therefore, Truman simply viewed Zhou's warning as "a bold attempt to blackmail the United Nations."[27] He and his advisors apparently did not perceive Zhou's verbal statement to Panikkar to be either "an announcement of intended entry or a threat to counter the U.S. operations militarily in North Korea."[28] Zhou's concern was influenced not only by the geopolitical importance of Korea to China's security but also by his perception of the United States as a foremost imperialist power.[29] It was this sense of immediate danger that prompted the Chinese government to take action, opposing the United States by helping North Korea. The UN command's crossing of the 38th Parallel represented both a failure of Zhou's efforts to deter such a military move and a clear test of his definition of such a move as a casus belli.[30] The deployment of U.S. forces gave substance to Zhou's fear of enemies amassing along the Sino-Korean border, if not in Manchuria itself. No longer could he and other CCP leaders, notably Mao, regard the Korean theater as an area of peripheral interest. Chinese intervention in the Korean War, as they saw it, was designed to guarantee China's territorial security.

On November 11, 1950, the Chinese government issued an unequivocal statement defining its position on the issue of the Korean War. "In order to achieve a peaceful settlement of the Korean question," the official statement declared, "it is essential, above all, to withdraw all foreign troops from Korea."[31] It further maintained that "the Korean question can be solved only by the people of North and South Korea themselves; that is the only way in which the Korean problem can be solved peacefully."[32] In his response to the UN's proposal for an immediate truce in mid-January 1951, Zhou denounced the plan, in a telegram dated January 17, asserting that the purpose of arranging a cease-fire first was merely to give U.S. troops some breathing space. He made it clear that any future peace talks would be contingent upon the withdrawal of UN military forces from Korea.[33]

Zhou considered that U.S. military and economic assistance to the GMD government had placed the CCP in a precarious position in the Chinese civil war. His personal efforts to achieve a political understanding with the U.S. government on the basis of American noninvolvement in China's internal affairs in the years between 1944 and 1947 had not been successful. Having failed completely in his attempts to reach a diplomatic accommodation with the United States in 1949, Zhou began to reassess the causes and implications of Sino-U.S. hostility and confrontation. Zhou's early analysis of China's external threats and his appraisal of U.S. intentions in East Asia and the Pacific region are contained in a number of official statements and political reports. He concluded that the United States was a serious menace to China's national security but that military confrontation between the two countries should be avoided through diplomatic efforts.

Zhou's evaluation of Far Eastern international relations had a great influence on Mao's decision to counter U.S. military expansion in Korea in October 1950. Zhou believed that there was a compelling reason for Chinese "volunteers" to engage the enemy forces across the Yalu River before they could invade China itself. One of Zhou's immediate tasks was to deter the United States from using or threatening to use atomic weapons against China. Furthermore, China could not tolerate the presence of hostile military forces on the Yalu River, within striking distance of the industrial base in Northeast China. In this particular case Chinese security interests were directly threatened by hostile forces; thus, China's national interests dictated its need to enter the Korean War. In spite of its internal vulnerabilities and the need for peaceful economic reconstruction, China chose the course of military intervention in Korea.

In retrospect the UN command's overoptimism and Western insensitivity were mainly responsible for the failure of Zhou's strategy of deterrence and, along with it, avoidance of a direct U.S. military confrontation. Tang Tsou has suggested in his work *The Failure of American Foreign Policy in China*: "If there remained, after the neutralization of the Formosa [Taiwan] Strait, any chance for Secretary Acheson to implement successfully his long-range policy of turning Chinese nationalism against Russia, it was destroyed by the administration's decision to cross the 38th Parallel."[34] The Korean War and China's intervention in it ensured the survival of the GMD government on Taiwan, and at the same time it hardened Sino-American disagreements. The United States, for its part, responded to China's intervention with a policy of isolating the Chinese Communist regime from the world arena and of containing any possible expansion of Chinese communism in Asia.

In May 1952 Secretary of State John Foster Dulles announced the U.S. policy of deterrence by massive retaliation. The only effective way to stop prospective aggressors, in Dulles's view, was to convince them in advance that, if they committed aggression, they would "be subjected to retaliatory blows so costly that their aggression [would] not be a profitable operation."[35] On February 2, 1953, President Dwight D. Eisenhower declared in his State of the Union Address that he was "issuing instructions that the Seventh Fleet no longer be employed to shield Communist China" from GMD military attacks.[36] On the possible consequences of the Indochinese War, Eisenhower told the American Society of Newspaper Editors on April 16, 1953, that "any armistice in Korea that merely released aggressive armies to attack elsewhere would be a fraud."[37] Two days later Dulles made a similar statement. It was his opinion that Communists in the Far East simply could not be allowed "to count on winning by shifting their strength first here, first there, and by focusing attack upon one or another free world position that is isolated. There is no longer that isolation."[38] During his visit to New Delhi in late May 1953 Dulles told Prime Minister Nehru explicitly that, if the Korean "fighting had to be resumed," the United States certainly "would go all out to win and would restrict neither its effort nor its weapons."[39]

With reference to Korea and later Indochina the U.S. government relied heavily on the threat of massive retaliation as an effective deterrent against China. There was an inclination at the highest levels of U.S. government to attribute the successful conclusion of an early Korean armistice agreement, signed at Panmumjom on July 27, 1953, to the effects of U.S. threats to broaden the Korean War to Manchuria and to resort to the atomic bomb. In a speech addressed to an American Legion Convention in St. Louis on September 2, 1953, Dulles warned that "there is the risk that, as in Korea, Red China might send its own army into Indochina. The Chinese Communist regime should realize that such a second aggression could not occur without grave consequences which might not be confined to Indochina."[40]

Dulles's statement appeared to take the United States' commitment to Indochina even further by implying that a Korean-type intervention on the part of the PRC would result in U.S. countermeasures against China itself. Later Dulles recaptured the central theme of his strategy in a speech addressed to the Council on Foreign Relations, meeting in New York on January 12, 1954. "Local defense," according to Dulles, was being "reinforced by the further deterrent of massive retaliatory power."[41] He added, however, that "the basic decision" made by the National Security Council was "to depend primarily upon a great capacity to retaliate instantly by means and at places of our choosing."[42] This strategy would follow "a selection of military means instead of a multiplication of means."[43] Dulles's rationale was simple and straightforward: Such a strategy was the modern way of getting maximum protection at a bearable cost against "an aggressive state, which was glutted with manpower."[44] He warned that Chinese open aggression in Indochina would certainly have "grave consequences which might not be confined to Indochina."[45]

The secretary's statement, in retrospect, further led to the deterioration of Sino-U.S. relations. His strong military posture, however, was somewhat tempered by that of the president himself. Eisenhower's personal reluctance to let Indochina become a second Korea led him to discourage direct U.S. intervention. On February 10, 1954, he said that he was doing what he could to avoid involvement: "No one could be more bitterly opposed to ever getting the United States involved in a hot war in that region than I am. Consequently, every move that I authorize is calculated, so far as humans can do it, to make certain that this does not happen."[46] In a press conference two days later, however, Eisenhower said that he agreed completely with what Dulles averred in his overseas press club speech. He indicated that it was not possible to lay down a general rule about what the United States would do but that the U.S. government was committed to "united action" against any Communist effort to overrun Southeast Asia.[47]

Between March and April 1954 Dulles conferred several times with Eisenhower about the effectiveness of air strikes and other means for supporting French efforts in Indochina, particularly a carefully considered defense program that would entail forming a regional security alliance for Southeast Asia. Eisenhower, in his book *Mandate for Change*, wrote that Dulles had concluded it would be impossible to get congressional authorization for the United States to act alone; it would be contingent, rather, upon meeting certain conditions. He argued, however, that Dulles should go ahead with his plan to "talk to other nations and tell them that if they would go along with our proposal we would be ready to participate in a regional grouping."[48] On June 3, 1954, Eisenhower told his chief advisors that he would approve U.S. military action in Indochina on certain conditions. One of these conditions was that he should be able to assure Congress that the United States "had allies such as Thailand, Australia, New Zealand, the Philippines, and above all, the bulk of the Vietnamese people, ready to join the United States in resisting"[49] overt Chinese Communist aggression. He made it clear that the United States would not undertake unilateral action to counter Chinese Communist hostilities.[50]

Against this background of conflicting signals sent by Eisenhower and Dulles, it is important to trace, if possible, when and under what circumstances Zhou decided to develop the diplomatic channel of direct communication with the United States. In retrospect, there were certain issues on which Zhou could not allow China's position to be compromised, even though, at the same time, he sought to achieve a balance of firmness and flexibility. One such issue was China's sovereignty over Taiwan. Although China's position was incompatible with U.S. foreign policy objectives, Zhou sought to create a favorable diplomatic atmosphere with a posture of flexibility as a first step toward normalizing Sino-American relations. In response to what he deemed aggressive initiatives by the United States in an area of primary interest to China, Zhou believed that it was important to establish normal channels of communication with Washington to avoid unnecessary military confrontation in Asia and the Pacific region. The presence of U.S. military bases around the periphery of China following the Korean and Indochinese wars were constant reminders of China's vulnerability.

Zhou's attempt to negotiate with the United States government certainly revealed a growing mood of realism in his conduct of Chinese foreign policy. Seeking to create the most favorable circumstances possible for the realization of China's foreign policy objectives, once again Zhou was ready to apply the pragmatic principle to his handling of Sino-American relations in the mid-1950s. He saw in U.S. foreign policy a serious challenge to China's national security and legitimate aspirations. Reduced tensions between China and the United States, in Zhou's view, rested on maintaining a regular dialogue with top U.S. authorities. His expectation was that the United States might be willing to negotiate on the normalization of Sino-American relations in exchange for China's commitment to Asian international stability and to a peaceful solution to the Taiwan issue.

The formation of the Southeast Asia Treaty Organization (SEATO) and the bilateral relations between the United States and its allies in Asia and the Pacific region brought large-scale U.S. military presence to the area, but it was perhaps no coincidence that Zhou should, in this foreign policy dilemma, resort to diplomatic negotiations rather than another military confrontation. The element of caution was the key to Zhou's diplomatic approach to the United States. Zhou insisted on diplomatic flexibility to maximize China's national interests. He envisaged diplomacy as an effective instrument of national policy and more than once stressed the importance of negotiating with the U.S. government. Aside from frequent expressions of hope for settling of the Taiwan region issue through negotiations with the United States, Zhou was ready to employ diplomacy whenever it could promote China's national interests and international status. During and after the 1954 Geneva Conference Zhou began to lay the groundwork for establishing a direct channel of communication with Washington.

Zhou's efforts to reduce tensions and to seek some kind of diplomatic accommodation between Beijing and Washington continued after the Korean War. The Indochina crisis, viewed against the backdrop of the broad U.S. threat of massive retaliation, posed a serious dilemma for Zhou. He could not discount the possibility of U.S. military intervention in Indochina, nor could he ignore the likelihood that the United States would use atomic weapons against targets inside China should the Chinese government decide to intervene in Indochina as it had done in Korea.[51] A Vietminh victory might prompt the dispatch of U.S. troops to Indochina, with or without British support. If the U.S. government committed its military strength to Indochina in support of the French troops, Zhou anticipated that China would be faced with the difficult choice of whether or not to intervene. His inclination was to avoid escalating the tension and, hence, to prevent Chinese involvement in another costly war with the United States. His emphasis on China's desire for a "peaceful" international environment and his proposal to end the war in Indochina were designed to minimize the possibility of triggering the "massive retaliation" so often threatened by Dulles.[52]

Concern for China's economic growth and its military weaknesses as well as his realistic appraisal of U.S. striking forces in Asia and the Pacific region weighed heavily on Zhou's mind at the time of the intensification of the Indochinese War and the convening of the Geneva Conference, held from April 26 to July 21, 1954. The growth of U.S. strategic airpower in the early 1950s had been formidable. Meanwhile, steps had been taken by the United States to reinforce its structure of overseas bases in Asia and the Pacific region, which could significantly extend the striking distance of U.S. airpower.

Not surprisingly, at the Geneva Conference Zhou had to weigh China's relations with the Vietminh against the consequences of any possible Sino-U.S. confrontation. He felt strongly that the best way to avoid a Korean-type war in a vital area immediately adjacent to China's southern frontiers was to neutralize Indochina. His six-point proposal to end the war in Indochina was presented at the conference on May 27, 1954.[53] He attached the highest priority to prohibiting the reintroduction of military personnel and armaments into Indochina; it was, he said, "the most important condition" for putting "an end to foreign interference there."[54] Point 3 of his proposal stipulated: "The introduction into Indochina from outside of all kinds of fresh troops and military personnel as well as all types of arms and ammunition is to cease with the cessation of hostilities throughout the territory of Indochina."[55] Zhou did everything possible to facilitate a negotiated settlement, and the success of his diplomatic maneuvers was underscored by the signing of the Final Declaration at Geneva on July 21, 1954, which pledged the signatories not to impair the sovereignty, independence, and neutrality of the three Indochinese states.[56] Provisions for neutralization were contained in the agreements dealing with the cessation of hostilities in Cambodia, Laos, and Vietnam. The Indochinese states were prohibited from entering into alliances, establishing foreign military bases, or building up unjustified military defenses.

Zhou's foreign policy strategy in relation to the Indochinese War was based upon the assumption that the United States was in the process of establishing an extensive system of political and military alliances and alignments in Asia and that this situation directly threatened China's national security and economic development. A neutralized Indochina, Zhou reasoned, could possibly prevent the U.S. intervention in the war between the French and Vietminh forces, which in turn might forestall a Sino-U.S. military confrontation.

On August 11, 1954, Zhou gave a report on China's foreign relations to the Thirty-third session of the Central People's Government Council.[57] He elaborated on U.S. air and naval forces in the Taiwan Strait area and their implications. On the issue of Taiwan Zhou's position was unequivocally uncompromising: "Taiwan is inviolable Chinese territory," said Zhou. "Its occupation by the United States absolutely cannot be tolerated, and it is equally intolerable to have Taiwan placed [under] United States trusteeship."[58] He continued: "The liberation of Taiwan is an exercise of Chinese sovereignty and China's internal affairs; we will brook no foreign interference. Any treaties concluded between the United States government and the Jiang Jieshi gang entrenched in Taiwan are illegal and void."[59] He warned, "If any foreign aggressors dare to try to hinder the Chinese people from liberating Taiwan, if they dare to infringe upon our sovereignty and territorial integrity, if they dare to interfere in our internal affairs, they must take all the grave consequences of such acts of aggression upon themselves."[60] This declaration was to become China's official position on the issue of Taiwan for years to come.

Zhou believed that the alliance building activities of the United States would serve only to increase tensions in Asia. "The aggressive circles of the United States," Zhou stressed, "have continually attempted to intervene militarily in China and threaten us with war from three fronts: Taiwan, Korea, and Indochina."[61] He added, however: "Now the Korean armistice and the restoration of peace in Indochina have gradually reduced tensions in Asia and, precisely because of this, the aggressive circles of the United States, to create new tension, seek to extend armed intervention by more intensive use of the Jiang Jieshi traitor gang, hiding in Taiwan, to wage a war of harassment and destruction against our mainland and coastal areas."[62] On September 23, 1954, Zhou made another important report to the first session of the First NPC in which he outlined China's policy priorities, both at home and abroad.[63] He reaffirmed the determination of the Chinese leadership to transform the country into "a socialist industrial country of prosperity."[64] To achieve this goal, he emphasized, there was an urgent need for "a peaceful environment and a peaceful world" in which to develop China's economy.[65]

On December 2, 1954, Secretary Dulles signed a treaty of mutual defense with Taiwan, and on December 8 Zhou declared that the treaty between the United States and Taiwan "can in no sense be called a defensive treaty; it is a treaty of naked aggression."[66] He warned the U.S. government that it would face "grave consequences" if it did not withdraw "all its armed forces" from Taiwan.[67] He further declared that the Beijing government was determined "to liberate Taiwan and liquidate the traitorous Jiang Jieshi clique."[68] Obviously, central to Zhou's policy strategy was how to deal with the United States and its extensive military presence in Asia. Even at this stage Zhou still entertained the hope that limited agreements with the United States remained possible and that the way to deal with U.S. military actions in Asia and the Pacific region was accommodation through negotiation. In spite of the escalating postures of threat, China's policy toward the United States under Zhou continued to be one of self-restraint. It might not be a pure coincidence that, Zhou was, at the same time, also leading the effort to implement China's five-year domestic economic plan. Clearly, he understood the importance of economic strength as an instrument of national policy.

The Asian-African Conference, held at Bandung, Indonesia, from April 18 to 24, 1955, proved an ideal forum for Zhou to pursue China's foreign policy objectives by peaceful means. It also provided Zhou with an unusual opportunity to make clear the Chinese government's intention to avoid direct military confrontation with the United States over the status of Taiwan. "The Chinese people," said Zhou on April 23, "are friendly to the American people. The Chinese people do not want to have war with the United States of America."[69] He added: "The Chinese government is willing to sit down and enter into negotiations with the United States government to discuss the question of relaxing tension in the Taiwan area."[70]

On July 25 Beijing and Washington issued a joint communiqué formally announcing the initiation of Sino-American negotiations, even though the U.S. government carefully qualified that any talks with China did not signify diplomatic recognition. On July 30 Zhou provided his assessment of the Sino-American discussions at the second session of the First NPC: "Provided that the United States does not interfere with China's internal affairs, the possibility of peaceful liberation of Taiwan will continue to increase."[71] He also suggested that, "if possible, the Chinese government is willing to enter into negotiations with the responsible authorities of Taiwan to map out concrete steps for Taiwan's peaceful liberation."[72] According to Zhou, "the tension in the Taiwan area, caused by the U.S. occupation of China's territory of Taiwan and its interference with the liberation of China's territory, was an international issue between China and the United States."[73] On the other hand, however, "the liberation of Taiwan . . . was an internal Chinese affair."[74] Against this background Zhou clearly defined the scope of the talks by stating that "these two questions could therefore not be mixed up; only the first question could be subject to Sino-American negotiation."[75]

Talks between the Chinese and U.S. governments at the ambassadorial level began in Geneva on August 1, 1955. The Chinese side proposed that the dispute between China and the United States, including that in the Taiwan region, should be settled through peaceful negotiations and without the use or threat of force.[76] The American side insisted not only that the renunciation of force should be a basic condition to the relations between the government of China and the Jiang regime in Taiwan but also that such a renunciation should not prejudice the U.S. "right to individual and collective self-defense" in the Taiwan area.[77]

These direct negotiations represented a major turning point in Zhou's approach to Sino-American relations. Zhou consistently regarded the use of diplomacy as an instrument of national policy and direct negotiation with the United States as a way of reducing international tension in Asia and the Pacific region. He also viewed U.S. military actions in Korea, in the Taiwan region, and elsewhere in Asia within the context of China's national security and, consequently, attempted to bring the U.S. government to the negotiating table to minimize the Sino-U.S. competition and rivalry. The United States was militarily powerful and dangerous, and, thus, greater access to U.S. foreign policymakers through the ambassadorial talks at Geneva, and later at Warsaw, was imperative. Zhou hoped that through his continuing explorations he might eventually find bases of common interest on which mutual understanding between China and the United States would be furthered and mutually satisfactory solutions developed. Even though Zhou's diplomatic initiative did not achieve his desired objectives, he did not seem to think that the whole effort was futile. His initiative had the potential for creating an opportunity to establish a workable relationship with the United States that would make military confrontation between the two countries less likely and also lay the groundwork for future Sino-U.S. diplomatic rapprochement.

Zhou was disturbed, however, by what he perceived to be U.S. interference in China's domestic affairs. In his report to the second session of the Second National Committee of the Chinese People's Political Consultative Conference on January 30, 1956, he presented the basis of his analysis of future relations between China and the United States.[78] According to Zhou, there were monopolist warmongers within the U.S. ruling circle. "There are also some more farsighted persons," he said, "who have gradually come to realize that the use of war and the threat of war, the advocacy of going to the 'brink of war,' and the continued adherence to a rigid policy of relying on 'strength' can only isolate the United States further. Therefore, they are asking for a more sober policy based on the recognition of realities."[79] He added: "There are also quite a few people in American industrial and economic circles who are dissatisfied with the U.S. policy of embargo and demand development of normal international trade. All this is welcome."[80] In his report delivered to the third session of the First NPC on June 28, 1956, Zhou reiterated his optimism regarding a peaceful solution to international problems. "Recently, statesmen in Great Britain and France indicated that, except fools, nobody likes war. That is correct,"[81] said Zhou. With regard to political leaders in Washington, he asserted that "only a part of them want to fight." "If there are no formal diplomatic relations," he noted, "intergovernmental contacts are helpful."[82]

The Sino-American ambassadorial talks, first at Geneva and then in Warsaw, were held more than 130 times at regular intervals beginning in 1955. As the only forum for direct Sino-American communication, these talks were always viewed by Zhou as a means of influencing the U.S. government to reduce its military presence in the Taiwan region, while American policymakers originally regarded them as a device for the repatriation of U.S. prisoners from the Korean War. According to Kenneth T. Young, "This diplomatic arrangement has become a workable and essential channel for reducing miscalculations, clarifying intentions, and explaining proposals."[83] He also observed: "Covering a broad range of issues and a dozen principal subjects, the talks have involved the use of power, clash of interests, and manipulation of confrontations between the two parties to advance the interests of one side or to avoid military collision between both."[84] Among the many challenges that Zhou confronted during this period were: how China's relations with the United States should be conducted; and what devices should be used to reach optimum understanding and cooperation. It was Zhou's intention first to establish and then to regularize face-to-face communication and discussion between the two countries in order to reduce unnecessary tensions.

The direct Sino-American negotiations initiated by Zhou amply reflected his desire to convince U.S. policymakers of the practical value of maintaining even marginal contact with Chinese representatives. In the process Zhou wanted to modify China's tone of hostility and moved pragmatically to probing and bargaining for bilateral agreements with the United States. It was through the Sino-American ambassadorial talks that Zhou became ready to commit to relaxing and eliminating tensions between Beijing and Washington regarding the Taiwan area. He formally suggested that China intended to liberate Taiwan even "by peaceful means."[85] It was also part of his strategy that through these bilateral talks China could expand the realm of diplomatic relations with the United States.[86] Both China and the United States might, in Zhou's view, be able to pursue converging interests in some sort of de facto accommodation without being trapped by the paralyzing dogma that East-West conflict was inevitable. By the end of 1956 Zhou had reverted to a more moderate position on Sino-American relations, which clearly reflected his realistic approach.

The corollary measures taken by Zhou during the period tended to suggest China's seriousness about negotiations. There was actually a reduction in the military budget, while an overall emphasis was placed on economic development. It would have been the greatest accomplishment for Zhou if the problem of Taiwan were actually resolved as well as the question of China's representation in the United Nations. In his numerous remarks his old posture of conciliation reappeared, but, undoubtedly, it was in a calculated form. In his report to the State Council on the Bandung Conference, Zhou stated, on May 13, 1955: "At the conference we put forward no proposals either against the occupation of Taiwan by the United States and its creation of tension in the Taiwan area or for the restoration to the PRC of her legitimate status in the United Nations."[87] He also indicated China's intention of extending terms for peaceful coexistence to the United States in a settlement of the Taiwan question. He did not want to see the conference "bogged down in disputes and antagonism on these two questions as the result of outside pressures."[88]

The ambassadorial talks began in Geneva on August 1, 1955, and were concluded there in December 1957, when U.S. ambassador U. Alexis Johnson was transferred to Thailand. More than seventy talks had taken place in Geneva, collectively referred to as the Geneva Talks, during which China's initiative to exchange journalists with the United States and other proposals for increasing bilateral contacts were all rebuffed by the U.S. government. After Johnson's departure the U.S. government tried to reduce its representation at the Geneva Talks to below the ambassadorial level. As a result, they were suspended for more than half a year.

In his annual report to the fifth session of the First NPC, delivered on February 10, 1958, Zhou commented on the U.S. pursuit of a de facto "two-China" policy.[89] "The United States holds ambassadorial talks with China," said Zhou, "and yet at these talks demands that China accept the *status quo* of its occupation of Taiwan. This is in substance an attempt to create 'two Chinas,' which is of course absolutely unacceptable to the Chinese side."[90] He went on to say: "That is why the method [U.S. efforts to bar China from the UN] used by the United States is first to create whenever possible a state of 'two Chinas' in certain international conferences and organizations so as to establish gradually a fait accompli of 'two Chinas' in international affairs."[91]

On the same occasion Zhou talked about U.S. allies' increasing reluctance to follow the lead of the United States. "The broad masses in the allied countries of the United States," claimed Zhou, "are opposing with growing vehemence their heavy burden of military expenses, the deployment of guided missiles in their countries, and the flight of United States airplanes carrying nuclear weapons over their heads."[92] He speculated: "This fact too compels the governments of these countries to grow more sober on the question of war or peace."[93] Despite Zhou's inclination to pursue peaceful coexistence through negotiations, the Chinese government formally announced on June 30, 1958, that it would abandon the ambassadorial talks altogether unless the U.S. government agreed to resume them on an ambassadorial level within fifteen days. It also stated that the American endeavor to bring about "a situation of 'two Chinas'" was "the crux of the reason for the failure" of the Geneva talks.[94]

On July 1, 1958, Dulles declared that the U.S. government would not "intend to be bound by" any such ultimatum from the Chinese,[95] but at the same time he opened the door by suggesting that, if China agreed to transfer the talks from Geneva to Warsaw, Jacob Beam, ambassador to Poland, would "personally" be designated as the U.S. representative in due course. The Chinese Foreign Ministry responded by asking, "If the United States can violate an agreement [to hold ambassadorial talks] for more than six months, why can't China demand to resume its implementation within fifteen days?"[96] U.S. officials continued, however, to delay the resumption of the Sino-American talks.

The advent of the Middle East crisis was used to further justify delaying action by the United States. It was not until the end of July, when high-level Sino-Soviet talks were about to take place in Beijing, that the State Department finally designated Beam as the chief U.S. representative. Under intense pressure from all sides, Dulles returned once again to the Sino-American negotiations. He indicated explicitly, however, that the United States would defend Quemoy with nuclear weapons if necessary. Zhou's response was that the two ambassadors meet in Warsaw to "settle" the Taiwan crisis.[97]

Sino-American talks at the ambassadorial level were resumed on September 15, 1958, now at Warsaw, at the height of the offshore islands crisis. After negotiation was under way the Soviet Union publicly supported China's territorial claims and its security against U.S. military attack. Ambassadors Beam and Wang Bingnan held several long, tense, and difficult sessions during the latter part of September and early October. The renewal of talks between Beijing and Washington underlined the desire by both sides to avoid major conflicts. The ambassadorial talks once again proved unsuccessful in bridging the basic differences between the two sides, but the diplomatic dialogue certainly helped defuse the offshore islands crisis. Zhou masterminded the negotiations through Ambassador Wang, who, as a long-term Party veteran, enjoyed his personal trust. In the spirit of mutual bargaining in good faith, Zhou tried to reach concrete agreements with the U.S. government through a give-and-take process of bridging differences and transacting compromises advantageous, in varying degrees, to both sides.

For all his apparent fluctuation between hostility and conciliation Zhou remained firm on the Taiwan problem throughout the 1950s and 1960s. In a public interview conducted by Edgar Snow in January 1961 Zhou outlined these prerequisites for meaningful Sino-American negotiations:

> All disputes between China and the United States, including the dispute between the two countries in the Taiwan region, should be settled through

peaceful negotiations, without resorting to the use or threat of force; and second, the United States must agree to withdraw its armed forces from Taiwan and the Taiwan Straits. As to the specific steps on when and how to withdraw, they are matters of subsequent discussion. If the United States government ceases to pursue the policy of aggression against China and of resorting to threats of force, this is the only logical conclusion which can be drawn.[98]

When asked by Snow whether these two principles had also been the major issues in the Sino-American ambassadorial talks, Zhou's answer was simply yes. He went on to say that "the first principle was put forward by China at the end of 1955. The second principle was put forward in the autumn of 1958 at Warsaw."[99] On the questions of the time and manner of U.S. withdrawal from Taiwan if the principles were agreed upon as the basis of future Sino-American negotiations, Zhou stated that "such questions would belong in the realm of diplomacy."[100]

The U.S. military presence in Taiwan, as Zhou saw it, was a concrete manifestation of U.S. hostility toward mainland China. As long as the United States refused to consider, even in principle, the possibility of military disengagement, the relations between the two countries would not improve. On the other hand, Zhou still believed that a solution to the problem of Sino-U.S. relations would ultimately be found. As he put it, "It is only a question of time."[101] It is interesting to note that Snow subsequently commented on Zhou's position on Sino-American relations by stating that "nearly all Chou's [Zhou's] arguments depend on the logic of nationalism, quite apart from Communism."[102]

During his interview with Snow, Zhou again attempted to make the distinction between treating Taiwan as an internal problem and as an international issue to justify Beijing's parallel talks with Taiwan and the United States. "We hold that the dispute between China and the Untied States in the Taiwan region," said Zhou, "is an international question; whereas military action between the Central Government of New China and the Jiang Jieshi clique in Taiwan is an internal question."[103] He reiterated that "the United States has maintained that the two questions are inseparable. We hold that they can and must be separated."[104] As such, Zhou believed that it was possible for China and the United States to hold ambassadorial talks and that, at the same time, dialogue could take place between the Chinese government and Taiwan authorities.

In the early 1960s Zhou continued to approach the Sino-American relationship with caution and self-restraint. In 1961, when the Laotian crisis raised new fears on both sides, Beam indicated to Wang at Warsaw that a failure to reach a cease-fire in Laos might result in U.S. military intervention. Through the ongoing ambassadorial meetings, and later with Ch'en Yi, the Chinese foreign minister, at the Geneva Conference, Zhou, as chief delegate, managed, behind the scenes, to inform the U.S. government that China was serious about its desire to negotiate an acceptable formula for neutralizing Laos. By so doing, it became possible for both China and the United States to defuse the crisis between them. In 1962, when China was deeply engaged in border disputes with India and the Soviet Union, U.S. authorities informed the Chinese government, through the Warsaw link, of its intention to discourage GMD leaders in Taiwan from launching a military attack on the mainland. The ambassadorial talks seemed to be a useful forum through which the Sino-American conflict in the Taiwan area was at least kept in check.

Nevertheless Zhou continued to regard the United States as a major threat to world peace in general and to China's national security specifically. In his report to the first session of the Third NPC on December 21, 1964, Zhou described the United States as "the most arrogant aggressor ever known in history, the most ferocious enemy of world peace, and the main prop of all the forces of reaction in the world."[105] Zhou also reiterated the central theme that "China stands for a settlement of the Indochinese question in accordance with the agreements of the two Geneva Conferences."[106] At the same time, he once again declared that the government of the PRC was "the only lawful government representing the entire Chinese people" and that "the U.S. armed forces must withdraw from Taiwan and the Taiwan Straits" prior to settlement of the Taiwan question.[107]

During the period of direct U.S. involvement in the Vietnam War in the mid-1960s Zhou carefully avoided provocative actions on the part of China. He even went so far as to warn Hanoi against military adventurism by making it quite clear that China would not intervene unless the United States attacked China or invaded North Vietnam. In fact, at no stage did Zhou advocate a firm commitment to military intervention on the Vietminh's behalf. His foreign policy strategy during this crucial period was to prevent a widening of the Vietnamese conflict that could involve direct Chinese confrontation with the United States. Clearly, China's national interest, not international proletarianism, dictated its course of action vis-à-vis the United States. In 1964 the Chinese representative at Warsaw proposed a bilateral agreement on "no first use of nuclear weapons."[108] On February 9, 1965, the Chinese government issued a statement on Vietnam: while it contained the customary reference to the "unshakeable international obligation" of socialist countries to assist North Vietnam, it did not commit to unity of action with the Soviet Union against

U.S. military forces.[109] In March 1965 Zhou asked Pakistan's president, Mohammad Ayub, to convey to U.S. President Johnson the message that "the situations in 1950 and 1965" were not similar. Moreover, "if the United States would not push the Chinese to the point of no return, the Chinese would abide by international obligations and responsibilities and would not get involved in any war with the United States."[110] In an interview with the Pakistani daily *Dawn* on April 10, 1966, Zhou reaffirmed China's resolve not to provoke a war with the United States.[111]

By mid-1966 Zhou had reason to believe, through the ambassadorial talks in Warsaw, that the United States was not planning to escalate the war in Vietnam indefinitely nor to launch a nuclear attack against China. In August 1966 the Mao-Lin coalition managed to win the foreign policy debate at the Eleventh Plenum of the Eighth Central Committee of the CCP after eighteen months of serious deliberations among top Party leaders. The Central Committee, in its final communiqué, stressed the danger of Soviet revisionism and promised only conditional support for North Vietnam. It is significant to note that even the war threat was blunted with the perfunctory statement that, should the Americans start a war against China, the Chinese were ready to meet them. Zhou urged, however, that China must continue a low-risk strategy of no direct confrontation with the United States. Also, China should not be forced to adopt a Sino-Soviet united front in support of North Vietnam.

While Zhou was trying to steer China along a prudent, non-interventionist course of action in foreign affairs to avoid direct miliary confrontation with the United States in Vietnam and elsewhere in Asia and the Pacific region, China made every effort to acquire a nuclear capability so as to strengthen its international position. China's several nuclear and thermonuclear weapons tests in 1966 and 1968 were obvious attempts to rectify the imbalance of the Sino-American power relationship. Zhou interpreted official U.S. statements that no mercy would be granted to China in the event of Chinese intervention in the Vietnam War to mean that there was no possibility of a limited war of the Korean type between a nonnuclear and a nuclear power. It was but natural that most of China's foreign policy statements relating to nuclear weapons placed special emphasis upon China's ability to break the nuclear monopoly of the two superpowers.[112] China's capacity for nuclear deterrence meant, to Zhou, relative freedom of action in the area of power politics.

Zhou's assessment of the international situation underwent quite a significant change. On October 1, 1968, he remarked that "a new historical stage of opposing U.S. imperialism and Soviet revisionism has begun"[113] and that the trend of both collusion and contention between the two superpowers had become a dominant factor in the international arena.[114] Zhou's phrase "a new historical stage" implied that the old world system in which the United States had been China's primary threat was undergoing major changes. As he saw it, the Chinese people must crush "U.S. imperialist and Soviet revisionist plots to divide the world."[115]

Such a reality presented both dangers and opportunities to China. The collusion of the two superpowers naturally rendered China's national security more precarious. On the other hand, if China could drive a wedge between them to intensify their conflicts and thereby prevent their collaboration, it could gain a breathing space and even possibly achieve its own desired international standing. Concerning the two superpowers, Zhou continued to hold the belief that it would be a matter of strategic need to prevent U.S.-Soviet collusion at the expense of China. To balance the relative power distribution between the two superpowers in order to improve China's national security and international position was central to his foreign policy orientation throughout his political career as the CCP's chief negotiator and China's principal policymaker, in spite of his lack of real success due to American rebuff.

Mao shared Zhou's general assessment of the recent international situation. He also agreed with him about distinguishing between China's primary and secondary enemies instead of confronting a dual adversary. Therefore, the possibility of détente with the United States was to be explored more vigorously. In retrospect, the year 1968 marked a major turning point in the implementation of Zhou's foreign policy toward the United States. During the next year and a half he proceeded cautiously but persistently to seek détente with Washington.

The United States also exercised considerable restraint in relation to the Chinese government in order to prevent a new Sino-American conflict in Vietnam. Even though the escalation of U.S. involvement in Vietnam and U.S. air actions near the Chinese border inevitably created serious tensions between the two countries, on numerous occasions the U.S. representatives at Warsaw assured their Chinese counterparts that the United States did not wish to pose a threat to the security of China and had no designs on the territory of North Vietnam.[116] These assurances undoubtedly contributed to easing Zhou's fears from 1966 on.

Basic Chinese and American interests and purposes, however, continued to clash in Vietnam and elsewhere. When U.S. forces invaded Cambodia, Zhou immediately backtracked in his pursuit of détente. Only after he was convinced that the United States was withdrawing its troops from Vietnam and Cambodia did he decide that the road was clear to make serious moves toward Sino-American détente. He continued to stress that de-escalation of American involvement in Vietnam was a prerequisite for improved relations between

Beijing and Washington. At times he seemed to place greater stress on this issue than on the unresolved question of Taiwan. During 1968 and 1969, when the U.S. government took the first steps toward withdrawal from Vietnam and proclaimed that it would reduce its military involvement throughout Asia, Zhou was prepared to enter into serious dialogue with the United States. In part, his move was dictated by the realities of deteriorating Sino-Soviet relations. Zhou entertained the hope that the United States would serve as a counterweight to Moscow.

Zhou's own institutional power base combined with Mao's influence gave his foreign policy line official blessing as well as actual legitimacy. The pragmatism displayed in this new phase of Chinese diplomacy reveals the efforts being made to take advantage of new opportunities offered by both domestic and international politics. At the same time, Beijing's decision to pursue a more active and wider-ranging diplomacy also reflects, to a considerable degree, Zhou's political ascendancy in the decision making process of the Chinese government. Moreover, the policy of promoting contacts and exchanges between China and the United States was bolstered in 1968 and 1969 by the reduction of U.S. global commitments, the corresponding extension of Soviet influence, notably in Asia, the Soviet invasion of Czechoslovakia, and the Sino-Soviet border clashes in March 1969.

The escalation of the conflict in Vietnam brought large-scale but unsuccessful U.S. military intervention. The United States' ultimate failure there and President Richard Nixon's decision to withdraw U.S. military forces from Indochina had a far-reaching impact not only in Southeast Asia but also on Sino-American relations. It is significant that Zhou's search for détente with the United States coincided with Nixon's decision to revise the U.S. postwar policy of containment in Asia. Nixon gave the first indication of a possible shift in policy in 1967 during his national election campaign. In a campaign speech he advocated the "development of regional defense pacts, in which nations undertake, among themselves, to attempt to contain aggression in their own areas."[117] He defined the improvement of U.S. relations with China as one of his long-term objectives. When Nixon assumed office in January 1969 he ordered a reexamination of U.S. foreign policies and carefully explored all possible new moves toward mainland China. Undeterred by the postponement of ambassadorial talks at Warsaw, Nixon managed, through other international intermediaries, to convey to Beijing Washington's desire to reopen dialogue and his plan to withdraw U.S. military forces form Vietnam.[118] On April 21, 1969, Secretary of State William Rogers acknowledged China's central role in the Asian-Pacific region and emphasized the U.S. desire to develop a constructive dialogue with Chinese leaders.[119] On May 24 Nixon told Rogers to get the

Chinese response through the Pakistani government about the talks with the United States.[120] In July, Nixon articulated, at Quam, the so-called Nixon Doctrine, calling for reduced U.S. military involvement in Asia.[121] This approach reflected a significant downgrading of the Chinese threat by U.S. foreign policymakers and indicated a reappraisal of their policy of containing China.

While visiting Pakistan, Nixon reiterated, in an August 1 meeting with the Pakistani president, Yahya Khan, the U.S. government's interest in having diplomatic dialogue with China.[122] In Bucharest he made a similar statement to Rumanian leader Nicolae Ceausescu.[123] On August 8 Rogers reaffirmed the U.S. government's intention to bring about a relaxation of tensions between the United States and China.[124] Nixon's article entitled "Asia after Viet Nam," published in the October 1969 issue of *Foreign Affairs,* clearly revealed the views he had held on China in the period just before his election.[125]

The first decisive demonstration of American goodwill did not actually occur until November, when the U.S. government announced the termination of regular patrolling by the Seventh Fleet in the Taiwan Straits. In a major foreign policy report to Congress on February 18, 1970, Nixon provided further clarification of U.S. foreign policy toward China, emphasizing the efforts of his administration to improve "practical relations" with the PRC.[126] He characterized those efforts that his administration had made in 1969 as "specific steps that did not require Chinese agreement but which underlined our willingness to have a more normal and constructive relationship."[127] He also made it clear that the United States had "no intention of taking sides" in the current Sino-Soviet dispute.[128] In addition, the U.S. government would do nothing to encourage Moscow's plan for the formation of an anti-China coalition of Asian states.[129] On the contrary, the United States would take certain actions in order to create broader opportunities for contacts between the Chinese and American peoples.[130] Not long thereafter Nixon tried, through Pakistani and Rumanian intermediaries, to assure the Chinese government that the United States desired to disengage from Vietnam and wanted to explore the possibility of a high-level official visit to Beijing.

At the Lushan Plenum, held from August 23 to September 6, 1970, Zhou was of the opinion that China should reach some kind of accommodation with the United States. While Zhou was prepared to negotiate directly with the United States on many major issues, he realized that a move toward diplomatic rapprochement with the United States would certainly alarm the Soviet leadership and increase tensions between China and the Soviet Union. Against this background he proceeded slowly and cautiously, knowing full well that his move involved taking calculated risks. Considering the advantages to be gained, Zhou obviously found the risks acceptable. Mao shared Zhou's desire for

Sino-American diplomatic rapprochement and, thus, such a course of action also received his blessing. On December 1, 1970, China's National Day, Mao invited Snow, the American journalist, to sit beside him on the public rostrum in Beijing.

On November 11 Zhou told the Pakistani chief of staff that, "in order to discuss evacuation of Chinese territories called Taiwan, a special envoy of President Nixon will be most welcome in Beijing."[131] In early December Zhou told Snow that China was ready to negotiate with the United States. The problem of Taiwan, however, once again posed a major obstacle. "The door is open," said Zhou in his interview with Snow. The question was whether or not "the U.S. is sincere about solving the problem of Taiwan."[132] On December 16 the United States government, through Pakistan, accepted Zhou's invitation to begin direct dialogue with China; the scope of the talks was defined to embrace "a broad range of issues which lie between the People's Republic of China and the United States, including the issue of Taiwan."[133] Later Zhou made a dramatic display of China's changed attitude toward the United States by inviting a U.S. Ping-Pong team to China for exhibition games. He personally met with the team on April 14, 1971, and proclaimed the visit the opening of "a new page in the relations of the Chinese and American people."[134] Interestingly enough, Secretary of State Rogers, at a press conference on April 23, declared his hope that this "new page" in Sino-American relations would become "a new chapter."[135]

From that point on events moved at a rapid pace. On June 11 Zhou formally accepted a U.S. proposal, transmitted to China earlier through the Pakistani channel, for Henry Kissinger to visit Beijing from July 9 through 11. The prospect of conducting face-to-face negotiations with Kissinger represented the culmination of Zhou's long-term efforts, dating back to his early days during the united front period, to win U.S. support. The Sino-American rapprochement could be most critical in curtailing Soviet expansion in Asia and beyond. More important, it would be a vindication of his long-standing foreign policy orientation. Kissinger, President Nixon's chief national security advisor and a distinguished scholar steeped in the history of European diplomacy, was the ideal match for Zhou in temperament, knowledge, and diplomatic skills. These activities constituted a rare moment in history when the objective conditions, key players, and goals pursued were perfectly synchronized and made significant changes in world affairs their subsequent encounters thus assumed legendary proportions.

The talks between Zhou and Kissinger, held first in July and then in October of 1971 at Beijing, were intended to prepare the way for Nixon's visit to China the following February and to explore each participant's views on international issues in a strategic context. "By tacit agreement," according to Kissinger, neither side actually "pressed controversial issues to the hilt."[136] During Kissinger's second visit Zhou specifically told the U.S. emissary that it was China's "actions" rather than its rhetoric that would really count.[137] By the same token Zhou expected the United States to substantiate its words with action in order to remove sources of tension between the two countries. As such, a new pattern of diplomatic dialogue for the normalization of state-to-state relations between China and the United States was established, with each side seeking to expand common ground to promote shared interests and to set aside differences, which could be adjusted later.

Zhou was fully cognizant of the fact that statesmen could not create reality. He frequently used the Chinese proverb that "the helmsman must guide the boat by using the waves; otherwise, it will be submerged by them" to justify his sense of timing and caution.[138] In the words of Zhou's biographer, Dick Wilson, "It is rare for the spokesmen of two giant opposing blocs at the highest level to be able to speak and understand each other's language as Zhou and Kissinger could."[139] On concrete issues both Zhou and Kissinger were realistic and conciliatory. On the U.S. draft of the communiqué to be issued during Nixon's visit to China, for instance, Zhou offered a unique suggestion. The draft, as it stood, was unacceptable, he said, and, unless the communiqué set forth the fundamental differences between the United States and China, it would be "untruthful."[140] A new draft stated the Chinese position but left a space blank for the Americans to insert theirs. Kissinger, upon reflection, accepted it.

In his toast at the first state banquet welcoming Nixon to China, Zhou stated that, despite ideological differences, his country and the United States could establish normal relations on the basis of the Five Principles of Peaceful Coexistence.[141] He hoped that, "through frank exchange of views between our two sides to gain a clearer notion of differences and make efforts to find common ground, a new start can be made in the relations between our two countries."[142] Zhou also made specific reference to his statement of 1955, in which he had said that "the Chinese people do not want to have a war with the United States and the Chinese government is willing to sit down and enter into negotiations with the United States Government."[143] He added, "This is a policy which we have pursued consistently."[144] It was Zhou's conviction that both the Chinese and American peoples were willing to promote normalized relations between their countries and work to relax existing tensions. "The people, and the people alone," said Zhou, "are the massive force in the making of world history. We are confident that the day will surely come when the common desire of our two peoples will be realized."[145] Nixon responded by stating that, if both countries could find common ground on which to work together, the chances for international peace could be improved. "What brings us together," he stressed, "is that we have common interests which transcend [our] differences."[146] This spirit—to seek common ground while reserving differences—remained intact throughout the subsequent negotiations between Zhou, on one side, and Nixon and Kissinger, on the other.

According to Kissinger, Zhou possessed "the sense of cultural superiority of an ancient civilization," and he could soften "the edges of ideological hostility by an insinuating ease of manner and a seemingly effortless skill to penetrate to the heart of the matter."[147] He also perceived that Zhou was realistic enough to know that China was not yet a superpower. "In fact, had China been stronger," noted Kissinger, "it would not have pursued the improvement of relations with us with the same single-mindedness. Peking [Beijing] needed us to help break out of its isolation and as a counterweight to the potentially mortal threat along its northern border."[148] It was equally true that U.S. foreign policy was rapidly adjusting to the conditions of a transitional period in world politics. In-depth analysis of strategic realities made Kissinger a pioneer in developing the Sino-American diplomatic rapprochement that was to dominate the international scene in 1972 and 1973. He opined that the United States "needed China to enhance the flexibility of our diplomacy. Gone were the days when we enjoyed the luxury of choosing the moment to involve ourselves in world affairs."[149] It was a matter of strategic necessity, for Kissinger, that the United States be compelled "to take account of other power centers and strive for an equilibrium among them."[150] Kissinger further noted: "The China initiative also restored perspective to our national policy. It reduced Indochina to its proper scale—a small peninsula on a major continent."[151]

China's position in Asia would, in Zhou's estimation, be threatened by either of the two superpowers or, worse still, by both, without the establishment of satisfactory relations with the United States. By steering China on a course that would facilitate diplomatic rapprochement with the United States, it would be possible to create a delicate strategic triangle among China, the United States, and the Soviet Union. Kissinger aptly observed that the Chinese leaders, notably Mao and Zhou, "were beyond ideology in their dealings with us," adding that their action "had established the absolute primacy of geopolitics."[152] More precisely, in Kissinger's words again, "They were in effect freeing one front by a tacit nonaggression treaty with us."[153]

Zhou sought diplomatic rapprochement with the United States partly to counter Soviet hegemonism and partly to increase the flexibility of China's diplomatic maneuvers. He understood that the most effective way to achieve his dual purpose was to identify areas of agreement between China and the

United States. Accordingly, he personally conducted negotiations with Kissinger and Nixon. He believed that China could benefit both diplomatically and strategically from improved Sino-American relations. Diplomatic rapprochement would not be possible, however, unless the United States made at least a symbolic concession to China on the issue of Taiwan in return for China's cooperation in opposing Soviet worldwide expansion.

For a man of Zhou's persuasion there was always a middle ground. Though Zhou urged compromise, he was by no means oblivious to the conflicting national interests of China and the United States. In fact, his whole approach to Sino-U.S. relations was predicated on the assumption that the Taiwan question was the crucial obstacle to their normalization. Recognizing conflicting national interests and making efforts to reconcile them were, as Zhou saw it, the essence of diplomacy. Therefore, while he insisted that the liberation of Taiwan was China's internal affair, he took care to make it clear that China would not liberate Taiwan through the use of force; on the contrary, it would be ready to engage in direct negotiations with Taipei in order to reunify the province with the rest of China peacefully. Even in demanding the withdrawal of U.S. military forces from Taiwan, Zhou's choice of words suggested that he was more concerned with obtaining a declaration of intent from the United States rather than immediate compliance with this precondition.

Zhou fully understood that, in order to achieve reconciliation with the United States, he must have a thorough knowledge of what Kissinger and Nixon were after; he would thereby be able to defer to their points of view at the appropriate moment while still preserving the substance of his own objectives. During their negotiations Zhou carefully tried to grasp the U.S. perspective and sought to identify possible areas of common ground between the two sides. Not surprisingly, he probed deeply in order to gauge both Kissinger's and Nixon's positions accurately.

In his toast at the first state banquet Zhou deliberately did not mention Taiwan. More significantly, he declared that force was inappropriate in solving outstanding disputes. "This only made explicit what we had learned privately," Kissinger wrote later on. "It was another, if implicit, assurance that we need no longer fear Chinese military intervention in Indo-china."[154] Kissinger assessed the event: "The overwhelming impression left by Zhou . . . was that continuing differences over Taiwan were secondary to our primary mutual concern over the international equilibrium. The divergence of views on Taiwan would not be allowed to disturb the new relationship that had evolved so dramatically and that was grounded in geopolitical interests."[155] From Zhou's point of view it was more appropriate for both China and the United States to put aside the issue of Taiwan for the time being so that their efforts toward normalizing relations would not be derailed and so that they could concentrate on their common interests. At the farewell party for Nixon held on February 28, 1972, Zhou remarked that "we . . . have already let the Taiwan issue remain for twenty-two years, and can still afford to let it wait there for a time."[156] Nixon was obviously receptive to Zhou's approach. His response was calculated to both encourage and reassure his host. "There is no reason," Nixon stated, "for us to be enemies. Neither of us seeks the territory of the other; neither of us seeks domination over the other; neither of us seeks to stretch out our hands and rule the world."[157]

In his direct negotiations with Nixon and Kissinger, Zhou focused on "the requirements of the balance of power, the international order, and long-term trends of world politics."[158] It was Kissinger's opinion that "both sides understood that, if they agreed on these elements, a strategy of parallel action would follow naturally; if not, tactical decisions taken individually would prove ephemeral and fruitless."[159] Containing Soviet global expansion remained the top priority in Zhou's foreign strategy. By implication, the primary issue was the maintenance of a worldwide balance of power. Zhou's immediate task was to identify areas in which Chinese and American interests coincided. Against this background Zhou and Nixon reviewed the current international situation, and Nixon outlined U.S. foreign policy for Zhou.

As Kissinger reflected on his numerous talks with Zhou and Mao, he summarized his observations by stating that "China was in the great classical tradition of European statesmanship. The Chinese Communist leaders coldly and unemotionally assessed the requirements of the balance of power, little influenced by ideology or sentiment."[160] He described them as "scientists of equilibrium, artists of relativity."[161] On the issue of China's opposition to great-power chauvinism or its antihegemonic position, Kissinger obviously understood his Chinese counterpart perfectly. He was led to remark: "Only one principle was inviolate. No nation would be permitted to be preeminent."[162] He correctly concluded that in the Chinese approach to foreign policy issues "national interests overrode ideological difference" and that "ideological slogans were a facade for considerations of balance of power."[163] Kissinger's assessment of Zhou is particularly interesting. Kissinger thought that Zhou had a "realistic" understanding of international relations but that his realism, however, was still framed by the correlation of Chinese "ideology" and "foreign policy"; it was based on a symbiotic relationship between so-called faith and disciplined mentality. "He was a dedicated ideologue," asserted Kissinger, "but he used the faith that had sustained him through decades of struggle to discipline a passionate nature into one of the most acute and unsentimental assessments of reality that I have encountered."[164]

As Zhou grew older, he put more and more effort into improving China's relations with the United States. The importance he attached to the changing international situation provided much of the conceptual framework of Chinese foreign policy after the Cultural Revolution in 1968. Central to his foreign policy analysis was the revised assessment of the real and potential threat of "U.S. imperialism," which led to a much clearer understanding of its declining influence in Asian international relations. From Zhou's point of view a flexible and creative Chinese diplomacy must address itself to the dual problems of containing the continuing expansion of Soviet power worldwide and restraining the U.S. commitment to Taiwan. The policy Zhou sought of opening communications with the United States was a means, in part at least, of gaining leverage with Soviet leaders in order to mitigate tensions between China and the Soviet Union.

Toward the end of 1968 Zhou concluded that the Soviet Union posed the greatest immediate threat to China, and he began to feel that some sort of U.S. military presence in Asia and the Pacific region would be desirable in order to create a counterweight to the Soviet Union. His search for a subtle balance of power between the two superpowers favorable to Chinese interests in East Asia was to be a key factor in the new orientation of Chinese foreign strategy vis-à-vis the United States. This strategic emphasis revealed China's opposition to hegemony and its advocacy of reduced of international tensions in the context of the evolving triangular relationship among China, the United States, and the Soviet Union. Zhou's new strategy also reflected his shift in emphasizing negotiations with the United States rather than continuing on a course of confrontation and isolation. China, as a new nuclear power, had not yet developed a coherent nuclear strategy in relation to either the United States or the Soviet Union. Of more immediate concern were the million hostile Russian troops stationed along the Soviet border with China. The Soviet Union had brought its strained relationship with China to a breaking point, and Zhou and Mao were compelled to regard the Soviet Union as the greatest menace to China's security. Meanwhile, it became more realistic for them to relax their vigilance against the U.S. threat once the Americans had begun to disengage from Vietnam and had promised to reduce their military forces elsewhere in Asia. The circumstances of the time made possible a dramatic change from confrontation to reconciliation in China's relationship with the United States, and the Chinese leadership, prompted by Zhou, was decisive and ready to seize the moment.

After a long and intense negotiating process of give-and-take between Zhou and Nixon, they signed the important diplomatic document called the *Shanghai Communiqué* on February 27, 1972.[165] It was a skillfully drafted instrument that set an entirely new framework for the Sino-American relationship. This joint communiqué listed and defined the points of difference as well as shared opinions between the two countries. Both Zhou and Nixon compromised on certain issues, but both also made clear that fundamental differences remained. This strategy harked back to that which Zhou had adopted in 1955 at the Bandung Conference—seeking agreements and shelving differences. The major distinction, however, was that the differences at the Bandung Conference had been left unrecorded in the Afro-Asian concord of Ten Principles, while the *Shanghai Communiqué* catalogued and set forth the discordant points at length. Both sides, recognizing certain common strategic interests, decided to subordinate other, less pressing concerns in order to build a new relationship.

The joint communiqué expressed the desire of both governments, each for its own reason, to put an end to the period of enmity and to strive for normal relations through a variety of channels, "including the sending of senior U.S. representatives to Beijing from time to time for concrete consultations."[166] The two sides also declared that they would conduct their relations on the basis of the Five Principles of Peaceful Coexistence, originally advocated by Zhou as early as December 1953, and that they were prepared to settle "international disputes without resorting to the use of threat of force."[167] Moreover, the two countries were determined to define a new order in Asia not on the basis of the preponderance of one power but, rather, on an equilibrium among nations. "Neither should seek hegemony in the Asia-Pacific region," the document stated, "and each is opposed to efforts by any other country or group of countries to establish such hegemony."[168] The joint communiqué added that "it would be against the interests of the peoples of the world for any major country to collude with another against other countries, or for major countries to divide the world into spheres of interest."[169]

On the question of Taiwan separate statements were issued. The Chinese side once again called for the progressive withdrawal of "all U.S. forces and military installations."[170] The United States, for its part, offered a major shift from its original position; the U.S. government formally recognized that the future of Taiwan was an internal matter and explicitly accepted the principle of one China. According to its statement, the U.S. government reaffirmed its interest "in a peaceful settlement of the Taiwan question by the Chinese themselves."[171] The *Shanghai Communiqué* successfully defused Taiwan as a source of tension between China and the United States, and it also established a new framework within which Zhou and Nixon could work in building a cooperative relationship that was characterized by increasingly parallel positions on Asian security problems.

After the signing of the *Shanghai Communiqué* in February 1972 by Zhou and Nixon, the most important follow-up discussions between the two took place in Beijing in January 1973. On this occasion, Zhou reiterated his view on Sino-American relations at length. Since they had come to know each other quite well over the course of their extended negotiations, Zhou and Kissinger had developed a sense of mutual respect and understanding. Following a lengthy exchange of views, a joint communiqué was announced on February 22 stressing that both sides agreed that "the time was appropriate for accelerating the normalization of relations."[172] Accordingly, diplomatic liaison offices were to be established in Beijing and Washington.

Even as Zhou's health deteriorated, he continued to labor for the improvement of China's relations with the United States, believing this to be fundamental to China's ability to carry out its domestic policy of Four Modernizations and to secure a proper role in a new world order. Most of Zhou's residual energy was, therefore, devoted to completing the long process of Sino-American diplomatic rapprochement and to giving hope to the Chinese people as they recovered from the ravages of the Cultural Revolution. Normalization and improvement of relations between China and the United States would come, Zhou strongly believed, as soon as both countries sincerely sought common ground.

Whatever tangible results had been achieved by the end of 1974 were directly attributable to Zhou's efforts. The new foreign policy line formulated by Zhou and sanctioned by Mao was intended to secure a major role for China on the stage of world politics. Its success meant the end of the U.S. containment policy vis-à-vis China and the beginning of a new era in Chinese foreign policy. The pursuit of a policy of normalization in China's relations with the United States also implied the shift to a more pragmatic bilateral connection with Washington as well as the establishment of a strategic triangle made up of China, the Soviet Union, and the United States, within which alliances would change depending on the issues at stake. In his last report to the NPC in January 1975 Zhou indicated that "there exist fundamental differences between China and the United States" in spite of the fact that the relations between the two countries "have improved to some extent."[173] He nevertheless optimistically predicted that the improved relations would continue "as long as the principles of the Sino-American Shanghai Communique are carried out in earnest."[174]

As Zhou pursued his new foreign policy orientation vis-à-vis the United States, the undergirding principle was that common interests transcended the conflicts and competition between China and the United States. Meanwhile, he also began to conceptualize a new world order to which all nation-states belonged whose preservation was vital for the security and prosperity of all member nations. Those conducting the foreign policy for independent member nations should, as he saw it, not only act to protect and promote the interests of their own nation but also to preserve the international community itself to benefit all its member states. Statesmanship in the world arena, therefore, required proper recognition of this important responsibility as well as the skill and judgment needed to safeguard the interests of the individual country within the system. In international affairs, Zhou held, a diplomat needed experience, judgment, and self-restraint in pursuing national interests and, moreoever, a desire to search for shared interests and common values between or among nation-states. Within this context it is interesting to note Kissinger's observation that the relationship between the United States and China would depend heavily on American "international performance." He remarked: "What the Chinese want from us is to maintain the world balance of power. If we do this, if we show we understand these problems, we will have a good relationship with the Chinese."[175]

Zhou was inclined to view international events as interconnected. The absence of a long-term foreign policy, as he saw it, could only lead to incoherent improvisation in a nation's decision making; in contrast, the existence of a long-term foreign policy provided a basis for taking diplomatic initiatives. If Zhou could not achieve successful rapprochement with the United States and failed to reach general agreement with Nixon as they searched for common moves to counter the effect of Soviet hegemonism, then the evolving global situation would not be shaped the way he preferred. He was fully aware of the fact that China's unilateral moves to address the numerous, and quickly changing, circumstances existing in the world would never be adequate. Therefore, he held fast to a cluster of values and strategies that included, among other elements, the employment of diplomacy in establishing normal relations between China and the United States, the pragmatic adjustment of national interests to international realities, and the optimum exploitation of U.S.-Soviet competition and rivalry for the benefit of China and other Third World nations. The subsequent step-by-step implementation of Zhou's foreign policy initiatives in relation to the United States and its resulting success was a high point in his long career as a pragmatic leader and statesman.

CHAPTER 9

The Third World in Zhou's Global Strategy

Prior to the founding of the Communist regime in China, Zhou effectively utilized the strategy of winning over the domestic "neutral," or "third," forces during the period from 1924 to 1949 as a means of gaining national political power. With the CCP's rise to power in October 1949 he expanded this strategy to the world arena. His experience in dealing with domestic middle-of-the-road forces convinced him of the importance of international neutral forces in promoting China's prestige and influence abroad and in strengthening its bargaining position with the West. With the end of the Korean War in 1953, and particularly with the opening of the Bandung Conference in April 1955, the world stage was ready for Zhou to internationalize his strategy.

The Bandung Conference marked a new emphasis in Chinese foreign policy under Zhou's guidance. Central to his policy design was the formation of an anti-imperialist and anticolonial united front of the nations of the Third World, supporting the policy of nonalignment as a device to enlarge the area of peace and neutrality in Asia and beyond. As China's new foreign policy perspectives were being defined and refined in the early 1950s, Zhou applied the CCP's domestic revolutionary experience to the international "middle forces," represented by the nonaligned nations of the Third World, using the united front as an instrument to counteract the military supremacy of the United States and the Soviet Union.

Zhou's most significant contribution to China's foreign policy initiative during this period lay in his articulation and advocacy of the Five Principles of Peaceful Coexistence as the theoretical foundation of China's relations with the Third World nations[1] as well as in his active role in the development of neutral forces by working with India, Burma, Cambodia, Laos, Indonesia, and Egypt. To implement this strategy Zhou worked on ways to deal with the immediate issues: first, how the new Chinese government should approach the nonaligned states; and, second, how China should handle the neutral forces in the international arena.

To understand Zhou's strategy fully, it is necessary to examine his views on the third forces. The united front was, by definition, composed of diverse elements, at least one-third of which were not wholly reliable. The very loose grouping of large numbers of Third World countries with different aspirations threatened to weaken the coalition and created the possibility of a split. For this reason Zhou concentrated on the task of examining the position of the middle forces, or the intermediate strata.[2] If the concept of the domestic united front was applicable to the field of international relations, there could also be some means of classifying the Third World forces on the basis of their social, economic, and political orientations. The bourgeois national leaders in the neutralist states had a dual nature; they were inclined both to resist imperialism and to capitulate to it. Because of this, any cooperative strategy had to be flexible and cautious. At times it might be necessary to struggle against them to protect the progressive forces and to compel them to resist imperialism. If these "unreliable forces" were not properly dealt with, the anti-imperialist forces would be weakened, and the united front would lose its vitality. Therefore, they had to be alternately challenged and wooed.

One of the key imperatives in Zhou's architecture of Chinese foreign policy was to thwart the efforts of major powers to encircle China with military bases or alliances. The security of the new China required dynamic strategies to counter the containment policy of the United States. The nonaligned countries of the Third World rejected the view that international peace would be based on a balance of power or that security could be ensured by countries joining power blocs and military alliances with the great powers. If the Third World nations could adopt a nonaligned policy of peace and neutrality, they, as a group, could play an important role in world affairs[3] through their joint efforts in struggling against imperialism in all its manifestations and in resisting all other forms of foreign domination. Moreover, Zhou considered that a global united front against neocolonialism and imperialism in the Third World could be a decisive factor in changing the bipolar balance of power. China, as a developing country, had its place in the Third World, and solidarity with Third World nations ought to be a basic principle in Chinese foreign policy. A commitment to peaceful coexistence with nonsocialist countries was necessary to stabilize Asian international relations.

From his earliest years as China's foreign minister and premier Zhou sought to establish bridges linking China to the outside world by means of diplomatic flexibility. He relied on negotiations, cultural exchanges, state visits, and personal diplomacy to achieve his foreign policy objectives. In pressing his anticolonial and anti-imperialist coalition in the Third World, Zhou's foreign strategy was carefully framed, and his approach remained astutely pragmatic. His efforts to establish government-to-government relations with Third World nations and to cement such relations with economic aid indicate that Zhou grappled with foreign affair issues from the perspective of geopolitics rather than ideology. He did not rely on dogmatic revolutionary rhetoric but sought, instead, to develop a sense of common interest and solidarity. He was highly sensitive to the imperialistic exploitation of Third World nations and his assessment of their common interests and of their role in contemporary international relations tended to focus almost entirely upon practical considerations. Realism required that he accept the unique local conditions of each Third World nation and the limits of China's national power. In his quest for China's national security and prestige Zhou understood the importance of making concessions for adjustments in light of the vital interests of other Third World nations. Therefore, pragmatic adaptation and strategic flexibility were key to Zhou's foreign policy, and China's own interests overrode ideological considerations related to the international Communist movement.

The zone of intensive Chinese involvement with Third World countries extended from Indochina to Southeast Asia, an area of some importance to China's territorial security. Many local wars of liberation of the postwar period had been fought within this zone, and it was here that the leading contingents of the anti-imperialist struggle had grown. It was within this zone that Zhou first tried to improve China's relations with non-Communist, nonaligned states. The principal goals of Zhou's diplomatic activities were to increase the security of China by creating "areas of peace and neutrality" on its periphery as well as by means of neutralization and treaties of friendship.[4] Through state-to-state relations and a heavy reliance on diplomacy, Zhou hoped, over the succeeding years, to mobilize the new forces in Asia, converting them from suspicious to cooperative partners.

Zhou's role in the process was that of a mediator attempting to induce both the Chinese people and their non-Communist, nonaligned neighbors to move in the direction of mutual understanding and concession. He thought that Chinese national interests could best be secured by the judicious application of the Five Principles of Peaceful Coexistence. As a new diplomatic move, the emphasis on peaceful coexistence complemented the practical need for cooperation between China and the Third World nations. Zhou's diplomatic approach to the Third World was based on the premise that its nations desired political independence and economic progress. During the early period Zhou was not only China's foreign minister and premier but also served practically as a roving ambassador for his country, traveling from one Asian capital to another in an attempt to deal with the Asian leaders personally whenever possible.

China's foreign policy orientation changed from an exclusive emphasis upon alliance with the Soviet Union to the formation of peaceful areas in China's neighborhood. As a result of applying the Five Principles of Peaceful Coexistence to South and Southeast Asia, China's relations with the neutralist states were substantially improved. Many Asian states not only supported Zhou's proposal for the neutralization of Indochina in 1954 but also endorsed the concept of areas of peace on the grounds that it could help them avoid Cold War entanglements so that they could concentrate, instead, on developing their economies and raising their low living standards. Such an approach was very convincing and persuasive, as China itself also stressed the importance of avoiding large-scale military confrontation with either of the two superpowers in order to mobilize its resources for economic development and industrialization.[5] The strategic aim of securing the withdrawal of the hostile Western military presence in Asia obliged Zhou to play down revolutionary objectives in nonaligned neighboring countries and to recognize the legitimate aspirations of the nonaligned states.

To win the trust of the nonaligned countries, Zhou opposed any course of action that threatened to disrupt Asian cooperation or to force China to take unilateral action that none of the new Asian states would support. Zhou carefully observed this basic rule, as far as possible, in his approach to maintaining China's close ties with India, Nepal, Burma, Cambodia, Laos, Indonesia, North Vietnam, and North Korea. Under Zhou's guidance, policy based on the twin elements of cooperation and accommodation was gradually developed in dealing with Third World countries. This policy of Five Principles of Peaceful Coexistence represented a dramatic switch from the tactic of using aggressive action by supporting wars of liberation—the line preached by Liu Shaoqi at the Trade Union in Beijing in 1949.[6] By following it, Zhou became quite successful in strengthening China's position abroad. A cordon sanitaire of nonaligned states was established, separating China from Western military bases. Furthermore, it effectively prevented the neighboring nations from forming an anti-Chinese front and, specifically, from participating in the U.S.-sponsored Southeast Asian Treaty Organization. It also guarded against the resurgence of the influence of Western powers, both hostile and friendly, in the former colonial countries. Zhou knew full well that a workable system of collective peace in Asia could not be achieved overnight. He painstakingly enacted every new step taken, every change made, in terms of China's security interest. In the final analysis this new foreign policy orientation proved particularly effective in safeguarding against the United States because the U.S. government was unable to persuade as many Asian states to join SEATO as it had hoped.

In his effort to maximize China's diplomatic flexibility abroad Zhou found the neutral leaders of the Third World to be useful instruments of foreign policy. Within an amazingly brief period of time after the founding of the Beijing regime, Zhou was able to win over the support of many Asian nations at both the Geneva and Bandung Conferences in 1954 and 1955. Through his continuing attempts to articulate and refine the objectives of Chinese foreign policy toward the Third World, two patterns of tactics emerged during this period, and Zhou employed them consistently in all his subsequent handling of international affairs. First, he extensively utilized the method of direct personal contact in his negotiations with foreign leaders both in China and abroad. Second, he consistently advocated the adoption of the Five Principles of Peaceful Coexistence as the basis of China's foreign relations.

The departure from the Soviet-leaning policy was evident in Zhou's increasingly vigorous advocacy of cooperation with its non-Communist neighbors. Peaceful settlement of international disputes and formation of the zone of peace and neutrality became a constant theme of Zhou's official statements and reports on China's foreign policy objectives during this period. Also, Zhou envisioned a far more central role for China in world affairs. "Without the participation of the PRC," he asserted on October 7, 1953, "it is impossible to settle many major international questions, above all, the questions of Asia."[7] Clearly, Zhou perceived that China should play an important role as the voice of the emerging nations of the Third World and that it could be a peacemaker and an arbiter of international affairs. At the Geneva and Bandung Conferences Zhou, as China's chief delegate, was instrumental in drafting the common principles of understanding adopted by the participating nations. He treated the small neighboring Asian states with consideration, avoided controversy whenever possible, and settled conflicts through diplomatic negotiations. His diplomatic labors earned him widespread respect and recognition. In retrospect, Zhou was astute in rejecting the rigid dogma of communism and Chinese revolutionary rhetoric in his efforts to grapple with the complex issue of China's relations with the emerging Third World. His cautious appraisal of reality led him once again to use pragmatism as a guide to China's actions.

Zhou already understood the importance of the Third World and its potential in international relations. He recognized the anticolonial sentiment of the newly independent states. Yet, his campaign for China's diplomatic diversification through alignment with Third World nations was at first thwarted by Mao's Soviet-leaning approach and by the elusive nature of the third force in the international arena.[8] His dialogue with neutral Asian leaders in 1954 and 1955 was made possible, and even necessary, because of the U.S. policy of containment and the expansion of the Cold War. Such international conditions made it desirable for Zhou to adjust the CCP's doctrinaire interpretation of international relations to world reality, and, in so doing, he opened up Chinese foreign policy for modification and pragmatic accommodation.

As early as 1953, Zhou's vision of a new foreign policy approach began to emerge in official statements, which asserted that diplomatic diversification could serve as a testing ground for Beijing's relations with Third World nations. There were two major reasons for such a diplomatic initiative. First, the ideas endorsed by the Party ideologues on China's foreign relations simply could not provide a dynamic basis for the nation to exert its influence in the international arena. Second, the Five Principles of Peaceful Coexistence were closely linked with Zhou and his State Council. Zhou indicated that, given the context of the new China's limited relations with the outside world, the State Council should be allowed to design a more flexible yet cautious approach to Third World nations. Zhou believed that China could be far more influential among these newly established nations if its international image and behavior were less militant and if its diplomatic thrust were aimed more toward improving state-to-state relations with them. Zhou began to busy himself with diplomatic activities designed to advance Chinese national interests through a series of boundary treaties and trade agreements with neighboring Asian countries. He became convinced that diplomatic maneuverability and the economic reconstruction of China should take precedence over proletarian internationalism and revolutionary rhetoric.

Up to the mid-1950s Zhou's perspective on international affairs was heavily oriented toward Asia. He had to acknowledge the existence of strains between the call for Communist world revolution and the need for peaceful coexistence. This conflict required constant rebalancing in China's relationships with non-Communist states of Asia. An important step in practicing pragmatism took place on April 29, 1954, when Zhou signed a treaty with India.[9] His effort to prevent a rift between his country and India over the status of Tibet was a key instance of his conciliatory approach to interstate relations. A second example of Zhou's pragmatism during this period was his proposal for the neutralization of Indochina. In 1954 and 1955 Zhou saw China's main foreign policy problem as the removal of the Western military forces and bases in Asia, which stood in the way of a "peaceful international environment." He valued the anticolonial and anti-Western potential of his Asian neighbors as highly as he did the surging nationalism of the entire Third World. He sought to exploit the conflicts between the Third World and the West in order to maximize China's diplomatic maneuverability. To this end Chinese diplomacy was to be conducted in such a way that the anticolonial and anti-imperialist sentiments among Third World nations could be solidified. Efforts were made by Zhou to localize conflicts in their regional settings, even though local issues frequently became helplessly entwined with the larger issues of the Cold War.

Zhou's foreign policy objective up to the mid-1950s was the creation of areas of peace in South and Southeast Asia, and the strategy to achieve this objective was based on the nonaligned international status of India, Burma, and Ceylon as well as on the neutralization of the three Indochinese states—namely, Cambodia, Laos, and Vietnam—as guaranteed by the 1954 Geneva agreements. In the mid-1950s Zhou occupied himself with China's national security and economic reconstruction. He was fully aware of the United States' military supremacy and extensive diplomatic activities in Asia. The U.S. policy of isolating China and the policy of peripheral military containment compelled Zhou to organize diplomatic opposition to the U.S. system of alliances in Asia and the Pacific region. He also felt that the key to economic and regional unity in Asia was China's ability to solve disputed issues peacefully, such as the dual nationalities of the ethnic Chinese and boundary demarcation. More so than his colleagues within the CCP hierarchy, Zhou was keenly aware of the need for a peaceful environment in which to undertake China's economic reconstruction. By surrounding itself with areas of peace, or buffer states, China could avoid costly military ventures.[10]

By the beginning of 1954 the international scene was in a state of flux. The Korean armistice enhanced China's prestige in Asia. This new status, combined with Zhou's calculated attitude of flexibility, opened new vistas in regard to Third World nations. As Zhou saw it, the widespread desire for an early settlement of the Vietnamese conflict, along with the need to bring about political settlement in Korea, created an opportunity for China to emerge onto the international stage in a newly cast role—that of a power broker. As such, China was able to make a strong bid for Asian leadership and for becoming representative of Asian interests in world affairs. Zhou realized that China, hoping for regional and international prestige and influence, must pass through at least three stages toward its national aspirations.

In the first stage the Chinese government must clearly define its national boundaries. Along China's long boundaries were many sovereign states. These boundaries were symbols of national power, independence, and China's ability to maintain its security; they were also traditional sources of international friction. Boundaries between China and its neighbors, such as India and the Soviet Union, were critical areas. The settlement of China's boundary disputes meant, for Zhou, not only increased national security but a more credible international position.[11]

During the second stage China should seek to establish a neutral belt of states as a zone of peace around China's periphery.[12] As long as the states bordering China were nonaligned, Zhou reasoned, they would naturally constitute a major obstacle to any expansionist design on the part of the Western powers. China's demand that its Asian neighbors not be used by any major power to pose a threat to its national security meant that China should be sensitive to the interests of its neighbors so as to win regional cooperation and to remove Western military forces and bases from Asia.

During the third stage China's efforts must transcend its territorial security and the creation of a regional belt of nonaligned states. China should search for a worldwide role. Zhou's foreign policy toward Third World nations was motivated in this regard by a strong desire to enhance his country's global influence and its flexibility of action in a world in which two superpowers enjoyed unchallenged supremacy. At this point extending Chinese political influence beyond Asia would become an important objective in Zhou's calculations concerning the Third World.

One of Zhou's foreign policy strategies in Asia was the neutralization of Indochina. The term *neutralization* may be defined as "a special international status designed to restrict the intrusion of specified state actions in a specified area."[13] Neutralism, in the present context, may be conceived merely as the practice of a foreign policy whereby a state does not ally itself with either of the rival superpowers as part of their competing collective security system. The policy was adopted by many smaller states in the early post-World War II period, and especially in the Third World.[14] India's prime minister Jawaharlal Nehru was the pioneer of this concept and practice. Although it is difficult to assess the extent of Nehru's direct or indirect influence on Zhou's thinking, clearly, Zhou was a strong advocate of neutralism.

In 1954 there was immediate concern that the Indochinese conflict might expand across the border into China, which could result in Chinese military involvement. In his negotiations with the West at the 1954 Geneva Conference, Zhou proposed the neutralization of Indochina to avoid any possible military confrontation between China and the Western powers.[15] Adoption of this policy was also intended to channel China's energy into its internal economic development. In Geneva Zhou went further than any other chief delegate in endorsing this principle. The neutralization of Indochina could accomplish the immediate objective of avoiding military conflicts between China and the

Western powers, but, more important, it could serve China's long-term need for transforming the Indochinese states into Zhou's projected area of peace.[16] Under such circumstances it was clear that improving China's relations with the states of Southeast Asia was certainly more beneficial than maintaining its subordinate role in current diplomatic initiatives undertaken with the Soviet Union. Zhou wanted to reach a negotiated settlement in Indochina, so he emphasized the need for mutual compromise that would reconcile French interests with the national aspirations of the Indochinese states. There was little prospect, however, that neutralization would be realized until much greater regional cooperation was achieved. Furthermore, all the major powers would have to respect the restraints that such a policy would impose on them.

Zhou remained committed to the goal of achieving neutralization in Indochina, particularly because he believed this to be of great importance to peace throughout Southeast Asia and to China's security. Zhou recognized that clashes of interest were inevitable in international relations. He did not expect the neutralization of Indochina to be accomplished quickly due to greater benevolence and altruism on the part of the major powers. Neutralization could occur only when a satisfactory balance of interests had been struck. The neutralization of Indochina depended upon the common desire of the major Geneva powers to remove the region's three states from the sphere of international rivalries and upon the determination and ability of Cambodia, Laos, and Vietnam to resist encroachments on their neutral status.

In his opening speech to the Geneva Conference on April 28, 1954, Zhou cautioned that, if the war in Indochina were left uncontrolled, it would remain a source of extreme instability. "The existence of this state of affairs and its further continuation," asserted Zhou, "hinder the peaceful settlement of urgent international questions, especially those of Asia, and aggravate uneasiness and tension in international relations."[17] At the third session, held on May 12, Zhou openly expressed his support for peaceful settlement of the Indochinese war. He also indicated that the important task of the Geneva Conference was to bring about a restoration of peace in Indochina by recognizing the "national rights" of the Indochinese peoples.[18] On May 27 Zhou formally presented to the conference his six-point proposal to end the war. He attached the highest priority to prohibiting reintroduction of military personnel and armaments into the region, calling this "the most important condition for putting an end to foreign interference there."[19]

After arriving at some basic understanding with Anthony Eden and George Bidault, the chief delegates from Great Britain and France, respectively, Zhou initiated a formal proposal for the withdrawal of Vietminh forces from Laos and Cambodia. On June 23 Zhou met with Pierre Mendes-France, the new French premier and foreign minister, in Berne, Switzerland, and discussed a number of issues vital to a negotiated settlement in Indochina. Both premiers agreed that a united government of Vietnam should be formed through a national election. More important was Zhou's statement that China would recognize the royal governments in Laos and Cambodia, provided that their "neutral status" was enforced.[20]

Zhou made short trips to New Delhi and Rangoon during the Geneva Conference to exchange views with Indian prime minister Nehru and Burmese prime minister U Nu, two leading proponents and practitioners of the principles of nonalignment as a legitimate approach to Cold War issues. His discussions with these neutral Asian leaders reinforced his belief in the practical value of establishing an area of peace and neutrality. Zhou saw Nehru as the most influential neutral leader in the world arena and sought his support in securing a Western guarantee to bar U.S. bases from Indochina, which would help to secure China's southern borders. Nehru viewed Zhou's approach to the neutralization of Indochina as a key to his own policy of collective peace through the enlargement of the areas of peace and nonalignment in South and Southeast Asia. On June 28, 1954, Zhou and Nehru issued a joint statement in which both premiers urged a "political settlement" for Indochina and neutral status for all three Indochinese states.[21] On June 28 Zhou arrived in Rangoon for talks with U Nu, and a joint statement was issued the following day declaring the right of the people of each nation to choose their own system and way of life without interference from other nations. The statement declared, moreover, that revolution was not for export and that outside interference with the expressed will of the people of any nation could not be tolerated.[22]

The success of Zhou's diplomatic endeavors was underscored by the signing of the Final Declaration at Geneva on July 21, 1954, which pledged the signatories not to impair the sovereignty, independence, and neutrality of the three Indochinese states. In his speech addressed to the last conference session, on July 21, Zhou aptly summed up the accomplishments of the conference: "The agreements that we have achieved carry concrete provisions for ending the Indochina war and lay down the principles for the settlement of the political question of Indochina. . . . We note that after the armistice the three states of Indochina will refrain from joining any military alliance and that the establishment of military bases on their respective territories by any foreign country will not be allowed. These agreements will enable the peoples of the three states of Indochina to engage in the construction of their respective countries in a peaceful environment."[23]

Zhou expected the neutralization plan to shield the three Indochinese states from fierce competition in the Cold War and world power politics.

Moreover, the neutralization of Indochina under the auspices of the Geneva Powers could be a flexible and useful instrument of diplomacy in avoiding an East-West military confrontation. In his report on China's foreign relations delivered to the Twenty-third session of the Central People's Government Council on August 11, 1954, Zhou elaborated on the Geneva agreements and their implications.[24] He emphasized the significance of the neutralization of Indochina for China in terms of its territorial security and economic interests. What interested him most was not the creation of a Communist state on China's southern borders; his chief concern was, rather, to ensure that there could be no Western military base anywhere near the southern rimlands of China. In addition, he stressed the positive effects a neutralized Indochina would have on overall Asian and international stability. According to Zhou, it was now possible to establish "an area of collective peace in Indochina and its surrounding countries."[25] If favorable international conditions prevailed, Zhou reasoned, such an area of collective peace could be enlarged to include other Southeast Asian countries, and countries throughout Asia, to help assure their peaceful coexistence free from outside interference.[26]

Zhou soberly warned, however, that a developing threat to this area of collective peace was imminent. "Clearly United States aggressive circles," said Zhou on August 11, 1954, "will not allow the smooth and thorough implementation of the agreements reached at the Geneva Conference. Recently, [they] have been actively goading Australia, New Zealand, Thailand and the Philippines, trying to bring around Britain and France, and even trying to prevail upon the Colombo Powers to form a so-called Southeast defense bloc."[27] He maintained, "It is not difficult to perceive that this bloc is being organized mainly against China and with the purpose of undermining the collective cooperation on the Indochina question of the various participating nations in the Geneva Conference. If any of the nations concerned should join the United States aggressive circles in these divisive activities, then the common cause of ensuring the restoration of peace in Indochina would be endangered and the implementation of the Indochinese armistice agreement might be disrupted."[28]

On September 23, 1954, Zhou made another important report, this time to the first session of the First NPC, in which he outlined China's policy priorities, both at home and abroad. He reaffirmed the determination of the CCP leadership to transform China into "a socialist, industrial country of prosperity."[29] To achieve this goal he stressed the urgent need for "a peaceful environment and a peaceful world" in which to develop China's internal economy.[30] He specifically mentioned that both Laos and Cambodia had committed themselves to not taking part in any "military alliance," adding that it was essential for Asian countries to strive jointly to defend "collective peace and security throughout Asia."[31] He offered three points, however, to demonstrate why SEATO was an aggressive alliance against the nonaligned Asian states. First, adherence by Thailand, along with the Philippines and Pakistan, was merely an extension of its previous relationship with the United States. Second, "Communist aggression" was "nonexistent" and a pretext: the fact that Thailand and the Philippines had not entered into diplomatic relations with China was also "only a pretext used by the governments of these two countries to justify their action in serving the aggressive forces of the United States."[32] Third, the treaty was an "alliance of colonial powers" that "supports the United States policy of making China the main object of hostility in the Far East . . . and facilitates the United States aggression against Asian countries from all directions."[33]

At a banquet for Nehru, Zhou said, "As a result of the Geneva Conference, there arises the possibility that the idea of establishing an area of peace in Southeast Asia, which was initiated by Prime Minister Nehru, may be realized."[34] He went on to say, "But the conclusion of the Manila treaty goes directly against this idea."[35] Nevertheless, Zhou reaffirmed, "We . . . are ready to work, together with India, in a common effort to overcome the difficulties, and to establish and extend an area of peace in Asia."[36] Later, in December 1954, Zhou and the visiting Burmese leader U Nu issued a joint communiqué. It reiterated many of the key elements of Zhou's foreign policy appraisal: "The two Premiers expressed the hope that in order to safeguard peace in Asia and the world, the Five Principles of Peaceful Coexistence would be widely accepted by all the countries of Asia and the world. The Premiers maintained that even countries now antagonistic to each other could establish normal, peaceful, and friendly relations if they would strive for that end with sincerity and good will."[37] The communiqué confirmed most of all the importance of the area of peace: "The two Premiers expressed their profound interest in the consolidation and enlargement of the area of peace. If the area of peace were consolidated and enlarged, the present international tension would gradually be relaxed, thereby lessening the likelihood of a new war and strengthening the cause of world peace."[38]

The first Afro-Asian Conference, held at Bandung, Indonesia, from April 18 to 24, 1955, marked the expansion of Zhou's interest in the Third World countries of Asia to a global scope. In his public speeches and private talks he stressed the theme of peaceful coexistence in contemporary international relations.[39] Zhou stated China'a belief that "states, large and small, strong and weak, must all enjoy equality, and their sovereignty and territorial integrity must be respected without fail."[40] At the Bandung Conference Zhou championed the virtues of moderation and reconciliation. He was recognized as a constructive

Third World leader when he and Nehru jointly promulgated the Five Principles of Peaceful Coexistence. Yet differences among social systems and political ideologies and the mutual apprehension and misunderstanding fostered by the former colonial powers tended to drive a wedge between participants. Throughout the conference Zhou was at his most conciliatory; he worked quietly and patiently to win over neutral leaders to become his partners in the campaign for peaceful coexistence. He tried his best to assure them that China harbored no aggressive or subversive designs for their countries. With a shrewd understanding of the practical value of past colonial experiences Zhou worked to broaden the common political ground between China and other Third World countries. He also forged new diplomatic relationships with nonaligned states such as Indonesia, Cambodia, Nepal, and Ceylon.

The keynote of Zhou's diplomatic line was set forth in a speech delivered at the Bandung Conference on April 19, 1955. The speech breathed conciliation and stressed China's interest in peace and its desire to act as a "good neighbor" in Asia. He indicated both hope for and obstacle to achieving unity among Third World nations and outlined China's wish to seek common ground in spite of existing differences.[41] "By following the principles of mutual respect for sovereignty and territorial integrity, non-aggression, noninterference in each other's internal affairs, equality, and mutual benefit," noted Zhou, "the peaceful coexistence of countries with different social systems can be realized."[42] In a later speech before the Political Committee of the Bandung Conference, on April 23, Zhou gave further assurances of China's intentions and reiterated its desire to recognize the equality of all nations, small and large.[43]

Until the Bandung Conference in 1955 China's contacts with African nations had been rather limited. Zhou's extensive discussions with the Egyptian leader Gamal Abdel Nasser and his invitation to all the delegates at the Bandung Conference to visit China reflected the diplomatic initiative by the Chinese government to diversify its relations with the outside world. In addition, Zhou used the Bandung Conference as a forum for expounding and advancing official Chinese viewpoints on a series of colonial and Cold War issues. He was certainly successful in broadening his personal contacts in the Third World.

The potential value of Third World nations made Zhou view international relations in terms of a multistate system rather than a rigid bipolar world order composed of only socialist and capitalist camps. With the Five Principles of Peaceful Coexistence as the basis of Chinese foreign policy Zhou tried to prevent Third World countries from aligning with the West. In his report to the NPC on May 13, 1955, he declared that "the Asian-Africa Conference inspired all oppressed nations and peoples in Asia, Africa, Latin America, and other parts of the world in the fight for independence and freedom."[44] This emphasis on the forces moving toward independence among the African states signaled the rise of the Third World as a new factor in international affairs.

On July 30, 1955, Zhou delivered the keynote speech on the current international situation and China's foreign policy to the second session of the First NPC. He noted that "the people demand the abolition of military blocs which create splits and hostility between nations" and that "the people of Asia and Africa, in particular, are opposed to such military blocs, since it is quite clear that the colonialists are using such military blocs as a means of setting up their colonial rule."[45] He went on to state: "Since the [Bandung] Conference, contacts between China and Asian and African countries have already expanded. We are prepared to continue to enlarge these contacts. We consider this to be beneficial to all parties concerned and also helpful to the promotion of world peace and cooperation."[46] He also examined the conditions in Indochina and characterized "the proposition of keeping neutrality" and "nonparticipation in military blocs" as "an important development in current international life."[47] He took the opportunity to reaffirm China's respect for the "neutral position" adopted by Asian countries. He expected that both Laos and Cambodia would closely associate themselves with the nonaligned states of South and Southeast Asia and would certainly reject any close link with either the United States or SEATO. The overall reduction of Western influence in the world constituted, in Zhou's estimation, the beginning of a new era in Chinese foreign policy.[48]

How to deal with the Third World nations during and after the Bandung Conference was the top priority in Zhou's global strategy. His policy orientation and tactics represent a good example of ideology yielding to pragmatism. Zhou elaborated his central theme of peaceful coexistence in various official statements and reports. On January 30, 1956, for example, he presented a political report to the National Committee of the Chinese People's Political Consultative Conference in which he stated that "we believe in the superiority of the socialist system. But we always maintain that revolution cannot be exported."[49] He added that "we advocate peaceful coexistence and peaceful competition between countries having different social systems, and that the people of each country should choose their political and economic systems and their way of life for themselves."[50] Zhou anticipated that in the future "there will certainly be more oppressed nations and countries who free themselves from colonial rule along paths of their own choosing. . . . We wish to make contacts with the leaders and peoples of all these countries in pursuance of the spirit of Bandung."[51] What is more significant is the fact that Zhou attributed the achievement of independence by former colonies and semicolonies to their national leaders. Rightly, he concluded, "these countries treasure the national independence they have achieved and are determined to safeguard their independence and sovereignty."[52] He saw their desire to uphold their national sovereignty and their adoption of the nonalignment policy as compatible. He was convinced that these countries "firmly maintain a position of neutrality and demand peaceful coexistence among all countries."[53] Thus, according to Zhou, "these countries, particularly India, as a great power, are playing an increasingly great positive role in the peaceful settlement of many major international questions."[54] He went on to say, "We have established friendly relations with them on the principle of peaceful coexistence, and are cooperating with them in many respects in the struggle for peace and international security."[55]

On June 28, 1956, Zhou made similar remarks on the subjects of nonalignment and peaceful coexistence in another major foreign policy statement addressed to the third session of the First NPC. According to Zhou, the nonaligned Asian countries wished to build up their own "independent national economies"; therefore, they desired "a peaceful international environment" in which to develop their respective projects at home.[56] Moreover, Zhou stressed the positive role played by the nonaligned states in the development of "a system of collective peace."[57]

Being an accomplished practitioner of personal diplomacy, Zhou always favored person-to-person contacts with the leaders of other states. In his statement he also emphasized the importance of such activities by asserting that "contact between the leaders of different countries is a very important measure for enhancing understanding and trust and easing tension."[58] He specifically pointed out that "we all remember clearly that an important landmark in the development of the friendly and cooperative relations between China and India, China and Burma . . . was the exchange of visits and issuance of joint statements by their leaders."[59] Therefore, he concluded, "we intend to make such contacts more extensively in the future."[60]

In line with his public pronouncements Zhou paid visits to India, Burma, Cambodia, and Nepal between mid-November 1956 and early February 1957. As he put it, the chief purpose of his visits was "to seek friendship, peace, and knowledge."[61] The warm reception Zhou received wherever he went reassured him that countries of different sociopolitical systems could indeed coexist in peace. Reporting on his visits to the National Committee of the People's Political Consultative Conference on March 5, 1957, Zhou noted that "in the many places we visited, whether in the daytime or at night, there were always thousands of people coming out, in spite of great heat or bitter cold, to cheer us, to greet us according to their various national customs."[62] He went on to say: "A keen feeling of closeness never left us during our visits to those countries. We felt very much like being in the homes of close friends, our kinsmen or brothers, and not in strange countries."[63]

During the period from 1953 to 1957 three basic facets of Zhou's approach to the Third World emerged: first, peaceful coexistence; second, the neutralization of Indochina; and, third, the formation and enlargement of areas of peace. All these developments led Zhou to continue his search for diplomatic flexibility and national security. His conciliatory line was consistent with his political style, and his practical approach to the Third World was the result of the interaction of political reality and national interest. As the Chinese premier and foreign minister, his primary objective lay in adopting foreign policy initiatives that could (1) facilitate the maintenance of national security, (2) provide opportunities to foster China's economic development, and (3) preserve a high degree of diplomatic maneuverability. China, in Zhou's view, required moderation in order to inspire the confidence of both Communist and non-Communist states throughout the Third World. Fundamental to Zhou's approach was an attempt to introduce rationality and pragmatism into Chinese foreign policy; furthermore, he emphasized the need to develop China's state-to-state relations with Third World nations.[64] Third World leaders and governments should not only be fully recognized but also encouraged to join in the effort to counter the global revival of colonialism and imperialism.

Zhou acknowledged that strains existed between world revolution and peaceful coexistence. Such international tensions required constant balancing and, in China's relationships with the non-Communist states, constant negotiating. His flexible foreign policy strategy was formulated within the context of Chinese national priorities and needs. Peaceful coexistence, according to Zhou, involved direct relations between China and non-Communist states, particularly in strategic areas, yet it was not designed to prevent Chinese support for "favorable developments" in non-Communist states. Such a policy added a degree of flexibility to China's foreign relations and provided not simply an instrument for dealing with conflict but also the basis for a genuine rational dialogue as well. In actual practice, the policy of peaceful coexistence was aimed at creating an environment in which China and other nations could regulate and restrain their differences and conflicting national interests.[65]

Zhou believed in international community—in its essential value, its existence, and its potential for growth. The reality of international community was based on the responsibility of each state to provide collective security; the need for it arose from the common interests of states. Foreign policy was thus directed, in Zhou's view, toward a growing awareness of interdependence between states and toward peaceful settlement of interstate disputes, territorial or otherwise. As might be anticipated from his emphasis on continuous adjustment, Zhou was inclined to take the present conditions of interstate relations as the point of departure from which a more desirable pattern of international relations in the Third World could be developed. His strategy did not require a revolutionary clean slate in order to prepare for a new world order.

In retrospect, it was not until 1954 that Zhou became an active participant in international conferences, exerting a tremendous impact upon Third World politics. Zhou's frequent references to common colonial experiences during and after the Bandung Conference reflected not only his explicit commitment to Third World unity and cooperation but also the growing influence that China expected to exert on the stage of international politics.[66] The practical value of cooperation between China and other Third World nations lay in the fact that it could help change the worldwide balance of forces and enabled the anticolonial and anti-imperialist united front, of which China was an integral part, to wage its initial struggle from a position of considerable strength.

Zhou knew that China's call for peaceful coexistence and equality between states could materialize only if the Third World nations were successful in forcing the Western powers to abandon their plans for war and economic exploitation. He also regarded the vital interests of the newly independent nations of the Third World as separate from those of the Communist bloc, as having a legitimacy of their own and the capacity to create a third force in the world arena, standing apart from both the socialist and capitalist camps while working for their national independence and economic development. Far from practicing a radical militant policy, Zhou valued the anti-imperialist and anticolonial struggle and the revolutionary potential of the Third World.[67] By keeping China the champion of the policy of peaceful coexistence, Zhou could make use of Beijing's enhanced prestige in the Third World to gain additional leverage in his ongoing negotiations with either of the two superpowers, or both, whenever necessary. Therefore, Zhou's attitude toward the Third World was the outcome of his realistic assessment of the policies of the two superpowers. If friendship, support, and influence could not be found within the two existing global alliance systems, they would have to be sought in the Third World.

While intensifying China's appeal to the leaders and governments of the Third World, Zhou also took full advantage of the Sino-Soviet military alliance to buttress China's international position. His emphasis on the Sino-Soviet alliance did not blur his pragmatic political calculation in a highly competitive international situation and obscure the rich possibilities open to Chinese diplomacy. His performance at the 1954 Geneva Conference, for example, was an act of brilliant diplomatic virtuosity, and he managed to bring to the Third World nations a sense of dignity and common historical experience.

The Bandung phase of Chinese foreign policy gained momentum with Zhou's 1956 trip to eleven countries in Asia and Europe for the purpose of broadening China's diplomatic horizon. In his report on March 5, 1957, Zhou specifically stressed the historical significance of the mid-1956 Suez Canal affair. The event, he explained, was "a great revelation to us, showing that although the Asian and African countries are not yet powerful in national strength, all aggression by the colonialists can be frustrated as long as we maintain our solidarity and remain firmly united with all peace-loving forces of the world and wage a resolute struggle."[68] As time went on, the Third World was no longer equated by Zhou with a zone of collective peace. Ultimately, it represented an integral part of the anti-imperialist and anticolonial front. By 1960 Zhou was ready to place Asia, Africa, and Latin America in the forefront against aggression and neocolonialism. Moreover, the Chinese government launched a systematic and far-reaching drive toward economic cooperation with other Third World governments. While these moves were in line with the new diplomatic initiatives expressed by Zhou at the 1955 Bandung Conference, they also reflected a new appreciation of both agricultural and construction as means of economic assistance. Although "revolutionary" prospects were "excellent" in Africa,[69] Zhou was careful to point out that the Chinese revolutionary experience could only serve "as a kind of reference" for the African peoples.[70] Conditions in China and any African nation were not identical; therefore, he was more interested in establishing closer diplomatic and economic relations with the African nations than in promoting revolution in them.

Zhou led a large Chinese delegation to Africa from December 1963 to February 1964. In June 1965 he made two visits, one to Tanzania and another to the United Arab Republic. During his tour of Africa Zhou stated at a press conference in Algiers, "China's experience in socialist revolution and socialist construction after its liberation can only serve as a kind of reference for the Algerian people, who are carrying their revolution forward and have taken the path of socialism under the leadership of the National Liberation Front [NLF] and President Ben Bella."[71] He went on to say that "conditions in China and Algeria are not quite the same: The Algerian people draw on their own experience from their revolutionary practice in accordance with revolutionary principles. This is most dependable and useful."[72] In his speech to NLF cadres on December 25, 1963, Zhou suggested that "the truth of revolution cannot be monopolized" and that "the revolutionaries of all countries will find the way for revolution suitable to the realities of their own country."[73] He qualified his remarks, however, by noting that the revolutionaries of all countries should "earn the support and respect of the popular masses so long as they rely on the masses and persevere in the revolution. Otherwise, they will be renounced, sooner or later, by the masses of the people."[74]

Algeria's independence was, for Zhou, a living symbol of a successful armed struggle. It was "a great event in the African national liberation movement."[75] Their country's independence, as Zhou told the Algerians, "has set for other African peoples a brilliant example of daring to wage an armed struggle and daring to seize victory, and indicates to oppressed nations throughout the world the correct road to winning independence and freedom."[76]

In Ghana, on January 15, 1964, Zhou stated that one of the key elements of Chinese foreign policy was " to support the African nations in opposing imperialism and old and new colonialism."[77] In his speech at Mogadishu on February 3, 1964, he urged solidarity of the Afro-Asian nations because "Asian and African peoples are brothers sharing the same life-breath and destiny. . . . It is our common fighting task to win and safeguard national independence and develop national economy and culture."[78] On the same occasion Zhou stressed the importance of "correct leadership," reliance on "the strength of the masses," and "careful utilization of natural resources."[79] In every African capital he visited Zhou reiterated, with different degrees of emphasis, his contention that imperialist powers were seeking to place Africa under new forms of political and economic control. He also pointed out that the struggle for political independence among Third World nations ought to be complemented by the policy of economic self-reliance.[80]

It is important to note that, at the start of his trip to Africa, Zhou announced a five-point program as the basis of the Chinese approach to the African nations. "China supports African peoples," declared Zhou, "in their struggle to oppose imperialism and colonialism, old and new, and to win and safeguard national independence."[81] He was careful to point out that his country was ready to support "the desire of African peoples to achieve unity and solidarity in a manner of their own choice."[82] More specifically, Zhou commended the "policy of peace, neutrality, and nonalignment" as a long-term strategy, not as a diplomatic maneuver.[83] The sovereignty of the African nations, he suggested, "should be respected by all other countries, and encroachment and interference from any quarter should be exposed."[84] Zhou's public position on the First Conference of Nonaligned States, held at Belgrade, Yugoslavia, from September 1 to 6, 1961, was both clear and supportive. "Being a committed country," Zhou told a press conference in Algeria on December 26, 1963, "China obviously will not participate in a conference of nonaligned countries. We support the result of the first conference of nonaligned countries in opposing imperialism, defending world peace, combatting colonialism, and supporting the national independence movement."[85] He added, however, "I believe that the second conference of nonaligned countries, should it take place, should follow the policy of the previous conference; otherwise, it would fail to play the progressive role of arousing the people of the world to struggle."[86] The Belgrade Conference had also, for Zhou, strengthened the basic notion of a viable third force in contemporary international relations at the expense of the "two camps" worldview.

While extending congratulations to every host country for having emancipated itself from colonial control, Zhou was careful to point out the need for continuing struggle along the road toward independence. Political independence was, according to him, only the first step in the fight against imperialism, for a new nation was still vulnerable to "the activities of aggression, intolerance, subversion, and infiltration by the imperialists and [other] foreign forces."[87] Only through the final defeat of imperialism and old and new colonialism would the African nations achieve liberation and independence.

It was during this tour through the African continent that Zhou pledged his government's commitment to equality and mutual benefit. In his public statements he frequently emphasized the theme of self-reliance as a means to political independence. According to Zhou, this was defined as primary reliance on a country's own efforts, people, and resources. Foreign economic aid with conditions attached should be avoided. It was within this conceptual framework that Zhou enunciated the eight principles governing China's aid to foreign countries, stressing the central theme of self-reliance.[88] The eight-point policy justified the small scale of Chinese foreign assistance and laid out the common interests shared by China and recipient countries in the Third World.

Zhou's comments on economic developments in the Third World were in line with his diplomatic mission. "First, the Chinese government always bases itself," he noted, "on the principles of equality and mutual benefit in providing aid to other countries."[89] He went on to say: "It never regards such aid as a kind of unilateral alms but as something mutual. Through such aid the friendly new emerging countries gradually develop their own national economies, free themselves from colonial control, and strengthen the anti-imperialist forces in the world."[90] According to Zhou, this was in itself "a tremendous support to China."[91]

The second principle was that, "in providing aid to other countries, the Chinese government strictly respects the sovereignty of the recipient country." Zhou added that it would never ask "for any privileges" or attach "any conditions."[92] Third, the Chinese government would provide economic aid "in the form of interest-free or low-interest loans" and "extend the limit for the repayment so as to lighten the burden of the recipient countries as far as possible."[93]

"In providing aid to other countries," according to the fourth principle, "the purpose of the Chinese government is not to make the recipient countries dependent on China but to help them embark on the road of self-reliance, step by step."[94] In other words, developing countries should rely on themselves for their economic transformation. By implication China required its own resources for domestic development. Thus, the Chinese government could anticipate limits to its massive aid operations, and most investment for economic development would have to be generated within the developing countries. Accordingly, the Chinese government would try its best, in line with Zhou's fifth principle, to help the recipient countries build projects that required "less investment while yielding quicker results, so that the recipient governments may increase their incomes and accumulate capital."[95]

According to Zhou's sixth and seventh principles, the Chinese government should provide "the best-quality equipment and material of its own manufacture at international market prices" as well as assume responsibility for training the personnel of the recipient country in order to fully master "any particular technical assistance" from China.[96] In line with the eighth principle the Chinese experts dispatched by their government "to help in construction in the recipient countries" were required to "have the same standard of living as the experts of the recipient country."[97] Therefore, technical assistance associated with training and common interests between Chinese experts and their African counterparts were emphasized. Local projects among Third World nations could thus be financed principally by indigenous resources or with modest Chinese support, either human or material or both. While extremely limited in scope, such aid to foreign countries was useful to China as a reminder to Third World governments of the options open to them should their policies prove consistent with Chinese interests.

In retrospect, Zhou's 1963-64 trip was a watershed in China's political and economic policies toward the Third World. Zhou was confident that the guidelines of China's economic policy could serve as an example to developing nations. In addition, the Chinese aid policy in itself contained many positive features. First of all, loan payment would take the form of supplies of local products or local currency. Second, Chinese agricultural production techniques were well suited to the economic conditions existing in most underdeveloped countries, which made Chinese aid policy that much more attractive. Finally, the Chinese tended to exclude from their aid packages materials that were readily available in the recipient country, thereby maximizing the effectiveness of any amount of aid. In addition, China's policy of technical cooperation, especially in the industrial field, normally would cover all stages of any particular project, including the selection of sites, the drawing up of blueprints, and the supply of all necessary equipment and spare parts.

Zhou's practical suggestions to Third World leaders and governments throughout the African tour revealed a number of themes derived from China's domestic experience—for example, the importance of making agriculture the foundation and industry the leading factor in economic development and the value of self-reliance. Economic perspectives ought to stem from political priorities rather than from domestic experience. Chief among them was a desire to expel Western influence from the Third World. In support of this aim Zhou was willing to accept almost any domestic economic system, provided that a Third World nation's foreign policy was sufficiently anti-imperialist. Therefore, the criterion for receiving aid was not based on a country's economic substructure but, rather, on its international stance.

At the end of his extensive tour of Africa, Zhou characterized the essence of his approach to Third World nations before the reception in the Great Hall of the People in Beijing on March 24, 1964. "The Chinese Communists have shared with you the experience of imperialistic aggression," said Zhou, "and therefore are sharing with you the common mission of opposing imperialism and old and new colonialism."[98] Later, in his report on the results of his visit to Africa, Zhou remarked on the unique quality of Chinese aid, which, though small in scope, was "reliable, practical, and conducive to the independent development of the countries concerned."[99] His comments on existing African political conditions were equally positive. "During our visit to the new emerging African countries," he said, "we were most deeply impressed by the profound change in the mental outlook of the African people. Their courage and enthusiasm, energy and vigor, bespeak the mettle of a people who have become independent and stood up on their own feet."[100] He added: "They dare to be the masters of their own house and to manage their own state affairs; they dare to despise their enemies and to fight all oppressors, old and new. This fighting spirit constitutes the fundamental strength for the establishment of all the new emerging states."[101] Zhou concluded his political analysis of the African continent by suggesting that, "with this fighting spirit, a people can defeat all schemes of the imperialists and old and new colonialists and overcome all difficulties and obstacles on their road of advancement. Africa today is no longer what it was in the late nineteenth and early twentieth centuries. It has become an awakened, militant, and advanced continent."[102]

In his report on the work of the government delivered to the NPC on December 21 and 22, 1964, Zhou examined recent developments in Algeria and the Congo and offered further comment on China's foreign policy. "The victory of the Algerian people in their national liberation war," noted Zhou, "has set a brilliant example for the national liberation movement in Africa."[103] The people of the Congo, as he saw it, would win their fight for independence and freedom "by strengthening their national unity and persisting in their long struggle."[104] On the issue of China's foreign aid policy Zhou indicated his government's intention to support "countries which are not yet independent in winning their independence,"[105] and such assistance was offered in the form of low-interest or interest-free loans.

On another occasion Zhou made an effort to draw a distinction between the Chinese policy of Afro-Asian solidarity and nonalignment. He pointed out that the two were directed toward the same ends, thus reaffirming Chinese support for nonalignment. "Afro-Asian solidarity," declared Zhou, "is a guarantee for the victory of the Asian and African countries and peoples in their common struggle against imperialism and old and new colonialism."[106] He then went on to say: "Solidarity has thoroughly crushed the imperialists' vicious scheme of making 'Asians fight Asians' and 'Africans fight Africans.' The nonalignment policy of peace and neutrality pursued by the Asian and African countries is in fact pointed at U.S. imperialism."[107] It was, to Zhou, a matter of certainty that in spite of "these different peculiarities between the endeavor of Afro-Asian solidarity and genuine nonalignment policy . . . they have common aims; both of them have been developed in the struggle against imperialism and their spearheads are directed against imperialism and old and new colonialism, headed by the United States."[108]

Many African countries gained their independence in 1960, and the others were expected to do so soon. Competing with both American and Soviet influence in the Third World, Zhou sought to build a broad coalition between China and Afro-Asian nations on the basis of government-to-government relations, granting technical and economic assistance, and forming new trade relations as well as strong support for national sovereignty and independence. As early as 1963, he proposed that a new Afro-Asian conference designed mainly to enhance unity between the African and Asian nations be staged. His extensive tour of the African continent in late 1963 and early 1964 was intended to stimulate support for such a conference. It was a matter of necessity for him to stress the common colonial experience and understanding of the legitimate aspirations among Third World nations.

It was in this area of common experience and shared aspirations that Zhou found the basis for forming a broad united front in the Third World against imperialism and colonialism, old and new. Mobilizing Africa in order to combat imperialism, colonialism, and later revisionism was one of Zhou's immediate objectives. In the period between early 1964 to mid-1965 Zhou made three trips to Africa and several more through the Asian world. Constant reference to the Third World as a new force in contemporary international relations indicated China's strong support for the African and Asian nations in their struggle to fight imperialism and colonialism. Zhou believed that the imperialists and colonialists had adopted a number of new policies—including the formation of military alliances, bilateral or unilateral; the establishment of military bases; and the use of economic and technical assistance programs—to perpetuate their control over the newly independent Third World nations.

Moreover, political independence, in Zhou's view, did not always mean the end of foreign rule, let alone foreign influence. The new forms of imperialism and colonialism were equally as vicious and dangerous as the old. Zhou frequently called upon African and Asian leaders to continue the relentless struggle to achieve their nations' true political independence, citing the cases of Algeria, Tanzania, among others, to underscore his faith in this outcome.

In early 1964 Zhou knew that most Asian and African nations were interested in convening a nonaligned conference. By this time, however, he was preoccupied with the Sino-Soviet conflict and attempted to exclude the Soviet Union from the second Afro-Asian conference,[109] to be held in Algiers on June 29, 1965. He maintained that the Soviet Union should not be included on the grounds that it was neither an African nor an Asian state. In late June fifteen African and Asian nations applied pressure to postpone the event, and Zhou tried his best to salvage the proposed conference. In the uncertain weeks that followed Zhou was compelled to reassess the validity of China's united front strategy, which had concentrated all its efforts on creating an ideologically diverse and loosely structured grouping of Afro-Asian governments. If the Afro-Asian nations would not be persuaded to adopt a common position criticizing the manipulation of the United Nations by a few great powers and supporting a resolution to condemn the U.S. military intervention in Vietnam, there would be little point in holding a "Second Bandung Conference" of Asian and African nations.

Zhou's decision to abandon the conference surfaced when he attacked Soviet "sabotaging activities" on September 8.[110] On this occasion Zhou said explicitly that it was a "question of principle" that the Soviet Union be excluded from the conference.[111] On October 26 the Chinese government, under Zhou's guidance, formally announced its decision to boycott a second Afro-Asian meeting. It was a logical decision on Zhou's part to prevent the Soviet Union from being invited to the conference on the grounds that it represented an expansionist European power against which, according to Zhou, all nations of Asia and Africa should wage a relentless, protracted struggle. To a certain extent Zhou's formulation of the worldwide anti-imperialist and anticolonial united front among Asian and African nations revealed China's more intensified position in the Sino-Soviet conflict. As expected, the Soviet Union was charged with holding onto the imperialist gains of its former czars; moreover, the Chinese government called for an end to this historically unfair distribution of territory.

The forces of international change, however, were far too numerous to control. China was a developing socialist country and was also fundamentally different from most Third World nations. It enjoyed a cultural heritage, endowment in resources, and military power that they would never know. Recent developments in Chinese missile and nuclear weapons technology gradually began to alter the strategic imbalance. Real threats to China's national security since the formation of a Communist regime in 1949 had come exclusively from the two superpowers. The first serious challenge came from the United States during the Korean War in the early 1950s, later from the Soviet Union, perhaps as early as 1964, when Soviet premier Khrushchev seriously considered an attack against China's budding nuclear capability. At the beginning of Sino-American détente in 1971 and 1972 Zhou approached Third World nations with a view to cementing common solidarity and jointly opposing neocolonialism and social imperialism. On the one hand, Zhou wanted to impress upon the African governments and Asian leaders both the speed and magnitude of China's industrial development; on the other hand, he had to avoid giving the impression that China had become just another industrial state devoid of sympathy for the economic problems of Third World nations.

In his political report to the CCP's Tenth Congress on August 24, 1973, Zhou described the awakening of the Third World and its growing influence in the worldwide struggle against imperialism and colonialism, especially against the "hegemonism and power politics" of the two superpowers.[112] According to Zhou, three worlds existed. The first was that of the two nuclear superpowers, the United States and the Soviet Union, which were contending for global hegemony. The Second World consisted of the industrial countries of Western Europe, Japan, Australia, and Canada. Associated with the second was the Third World, made up of the poor, developing nations of Asia, Africa, and Latin America.

Because of the recent Soviet practice of social imperialism, the two superpowers had become essentially alike; they, as two imperialist world powers, were competing with each other to establish hegemony over the rest of the world. As a result, Zhou reasoned, the Third World nations should make concerted efforts "to win and defend national independence and safeguard state sovereignty and national resources" against threats and exploitations from the two superpowers.[113] Moreover, Zhou downplayed China's support for guerrilla and insurrectionary groups in Southeast Asia and backed a proposal by the Association of Southeast Asian Nations (ASEAN)—which included Indonesia, Malaysia, the Philippines, Singapore, and Thailand—to turn the region into a "zone of peace, freedom and neutrality" guaranteed by the major powers.

It was Zhou's conviction that his country's relations with the member states of ASEAN should be based on mutual support for regional peace and stability. Both the joint communiqué with Malaysia and, more specifically, Zhou's speech at the welcoming banquet for Malaysian prime minister Tun Razak on May 28, 1971, indicated clearly that Chinese support for the Malaysian government would have nothing to do with that country's domestic policies. The government of Malaysia was praised, however, for certain aspects of its foreign policy, notably its active participation in "the activities of the Third World countries" and its opposition to "great-power hegemonism and power politics."[114] More significantly, the Malaysian government's call for a zone of peace and neutrality was appreciated and encouraged. But, most important of all, such positive views and comments were placed in the context of Third World nations having "become the main force in the united struggle of the people of the world against hegemonism."[115] The Southeast Asian political context could be seen as a reflection of the existing global situation. "The realities of Southeast Asia," said Zhou, "show that superpower aggression and expansion are the main source of danger to peace and security in this region."[116] He suggested, on a more positive note, that the Chinese people "are convinced that, as long as the Southeast Asian peoples strengthen their unity and persist in struggle, they will certainly be able to frustrate superpower schemes and safeguard their own independence and sovereignty."[117]

Along with China's border clashes with the Soviet Union in the late 1960s and diplomatic rapprochement with the United States in the early 1970s, Zhou had to contend with the détente between the two superpowers. He also had to deal with those Third World nations that still regarded China with varying degrees of distrust, suspicion, and fear. There were, however, countries in the Third World that, over the years, had developed close ties with China and could be regarded by Zhou as China's friends and allies, but even these countries—which included Burma, Nepal, Cambodia, Laos, Egypt, Algeria, Tanzania, and Cuba—considered their connection to China as an instrument with which to gain their own national and strategic objectives rather than as signposts of Chinese presence in South Asia, Southeast Asia, Africa, or Latin America. Furthermore, a new distinctive element in this Third World anti-imperialist and antihegemonist struggle was the intensified fight in the realm of economics. Increasingly, some Third World nations could use their raw materials, especially oil, as powerful weapons against both imperialism and hegemonism. It was perhaps the rich countries in the West and Japan that most depended on the poor, developing nations of the Third World.

In addition, growth in the ranks of the Third World nations changed the makeup of the United Nations. The UN, as an international voting machine, could no longer be manipulated by a few major powers or used especially as a tool of the two superpowers in their contention or collusion for world hegemony. By promoting their unity and making concerted efforts, China and the Third World nations could certainly demonstrate the magnitude of their voting strength at each session of the UN's General Assembly. In order to manage their own affairs the Third World nations could establish or reinforce regional organizations that excluded the two hegemonic powers and transform others that had formerly been dominated by the big powers.

According to Zhou, the Third World had entered the international arena and was now playing an increasingly important role in it.[118] The series of major international conferences between 1973 and 1975 pointed to a new trend in the world arena: not the superpowers but, instead, the Third World nations played the main part collectively. It was Zhou's opinion that China was "a developing socialist country belonging to the Third World" and that the Third World was "the main force in combatting colonialism, imperialism and hegemonism."[119]

CHAPTER 10

Nuclear Weapons and the United Nations in Zhou's Foreign Policy Strategies

The incentives for China to develop its nuclear weapons were numerous, and Beijing's acquisition of nuclear weapons was subject to a set of foreign policy calculations and cost considerations. Zhou apparently concluded that it was essential for China to pursue an active nuclear weapons development program. The success of the program in the mid- and late 1960s was in large measure due to Zhou's leadership.

After the Korean War and throughout the 1950s Zhou continued to be concerned about the U.S. military threat. When the Sino-Soviet conflict was becoming increasingly serious in the early 1960s, Zhou had reason to worry about the perceived dual threat to China from both U.S. and Soviet stockpiles of nuclear weapons and their intercontinental delivery systems. The Nuclear Test Ban Treaty initiated by the United States, Great Britain, and the Soviet Union in July 1963 clearly implied that the Soviet Union was unwilling to assist China in becoming an independent nuclear power. Prior to 1963 Moscow had provided China with limited scientific and technological assistance to develop its nuclear weapons.[1] After the nuclear test ban the Soviet Union showed interest in supporting Zhou's 1959 proposal for a "nuclear free" zone in the Far East and the Pacific region[2] but was very sensitive to China's possible emergence as a nuclear power. That Zhou had earlier opposed the development of a nuclear arsenal by the nuclear powers and was now, in the mid-1960s, seeking to transform China into a nuclear power was primarily a result of China's fears about its own survival. Zhou made it very clear that China sought nuclear weapons only as a "means" of ending the Western nations' "monopoly" over them as well as their "use" of such weapons as a threat against China.[3] China successfully detonated its first atomic bomb on October 16, 1964, and within hours Zhou called for a world summit conference to ban the use of nuclear weapons and, ultimately, to eliminate them.[4]

Zhou's new foreign policy strategy during this period was aimed at reducing the possibility of Soviet-American détente at the expense of China and at mitigating the consequences should détente be unavoidable. The fact that China now was a nuclear power did not help it gain entry into the United Nations. Zhou wanted very much for the new Chinese government to be recognized internationally. He felt that the PRC was the sole legitimate government of China and that the UN was obligated to recognize all the legitimate rights to which China was entitled. Implied in this approach was the contention that Taiwan was not an independent nation but, rather, an integral part of China. As such, the PRC should occupy the seat of a veto-wielding power as one of the "big four" on the Security Council. Nevertheless, the PRC had to wait for twenty-two years before it could assume its seat in the UN. As a result, the "United Nations factor" was to remain a constant element in the PRC's policy deliberations. For more than two decades, from 1949 to 1971, Zhou tried his best to orchestrate Beijing's extensive efforts at enlisting international support for the PRC's admission into the United Nations.

Zhou's Approach to Nuclear Weapons

Zhou believed that the dynamism of foreign policy was determined by the relationship between ends and means. If the ends were set either too high or too low in relation to the available means, the balance would not be productive. Moreover, his belief in the nation-state as the basic frame of reference for setting China's foreign policy objectives such as national security and international influence led him constantly to adapt China's national power to the existing international situation. Military might was definitely an important factor, however, in conducting of diplomatic negotiations.[5] He did not believe in the use of military force as an instrument of aggression but, rather, as a measure to achieve the calculated political and psychological effects in China's diplomacy.

As early as in October 1954, the PRC concluded an agreement with the Soviet Union for the establishment of a joint Scientific and Technical

Commission. The CCP's Politburo made the decision to build atomic weapons in mid-January 1955. On October 15, 1957, another agreement on new technology for national defense was signed by the two countries. According to this new agreement, the Soviet Union was "to provide China with a sample of an atomic bomb and technical data concerning its manufacture."[6] The strategic weapons program was accelerated as the Sino-American conflict intensified in Asia and the Pacific region. The U.S. nuclear threat convinced Zhou and other CCP leaders that China had no choice but to devote its resources to an active nuclear weapons program. On July 1, 1958, Beijing Radio reported that the PRC's first experimental atomic reactor had begun operation[7] and that the Chinese government was looking forward to becoming a member of the exclusive "nuclear club."

During the period from 1958 to 1960, with substantial Soviet assistance, China developed the mining and industrial infrastructure for uranium processing and enrichment.[8] From 1960 to 1962 the Chinese leaders engaged in major debates on the priority of the nuclear weapon efforts and concluded that the uranium mines and processing plants should be brought into good productive order. In November 1962 they instituted a fifteen-member Special Commission, under Zhou's direction, to supervise the PRC's nuclear weapons program. In early 1963 Zhou, representing the commission, visited the Fifth Academy, the missile division, and directed the missile specialists to build four types of strategic surface-to-surface missiles in eight years.[9] In July 1964 Zhou instructed the Second Ministry to combine the nuclear weapon with a guided missile.[10] It was obvious that in the early 1960s Zhou gave very high priority to the nuclear weapons program and to multiorganizational cooperation.[11] Even after the Soviet Union withdrew its technical assistance in 1963, Zhou continued to push the nuclear development program forward by stressing China's need for "self-reliance."

During the Cold War years nuclear weapons were perceived to be an indispensable prerequisite for great power status. Zhou considered international relations an arena in which every participating country attempted to increase its own power and influence at the expense of the others; therefore, as long as nuclear weapons were exclusively possessed by Western nations, China had no choice but to follow a nuclear military course. Zhou fully understood the importance of possessing nuclear weapons as a deterrent to potential foreign aggression.

A form of minimum nuclear deterrence, in Zhou's estimation, was needed to increase China's bargaining power with both the United States and the Soviet Union. According to Field Marshal Bernard Montgomery, Zhou indicated that the Chinese government decided "to proceed with plans for developing nuclear weapons for the armed forces."[12] The strategy was for China to create a force of high-yield, moderately accurate nuclear weapons that could, with reasonable certainty, survive and retaliate if China should ever suffer a U.S. nuclear attack. "China would develop them [nuclear weapons] herself with her own scientists," according to Alice L. Hsieh, "and had not asked for, nor was she receiving, any help from Russia."[13] Zhou was determined that China should join the nuclear club by exploiting its nascent nuclear capability and by continuously enhancing its modest nuclear delivery capability. Without nuclear weapons of its own the nation would be severely curtailed in the conduct of its foreign policy objectives—namely, incorporating Taiwan into Chinese territorial domain and achieving great power status.

When the Nuclear Test Ban Treaty was signed in Moscow on August 5, 1963, by the United States, the Soviet Union, and Great Britain, Zhou's response was swift and clear: "This is to keep a monopoly of atomic might between the two superpowers," he said.[14] The primary purpose of this treaty, as he saw it, was to reach a partial ban on nuclear tests so as to prevent all the other countries, including China, from increasing their defense capability. There would be no nuclear disarmament, Zhou declared, because the United States and the Soviet Union would "continue to stockpile nuclear weapons."[15] He derided the treaty, saying, "It is like the bandit who sets fire to a house but does not allow an honest man to light a candle."[16] In the final analysis Zhou regarded it as a clear indication of Soviet-American collusion against China's national interest. The only meaningful nuclear test ban treaty, according to Zhou, would be the total and complete destruction of nuclear weaponry, with the immediate establishment of nuclear-free zones as a preliminary step. The Nuclear Test Ban Treaty, according to a statement issued by the Chinese government on July 31, 1963, "completely divorces the cessation of nuclear tests from the total prohibition of nuclear weapons, legalizes the continued manufacture, stockpiling and use of nuclear weapons by the three nuclear powers, and runs counter to disarmament."[17]

On October 16, 1964, China exploded its first atomic bomb at Lop Nor in Sinkiang Province, thereby promoting itself to the level of an atomic power. The Chinese government issued a statement that day, declaring, "This is a major achievement of the Chinese people in their struggle to increase their national defense capability and oppose the U.S. imperialistic policy of nuclear blackmail and nuclear threats."[18] It went on to state: "To defend oneself is the inalienable right of every sovereign state. . . . China cannot remain idle and do nothing in the face of the ever-increasing nuclear threat posed by the United States. China is forced to conduct nuclear tests and develop nuclear weapons."[19] With special reference to the nuclear weapons the statement stressed that "China will neither commit the error of adventurism nor the error of capitulationism."[20] It also proclaimed that "China will never at any time under any circumstance be the first to use nuclear weapons."[21]

In his letter addressed to government heads of the world on October 17, 1964, Zhou proposed that an international conference be convened to discuss the question of nuclear weapons. As a first step, this summit conference "should reach an agreement to the effect that the nuclear powers and those countries which may soon become nuclear powers undertake not to use nuclear weapons, neither to use them against non-nuclear countries and nuclear-free zones, nor against each other."[22] Zhou also made it clear that China's long-term effort was "to work for the complete prohibition and thorough destruction of nuclear weapons through international consultation."[23]

To support its foreign policy objectives China already possessed the largest conventional military forces in the world. Zhou's advocacy of nuclear disarmament on his terms could have led to a change in the global balance of power in China's favor. His proposal for an international conference to discuss nuclear weapons and nuclear disarmament was immediately relayed to the U.S. president, Lyndon Johnson, through the ambassadorial channel that the two countries had maintained in Warsaw. The Chinese ambassador to Poland, Wang Guo-quan, delivered Zhou's letter to the U.S. ambassador, John M. Cabot, for transmittal to the White House.[24] According to State Department officials, "It was the first time that the Warsaw channel had been used for a direct communication between the heads of the two governments."[25] Zhou's proposal for nuclear disarmament was dismissed by Secretary of State Dean Rusk as a propaganda "smoke screen."[26] In retrospect, this was an unequivocal rejection by Washington of Zhou's call for a summit meeting to outlaw nuclear weapons.

An independent Chinese nuclear course, for Zhou, could be justified by the need for retaliatory preparedness against either of the two superpowers, or both. The presence of an enemy, or even two adversaries against which a nuclear defense was required, became a strong stimulus to a stepped-up nuclear program in China in the mid-1960s. China could not afford to confine its efforts merely to the conventional preparations for a war with the United States. Fully equipped divisions, and a large number of them, were necessary to counter the short-range U.S. military threat. Forces had to be developed for a land war in Asia and the Pacific region, but, whether or not China's deterrence was sufficient, it had to take precedence over the nation's defense. From 1964 on an atomic strike force was apparently part of the Chinese military design. Zhou continued to press for the buildup of China's nuclear weapons and also to develop a satisfactory delivery system for them. China could have the means of practicing "minimal deterrence" as soon as it had the elements of nuclear coercion at its disposal. This calculation spurred Zhou to accelerate the nuclear weapons program with the expectation that changing military technology would ultimately make China's nuclear deterrent viable.

Within hours of China's first atomic detonation on October 16, 1964, Zhou issued another directive to the Chinese specialists "to make a breakthrough on the hydrogen bomb project."[27] In March 1965 the guidelines for the East Wind (Dong-feng) missile program and other missile technologies were approved by the fifteen-member Special Commission, chaired by Zhou himself. Two other detonations on May 9 and on December 28, 1966, paved the way for the test of a multistage-type, three-megaton device on June 17, 1967. By 1966 China had become a full-fledged nuclear power.

Zhou was constantly trying to balance the need for acting forcefully to protect the vital interests of China with the need to adopt in time a more flexible strategy of conciliatory diplomacy. He was well aware that under most circumstances a suitable blend of these two approaches was likely to yield the best results. Pursuing negotiations with the United States together with a long-range strategy of mutual accommodation vis-à-vis the other nuclear powers, in Zhou's estimation, could prevent a needless waste of China's national resources, while military capability and political resolve could provide Chinese diplomacy with the necessary foundation. Zhou's proposal for nuclear disarmament was also intended to appeal to those nonnuclear countries that desired legitimate voices in the discussion of nuclear disarmament. By so doing, Zhou sought to bring great pressure to bear upon the nuclear powers, especially the United States and the Soviet Union. He anticipated what the outcome might be if China took a conciliatory stand vis-à-vis the Western nuclear powers.

Zhou's strong support for China's independent nuclear capability was not based purely on military considerations. He viewed China's nuclear arsenal as both a military and political instrument. In his report to the Third NPC on December 30, 1964, Zhou asked a series of simple but rousing questions regarding the success of China's first atomic detonation. Positive answers to these questions, as Zhou anticipated, would rally the morale and solidarity of both the Chinese leadership and people. "Have we not exploded an atomic bomb?" asked Zhou. "Has not the label, 'sick man of the east,' fastened on us by westerners, been flung off? Why can't the proletariat of the East accomplish what the bourgeoisie of the West has been able to?"[28] The aspirations and psychology of the Chinese people changed with time and circumstances. Great power status became synonymous with independent nuclear capability. China could not aspire to play an important role in contemporary international affairs without strategic nuclear weapons and nuclear delivery capability. Both international prestige and national security dictated that Zhou and other CCP leaders develop China's nuclear weapons.

Zhou, confronted as he was with the possibility of U.S. nuclear attack and the enormity of Soviet nuclear power, managed to qualify tactical caution with strategic boldness. He took great pains to avoid direct confrontation with the United States. By means of low-risk diplomacy he was able to take advantage of China's ambassadorial discussions with the United States by engaging in a carefully controlled probe of U.S. intentions with reference to Taiwan. In a statement on Chinese foreign policy on April 10, 1966, Zhou reaffirmed his country's intention not to provoke a war with the United States. On the other hand, he also warned that China would be prepared for such a war regardless of the types of strategic weapons to be used by the Americans.[29]

Throughout the 1960s China did not possess a significant nuclear arsenal. Although China's conventional forces were substantial, they could not be used to liberate Taiwan or remove the U.S. military bases from the Asian rimlands. The acquisition of nuclear weapons constituted a major factor in Zhou's foreign policy calculations. He sought both atomic and nuclear weapons as a primary means of forestalling a Sino-American war and of waging it if one was started by the United States. The theme of deterrence by the weak of the strong was defined and refined by the CCP leaders to protect China's nuclear weapons and installations from enemy attack under these circumstances. They tried to determine with certainty where, when, how, and in what measure nuclear weapons would be employed to defend the Chinese people and cities. In his memoirs Nie Rongzheng, who headed the Defense Science and Technology Commission, thought that the development of strategic rocket forces had enabled China "to own the minimum means to stage a counterattack in case our country suffered a surprise nuclear attack by the imperialists."[30] This meant nuclear retaliation at a time and against targets of China's own choosing.

A deep sense of diplomatic isolation, growing doubts about relying on the Soviet deterrent against the United States, the fear of a Sino-American military confrontation over the status of Taiwan, and the increasing confidence in China's technical capabilities for nuclear weapons development all contributed to convincing the Chinese leaders of the desirability of maintaining an independent nuclear arsenal. When the Soviet Union refused to provide China with the necessary assistance for the development of its nuclear capability, the Chinese government interpreted the Soviet decision as being inspired by the policy of détente between Moscow and Washington and as being "aimed at depriving the Chinese people of their right to take steps to resist the nuclear threat of U.S. imperialism."[31] Zhou regarded China's successful nuclear weapon tests in 1966 and 1967 as a victory for Third World nations because they destroyed the notion that only advanced nations could develop such weapons. He saw China's independent nuclear force as a counterdeterrent that could prevent the more powerful nations from interfering with China's policies. With a device deliverable by both airplane and missile China acquired new political strength for its diplomatic activities in Asia and the Pacific region. For the first time China could end the Western nations' monopoly of nuclear weapons and of their employment as a threat against China and its allies in Asia.

China's tripolar balance with the United States and the Soviet Union was both difficult and complicated. Such a balance, if achieved, would allow competitive coexistence and prevent military conflicts. Zhou's perception of a new global balance, delicately calibrated to avoid the direct use of military force, carried important implications for China's nuclear deterrence posture and the evolution of its military strategy. China, as a force forming the pattern of the strategic triangle of deterrence, gained an opportunity to improve its own position, reduce international tension, and avoid the possible cause of another world war, as Zhou frequently articulated. For more than two decades he had carefully calculated the changes of balance of power brought about by nuclear weapons. He expected that China's possession of an independent nuclear deterrent could pay off handsomely in both political and military spheres. "China's capability does not have to be measured against formidable Western forces," according to R. N. Rosecrance, "but rather against the sensitivities of Asian states already sharpened to a fine point by inordinate fears of nuclear war. In the Chinese instance, nuclear capability may produce dividends not found in other contexts."[32] Rosecrance concluded that "the Chinese may use nuclear weapons symbolically to further political penetration of Asia and to enhance overall international status."[33]

Once China had acquired a level of nuclear deterrence adequate to resist military pressure from both Washington and Moscow, Zhou could begin to utilize this increased leverage in his negotiations with both powers. Even Sino-American diplomatic rapprochement was possible. Deterrence was the product of two elements: a strategic weapon and an aptitude for making decisions. The threat of the use of nuclear weapons must be backed up by resolve of the policymakers. China's march to nuclear power under Zhou's guidance was not so much the miliary expression of an expansionist foreign policy but, rather, part of a broader political plan designed to minimize the U.S. threat of nuclear attack against China. In preserving China's freedom for pursuing its national strategic goals, the nuclear monopoly long enjoyed by both the United States and the Soviet Union was a major obstacle.

In the period from 1964 to 1970 China carried out eleven nuclear test explosions, ranging in yield from twenty kilotons in December 1964 to over three megatons in October 1970. By 1970 it was known to be constructing copies of the Tu-16 Badger medium bomber with a range of fifteen hundred miles. In addition, a booster assembly had been developed for firing intermediate range ballistic missiles (IRBMs) with a two thousand-mile range.[34] Clearly, Zhou was well aware of the vulnerability of China's cities and installations as targets of potential enemy attacks. During the 1960s the Chinese nuclear deterrence strategy was essentially designed to encounter the perceived U.S. threat. In the early 1970s the focus of China's strategy shifted to the Soviet menace. The Chinese intercontinental ballistic missile (ICBM) program was halted and the medium-range ballistic missile (MRBM) and IRBM programs expanded, thereby indicating a reduced concern about the United States.

Such a nuclear capability was perceived by Zhou as a means of achieving a degree of military balance of power vis-à-vis the Soviet Union, rather than as a means of dealing with China's neighbors. Zhou was seeking every possible way to persuade the small and medium-sized nations of the Second and Third Worlds to renounce miliary solutions for international disputes. For China to play a meaningful role in the global balance of great powers it was necessary to strengthen its relations with these Second and Third World nations. Zhou's invitation for the United States and the Soviet Union to join China in declaring that they would never be the first to use nuclear weapons was a carefully crafted strategy to win the support of the nonnuclear countries. In his interview with James Reston, a well-respected columnist for the *New York Times*, in Beijing on August 9, 1971, Zhou reiterated China's fundamental position on the control of nuclear arms. "We are not a nuclear power," said Zhou.[35] He then went on to explain: "We are only in the experimental stage. And what is more, that has been the case throughout the period from 1964 to the present, seven years already. We will not test when there is no need. We know it is quite expensive and a waste."[36] The two superpowers, in Zhou's view, had already embarked on the mass production of nuclear weapons and simply could not "get down from the horse,"[37] even though neither the United States nor the Soviet Union could monopolize nuclear weapons. Zhou justified China's nuclear weapons program by insisting, "We are forced to do so in order to break the nuclear monopoly."[38]

In retrospect, Zhou's position on the issue of nuclear weapons provides a useful illustration of how the forces of military rationale, nationalistic drives, and unique international circumstances all converged and propelled China into developing an independent nuclear capability. Thus, the series of five-year economic plans, the large defense budgets, and the atomic and nuclear tests were all part of Zhou's broad plan to develop the strategic undergirding for China's foreign policy. The nuclear weapons program under Zhou's direction and support was, therefore, not an accidental occurrence. The continued existence of the PRC as a global power, in Zhou's view, depended quite as much upon its ability to attract allies and to win friends in the world community as on its military strength and strategy. And the ultimate objective of Zhou's diplomatic maneuvers and military programs was to secure China's sovereignty and independence.

In his analysis of nuclear weapons and U.S. foreign policy Henry Kissinger argued: "Foremost among the attitudes which affected the making of our policy is American empiricism and its quest for certainty: nothing is 'true' unless it is part of experience. This makes for the absence of dogmatism and for the ease of social relations. But it has pernicious consequences in the conduct of policy."[39] He then went on to say: "Policy is the art of weighing possibilities; mastery of it lies in grasping the nuances of possibilities. To attempt to conduct it as a science must lead to rigidity."[40]

Zhou's pragmatism fostered a fundamental respect for the complexity of nuclear threat and retaliation. In the new world order of nuclear powers Zhou recognized the need for a different set of instruments and plans to promote Chinese national security and defense. He never evaded difficulty; he wrestled, poked around, and attempted metaphors, but he never tried to make things simpler than they were. He expounded a central theme that showed, in accordance with practical priorities, how a policymaker's judgment could directly advance the security interest of his nation. At the same time, Zhou was ready to embark on a diplomatic course of self-restraint, searching endlessly for the mechanisms and conditions that would enable him to establish dialogues with world leaders to discuss the issues of nuclear weapons and the formation of nuclear-free zones.

The theme, tempo, direction, and approach to the question of nuclear weapons evolved on the basis of Zhou's experience. Evaluating what would be important to China's national defense and its relations with Western nuclear powers and to deciding undertake or reject certain initiatives were handled pragmatically. At the core of his thought and practices was the unshakable conviction that the primacy of national strategic interests determined and shaped the adaptation process of foreign policy, through which concrete solutions to China's relations with the nuclear powers could be formulated. The nature of Zhou's brand of pragmatism led him to accept the practical value of change as a process and to obtain answers to specific questions about when and where such change might foster adaptability. It was always essential for China to respond creatively to environmental pressures within its national boundaries and beyond. An evolutionary drop-by-drop drive for China's national security and major power status materialized under Zhou's guidance through the development of the nuclear weapons program. Adaptation was a rational function of a cautious foreign policymaker and a general quality of statecraft. Using the term *adaptation* in the context of statecraft, in Zhou's view, conveyed the idea that a diplomat should seek the optimal adjustment of legitimate conflicting interests.

Zhou and the Restoration of China's Seat at the United Nations

In a cable dated November 18, 1949, addressed to Trygve Lie, secretary-general of the United Nations, Zhou stated that the Central People's Government of the PRC "is the sole legal government representing the entire people" of China.[41] By implication the UN should expel the Guomindang government, which had already lost the right to speak for the Chinese people, and restore China's seat and legitimate rights to the PRC. All decisions by the UN and its specialized agencies without the participation of "the lawful representatives" of the PRC were illegal and, therefore, null and void. On January 19, 1950, Zhou sent another cable, requesting that UN officials reply to his demand for the immediate replacement of the delegation of the GMD government with a new delegation appointed by the PRC.[42] On October 10, 1954, Zhou cabled UN secretary-general Dag Hammarskjöld, elaborating seven facts relative to "the armed aggression" committed by the United States against Taiwan and demanding that the United Nations "stop [the] aggressive action by the U.S. Government in interfering with Chinese people's liberation of Taiwan."[43]

After the signing of the U.S.-Taiwan Pact on December 2, 1954, Zhou issued a lengthy statement on December 8 and invoked the UN Charter in denouncing the pact. He argued that the so-called treaty of defense between the United States and Taiwan was "diametrically opposed to the purposes and principles which the United Nations Charter proclaims . . . [and] cannot possibly promote peaceful coexistence between nations."[44]

On January 19, 1955, President Eisenhower announced at a news conference that he hoped the United Nations would exercise its good offices to maintain a cease-fire in the Taiwan Straits.[45] Zhou replied on January 24 that the so-called cease-fire between the PRC and the Jiang Jie-shi "traitor gang" was "an intervention in China's internal affairs for the alienation of China's territory."[46] On January 31 the UN Security Council passed a resolution by New Zealand to invite the PRC to discuss hostilities in certain islands off the coast of mainland China. In a cable replying to the secretary-general's invitation Zhou indicated that the New Zealand resolution constituted an interference in

China's domestic affairs and therefore was a violation of the UN Charter. He also contended that "what is intolerable is the fact that the PRC, representing the six hundred million Chinese people, is up to now still deprived of the legitimate position and rights in the United Nations."[47] Further, he added: "At the same time, it must be pointed out that without the representative of the PRC participating in the name of China . . . all decisions taken in the Security Council on questions concerning China would be illegal and null and void."[48]

The United States was seriously concerned about the possible international influence of Chinese communism, especially the expansion of this influence into the United Nations and its specialized agencies. Furthermore, in the Cold War environment the GMD government in Taiwan enjoyed solid U.S. domestic support. Throughout the Eisenhower Administration the U.S. delegation to the United Nations exerted all its influence in enlisting support against the Soviet resolution for replacing the Taiwan government with the PRC. Every year the PRC was criticized as an outlaw nation whose admission to the United Nations would conflict with the principle of that international body as an instrument of world peace. The United States consistently proposed a resolution calling for the postponement of any action until the next year, and the UN General Assembly annually adopted it. The vote against the moratorium, however, was slowly gaining. As a result, the technique of annually postponing any action appeared to lose its popularity.

China's international prestige improved tremendously after Zhou's success at the Bandung Conference on Afro-Asian unity in April 1955. As more and more former colonies in Asia and Africa became independent and joined the United Nations, the moratorium against considering changing China's representation in the United Nations received less and less support. The UN and its specialized agencies, in Zhou's view, constituted an arena in which the PRC, if admitted, could play the role of a major power. In his report to the NPC, delivered on February 10, 1958, Zhou said, "In the United Nations, the United States has met with growing opposition in obstructing the restoration to China of its legitimate rights, and it has come to see that it is impossible to ban China from the United Nations forever."[49]

Fifteen African nations plus Cyprus were admitted to the United Nations in September 1960. The U.S. government, however, continued to support the Taiwan government under Jiang. Consequently, the question of Chinese representation became a substantive question that, according to Article 18, paragraph 2, of the UN Charter, required a two-thirds majority vote of the General Assembly to be changed. On December 14, 1961, the General Assembly passed a five-nation resolution supporting the U.S. position by a large margin, with sixty-two yes and thirty-four no votes and seven nations abstaining. On December 21, 1961, the Chinese Ministry of Foreign Affairs issued a statement strongly criticizing the five-nation resolution as "illegal and null and void" because the resolution "tramples upon the UN Charter and infringes on China's sovereignty."[50]

As time went on, a seat in the United Nations, even one with the "veto power," would not have added much to China's already growing power status. At the Geneva Conference on Laos between May 1961 and July 1962, the PRC was acknowledged as a key participant and was instrumental in reaching the agreement to neutralize Laos.[51] The style of Chinese diplomacy during this critical period fully reflected Zhou's approach to the world organization: he was agile, flexible, and, above all, tough-minded. He saw no reason to petition the world for their acceptance and recognition of the PRC, and, to him, any revision of the UN Charter without the PRC's participation would be illegal and void. Still, he welcomed the initiatives offered for the PRC's membership at the United Nations from other countries. In fact, he made special efforts in the early 1960s to win the support of the developing nations. Between December 14, 1963, and February 29, 1964, Zhou himself toured ten African countries, Albania, and three Asian nations. While he was in Africa, France agreed, on January 9, 1964, to recognize the government of the PRC.

The PRC successfully detonated its first atomic bomb on October 16, 1964, which was a great boost for its international prestige as the first nonwhite, non-Western member of the "nuclear club." On January 24, 1965, Zhou criticized the United Nations' practice of discrimination against newly emerging Afro-Asian countries such as the Congo, Vietnam, and Laos. "The United Nations," stated Zhou, "has committed too many mistakes. It has utterly disappointed the Asian and African countries."[52] He also suggested the reorganization of the United Nations to make it conform to the "aspirations of the Asian and African countries."[53] Zhou argued that this international organization must free itself from control by the major powers to better reflect the balance of global forces.

From November 1949 to the early 1960s Zhou sent numerous communications to the United Nations, most of which were concerned primarily with the question of restoring China's lawful seat in the United Nations, complete with the veto power. He demanded the seating of PRC's delegation to replace that of the GMD government in Taiwan. He acted essentially through UN organs and followed the organization's established procedures. He endeavored to keep the United Nations channel open for the PRC and frequently announced China's support of the UN Charter. While Zhou wanted to regain China's legitimate seat in the United Nations; more important, he also recognized the UN's importance to many new Afro-Asian nations. His frequent invocation of the UN Charter's purposes and principles was intended to demonstrate China's peaceful intentions and to gain sympathy and support from Third World nations. At the same time, in all his communications with the principal organs of the United Nations, Zhou never failed to declare that all decisions made by the United Nations without the PRC's participation were null and void, as far as China was concerned.

Zhou told American journalist Edgar Snow in October 1970 that the future of the United Nations was difficult to predict. There was the possibility that it might suffer the same fate as the League of Nations, which had failed to practice the principle of equal sovereignty in international relations.[54] For the PRC to join the United Nations, Zhou claimed, it was necessary not only that all membership rights be restored, including a permanent seat on the Security Council, but also that the Taiwan government be ousted from that international body. In his interview with Yoshikatsu Takeiri, chairman of Japan's Clean Government Party (Komeito) in late June 1971, Zhou tied the PRC's United Nations seat to Taiwan's ouster.[55] His reply to the question "What steps do you think are necessary in order to get China back into the United Nations?" was that "the legal position of the PRC must be restored, and Jiang Jie-shi driven out of the United Nations."[56] Furthermore, he considered these tasks the responsibility of the United Nations and its various member countries. On this occasion, while Zhou expressed China's gratitude to nations that advocated restoring its legal position in the United Nations, he declared that "we ourselves do not make any demands."[57]

In his lengthy 1971 interview with James Reston, Zhou reiterated his position on the problem of China's UN membership. As expected, he expressed great concern about the proposal for admitting the PRC into the United Nations while allowing Taiwan to retain its General Assembly seat. "A confused debate," Zhou asserted, "is bound to take place in the United Nations and in the international arena."[58] Zhou unequivocally stated: "Should a state of two Chinas or one China, one Taiwan appear in the UN, or a similar absurd state of affairs take place in the UN designed to separate Taiwan from China to create a so-called independent Taiwan, we will firmly oppose it and under those circumstances we will absolutely not go into the UN"[59] Zhou insisted that Taiwan "must be a part of China. But if in the UN resolution there is anything to the effect that the status of Taiwan remains to be determined, then we will not go in."[60] Between 1969 and 1971 the PRC established formal diplomatic relations with Italy, Equatorial Guinea, Ethiopia, Chile, Kuwait, Cameroon, San Marino, and Canada. The eighteen-nation draft resolution for Chinese representation was passed by the UN General Assembly on October 25, 1971. It voted to seat the PRC and to expel the Taiwan government from the United Nations.

For more than two decades Zhou had maintained a positive attitude toward the United Nations as a world organization. Though standing outside that body, the PRC could still participate in such important international talks as the 1954 Geneva Conference on Indochina, 1955 Bandung Conference on Afro-Asian unity, and 1961-62 Geneva Conference on Laos. As a political forum, the United Nations, according to Zhou, could in many ways serve the Chinese in attaining his foreign policy objectives. Outside the United Nations the PRC had been able to enjoy peaceful coexistence with Third World nations. At the same time, Zhou assessed the general debates and the voting trends on major issues in the annual sessions of the United Nations. The yearly vote on the question of the PRC's seat in the United Nations had become a useful indicator for measuring the Chinese government's international status and for evaluating the degree of success or failure of Zhou's approach to foreign relations. "Zhou had not set China's objectives in the context of the UN and had no reason to do so, while it remained outside. But its obvious interest in the Security Council seat, together with its insistence on full international participation in discussion of such matters as nuclear disarmament," as Steven FitzGerald has observed, "raised the possibility that it might consider the UN the kind of forum in which the balance it sought could be made to operate, with small power participation, to the ultimate advancement of the effectiveness of that body."[61]

In his interview with Moto Goto, managing editor of Japan's *Asahi Shimbun* (Morning News) in Beijing on October 28, 1971, three days after the UN General Assembly's vote to replace Taiwan with the PRC, Zhou outlined China's cautious approach to the issue: "In connection with our attitude toward the United Nations, there is an old Chinese saying which goes, 'Be careful when facing a problem.' We do not have too much knowledge about the United Nations and are not too conversant with the new situation which has arisen in the United Nations."[62] He made it clear, however, that "this does not mean . . . that we do not have self-confidence; it means that caution is required and we must not be indiscreet and haphazard."[63] China's entry into the United Nations was due in large measure to the support of the Third World nations. It was natural that Zhou positioned China as their champion. He articulated China's intention to uphold the principle that "all countries must be uniformly equal. We must particularly and without fail respect the opinion of the small and medium-size nations."[64] He asserted: "If the statements of the small and medium-size countries are ignored and if things are decided only on the basis of statements by the major powers, this violates the premise that small, medium and major nations are uniformly equal."[65]

Zhou concluded his interview with Goto by reiterating his central theme on the United Nations: "Our principles are clearcut ones. We are opposed to the 'major powers,' to power politics and to domination. We will not become a major power under any circumstances."[66] Zhou wanted to ensure that China's position on the United Nations and its major functions was clear; also, he would make use of the chance for creating a new voting bloc within the UN General Assembly against the great powers. The PRC's presence in the United Nations could strengthen its influence on developing nations, if China were successful in forging a unity among them. With a new international arena open to China through its membership at the United Nations, Zhou was quick to use this opportunity to expand his diplomatic strategy. He planned for China to continue following a flexible and pragmatic approach within the United Nations. In his interview with Neville Maxwell, an English journalist and scholar, on November 9, 1971, Zhou reiterated that, as a UN member, China would adhere to "the principle of equality of all states."[67] His recognition of the Third World nations' political influence was certainly in line with existing realities in the international environment.

Once Zhou perceived the changing nature of the global balance of power, he was quick to exploit the new possibility and to integrate his assessment of the international situation into his analysis of China's foreign policy priorities. Having detected signs of growing opposition to the practices of the two superpowers, notably within the ranks of the developing nations, Zhou shifted his focus from imperialism to superpower hegemonism. Contradiction and collusion by the two superpowers in their scramble for world hegemony and spheres of influence thus remained the central theme of Zhou's foreign policy assessment and orientation.

Zhou held that Chinese national objectives, such as national independence and security as well as the PRC's legitimate membership in the United Nations, must be reached through foreign policy strategies formulated on the basis of a realistic appraisal of both domestic and international conditions. He recognized from the outset that the result of the East-West struggle, and the PRC's influence upon it, would depend increasingly on relations between the industrial states and the underdeveloped world. Thus, using the collective strength of Third World as a means to achieve a set of broad global objectives was a significant feature of Zhou's strategy vis-à-vis the United Nations.

Zhou actively sought support and cooperation from the small and medium-sized states for the PRC's views on matters affecting the global balance of power. With the entrance of China into the United Nations the developing nations had a new champion to rally around so as to bring their influence to bear upon the UN General Assembly. China was quite ready to settle into playing a full part in international affairs within the framework of the United Nations and to speak and act in the style of an international power. The United

Nations, in Zhou's opinion, could be the most useful theater for China's foreign policy operations and for enhancing its international prestige and influence; China used the setting to broaden its contacts and support, hone its diplomatic skills, and play its negotiating games.

Conclusion

The vast canvas of contemporary international relations was crowded with political and military strategies and peopled with diplomats, power holders, policymakers, and advisors. Its themes of peace, war, international order and arms control, alliance and counteralliance, independence and reliance, emerged and vanished, only to surface again in a different context and with altered significance. Individual's acts could overtake them and run far beyond their personal destinies and into the flow of history. Zhou's emphasis on understanding and dealing with the world arena was rooted in experience and expressed in actions that were dictated by experience, which for him did not take the form of discrete events. It was, rather, dynamic, flowing, continuous, a process in which the human mind played an active part. Among the most notable elements in the realm of total experience, as Zhou saw it, was human activity. A person interacts with his or her environment. Thus, if international realities were properly understood, one could deal with the international environment in a creative fashion. Most of all, Zhou's ability to deal with the international community lay in his appreciation of the connections between thought and action and his refusal to separate one from the other. Dealing with political experience was a continual process of testing, experimenting, and adapting to a subject that was not static but, rather, filled with contingencies. Finality and certainty were impossible, and international trends were ever changing, dynamic, and always flowing. The test of human activity, therefore, lay in its practical consequences.

Zhou himself was meticulous and cautious, and he always tried to frame China's approaches to nuclear weapons and UN membership on the basis of his knowledge and understanding of the international situation, China's national needs, and the sharp rivalries and competitions existing in the world arena. The prudent foreign policymaker, in a well-conceived diplomatic and strategic move, could gain desired results. In pursuing China's legitimate role in the United Nations, Zhou sought something beyond his country's international position and influence; he believed that the UN ought to be strengthened by international law, cooperation, and authority of sanction adequate to support the common judgment rendered by the international body.

Perhaps a world torn by ideological struggles and military conflicts between the industrialized West and the Third World nations was exactly the kind of world in which China could play most effectively its two best cards: its Marxist-Leninist revolutionary and anti-imperialist ideology and its ability to intensify political, economic, and military disorders of various magnitudes throughout the world. For instance, some Third World nations could use their raw materials, especially oil, as a powerful weapon against both imperialism and hegemonism. In addition, growth in the ranks of the developing nations changed the makeup of the United Nations; this international body, as a voting machine, could no longer be manipulated by a few major powers or used as a tool of the two superpowers in their struggles over world hegemony. One important factor contributing to China's rise as a major force in international politics was, according to Zhou, its acquisition of a nuclear capability. Apart from promoting China's great power status, the Chinese nuclear force could also erode U.S. commitment to Taiwan and undermine the Soviet nuclear blackmail of China.

The focal point of Zhou's approach to the United Nations and nuclear armament was the search for common interests derived from mutual adjustment and understanding. In conducting China's foreign policy, Zhou stressed diplomatic flexibility; as he saw it, a sound foreign policy should be adjustable in proportion to its utility and workability based on a realistic appraisal and a series of actual experiments. It was Zhou's personal conviction that the CCP leaders should never lose sight of the world power equation and, along with it, the evolving structure of international systems. In consequence, it was essential for China to do everything possible to bring about a change in its relations with the nuclear powers. Any foreign policy planning, Zhou reasoned, should provide several possible courses of action. The one that was considered the best under the existing circumstances could be carried out in an orderly fashion. If the premises upon which it had been founded had by then changed because of new developments, an alternative policy option, better suited to those developments, would replace the previous one. But every alternative would be designed to advance China's national security, independence, and legitimate international position. Zhou also believed that it was irrational to separate ends from the means to attain them. In the field of foreign policy every decision conditioned the policymaker with respect to what followed. Every decision was a prelude to the next and a consequence of the one before; every decision was an end with respect to what preceded and a means, a cause, of what followed. Thus, Chinese foreign policy required the constant reassessment of its tangible results.

Zhou regarded China's relations with other states, nuclear and nonnuclear ones, as a series of mutual adjustments and accommodations, and upheld the efficacy of diplomacy as an instrument of China's national policy. Diplomacy gave him another means of modifying some of the characteristic features of interstate relations. With the development of China's nuclear weapons program as well as its entry into the United Nations, the diplomacy's usefulness, for Zhou, lay in its suitability and adaptability to the fluctuating conditions of a world in which both national security and prestige determined China's foreign policy objectives. More important, Zhou viewed international cooperation, diplomacy, balance of power, and nuclear disarmament as essential elements of statecraft. Indeed, statecraft remained a constant concern to Zhou. He shared a traditional distrust of the mere exercise of theoretical reasoning uninformed by either virtue or insight with a long line of Chinese statesmen throughout history who referred disdainfully to this style of practice as mere skill (shu). By implication, those who attached a higher meaning, and more lofty objectives, to statecraft would be seeking the ultimate goal of establishing a more stable and harmonious national and international order.

CHAPTER 11

Conclusion: The Foundations of Chinese Foreign Policy under Zhou's Guidance

Zhou's perception of postwar international relations was grounded in genuine realism, the legacy of his early exposure to Chinese pragmatic philosophy and the later influence of a flexible, Leninist strategy. World War II and the subsequent Cold War between the Western alliance and the Communist bloc intensified his concerns about China's sovereignty, independence, security, and economic growth. As premier and foreign minister, Zhou focused on the conduct of diplomacy, Cold War politics, and the nation-state system. His basic philosophy required that CCP leaders make a concerted effort to select a set of national objectives that could be successfully pursued in the existing international environment.[1] Moreover, they would be responsible for making these national objectives understood in the domestic and international arenas. Recognizing the dynamic nature of the contemporary international environment, Zhou believed that the new China's foreign policy must be grounded in reality rather than political ideology. Therefore, a balanced approach to the formulation of foreign policy would have to include a proper understanding of the process of international relationships as well as of the internal and external conditions affecting nations. In other words, CCP leaders must take into account the fact that any international situation was defined by evolving relationships between nation-states, and they must be able to perceive accurately the direction of the change as well as the situation at a particular moment.

Implied in this premise was the view that Chinese foreign policy objectives should be made on the basis of a careful assessment of the possible outcome of a given international situation and that CCP leaders must be ready to steer their policy toward a course of stability and moderation at every opportunity.

By utilizing available information about Chinese foreign policy objectives in the recent past, this chapter examines and interprets trends in the present to predict a range of possible courses for the near future. It cannot, however, forecast with certainty which of these prospects will in fact materialize nor foresee all the possibilities. It is hoped that a careful analysis of Zhou's legacy may at least help to increase our knowledge and understanding of present Chinese foreign policy objectives. The discussion begins with Zhou's basic perceptions of the nature of interstate relations and of the complexities of China's relations with the outside world.

The concept of the nation-state was fundamental to Zhou's political thinking and analysis,[2] and to Zhou China's intentions were clear: like other states, China had to occupy itself with matters of national defense while seeking to enhance its own interests. Consequently, the Beijing government had to accept the existing international state system and to engage in foreign relations of a traditional kind.

Among the operational principles significant to Zhou's conduct of foreign relations, first and foremost was national independence. This involved, on the one hand, the basic notion of national sovereignty—that, within the territorial confines of an internationally recognized state, the power of the legitimate authorities was supreme—and, on the other hand, the concept of freedom of action, which claimed that the state must be permitted a certain scope within which to pursue its objectives in representing the national interest. Therefore, Zhou believed, China must always be free to act in what it viewed as its best interests.

In line with this basic premise Zhou saw the need to develop China's national strength sufficiently so as to steer its own course and not have to tie itself to the foreign policy of any other state. Restrictions on China's freedom of diplomatic maneuverability would diminish its international prestige and influence. Given ever-changing conditions in the international arena, China must be prepared to seize opportunities as they arose to enhance its stature and to maximize its diplomatic maneuverability in order ultimately to exert more influence on the international scene and, more important, on superpower politics. "With respect to foreign relations," said Zhou as early as in April 1949 in his Report on Problems Concerning Peace Talks with the GMD Government, "we uphold China's national independence and the principles of independence and self-reliance."[3] This central theme was reiterated in his foreign policy statement on April 30,

1952.[4] Implicit in these statements was Zhou's conviction that the advancement of China's self-interest was to be attained through a well-defined foreign policy based on national security, maneuverability for Chinese diplomacy, and knowledge of the nature of power politics.

Power politics required a series of negotiations among nation-states. Although Zhou believed that nations might share at least a common interest, various other interests would diverge. Furthermore, common interests of the world community as a whole might be too tenuous to rely on in determining political action. A statesman should be able to reach the best possible compromise. The most difficult part of pursuing general interests was finding a compromise among mutually hostile special interests. Moreover, power politics to Zhou always meant the use of power by the strong and rich to dominate, influence, and exploit the weak and poor.[5] Throughout history power politics revolved around the control of spheres of influence, the balance-of-power strategy, and a great variety of instruments of foreign policy ranging from economic dominance; cultural, religious, or ideological influence; to the last resort, the use of, or threat of, force.

In Zhou's view the resurgence of Chinese nationalism in the mid-twentieth century produced an increasingly effective counterforce to foreign domination. The Chinese people wished to liberate themselves from any form of foreign exploitation and domination and to satisfy their economic, political, and cultural potential, which had been suppressed for so long. Zhou strongly believed that each nation-state had the right to find its own destiny and to evolve, in the light of its own experience, the foreign policy strategy best suited to its needs.[6] He believed in working for global stability and peace, which he knew would require some form of international cooperation. In short, for Zhou, power politics meant having fluid interstate relations, shifting alignments, and, above all, the primacy of national interests. Regional and international cooperation could be achieved only by mutual accommodation; only through this process, Zhou contended, could a problem be resolved in the context of a common interest as defined by a broad, complex interplay of domestic and international needs.

This thinking led to Zhou's second operational principle, the importance of negotiation.[7] In his efforts to guide the new regime of the PRC in establishing its rightful place in the international environment and to maximize its national interests, Zhou employed negotiation extensively. What Zhou sought was an end to China's inferior international status and the assurance that his country could no longer be "pushed around"; he also rejected close alignments with foreign powers, which could restrict China's maneuverability. The proper approach to dealing with the outside world, for Zhou, required a dispassionate examination of both the workings of international relations and the objectives of China's foreign policy, and negotiation was the necessary tool for reconciling conflicts between the two elements.

Zhou's third operational principle was his pragmatism.[8] His emphasis was on how interstate relations could best be conducted for conflict resolution. With respect to the strategic triangle, Zhou's foreign policy orientation was built upon his vision of a post-Cold War world in which China could connect the mature nation-states of the old world with the newly independent nations of the Third World and act to counterbalance the hegemony of the two superpowers. Moreover, the power relationship between the two superpowers and the shift in the strategic balance would increase China's options in a changing world; China could have the choice of pursuing independent and bilateral relationships, one with the United States and the other with the Soviet Union.

Should this not occur, Zhou calculated, there would still be sufficient basis for China to form a common front against the two superpowers with other nations in the Third World and in Western Europe, which would presumably become increasingly alarmed by both Soviet and American hegemonism. By following the pragmatic approach and by developing a triangular relationship with the two superpowers, China could derive considerable diplomatic leverage from the contention between the United States and the Soviet Union without having to take sides. In the competition for power and influence among China, the Soviet Union, and the United States, Zhou preferred traditional diplomacy to revolutionary rhetoric. By the logic of competition and cooperation within a multistate system, diplomacy was regarded by Zhou as a potentially useful instrument in interstate relations, one that could help China adjust its interests to the changing international environment. What was the use of Communist dogmas if China's course of action in the world arena was rigidly restricted by them? Zhou's extensive firsthand knowledge of the workings of the international system buttressed his sense of realism in his pursuit of China's foreign policy objectives and national security.[9]

Finally, it was important, in Zhou's view, to adopt policies that would ensure national survival in the face of the threat of diplomatic isolation and the possibility of foreign attacks. But Zhou would have denied that some of the practical concessions he had to make represented a radical change of assumptions or goals. At the early stage in his formation of strategy vis-à-vis the two superpowers, Zhou had clearly recognized the realities of a bipolar system in the postwar period and held that interstate conflicts arose from the multiplicity of national interests. He never intended to allow China to lose its freedom of action, and he never gave up his conviction that Chinese interests could not and would not be best served by tying China's foreign relations exclusively to the Soviet Union and its power orbit. Hence, the fourth, and perhaps the most important, of Zhou's operational principles was achieving national security.

It was not easy to define in general terms the elements that constituted China's national security, for much depended on the concrete problems the country was facing during a particular point in time. Certainly, China's ability to bargain with the two superpowers, for instance, was severely restricted by its limited military strength. Inasmuch as China's security depended on a bipolar struggle between the two superpowers and the system of alliance, it had been Zhou's initial task in the early 1950s to find a common ground between China and the Soviet Union to frustrate hostile American strategic designs against China.[10] Zhou, however, never lost sight of fundamental Chinese interests, and he came to believe that China's influence in Asia and beyond would depend much more upon its reputation for moderation than upon its military capabilities, due to many Third World countries' prewar colonial experiences. China had to act as a reconciling influence and to be flexible. Moreover, China would have to avoid maintaining exclusively ideology-oriented relations with the Soviet Union and its satellite states in Eastern Europe.

Zhou's endless search for diplomatic dialogue with the United States in the mid-1950s and again in the late 1960s unmistakably reflected his characteristic approach to the issue of national security and, along with it, China's relations with the Soviet Union and the United States. Any deep-seated suspicions of the West would inevitably inhibit the ability to shift to new policies—necessary for China's security—unless there were compelling domestic considerations and external circumstances. By the end of the 1960s, as a result of the Soviet invasion of Czechoslovakia in 1968 and the Sino-Soviet clashes in 1969, Zhou carefully reexamined the critical factors of China's security needs in light of the pressures exerted by Soviet diplomatic and military moves. He came to the conclusion that the Soviet Union was likely to be the greatest threat to China's national security.[11] For this reason alone, he reasoned, China should never let itself be placed in a vulnerable position in which it might lose its diplomatic maneuverability or be isolated by either or both of the two superpowers.

Despite these difficulties, Zhou retained his sense of realism and caution and devoted much of his energy to seeking a favorable triangular relationship with the two superpowers. While maximizing whatever power potentialities China had, Zhou relied especially on patient negotiations with both Washington and Moscow and tried to bring the ends and means of China's foreign policy into harmony with its available resources. Zhou's steady pursuit of national security over a period of more than four decades also reflected his belief in the interrelatedness of continuing to enhance China's self-interests while adroitly practicing pragmatism in the field of foreign affairs.

National security could not be attained if China were relegated to diplomatic isolation, nor could China continue to mature politically while ignoring the fact of its economic interdependence in international relations. National security interests required a foreign policy directed toward decreasing China's confrontations, military and diplomatic, with the two superpowers and increasing its capacity for extensive cooperation with leaders and governments of the Third World. If China relied upon a strong ally as the principal supporter of its security, Chinese foreign policy objectives would become overshadowed, if not completely determined, by its dependence on such an alliance. The resulting foreign policy, by necessity, would be geared toward strengthening the bonds between the two states, frequently to the disadvantage of the weaker partner, as the Sino-Soviet alliance exemplified throughout the 1950s. If, on the other hand, the purpose of Chinese foreign policy were to assert its independence, then, obviously, flexible diplomatic maneuverability would be the best possible instrument. National independence meant more to Zhou than self-identity; it also meant freedom from foreign control. Therefore, in exercising diplomatic flexibility, both caution and prudence were required, which, in turn, might take the form of compromise and conciliation as an attempt to curb those trends and forces that could threaten China's security. Against this background national security became the all-absorbing focus of Chinese foreign policy under Zhou's guidance.[12]

According to Zhou, a sound foreign policy was based on the policymakers' hierarchy of alternatives, the formulation of well-conceived plans, and the need to choose the best actions to achieve the most efficient outcomes in terms of the ends sought. A thorough knowledge of the operation of the international state system was the key to a policymaker's understanding of contemporary international relations. For Zhou the basic unit of international relations remained the nation-state.[13] Therefore, each nation-state was expected to act in a fashion that would maintain the conditions that could ensure its continued existence as a sovereign entity. Sovereignty here referred to the supreme authority that a state possessed within its boundaries and its freedom to act in external relations and foreign policy without being interfered with or manipulated by another state. National security—political, military, and economic—was the sum of a state's vital interests. Against this background the nation-state required adequate power in order to manifest itself fully.

The basic ingredient of power was the military. Zhou recognized the importance of alliance, diplomacy, and skill in negotiations as well as of anticolonial and anti-imperialist, antihegemonic sentiments, and he used them all.[14] In the international system, however, power remained an embodiment of national capabilities and forces that each state would use as it saw fit, and the structure of the game of power was still the military alliance.

In the early 1950s the strategic-diplomatic game was still conducted by Zhou within the framework of the bipolar system. At this crucial stage of the Cold War, in the immediate postwar years, it was Zhou's belief that an alliance with the Soviet Union could serve both as the basis for the integration of China into the Communist bloc and as the focal point of China's quest for greater international prestige and influence through conventional diplomatic means. In the face of Cold War realities and the U.S. policy of containment, a Sino-Soviet alliance was the only possible key to China's security policy because Moscow would provide Beijing with security guarantees and tangible benefits from economic assistance. In his direct negotiations with the Soviet authorities in Moscow in the winter of 1949-50, Zhou made certain that China, along with the Soviet Union, would resist the threats posed by the United States and its allies in the Far East and the Pacific region. Thus, Zhou's diplomatic priorities during the early years of the PRC were closely allied with those of the Communist bloc.[15]

In retrospect, realism was the constant element inherent in the dynamic nature of a "security-centered" foreign policy, as practiced by Zhou. It is plain that the diplomatic moves and foreign strategies that Zhou devised for China to manage its relations with the two superpowers were, from the beginning, driven by the imperatives of national security. The efforts to promote China's national security increased the need for pragmatic accommodation, and, ultimately, such efforts resulted in greater flexibility in developing Chinese foreign policy. Zhou believed that China's security rested on many resources: human, material, technological, political, and military. Among its most important assets was the ability to organize these resources, to arrange them into a coherent, productive pattern.[16]

This organizational capacity was a prime factor in the management of national security. It rested primarily on the wisdom, judgment, and prudence of the nation's policymakers. Yet no less important were the means that were employed by these policymakers. The judicious reconciliation of ends and means was of critical importance in conducting foreign affairs in Zhou's view. Since national purposes could not be equally served by all available means, he was convinced that national purposes had a tendency to determine means. Moreover, national security could be defined and refined: each action taken, each decision made, each relationship between ends and means established that was in line with China's national security, made it more likely that subsequent actions would also be in accord with the nation's security. Within this context Zhou's diplomatic strategy can be characterized as the product of a particular time, place, array of circumstances, and set of relationships between ends and means.

The foundations of Chinese foreign policy under Zhou's guidance came to rest on the following five fundamental principles: (1) restoration of China's national sovereignty, independence, and security; (2) formation of the "areas of peace and neutrality" in the immediate vicinity of China to ensure the primacy of a "peaceful environment" for economic development; (3) peaceful coexistence as the guiding rule of China's interstate relations; (4) creation of a worldwide coalition against imperialism, neocolonialism, and hegemonism; and (5) balancing global influence between the two superpowers to achieve China's proper strategic triangle.

Restoration of China's National
Sovereignty, Independence, and Security

The restoration of China's sovereignty and independence was certainly Zhou's primary foreign policy objective. In this respect national aspirations and diplomatic actions were inextricably intertwined because restoration meant the recovery of China's independence as well as its equality with other major powers. Although Zhou frequently spoke about proletarian internationalism, he was careful to establish a hierarchy of Chinese priorities even before the rise of the CCP to national power. Each sovereign, independent nation-state was, in Zhou's view, a distinct monopolistic center of force and of the formulation of policies both at home and abroad. "With respect to foreign relations," he declared on April 17, 1949, "we have a basic stand: we uphold China's national independence and the principles of independence and self-reliance."[17] He also indicated that "on questions of principle, we are firm—absolutely firm," that "China cannot be bullied," and that "no country may interfere in China's internal affairs."[18] Therefore, he cautioned the Chinese people against formulating the new China's foreign policy with a dependence on foreign aid. "We should not be dependent," said Zhou, "even on the Soviet Union and the New Democracies. If we only relied on aid from abroad, what could we accomplish?"[19]

What Zhou meant by "foreign aid" at that early stage in the evolution of Chinese foreign policy was a temporary arrangement or expedient solution. He also clearly enunciated at the time the importance of equality in China's relations with other states: "We are willing to cooperate with all countries that treat us as equals. We don't discriminate against foreigners or engage in provocation, but we must take a firm stand; otherwise we will become wholly dependent upon them."[20]

After the founding of the PRC in October 1949, Zhou began to take concrete steps to enhance the new China's security interests. From his perspective the Chinese Communist victory had been achieved independently, without any substantial support from the outside world, through long years of military and political struggle. At this early phase two central themes emerged in Chinese foreign policy: the search for national security, as exemplified by Zhou's efforts to enter into an alliance with the Soviet Union, and the drive for greater independence in the world arena, evidenced by Zhou's attempts to diversify China's relations with non-Communist states in Asia and beyond. In retrospect, Zhou laid the foundations for a realistic course of foreign policy for the fledgling government of China: to utilize the Sino-Soviet alliance to maximize China's security interests in the face of the U.S. policy of containment, if not open hostility by the United States.[21]

While he cautiously hoped that the linkage with the Soviet bloc could be effectively maintained, Zhou was prepared to explore China's diplomatic contacts with Third World nations. Obstacles to such a dual maneuver were numerous, and even Zhou at times was uncertain about the path he had chosen. The timing of his diplomatic endeavors and his development of a proactive global strategy were indications of Zhou's constant preoccupation with China's security interests. The steps he took to cement China's close relations with the Soviet Union, including a treaty of alliance in the winter of 1949-50, and his subsequent diplomatic moves in developing China's relations with Third World nations in the years from 1953 to 1958 best illustrate Zhou's sense of priority, even urgency, and, above all, his attempt to balance the equation between ends and means. Cold War politics and the complexity of interstate relations convinced him of the practical value of concentrating on what was immediately necessary and attainable rather than on what was ideologically desirable.

On various official occasions the main points in Chinese foreign policy were articulated by Zhou in his reports on the government's activities. Throughout the 1950s Zhou stressed the primacy of national interests based on political, economic, strategic, and diplomatic considerations. As he saw it, the international status of the new China was to depend upon four interrelated elements: (1) the strengths and weaknesses of China; (2) the strengths and weaknesses of the Soviet Union and the Socialist states; (3) the strengths and inherent problems of Third World nations; and (4) the strengths and weaknesses of the Western states. Zhou was primarily concerned with those factors and forces that would affect China's external relations and shape the options available in his search for national security and China's sovereignty and independence.[22]

In spite of efforts made to build up China's military capability, its internal stability, and its economic and industrial productivity, Zhou recognized the simple fact that China's strengths remained inadequate. Therefore, it was important to increase the nation's power base through rapid industrial and economic modernization and the development of nuclear weapons. Additionally, such a power base must be protected and strengthened continuously through diplomatic alliances. To ensure China's security in Asia and its independence as a global power, an alliance with the Soviet Union could counteract the threat to China's nationhood posed by Japan and the United States. Zhou pursued this fundamental foreign policy objective with great tenacity. China and the Soviet Union agreed to "undertake in the spirit of friendship and cooperation and in conformity with the principles of equality, mutual benefit, mutual respect for national sovereignty and territorial integrity, and noninterference in the national affairs" of the other state "to develop and consolidate" Sino-Soviet "economic and cultural ties."[23]

The principles of state sovereignty, national independence, and security could not be compromised, in Zhou's opinion. Certain aspects of an alliance with the Soviet Union would, in the long run, constrain China's freedom of maneuverability and its autonomy. Likewise, bipolarity would affect China's foreign policy behavior. While the broad interests and purposes of China and the Soviet Union coincided, there remained other differences of interests, perspective, and policies that would inevitably generate conflicts.

As a chief architect of China's foreign policy, Zhou had to examine in depth the tendency of international politics toward recurrent disorders and power struggles.[24] Based on his knowledge and understanding, he needed to make judicious strategic choices to promote China's security interests. Insofar as Zhou might make national and strategic choices or interpretations different from those of Party ideologues, there could never be definitive solutions to the dilemmas of contemporary international politics, only endless experimentation and adaptation reflecting the full range of possibilities affected by time, place, and circumstance. Thus, foreign policy was extremely complex and involved multiple factors; it required constant reflection and reevaluation of the general and specific international circumstances.

Formation of "Areas of Peace and Neutrality" in the Immediate Vicinity of China

In the early 1950s Zhou strongly advocated for the nonaligned states to be employed to improve China's diplomatic position.[25] To reduce Western influence in China's neighboring states and to maximize its diplomatic flexibility,

Zhou began to emphasize the relevance and necessity of "winning over" the international "middle-of-the-road" forces. His main foreign policy objective was to form a neutral belt of states as an area of peace between China and the Western coalition. To achieve this end the Chinese government, under Zhou's guidance, was ready to accept the concept of nonalignment as a legitimate approach to Cold War issues. Zhou also envisioned enhancing China's international status by improving diplomatic relations with nonaligned states. Thus, he encouraged the formation, preservation, and enlargement of the area of peace composed of such countries as Burma, Cambodia, Ceylon, India, Indonesia, and Nepal. He recognized the importance of the "uncommitted countries" and devoted much attention to their growing role in fortifying "the international forces of peace."[26]

Zhou's objective in forming an area of neutral states in Asia was completely in harmony with China's overall strategy during the post-Korean War period, which was to use diplomacy to thwart any significant extension of hostile power in the immediate vicinity of China, especially by encouraging the development of neutralism. As a first step toward maintaining China's national security, Zhou wanted to have China's frontiers surrounded, insofar as possible, with numerous areas of peace. As long as the states bordering China were nonaligned, Zhou reasoned, they would naturally constitute a major obstacle to the expansionist designs of the Western powers.

Zhou was disturbed by the colonial war in Indochina in the early 1950s; he could not rule out the possibility of an American escalation of the war in an effort to secure more favorable terms for France. The explicit threat by the United States of "intervening" in the Indochinese conflict in the spring of 1954 heightened Zhou's apprehensions about another Korea-type war in a vital area adjacent to China's southern frontier. The presence and expansion of hostile Western military forces in Indochina could directly threaten the security of China's Yunnan and Guangxi Provinces. In light of this new development Zhou was prompted to reassess China's position. If the United States committed its overwhelming military strength to Indochina in support of the French Union troops, Zhou anticipated that China would be faced with the dilemma of whether or not to intervene. China's military weakness, as compared with American nuclear strike forces in Asia, rendered a direct military confrontation with the United States both risky and undesirable. Thus, Zhou felt that the best way to avoid such a possibility was to neutralize Indochina.

Not surprisingly, the key to Zhou's overall Asian political strategy was to reduce Western influence in Indochina through diplomatic channels. As a first step, Zhou sought to detach the three Indochinese states from the Western system of military alignments. On a larger scale he envisaged the formation of an area of peace composed of all the nonaligned states in South Asia. The application of neutrality to Indochina was to lay the foundation upon which a grander area of peace would be built in Southeast Asia.[27] It should be noted, however, that, whereas the neutralization of Indochina was Zhou's preferred goal, in practice he was faced with the choice either of a divided Vietnam in which the North would be Communist and the South pro-Western or of a prolongation of the war with the Americans, who would probably replace the French. The fact that he promoted the former clearly demonstrates the prior claim that China's needs for national security and economic development took precedence over its longer-term aspirations of developing a regional area of peace.

On September 23, 1954, Zhou made a major report on the government's activities to the first session of the First NPC in which he outlined China's policy priorities. He specifically pointed out that it was essential for Asian countries to strive jointly to defend their "collective peace and security" throughout the continent.[28] In his pursuit of Chinese foreign policy objectives, Zhou was convinced more than ever that China's interests could best be served by creating areas of peace in the immediate vicinity of China. Thus, the neutralization of Indochina, to Zhou, not only served as a temporary instrument to avoid conflicts between China and Western powers but was also a long-range device for transforming the three Indochinese states into his projected area of peace. In an important foreign policy statement addressed to the third session of the First NPC on June 28, 1956, Zhou reiterated the positive role played by the nonaligned states in the development of "a system of collective peace." This trend greatly reinforced, in Zhou's own words, "the international forces of peace."[29]

China's economic development had been severely inhibited during the first half of the twentieth century by internal disorders, foreign exploitation, and the lack of capital and a clear plan. After the CCP's rise to national power, economic development and modernization was one of Zhou's domestic objectives. The great internal adjustment known as the First Five-Year Plan was intended to industrialize China. It called for state control over economic expansion through centralized planning and the socialization of enterprises. Financing of the economic plan was made possible through a nationwide imposition of austere living standards, which were intended to prevent the loss of any possible surplus of national revenue through personal consumption.[30] The fulfillment of the plan demanded specific conditions of internal stability and external security. Hence, Zhou's search for a peaceful international environment became a primary objective of Chinese foreign policy.

Zhou anticipated that it would take at least three five-year plans to transform China from an agricultural country into an industrial one. In his report to the first session of the First NPC on September 23, 1954, Zhou reaffirmed the determination of the Chinese leadership to transform the country into a socialist industrialized country of prosperity. To achieve this goal he stressed the urgent need for "a peaceful environment and a peaceful world" in which to develop China's domestic economy.[31]

On numerous occasions Zhou carefully assessed the importance of having a favorable international environment.[32] The State Council, under his guidance, focused on the nation's economic reconstruction and on the implementation of its five-year plans. China's drive toward a modern economy was, in part, a drive for major power status. Therefore, one of Zhou's foremost tasks was the systematic and orderly modernization of China's economy and technology during the post-Chinese civil war and post-Korean War period. These emphases underscored what Zhou perceived to be the priorities of Chinese foreign policy. When the growing influence of neutralism in the Third World is viewed against this background, it is easy to understand why Zhou's foreign policy approach was to become increasingly concerned with areas of peace and with proposals for neutralizing Indochina.

Peaceful Coexistence as the
Guiding Rule of China's Interstate Relations

Zhou was under considerable pressure to manage China's relations with both Communist and non-Communist states. His personal attempts to establish workable relations with the uncommitted Asian states were carefully conducted within the conceptual framework of peaceful coexistence, which, in Zhou's judgment, was the best way of dealing with the international middle-of-the-road forces. The theme of peaceful coexistence was first enunciated in his report to the national Committee of the People's Political Consultative Conference on February 4, 1953. In his report Zhou affirmed his basic premise that "countries with different systems can co-exist peacefully."[33] Later he was prepared to accord the theme of peaceful coexistence the formal status of an official policy line in the context of relations between China and the nonaligned Asian states.

On December 31, 1953, Zhou declared the Five Principles of Peaceful Coexistence the guidelines of China's external relations and foreign policy.[34] Its tenets were incorporated into the preamble of the Sino-Indian Agreement on Trade and Intercourse between the Tibet Region of China and India and signed by both sides on April 29, 1954.[35] In a speech addressed to the third plenary session of the Geneva Conference on May 12, 1954, Zhou announced China's willingness to observe the Five Principles of Peaceful Coexistence for the purpose of maintaining peace and security in Asia. He also urged that the Asian states should solve their disputes through peaceful negotiations and establish "normal economic and cultural relations on the basis of equality and mutual benefit."[36] By doing so, it would then be possible to avoid "the neocolonialist exploitation of the unprecedented catastrophe of Asians fighting Asians and to achieve peace and security."[37] Zhou's public renunciation of the use of revolution as an instrument of national policy was a logical extension of his desire to improve China's diplomatic relations with non-Communist countries in Asia and beyond.

Zhou's proclamation of the Five Principles of Peaceful Coexistence, his circumspect and amicable presentation of China's proposal for the neutralization of Indochina at the 1954 Geneva Conference, and the improvement of Beijing's bilateral relations with non-Communist countries all heralded an entirely new phase in Chinese foreign policy. This distinctive stage was characterized, in Zhou's own words, by "a policy of peaceful coexistence."[38] China's official line of the Five Principles of Peaceful Coexistence was formally endorsed by Soviet leaders on October 11, 1954. Both China and the Soviet Union agreed to undertake a joint peaceful approach to "international problems, especially those of Asia."[39]

At the 1955 Bandung Conference Zhou played the role of a peacemaker, working quietly and patiently to win over the leaders and governments of Asian and African nations and urge them to become his partners in the campaign for peaceful coexistence. At the same time, the conference provided Zhou with an opportunity to project and foster an image of Chinese moderation and reasonableness in relation to concrete problems involving both China and other participating nations. In his keynote speech addressed to the full conference on April 19, 1955, Zhou reiterated his central theme of peaceful coexistence. "By following the principles of mutual respect for sovereignty and territorial integrity, noninterference in each other's internal affairs, equality, and mutual benefit," said Zhou emphatically, "the peaceful coexistence of countries with different social systems can be realized."[40]

Was Zhou genuinely dedicated to the Five Principles of Peaceful Coexistence? If he was indeed pursuing a policy of peaceful coexistence, was it a policy inspired by the Marxist-Leninist guide to action, or was it primarily shaped by the self-interest of the state? If Zhou were to improve China's relations with non-Communist states in Asia to play a constructive role in the world arena, he must reconcile Marxist-Leninist doctrines with Chinese national priorities.

First, China's security interests and its ideology were not entirely separable, except for analytical purposes. Second, Zhou's approach to

Marxism-Leninism was characterized by a curious unity of opposites: rigidity in dialectics and flexibility in practice. Indeed, there was a wide disparity between Beijing's official ideology and Zhou's actual conduct of foreign relations and diplomacy. Third, historical events and international circumstances compelled Zhou to reconcile national and strategic interests in the context of reality. In the final analysis he had to define and refine China's own brand of ideological persuasion and the proper course of its foreign policy. He drew his lessons not only from the ideological font of Marxism-Leninism but also from his extensive experience in revolutionary struggle and postrevolutionary diplomatic activities. True Marxist-Leninists, for Zhou, were guided by methods and strategies in keeping with their actual material conditions and from their own practical observations and experiments.[41]

The basis of Zhou's thought was his dispassionate assessment of interstate relations and their major manifestations. The rational conduct of foreign policy, according to Zhou, meant working out an adjustment between national aspirations and the sovereign rights of other nation-states. It became his task to shift China's emphases from ideological doctrine to bringing about a greater understanding of the problems of Asia and to further efforts toward peace and cooperation. He saw the Five Principles of Peaceful Coexistence as the vehicle for this change. Given that China's foreign policy was an instrument for enhancing its economic growth, he must work toward maintaining peaceful internal and international conditions and promoting trade relations with both Communist and non-Communist states. Obviously, the promotion of peace and order in Asia would be advantageous to China's domestic economic reconstruction.

On January 30, 1956, Zhou presented a political report to the second session of the Second National Committee of the Chinese People's Political Consultative Conference in which he stated: "We believe in the superiority of the socialist system. But we always maintain that revolution cannot be exported."[42] He went on to say: "We advocate peaceful coexistence and peaceful competition between countries having different social systems and believe that the people of each country should choose their political and economic systems and their way of life for themselves."[43] He urged Asian states to cooperate in seeking common measures to safeguard Asian international order and security.

It was imperative, in Zhou's view, to improve and expand China's normal state-to-state relations with countries willing to subscribe to the Five Principles of Peaceful Coexistence. Not only did he make every effort to convince Third World leaders of the "peace intention" of China, but, more important, he felt that they would share his basic approach. On June 28, 1956, when Zhou delivered a foreign policy report at the third session of the First NPC, he asserted that the nonaligned countries of Asia wished to build up their own independent national economies and, therefore, desired "a peaceful environment" in which to develop their respective projects.[44]

Creation of a Worldwide Coalition
against Imperialism, Neocolonialism, and Hegemonism

Zhou's overall approach to Third World nations in the period from 1955 to 1975 can perhaps best be seen as an attempt to apply the united front strategy on the international level. His major objective was to achieve the broadest possible alignment of international forces against imperialism, neocolonialism, and hegemonism. In dealing with Third World nations, Zhou tended to focus on their local nationalistic aspirations and their fears of renewed foreign domination and control. He believed that the common "colonial experience" and opposition to any form of "foreign intervention" was the unique bond between China and the Third World.[45] Unity of action among Third World nations, Zhou reasoned, was certainly a mighty weapon, which could not only provide China with an effective defense against diplomatic isolation but also protect the nation from imperialism, neocolonialism, and, after 1970, hegemonism and superpower politics. Therefore, Zhou utilized the international united front approach to resist the imperialists, neocolonialists, and hegemonists by winning over to China's side as many Third World nations as possible. Careful study of Zhou's practices demonstrates a clear similarity between his domestic united front techniques of the earlier periods (discussed fully in chap. 4) and the international united front he engineered in the 1950s and 1960s.

In the wake of the Korean War in the early 1950s and with the overwhelming need to improve China's political, social, and economic conditions, Zhou adopted a realistic foreign policy as a counterforce against the United States and its system of alliance. His policy of diplomatic diversification in the mid-1950s and again in the early 1960s demonstrated China's sensitivity to changes in the global bipolar power configuration. This foreign strategy was designed to reduce the dangers of confronting a superpower adversary. At the same time, the foundations of Chinese foreign policy were laid for the future. Despite the difficulties confronting him in Asia and beyond, Zhou was confident that he could succeed in achieving China's foreign policy objectives. He relied upon two instruments, the system of alliance and the international united front, to promote China's territorial security and to win a respected place for his country in the world community. The international united front was defined in broad terms as encompassing almost any nationalist, anti-imperialist, and anticolonial force.[46] It thus became the chief device for combatting Western influence and for advancing China's prestige among the newly emerging nations of the Third World.

Zhou's analysis of the "capitalist world" was centered on one central theme—that it was divided and not a solid, impenetrable bloc. As he put it, the old world of capitalist countries was divided into three categories: first, the bellicose forces that would not hesitate to go to war against China; second, the forces that stood for maintaining the status quo; and, third, the forces that stood for preserving peace.[47] Based on this premise, Zhou laid down China's foreign policy strategy as follows: to win over the peace forces, to influence the status quo forces, and to isolate the forces bent on war against China.[48]

To strive to come together with all those who could be united, Zhou was inclined to create a kind of symmetry between his past experience in domestic united front policies and current international conditions. Influenced by Lenin's teaching on flexible strategies and the theory of imperialism, Zhou displayed an appreciation for the practical value of the experiences of underdeveloped countries of Asia, Africa, and Latin America as the real forces of the anti-imperialist and anticolonial movement.[49] While he was trying to win over Third World leaders and governments, he was careful not to exert undue pressure or to behave in too domineering a way. A key principle of the domestic united front had been the hegemony of the CCP, but Zhou cautiously avoided transferring this distinctive feature into the international arena. He judged that the success of the united front policy had to be based on persuasion and genuine cooperation instead of manipulation.

The overriding objective was for China to convince as many different nation-states as possible to oppose imperialism and neocolonialism.[50] As such, Zhou's operational approach was both simple and effective. If a country were allied with the West, Zhou would attempt to neutralize it and to transform it into a middle-of-the-road force. If a country were already sufficiently neutral, he then sought to bring that country into a closer relationship with China. In his dialogues with Third World leaders Zhou tried to capitalize on the widespread opposition to imperialism and neocolonialism. The self-restraint he showed in dealing with Third World nations was intended to minimize obstacles to the formation of a global united front against imperialism and neocolonialism. His interest in the Third World as a growing force in contemporary international relations was critical to China's improved relationships with non-Communist states of the Third World.

Zhou's ability to deal with Third World nations, especially those of Asia and Africa, provides a classic example of his effective use of the united front formula. It is evident, however, that the united front method was not merely a temporary strategic measure for the short term. On the contrary, the united front approach was raised to a new level of importance by China's attempts to develop diplomatic rapprochement with the United States in 1971 and 1972 and by its foreign relations with some countries of the Second World in the early 1970s as part of Zhou's strategy to counterbalance the power of the Soviet Union. It is clear that the strategy of a united front was not limited to any particular geographical area but could be applied with great flexibility to a wide variety of situations. In a sense the united front approach was a significant link between Zhou's revolutionary experience in the national and civil wars and his task of conducting China's foreign policy.

In retrospect, Zhou's efforts in winning over Third World nations represented a major initiative in Chinese foreign policy in the late 1950s and early 1960s. Bold experiments in the field of foreign policy had to be tried when the international environment presented favorable conditions for success, and practicality was judged a more important consideration than abstract principles.

Though Zhou concentrated on the issues of China's common experience with Third World nations, he was careful not to alienate the medium and small European nations, especially those in Western and Eastern Europe.[51] According to Zhou's analysis, the composition of the international united front should be determined by the specific global conditions. When the Sino-Soviet conflict became apparent in the early 1960s, Zhou changed the emphasis and targeted adversary of the united front approach, even though the struggle was still against hegemonism and the power politics of the superpowers. In the 1960s the united front strategy was employed against the United States and the Soviet Union. In a world dominated by these two countries it was necessary for China to unite with as many small and medium nations as possible against superpower hegemonism.[52]

In the early 1970s the concept of "great disorder," to use Zhou's words, became the most distinctive element in Zhou's analysis of the international situation. Such great disorder was "a good thing" for the people of the world.[53] It would throw the enemies into "confusion" and cause "division among them." International turmoil would also arouse the people, "thus helping the international situation develop further in a direction favorable to the people and unfavorable to imperialism, modern revisionism, and all reactionaries."[54] The relaxation of tensions between the two superpowers was, in Zhou's view, at best a temporary and superficial phenomenon.

Having detected signs of a growing opposition throughout the world to the policies of the two superpowers, notably within the ranks of the Third World nations, Zhou decided to shift the focus of his foreign strategy from "imperialism" to "superpower hegemonism" and from "oppressed" to "small and medium powers." Once Zhou perceived changing characteristics of the global balance of power, he was quick to exploit the new tendencies and to integrate his new assessment into his formulation of China's foreign policy objectives. In his report to the Tenth Party Congress on August 24, 1973, Zhou declared that "countries want independence, nations want liberation, and the people want revolution."[55] He also placed great emphasis on exploiting the antihegemonic struggle and justified any compromises that were required by such a foreign policy strategy.

The central theme of China's external relations and foreign policy was still based on uniting and struggling. Zhou perceived that there was a broad united front against the hegemonism of the superpowers, that there were a number of united fronts on specific issues against the two superpowers, and that these united fronts were as important in the current situation as were the more direct anti-imperialist and anticolonial struggles. Against this background Zhou quoted Lenin to buttress his analysis that imperialism meant "the rivalry between several Great Powers in the striving for hegemony."[56] He recognized the importance, in this context, of the growing independence of Soviet and American allies in Eastern and Western Europe, respectively.

Balancing Global Influence between the Two Superpowers to Achieve China's Proper Strategic Triangle

To maintain China's national security, especially in view of its extensive common border with the Soviet Union, Zhou perceived the need to prevent "U.S.-Soviet collusion" at the expense of China. This premise shaped his foreign policy orientation of balancing the relative power distribution between the two superpowers for the improvement of China's international position. During the entire period of his tenure as premier of the State Council, the predominant characteristic of Zhou's approach to foreign policy was the perceptible change from achieving the ideologically motivated revolutionary goals of the Party to carrying out the national security responsibilities of the government. This approach allowed him considerable freedom in defining China's relationships with the two superpowers.

When China emerged from the isolation of the Cultural Revolution in the late 1960s, it was possible for Zhou to pursue a foreign policy nearly opposite of what had come before. He believed that, as China became more conciliatory toward other states, this attitude should also be extended to China's dealings with the two superpowers.[57] The security interests of China had once depended on the Sino-Soviet system of alliance in the 1950s; in the late 1960s and early 1970s Zhou carefully shifted from this bilateral relationship to a strategic triangle made up of China and the two superpowers, within which the pattern of coalition could change depending on the issues at stake.

Zhou calculated that China could serve its own diplomatic and strategic interests best by maintaining a suitable distance from the United States and the Soviet Union rather than by allying with either one of them. In fact, China might even hold the pivotal position by tilting in favor of either one as the Chinese government saw fit in order to counteract any potential danger that might be imposed by the excessive power and influence of the other in the world arena. The main challenge, according to Zhou, was how China could live with the two superpowers without viewing every dispute as a provocation and without creating additional sources of tension. China's security could thus hinge on some sort of balance of power among the three components of the triangle, its own position being strengthened by the equilibrium between the combined power of China and the Third World nations and that of the two superpowers.[58]

The skillful use of diplomacy was one of the major means to achieve such a balance. Within this context Zhou urged CCP leaders to shift from their preoccupation with ideology to focusing instead on foreign policy results. Efforts should be made, he argued, to stabilize the international order by supporting the legitimate aspirations of Third World nations and by preventing the two superpowers from excessively expanding their respective power orbits in the world arena. This shift in Zhou's foreign policy orientation represented both an important phase of the continuing process of policy evolution and a break with the Communist bloc. As always, the determining factor was the need to maintain international order and stability to achieve the systematic advancement of China's interests.

Zhou also came to see that the economic development and national security of China ultimately required nonhostile relations with both superpowers. To accomplish this end China would have to be able to exploit tensions between the two superpowers in the world arena. China's relative military strength and its diplomatic maneuverability were two critical factors in seeking to maintain this delicate balancing act. A triangular relationship, in principle, would encourage two partners to join together against one, particularly if the third appeared unduly aggressive or interfered in the spheres of influence of the others, such as China's sphere in Asia, the Soviet Union's sphere in Eastern Europe, or the United States' sphere in the North Atlantic and the Western Hemisphere. Restraints would logically derive from a nation's fear of becoming isolated diplomatically and strategically. If, for instance, a large-scale war involving China and either of the two superpowers were to occur, China and its rival power could be so severely devastated that the noninvolved superpower would emerge the victor, even if the noncombatant were initially not the strongest of the three. Therefore, if China could avoid military confrontation with the two superpowers, it would greatly expand its ability to maneuver diplomatically. Zhou's negotiations with both Moscow and Washington in the late 1960s and early 1970s serve to illustrate his realistic assessment of the triangular relationship.

Zhou's new strategic emphasis helps explain his sensitivity to possible U.S.-Soviet collusion or détente during the last several years of his life. It also provides some fresh insights into Soviet concerns about improved Sino-U.S. relations. It certainly makes U.S. support of polycentric tendencies within the Communist bloc more readily understandable. Most important of all, it perhaps explains the caution exhibited by all three countries involved in this strategic triangle. To establish a workable triangular relationship, Zhou felt that China should define as clearly as possible, along with the two superpowers, new parameters of legitimate interests in Asia and beyond for China, the Soviet Union, and the United States.

The rise of China and its open conflict with the Soviet Union in the mid- and late 1960s constituted a major part of the emerging multipolar pattern in international relations. Therefore, the idea of a new role for China in the world power equation and in the evolving structure of the international system was certainly obvious to Zhou. It was also his basic notion that all Chinese diplomatic moves and countermoves should be oriented toward the eventual achievement of China's equal distance from the two superpowers. Zhou emphasized the means of creating opportunities for improving or at least expanding China's relations with both superpowers. Along this strategic line Zhou sought to improve China's diplomatic bargaining position with either of the two superpowers or both. International circumstances were constantly changing and evolving, largely because the two superpowers were busily carrying out their own agendas. A proper triangular relationship among China, the United States, and the Soviet Union was for Zhou a prerequisite for a new and stable world order. His adroit calculation of the balance between the available means and the desired ends remained the key to a realistic assessment of China's relationships with the two superpowers.[59]

If the CCP had not won the Chinese civil war, Zhou might never have gone beyond the role of Yenan's chief negotiator and its top liaison officer at the wartime capital Chongqing. In his capacities as the foreign minister of the PRC from October 1949 to February 1958 and as premier from October 1949 until his death on January 8, 1976, Zhou became virtually indispensable to the conduct of Chinese foreign policy.

In the last two years of his life ill health due to lifelong overwork steadily undermined Zhou's vitality. The message and metaphor of a poem Mao wrote to the dying Zhou in 1975 is revealing and instructive in terms of their personal relationship and common political goal:

> Loyal parents who sacrificed so much for the nation
> never feared the ultimate fate.
> Now that the country has become Red,
> who will be its guardian?
> Our missions, unfinished, may take a thousand years.
> The struggle tires us, and our hair is gray.
> You and I, old friends, can we just watch our efforts
> being washed away?[60]

Zhou maintained to the end of his career and his life a keen interest in foreign policy and a vast knowledge of international affairs. His death on January 8, 1976, was a major turning point in the history of Chinese foreign policy both for what it took away and what it left behind.

NOTES

Introduction

1. For useful elaborations of the nature of foreign policy process, see Richard C. Snyder, H. W. Bruck, and Burton Sapin, *Decision-Making as an Approach to the Study of International Politics* (Princeton, N.J.: Princeton University Press, 1954), pp. 1-55; and Joseph Frankel, "Towards a Decision-Making Model in Foreign Policy," *Political Studies*, vol. 7, no. 1 (February 1959): pp. 1-11.

2. On the essential elements of foreign policy, refer to Feliks Gross, *Foreign Policy Analysis* (New York: Philosophical Library, 1954), especially chaps. 1, 3, 6; and Kenneth W. Thompson and Roy C. Macridis, "The Comparative Study of Foreign Policy," in *Foreign Policy in Modern Politics*, ed. Roy C. Macridis (Englewood Cliffs, N.J.: Prentice-Hall, 1958), pp. 1-28.

3. For an excellent discussion of the meaning of diplomacy, see Harold Nicolson, *Diplomacy* (London: Oxford University Press, 1937), p. 15; and Sir Ernest Satow, *A Guide to Diplomatic Practice* (London: Longman's Green, 1957), pp. 1-3.

4. For a general survey of Zhou's pragmatism and of his pragmatic approach to China's foreign relations and diplomacy, see Lucian W. Pye, "On Chinese Pragmatism in the 1980s," *China Quarterly* (hereafter cited as *CQ*), no. 16 (June 1986): pp. 220, 226; and Ronald C. Keith, *The Diplomacy of Zhou Enlai* (New York: St. Martin's Press, 1989), pp. 3-6, 8-11.

Chapter 1

1. For details of Zhou Enlai's background, see Howard L. Boorman, ed., *Biographical Dictionary of Republican China* (New York: Columbia University Press, 1967), pp. 392-93; Kai-yu Hsu, *Chou En-lai: China's Gray Eminence* (Garden City, N.Y.: Doubleday, 1968); Tien-min Li, *Chou En-lai* (Taipei: Institute of International Relations, 1970); Donald W. Klein and Anne B. Clark, eds., *Biographic Dictionary of Chinese Communism, 1921-1965*, 2 vols. (Cambridge, Mass.: Harvard University Press, 1971), vol. 1, pp. 204-19; Jules Archer, *Chou En-lai* (New York: Hawthorn, 1973); Ching-wen Yen, *Zhou*

Enlai ping-zhuan (Biography of Zhou Enlai) (Hong Kong: Po Wen Books, 1974); John C. Roots, *Chou: An Informal Biography of China's Legendary Chou En-lai* (New York: Doubleday, 1978); Dick Wilson, *Zhou Enlai: A Biography* (New York: Viking, 1984); and Steven Goldstein, "Zhou Enlai and China's Revolution: A Selective View," *CQ*, no. 96 (December 1983): pp. 720-30.

2. For more information on the early life of Zhou Enlai, see Hsu, *op. cit.*, chap. 1; Hu Hua, *The Young Comrade Zhou Enlai* (Beijing: China Youth Press, 1977); *The Story of Premier Zhou's Childhood* (Shengyang: Liaoning People's Press, 1979); Huai En, *The Youth of Zhou Enlai* (Chongqing: Sichuan People's Press, 1980); Hu Hua, *The Early Life of Zhou Enlai* (Beijing: Foreign Languages Press, 1980), Wilson, *op. cit.*, chaps. 1-2; Chae-jin Lee, *Zhou Enlai: The Early Years* (Stanford, Calif.: Stanford University Press, 1994); and Suyin Han, *Eldest Son: Zhou Enlai and the Making of Modern China, 1898-1976* (New York: Hill and Wang, 1994), chaps. 1-4.

3. On Zhou's foster mother, see Hsu, *op. cit.*, pp. 7-8; Kai-yu Hsu, "Chou En-lai: The Indispensable Man of Compromise," *New Republic*, vol. 156, no. 14 (April 8, 1967): p. 21; and Hu Hua, *The Young Comrade Zhou Enlai*, p. 3.

4. Wilson, *op. cit.*, p. 26.

5. For more information about Zhou's training at Nankai, see Hu, *The Young Comrade Zhou Enlai*, pp. 11-12; K. Hsu, *op. cit.*, pp. 11-14; Li, *op. cit.*, pp. 20-21; Huai, *op. cit.*, pp. 30-31; Wilson, *op. cit.*, chap. 2; and Lee, *op. cit.*, chap. 2. On Zhou and the founding of the Respect Work and Enjoy Fellowship Society, see Wilson, *op. cit.*, pp. 31-32.

6. See, for example, Zhou Enlai, "Wo-zhi ren-ge-guan" (My View of Human Character, October 1916), *Zhou-Zong-li qing-shao-nian shi-dai shi-wen-shu-xin-ji* (Poems, Essays and Letters Composed and Written by Premier Zhou at a Young Age), ed. Huai En (Sichuan: Ren-min-chu-ban-she, 1979), p. 97; hereafter cited as *PELZ*.

7. For more information on "practical learning" (*she-xue*), see Ch'i-chao Liang, *Intellectual Trends in the Ch'ing Period*, trans. Immanual C. Y. Hsu (Cambridge, Mass.: Harvard University Press, 1959), pp. 3-4; Wm. Theodore de Bary and Irene Bloom, eds., *Principle and Practicality: Essays in Neo-Confucianism and Practical Learning* (New York: Columbia University Press, 1979), pp. 37-38, 61-62; and Wm. Theodore de Bary, *The Unfolding of Neo-Confucianism* (New York: Columbia University Press, 1970), pp. 202-3.

8. See Liang, *op. cit.*, p. 45; and de Bary and Bloom, *op. cit.*, pp. 69-70.

9. Liang, *op. cit.*, pp. 3-4, 6, 21, 24; and Etienne Balazs, *Political Theory and Administrative Reality in Traditional China* (London: School of Oriental and African Studies, University of London, 1965).

10. For more information on Gu Yanwu's life and major writings, see Arthur W. Hummel, ed., *Eminent Chinese of the Ch'ing Period (1644-1912)* (Washington, D.C.: Library of Congress, 1943), pp. 421-26; Liang, *op. cit.*, pp. 29-32; Wm. Theodore de Bary, Wing-tsit Chan, and Burton Watson, eds., *Sources of Chinese Tradition*, 2 vols. (New York: Columbia University Press, 1960), pp. 607-11; de Bary and Bloom, *op. cit.*, pp. 327-29, 400; Willard J. Peterson, "The life of Ku Yen-wu, Part 1," *Harvard Journal of Asiatic Studies*, no. 28 (1968): pp. 114-56; Wade Baskin, ed., *Classics in Chinese Philosophy* (New York: Philosophical Library, 1972), pp. 613-15; and Wm. Theodore de Bary, *Neo-Confucian Orthodoxy and the Learning of the Mind-and-Heart* (New York: Columbia University Press, 1981), p. 171.

11. Liang, *op. cit.*, p. 32.

12. *Ibid.*

13. See James Legge, trans., *The Chinese Classics: Confucian Analects, the Great Learning, The Doctrine of the Mean* (Hong Kong: Hong Kong University, 1968), vol. 1, chap. 6, p. 388.

14. *Ibid.*, chap. 14, p. 178.

15. For more information on Wang Fuzhi's life and major works, see Hummel, *op. cit.*, pp. 817-19; Yu-lan Fung, *A History of Chinese Philosophy*, trans. Derk Bodde, vol. 2 (Princeton, N.J.: Princeton University Press, 1953), pp. 630-32, 641-43, 648-49; Liang, *op. cit.*, pp. 38-40; de Bary, Chan, and Burton, *op. cit.*, pp. 597-606; Wing-tsit Chan, *A Source Book in Chinese Philosophy* (Princeton, N.J.: Princeton University Press, 1963), chap. 36; de Bary, *Founding of Neo-Confucianism*, pp. 473-90; Ian McMorran, "Wang Fu-chih and the Neo-Confucian Tradition," in *ibid.*, pp. 313-467; Ssu-yu Teng, "Wang Fu-Chih's Views on History and Historical Writing," *Journal of Asian Studies*, vol. 28, no. 1 (November 1968): pp. 111-23; and Baskin, *op. cit.*, pp. 617-22.

16. See Wang Fuzhi, "Si-wen-lu wai-pian" (Supplementary Chapter of the Records of Thinking and Queries); quoted in Yang Rong-guo, et al., *Jian-min Zhong-guo zhe-xue-shi* (Brief History of Chinese Philosophy) (Beijing: Ren-min-chu-ban-she, 1973), p. 314.

17. For more information on Wang's notion of the inapplicability of ancient institutions to modern times, see Baskin, *op. cit.*, pp. 619-21; and Chan, *op. cit.*, p. 693.

18. Quoted in Jerome Ch'en, *Mao and the Chinese Revolution* (New York: Oxford University Press, 1965), p. 12.

19. See Wang Fuzhi, "Zheng-meng-zhu" (Commentary on Zhang-zai's Rectifying Obscurities); quoted in Liang, *op. cit.*, p. 39.

20. Quoted in Liang, p. 39.

21. On the young Zhou's study of Gu's and Wang's works, see K. Hsu, *Chou En-lai*, p. 9; Li, *op. cit.*, p. 16; and Takashi Nishikawa, *The Path of Zhou Enlai* (Tokyo: Tokuma shoten, 1976), p. 16.

22. Zhou Enlai, "Dong-quan-mu-fan-xue-xiao di-er-zhou-nian ji-nian-ri gan-yan" (Reflections on the Second Anniversary of the Eastern Gate Primary School, October 12, 1912), *PELZ*, p. 8; and Zhou Enlai, "Cheng-neng-dong-wu-lun" (Talk on Sincerity as a Way to Move Things, May 15, 1916), *ibid.*, p. 55.

23. Hu, *Young Comrade Zhou Enlai*, p. 9; and Wilson, *op. cit.*, p. 24.

24. Zhou Enlai, "Reflections on the Second Anniversary of the Eastern Gate Primary School" *op. cit.*, p. 5.

25. *Ibid.*, p. 4.

26. See Zhou Enlai, "Laozi zhu tui-rang, He-xi-li zhu jing-zheng, er-shui-shu-shi, shi-yan-zhi" (Laozi in Favor of Yielding, Huxley Advocating Competition: Which View Is Right? Let Me Discuss the Question, March 20, 1916), *PELZ*, p. 43; and Wu Hao (Zhou Enlai), "Zong-jiao-jing-shen yu Gong-chan-zhu-yi" (The Religious Spirit and Communism), *Shao-nien* (The Youth), no. 2 (September 1922), in *Zhou Enlai tong-zhi lu-Ou wen-ji* (The European Correspondence of Comrade Zhou Enlai), 2 vols. (Beijing: Wen-wu chu-ban-she, 1979), vol. 1, p. 241; hereafter cited as *ZELWJ-1* or *ZELWJ-2*.

27. Zhou Enlai, "Talk on Sincerity," p. 55.

28. Zhou Enlai, "Reflections on the Second Anniversary of the Eastern Gate Primary School," p. 5. On Gu's idea of broad knowledge and of the sense of shame, see "A Letter to a Friend Discussing the Pursuit of Learning"; quoted in Baskin, *op. cit.*, pp. 614-15.

29. Zhou Enlai, "Reflections on the Secondary Anniversary of the Eastern Gate Primary School," p. 4.

30. *Ibid.*, p. 5; and Zhou Enlai, "Laozi in Favor of Yielding," p. 43.

31. On the issue of Darwinism and its influence in China, see Yan Fu, *Tian-yan-lun* (The Theory of Evolution) (Taipei: Shang-wu Publishing Co., 1967); Reeve Pusey, *China and Charles Darwin* (Cambridge, Mass.: Council on East Asian Studies, Harvard University Press, 1966); and Benjamin Schwartz, *In Search of Wealth and Power and the West* (Cambridge, Mass.: Harvard University Press, 1964), chaps. 3, 4. On the young Zhou's awareness of Darwin and Darwinism, see Hsu, *Chou En-lai*, p. 9; and Wilson, *op. cit.*, p. 25.

32. See Charles Darwin, *On the Origin of Species* (Cambridge, Mass.: Harvard University Press, 1966); and T. H. Huxley and Julian Huxley, *Evolution and Ethics, 1893-1943* (London: Pilot Press, 1947). Huxley's *Evolution and Ethics* was translated by Yan Fu in 1897.

33. Zhou Enlai, "Laozi in Favor of Yielding," pp. 41-42, 43.

34. Zhou Enlai, "Talk on Sincerity," p. 54.

35. Huxley, *op. cit.,* p. 64.

36. *Ibid.,* p. 51; and Pusey, *op. cit.,* pp. 160-61.

37. Huxley, *op. cit.,* pp. 81-82.

38. Zhou Enlai, "Laozi in Favor of Yielding," *op. cit.,* p. 43.

39. For more information on experimental philosophy, see John Dewey, *Reconstruction in Philosophy* (1920; reprint, New York: New American Library, 1950); John Dewey, *Human Nature and Conduct* (1921; reprint, New York: Henry Holt, 1944); John Dewey, *The Quest for Certainty* (New York: G. P. Putnam's Sons, 1960); and John Dewey "Social Philosophy and Political Philosophy," *Xin-qing-nian* (New Youth), vol. 7, no. 1 (December 1919): pp 121-34; and *ibid.,* vol. 7, no. 2 (January 1920): pp. 163-82.

40. John Dewey, "New Culture in China," *Asia,* vol. 21, no. 7 (July 1921): p. 586.

41. *Ibid.,* p. 581.

42. For more information on Dewey's lectures at Beijing University in the winter of 1919 on his experimental philosophy, see Chow Ts'e-tsung, *The May Fourth Movement: Intellectual Revolution in Modern China* (Cambridge, Mass.: Harvard University Press, 1960), pp. 219-20, 223-24, and 228-30.

43. Hu Shi, *Hu Shi wen-xuan* (Selected Works of Hu Shi) (Taipei, 1962), p. 294; hereafter cited as *HSWX.*

44. Hu Shi, "An Introduction to My Own Thought," *ibid.,* p. 3. On Hu's pragmatic approach and his interpretation of Dewey's experimental philosophy, see Jerome B. Grieder, *Hu Shih and the Chinese Renaissance* (Cambridge, Mass.: Harvard University Press, 1970), pp. 113-21.

45. Hu Shi, "Shi-yan zhu-yi" (Pragmatism), *Hu Shi wen-cun* (Collected Essays of Hu Shi), 4 vols. (Shanghai: Ya-dung-shu-quan, 1926), collection 1, chap. 2, p. 295; hereafter cited as *HSWC.* This article was originally published in *New Youth,* vol. 6, no. 4 (April 1, 1919), pp. 342-59.

46. *HSWC,* p. 295.

47. *Ibid.,* p. 294.

48. *Ibid.*

49. *Ibid.,* p. 69.

50. *Ibid.*

51. Pusey, *op. cit.,* p. 444.

52. Hu Shi, "duo-yan-jiu-xiu wen-ti, shao-tan-xiu 'zhu-yi'" (Study More Problems, Talk Less of 'Ism'), *Mei-zhou ping-lun* (Weekly Critic), no. 31 (July 20, 1919); also see *HSWC,* vol. 2, pp. 147-53.

53. Hu Shi, "xin-si-chao di yi-yi" (The Meaning of the New Thought, November 1, 1919), *New Youth,* vol. 7, no. 1 (December 1, 1919); an abridged English

translation of this article may be found in Ssu-yu Teng and John K. Fairbank, *China's Response to the West: A Documentary Survey, 1839-1923* (Cambridge, Mass.: Harvard University Press, 1954), pp. 252-55; also see Chow, *op. cit.*, p. 218.

54. *HSWC* (Shanghai, 1926), vol. 2, p. 151; also see Maurice Meisner, *Li Ta-chao and the Origins of Chinese Communism* (Cambridge, Mass.: Harvard University Press, 1967), p. 107.

55. See Fei Fei (Zhou Enlai) and his essay in *Shao-nian* (Youth), no. 6, n.d., *ZELWJ-1*, p. 255.

56. *Ibid.* For Hu's views on politics and political process in the early and mid-1920s, see Grieder, *op. cit.*, pp. 194-225.

57. Zhou Enlai, "Laozi in Favor of Yielding," p. 43.

58. Zhou Enlai, "Reflections on the Second Anniversary of the Eastern Gate Primary School," p. 5.

59. Zhou Enlai, "Talk on Sincerity," p. 55.

60. Zhou Enlai, "Laozi in Favor of Yielding," p. 43.

61. Zhou Enlai, "Reflections on the Second Anniversary of the Eastern Gate Primary School," p. 5.

62. See Liang, *op. cit.*, p. 22; and de Bary and Bloom, *op. cit.*, pp. 47-48.

63. Zhou Enlai, "Reflections on the Second Anniversary of the Eastern Gate Primary School," p. 5.

64. Zhou Enlai, "Guidelines for myself, March 18, 1943," *Selected Works of Zhou Enlai* (Beijing: Foreign Languages Press, 1981), p. 144; hereafter cited as *SWZEL-1*.

65. Zhou Enlai, "Talk on Sincerity," p. 55.

66. Zhou Enlai, "Reflections on the Second Anniversary of the Eastern Gate Primary School," p. 5. On Zhou's youthful patriotism, see his essays "Cun-ri-ou-cheng" (Notes on a Spring Day, October 1914), *PELZ*, p. 12; and "My View of Human Character," *ibid.*, pp. 98, 99.

67. Zhou Enlai, "Talk on Sincerity," p. 54.

Chapter 2

1. See, for example, Zhou Enlai, "Xi-Ou dui-E due-De zhi fang-lu" (The Strategy of Western Europe toward Russia and Germany, May 24, 1921), *ZELWJ-1*, p. 26; "Hua-fu hui-yi-zhong zhi Ying-Fa zhan-lu" (Anglo-French Military Strategies at the Washington Conference, Part 2, January 22, 1922), *ibid.*, p. 174; and "Shang-Xi-li-xi-ya zui-jin zhi luan-xiang" (Recent Confusing Situation in Upper Silesia, July 14, 1921), *ibid.*, p. 58.

2. See Zhou Enlai, "Sheng-dan-jie-qian zhi Ying-Fa hui-yi" (The Anglo-French Conference prior to Christmas Day, February 11, 1922), *ibid.*, pp. 184-85; and "Yi-jiu-er-er-nian kai-mu-hou zhi Ou-zhou" (Europe after the Opening of the 1922 [Washington] Conference, February 20, 1922), *ibid.*, pp. 189-90.

3. See, for example, Zhou Enlai, "The Strategy of Western Europe toward Russia and Germany," *op. cit.*, p. 27; "Yin-Fa yu-lun zhi yi-ban" (Anglo-French Comments [on the Issue of Upper Silesia], July 11-12, 1921), *ZELWJ-1*, p. 55; "Min-zu zi-jue yu Shang Xi-li-xi-ya wen-ti" (National Self-Determination and the Problem of Upper Silesia, December 11, 1921), *ibid.*, pp. 154, 155.

4. Zhou Enlai, "Recent Confusing Situation in Upper Silesia," pp. 58-59; "Xie-yue-guo zhui-gao-hui-yi yan-ji" (Postponement of the Allied Powers' Supreme Command Conference, July 13, 1921), *ZELWJ-1*, p. 57; and "Ou-zhan-hou pei-kuan wen-ti zhi jin-xun" (The Recent News about the Post-European War Reparations Problem, June 20, 1921), *ibid.*, pp. 64, 65. Also see "Ying-guo due-De zhi tai-du" (Britain's Attitude toward Germany, June 12, 1921), *ibid.*, p. 41; and "Yin-Fa zui-jin yi-jian ju-yu" ("Recent Differences of Opinion between Britain and France, July 10, 1921"), *ibid.*, p. 53.

5. *Ibid.*; and "Recent Confusing Situation in Upper Silesia," p. 58; "Ying-Fa liang-guo jiao-she zhi jing-guo" (The Anglo-French Negotiations, October 3, 1921), *ZELWJ-1*, p. 105; "Jia-en hui-yi zhi hou-ban-mu" (The Latter Half of the Cannes Conference, March 19, 1922), *ibid.*, p. 203; and "Europe after the Opening of the 1922 Conference," p. 192.

6. See Zhou Enlai, "Lin-pu-li hui-yi zhi qing-xing" (The Circumstances of the Limburg Conference, June 20, 1921), *ZELWJ-1*, p. 65; "Bu-lie-dian-di-guo zhi wai-jiao-nei-zheng" (Foreign Relations and Home Administration of the British Empire, September 6, 1921), *ibid.*, p. 86; "Britain's Attitude toward Germany," p. 41; "Recent Differences of Opinion between Britain and France," p. 53; and "News about the Post-European War Reparations Problem," p. 64.

7. Zhou Enlai, "Shang Xi-li-xi-ya wen-ti zhi fu-za" (The Complexity of the Problem of Upper Silesia, July 12, 1921), *ZELWJ-1*, p. 55; "Strategy of Western Europe toward Russia and Germany," p. 26; "Recent News about the Post-European War Reparations Problem," p. 64; "Allied Powers' Supreme Command Conference," p. 57; and "National Self-Determination and the Problem of Upper Silesia," p. 155.

8. See Zhou Enlai, "Mei-Ri zhi jiao-she [yu] Shan-dong wen-ti zhi chu-wai" (U.S.-Japanese negotiations [and] exclusion of the Shan-dong problem, September 14, 1921), *ZELWJ-1*, p. 99.

9. See Zhou Enlai, "Strategy of Western Europe toward Russia and Germany," pp. 26, 27.

10. *Ibid.* Zhou Enlai, "De-guo dui-yu Lian-he-guo zhi yi-jian" (Germany's Views on the League of Nations, June 22, 1921), *ZELWJ-1,* p. 40; "Recent Differences of Opinion between Britain and France," p. 55; "Shang-Xi-li-xi-ya-an zhi yi-jiao" (Transfer of the Case of Upper Silesia, December 5, 1921), *ZELWJ-1,* p. 108; and "Europe after the Opening of the 1922 Conference," p. 189.

11. See Zhou Enlai, "De-guo pei-kuan-wen-ti zhi jue-lie" (The Breakdown of the Problem of German Reparations, March 19, 1921), *ZELWJ-1,* p. 22; "Britain's attitude toward Germany," p. 41; Zhi-De ai-di-mei-dun-shu zhi nei-rong" (Contents of the Ultimatum Delivered to Germany, June 28, 1921), *ZELWJ-1,* p. 50; "National Self-Determination and the Problem of Upper Silesia," p. 155; and "Zai-bing pei-kuan wen-ti yu Ying-Fa" (Britain, France, and the Problems of Disarmament and Reparations, February 5, 1922), *ZELWJ-1,* p. 178. Also see "Anglo-French Negotiations," p. 105.

12. See, for example, Zhou Enlai, "Strategy of Western Europe toward Russia and Germany," pp. 26, 27.

13. Zhou Enlai, "Recent Confusing Situation in Upper Silesia," p. 58; and "Ying-Fa wen-ti zhu-jin zhi qu-shi" (Recent Trends in the British-French Problems, February 23, 1922), *ZELWJ-1,* p. 196.

14. Zhou Enlai, "Lun-dun hui-yi zai-kai-mu zhi jing-guo" (The Reopening of the London Conference, June 27, 1921), *ZELWJ-1,* p. 48; "British-French Conference prior to Christmas Day," p. 184; and "Recent Trends in the British-French problems," p. 196.

15. See Zhou Enlai, "Latter Half of the Cannes Conference," p. 203; "Recent Differences of Opinion between Britain and France," p. 53; "Foreign Relations and Home Administration of the British Empire," p. 86; "Europe after the Opening of the 1922 Conference," p. 191; "Europe after the 1922 Conference, March 1, 1922," p. 195; and "Ying-guo jin-ri dui-E zhi-ji-xu" (England's Urgent Need from Russia, March 25-28, 1922), *ZELWJ-1,* pp. 217, 221.

16. See Zhou Enlai, "De-guo-pei-kuan que-shu zhi jue-ding" (The Decision on the Exact Amount of German Reparations, May 22, 1921), *ZELWJ-1,* p. 3; "Fa-guo dui pei-kuan zhi chou-hua" (France's Plan for Reparations, June 12, 1921), *ibid.,* p. 40.

17. Zhou Enlai, "Shang-Xi-li-xi-ya Zhi jin-xun" (Recent News about Upper Silesia, June 16, 1921), *ibid.,* p. 62; "Recent Differences of Opinion between Britain and France," p. 53; "The Circumstances of the Limburg Conference," p. 64; and "Latter Half of the Cannes Conference," p. 203.

18. See, for example, Zhou Enlai, "Recent Differences of opinion between Britain and France," p.53; "Latter Half of the Cannes Conference," p. 203; "Ou-zhan-

hou zhi Ou-zhou wei-ji" (Crises in Postwar Europe, March 12, 1921), *ZELWJ-1*, pp. 2-3; and "Europe after the Opening of the 1922 Conference," p. 190.

19. Zhou Enlai, "Recent Differences of Opinion between Britain and France," p. 53; "Circumstances of the Limburg Conference," p. 64; "Postponement of the Allied Powers' Supreme Command Conference," p. 58; "Latter Half of the Cannes Conference," p. 203; and "Anglo-French Conference prior to Christmas Day," pp. 182, 183.

20. Zhou Enlai, "Recent News about the Post-European War Reparations Problem," p. 64; "Anglo-French Conference prior to Christmas Day," p. 183; "Contents of the Ultimatum Delivered to Germany," p. 50; "Foreign Relations and Home Administration of the British Empire," p. 86; "Anglo-French Military Strategies at the Washington Conference," p. 175; "Latter Half of the Cannes Conference," p. 203; and "Fu-pi-sheng-zhong zhi De-yi-zhi" (Germany under the Sound of Restoration, October 19, 1921), *ZELWJ-1*, pp. 116, 117.

21. See Zhou Enlai, "Postponement of the Allied Powers' Supreme Command Conference," p. 57; "Recent Confusing Situation in Upper Silesia," p. 58; "Recent News about Upper Silesia," p. 63; "Circumstances of the Limburg Conference," p. 64; "Anglo-French Strategies at the Washington Conference," p. 169; and "Europe after the Opening of the 1922 Conference," p. 191.

22. Zhou Enlai, "Britain's Attitude toward Germany," p. 41; "Reopening of the London Conference," p. 48; "Recent Differences of Opinion between Britain and France," p. 53; "Anglo-French Negotiations," p. 105; "Lao-te Qiao-zhi guo-hui yan-shui" (Lloyd George's Speech Addressed to Parliament, February 10, 1922), *ZELWJ-1*, p. 183; "Europe after the Opening of the 1922 Conference," pp. 190, 191; and "Recent Trends in British-French Problems," p. 196.

23. See Zhou Enlai, "Breakdown of the Problem of German Reparations," p. 22; "Germany under the Sound of Restoration," p. 116; "National Self-Determination and the Problem of Upper Silesia," p. 155; "Europe after the Opening of the 1922 Conference," pp. 191, 195.

24. Zhou Enlai, "Circumstances of the Limburg Conference, p. 65; and "National Self-Determination and the Problem of Upper Silesia," p. 155.

25. Zhou Enlai, "Anglo-French Military Strategies at the Washington Conference," p.174; "Europe after the Opening of the 1922 Conference," p. 194; and "Recent Confusing Situation in Upper Silesia," p. 58.

26. See, for example, Zhou Enlai, "Circumstances of the Limburg Conference," p. 65; "National Self-Determination and the Problem of Upper Silesia," p. 155; "The Anglo-French Conference prior to Christmas Day," p. 182; and "Recent Differences of Opinion between Britain and France," p. 54.

27. Zhou Enlai, "National Self-Determination and the Problem of Upper Silesia," p. 155; "Europe after the Opening of the 1922 Conference," p. 191; "Breakdown of the Problem of German Reparations," p. 22; and "Recent Differences of Opinion between Britain and France," p. 54.

28. Zhou Enlai, "Recent News about the Post-European War Reparations Problem," p. 64; "National Self-Determination and the Problem of Upper Silesia," p. 155; and "Europe after the Opening of the 1922 Conference," pp. 191, 192.

29. See Zhou Enlai, "Circumstances of the Limburg Conference," p. 65; "Foreign Relations and Home Administration of the British Empire," p. 86; and "The Anglo-French Conference prior to Christmas Day," p. 183.

30. Zhou Enlai, "Xiang-dang-shou-duan zhi shi-xian" (Practical Realization of the Proper Methods, May 20, 1921), *ZELWJ-1*, p. 24; "Britain's Attitude toward Germany," p. 41; "Recent Differences of Opinion between Britain and France," p. 53; "Foreign Relations and Home Administration of the British Empire," p. 86; "National Self-Determination and the Problem of Upper Silesia," p. 155; "Si-guo-xie-ding yu Mei-Fa" (The U.S., France, and the Four-Power Agreement, February 7, 1922), *ZELWJ-1*, pp. 180, 181; "Europe after the Opening of the 1922 Conference," p. 194; "Dai-xi-yang-shang zhi Tai-ping-yang hui-yi-quan" (The Pacific Conference Viewed from the Atlantic Ocean [Part 2], January 10, 1922), *ZELWJ-1*, p. 186; and "Latter Half of the Cannes Conference," p. 203.

31. *Ibid.*, p. 203; also see Zhou Enlai, "Practical Realization of the Proper Methods," p. 24; "Reopening of the London Conference," p. 48; "Recent News about the Post-European War Reparations Problem," p. 64; "Europe after the Opening of the 1922 Conference," p. 195.

32. Zhou Enlai, "Practical Realization of the Proper Methods," p. 24; and "Europe after the Opening of the 1922 Conference," p. 194.

33. Zhou Enlai, "Recent Differences of Opinion between Britain and France," p. 55; "Postponement of the Allied Powers' Supreme Command Conference," p. 57; "Anglo-French Negotiations," p. 105; and "National Self-Determination and the Problem of Upper Silesia," p. 155.

34. See, for example, Zhou Enlai, "Foreign Relations and Home Administration of the British Empire, p. 86; "Anglo-French Conference prior to Christmas Day," pp. 183, 184, 185; and "Recent Trends in British-French Problems," p. 196.

35. Zhou Enlai, "Recent News about the Post-European War Reparations Problem," p. 64.

36. See Zhou Enlai, "Britain's Attitude toward Germany," p. 41; "Recent Differences of Opinion between Britain and France," p. 53; and "Europe after the Opening of the 1922 Conference," p. 194.

37. See Lord Palmerston's reply to his critics in the House of Commons, March 1, 1848, as quoted in Kenneth Bourne, *The Foreign Policy of Victorian England, 1830-1902* (Oxford: Clarendon Press, 1970), p. 46.

38. Zhou Enlai, "Breakdown of the Problem of German Reparations," p. 23; "Strategy of Western Europe toward Russia and Germany," p. 26; and "Recent Differences of Opinion between Britain and France," p. 52.

39. *Ibid.;* "Lloyd George's Speech Addressed to Parliament," p. 183; "Europe after the Opening of the 1922 Conference," p. 195; and "Latter Half of the Cannes Conference," p. 203.

40. See, for example, Zhou Enlai, "Anglo-French Conference prior to Christmas Day," pp. 183, 185; also see "Foreign Relations and Home Administration of the British Empire," p. 86.

41. Zhou Enlai, "Recent Differences of Opinion between Britain and France," p. 53; "Complexity of the Problem of Upper Silesia," p. 55; "Postponement of the Allied Powers' Supreme Command Conference," p. 57; "Anglo-French Negotiations," p. 105; and "Anglo-French Strategies at the Washington Conference," p. 175.

42. See, for example, Zhou Enlai, "Britain's Attitude toward Germany," p. 41; "Complexity of the Problem of Upper Silesia," p. 53; "Ba-li hui-yi-zhong zhi Ying-Fa xiao-chong-tu" (Minor Conflict between Britain and France at the Paris Conference, October 4, 1921), *ZELWJ-1*, p. 106; "National Self-Determination and the Problem of Upper Silesia," p. 155; and "Britain, France, and the Problems of Disarmament and Reparations," p. 178.

43. Zhou Enlai, "Complexity of the Problem of Upper Silesia," p. 54; "Circumstances of the Limburg Conference," p. 65; and "Europe after the Opening of the 1922 Conference," p. 195; "Minor Conflict between Britain and France at the Paris Peace Conference," pp. 107-8; and "Lloyd George's Speech Addressed to Parliament," pp. 182, 183.

44. Zhou Enlai, "Recent Confusing Situation in Upper Silesia," p. 58; "Jin-liang-yue-jian zhi Xi-Ou da-shi-ji" (Major Events in Western Europe during the Past Two Months, October 2, 1921), *ZELWJ-1*, p. 103; "U.S., France, and the Four Power Agreement," p. 180; and "Anglo-French Strategies at the Washington Conference," p. 174.

45. Zhou Enlai, "Ou-zhan-hou zhi Ou-zhou wei-ji" (Crises in Postwar Europe, March 23, 1921), *ZELWJ-1*, p. 4.

46. See, for example, Zhou Enlai, "Recent News about Upper Silesia," p. 62; and "Dai-xi-yang-shang zhi Tai-ping-yang hui-yi-quan" (The Pacific Conference Viewed from the Atlantic Ocean [Part 1], January 1, 1922), *ZELWJ-1*, p. 164.

47. Zhou Enlai, "Practical Realization of the Proper Methods," p. 24.

48. Zhou Enlai, "Recent News about Upper Silesia," p. 62; "Anglo-French Strategies at the Washington Conference, p. 175; "The Anglo-French Conference prior to Christmas Day," p. 184; and "Latter Half of the Cannes Conference," p. 204.

49. Zhou Enlai, "Recent News about Upper Silesia," p. 62; "Minor Conflict between Britain and France at the Paris Conference," pp. 107-8; and "Recent Trends in British-French Problems," p. 196.

50. See Zhou Enlai, "Recent News about Upper Silesia," p. 62; "Bai-li-an zhi zai-bing yan-shui" (Briand's Speech on Disarmament, January 21, 1922), *ZELWJ-1*, pp. 170, 171; and "Europe after the Opening of the 1922 Conference," p. 191.

51. Zhou Enlai, "The Pacific Conference Viewed from the Atlantic Ocean," p. 163; "Anglo-French Military Strategies at the Washington Conference," p. 169; "Europe after the Opening of the 1922 Conference," p. 195; and "Latter Half of the Cannes Conference," p. 204.

52. *Ibid.*

53. See Zhou Enlai, "Europe after the Opening of the 1922 Conference," p. 195; and "Latter Half of the Cannes Conference," p. 203.

54. Zhou Enlai, "Recent Differences of Opinion between Britain and France," p. 53; and "Anglo-French Conference prior to Christmas Day," p. 182.

55. Zhou Enlai, "The Complexity of the Problem of Upper Silesia," p. 55; and "Anglo-French Negotiations," p. 105.

56. Zhou Enlai, "U.S.-Japanese Negotiations [and] Exclusion of the Shan-dong Problem," p. 98; "Pacific Conference Viewed from the Atlantic Ocean (Part 2), January 10, 1922," p. 186; and "Dai-xi-yang-shang zhi Tai-ping-yang-wen-ti" (The Pacific Question at the Atlantic Conference, December 30, 1921), *ZELWJ-1*, p. 161.

57. Zhou Enlai, "Ying-Mei zhi zheng-zhi" (American-Anglo Dispute, September 14, 1921), *ibid.*, p. 99; and "Gong-quan-shui sheng-chang Mei-guo zhi you-lai" (Origin of the Concerted Control Theory Popularly Introduced in the United States, December 17, 1921), *ibid.*, p. 159.

58. Zhou Enlai, "American-Anglo Dispute," p. 99. On the issues of warlord governments and Sino-Japanese relations in the mid- and late 1910s, see James E. Sheridan, *Chinese Warlord: The Career of Feng Yu-hsiang* (Stanford, Calif.: Stanford University Press, 1966), chap. 1; Lucian W. Pye, *Warlord Politics: Conflict and coalition in the Modernization of Republican China* (New York: Praeger Publishers, 1971), chaps. 1, 2, 8; Hsi-ping Shao, "Tuan Chi-jui, 1912-1918: A Case Study of the Military Influence on the Chinese Political Development" (Ph.D. diss., University of Pennsylvania, 1976), chaps. 2, 3, 6, epilogue; Hsi-sheng Ch'i *Warlord Politics in China, 1916-1928* (Stanford,

Calif.: Stanford University Press, 1967), chaps. 8, 9; Madeleine Chi, *China Diplomacy, 1914-1918* (Cambridge, Mass.: Harvard East Asian Research Center, 1970), chaps. 1-3; and Hsi-ping Shao, "From the Twenty-one Demands to the Sino-Japanese Agreement, 1915-1918: Ambivalent Relations," in *China and Japan: Search for Balance since World War I,* ed. Alvin D. Coox and Hilary Conroy (Santa Barbara, Calif.: Clio Books, 1978), pp. 35-51.

59. Harley F. MacNair and Donald F. Lach, *Modern Far Eastern International Relations* (New York: Octagon Books, 1975), p. 117; also see Zhou Enlai, "Si-guo-xi-ding zhi you-lai" (The Origins of the Four-Power Agreement, February 6, 1922), *ZELWJ-1,* p. 180; and "U.S., France, and the Four-Power Agreement," p. 181.

60. See Zhou Enlai, "Origins of the Four-Power Agreement," p. 181.

61. *Ibid.*

62. Zhou Enlai, "Origin of the Concerted Control Theory Popularly Introduced in the United States," pp. 158, 159.

63. Zhou Enlai, "American-Anglo Dispute," p. 98; "The Pacific Conference Viewed from the Atlantic Ocean," p. 86; and "Fa-zong-li yi-fan-feng-shun" (The French Premier [Briand] Had Favorable Winds in His Sails, January 1, 1921), *ZELWJ-1,* p. 163.

64. See Zhou Enlai, "Ge-guo dui-Mei-zhi-hui-da" (The Replies of Various Countries to the American-Proposed Conference, September 12, 1922), *ibid.,* p. 96; "Origin of the Concerted Control Theory Popularly Introduced in the United States," p. 160.

65. *Ibid.,* p. 159; and "The Pacific Conference Viewed from the Atlantic Ocean (Part 2)," p. 186.

66. Zhou Enlai, "Origin of the Concerted Control Theory," p. 159.

67. Zhou Enlai, "U.S., France, and the Four-Power Agreement," pp. 180, 181.

68. *Ibid.,* p. 181.

69. Zhou Enlai, "Origin of the Concerted Control Theory," p. 159.

70. *Ibid.*

71. Zhou Enlai, "U.S.-Japanese Negotiations [and] Exclusion of the Shan-dong Problem," pp. 98, 99.

72. Zhou Enlai, "Anglo-French Military Strategies at the Washington Conference," p. 174; "Recent Confusing Situation in Upper Silesia," p. 58; and "U.S., France, and the Four-Power Agreement," p. 180.

73. See Zhou Enlai, "National Self-Determination and the Problem of Upper Silesia," p. 155; "Breakdown of the Problem of German Reparations," p. 22; and "Recent Differences of Opinion between Britain and France," p. 53.

74. See, for example, Zhou Enlai, "Britain's Attitude toward Germany," p. 41; "Circumstances of the Limburg Conference," p. 65; "The Anglo-French

Conference prior to Christmas Day," p. 182; "Europe after the Opening of the 1922 Conference (Part 2)," p. 195; "The Pacific Conference Viewed from the Atlantic Ocean (Part 2)," p. 186; and "Europe after the Opening of the 1922 Conference," pp. 191, 194, 195.

75. See, for example, Zhou Enlai, "The Recent News about Post-European War Reparations Problem," p. 64; "Germany under the Sound of Restoration," p. 116; and "Europe after the Opening of the 1922 Conference (Part 1)," p. 191.

76. Zhou Enlai, "The Anglo-French Conference prior to Christmas Day," pp. 184, 185; "Anglo-French Negotiations," p. 105; "Recent Trends in British-French Problems," p. 196; "Latter Half of the Cannes Conference," p. 203; "Britain's Attitude toward Germany," p. 41; "The Complexity about the Problem of Upper Silesia," pp. 62-63; and "Jin-dong wen-ti yu Ying-Fa tai-du" (The Near Eastern Question and the Attitudes of Britain and France, August 7, 1921), ZELWJ-1, p. 76.

77. See, for example, Zhou Enlai, "Practical Realization of the Proper Methods," p. 24; "Britain's Attitude toward Germany," p. 41; "Recent Differences of Opinion between Britain and France," p. 53; "The Recent News about the Post-European War Reparations Problem," p. 64; "Britain, France, and the Problems of Disarmament and Reparations," p. 176; "U.S., France, and the Four-Power Agreement," p. 180; "Lloyd George's Speech Addressed to Parliament," p. 183; and "Europe after the Opening of the 1922 Conference (Part 2)," p. 194.

78. Zhou Enlai, "Postponement of the Allied Powers' Supreme Command Conference," p. 57; "The Anglo-French Negotiations," p. 105; "Britain, France, and the Problems of Disarmament and Reparations," p. 178; and "Anglo-French Conference prior to Christmas Day," p. 184.

79. Zhou Enlai, "Foreign Relations and Home Administration of the British Empire," p. 86; "Germany under the Sound of Restoration," p. 116; "The Complexity of the Problem of Upper Silesia," p. 53; "Lloyd George's Speech Addressed to Parliament," pp. 182, 183; "Europe after the Opening of the 1922 Conference," pp. 190, 191.

80. Zhou Enlai, "Strategy of Western Europe toward Russia and Germany," p. 26; "Anglo-French Military Strategies at the Washington Conference," p. 174; and "Britain, France, and the Problems of Disarmament and Reparations," p. 176; and "Europe after the Opening of the 1922 Conference," p. 189.

Chapter 3

1. On the issue of the May Fourth Movement of 1919, see Chow, *The May Fourth Movement: Intellectual Revolution in Modern China* (Cambridge, Mass:

Harvard University Press, 1960), chaps. 4-6; Lucian Bianco, *Origins of the Chinese Revolution, 1915-1949* (Stanford, Calif.: Stanford University Press, 1971), chap. 2; and Vera Schwarcz, *The Chinese Enlightenment: Intellectuals and Legacy of the May Fourth Movement of 1919* (Berkeley: University of California, 1986), chap. 1.

2. Zhou Enlai, "Wu-ti" (Song of the Great River Sung, September 1917), *In Quest-Poems of Zhou Enlai*, trans. Nancy T. Lin (Hong Kong: Joint Publishing Company, 1979), pp. 9, 13; also see *PELZ*, pp. 135-36; and Dick Wilson, *Zhou Enlai: A Biography* (New York: Viking), p. 37.

3. Kai-yu Hsu, *Chou En-lai: China's Gray Eminence* (Garden City, N.Y.: Doubleday, 1968), p. 20; and Wilson, *op. cit.*, p. 40. On Kawakami's basic concepts, see David John Lu, *Sources of Japanese History*, 2 vols. (New York: McGraw-Hill, 1973), vol. 2, pp. 121, 122, 124-26; and Wilson, *op. cit.*, p. 44.

4. Ch'en Duxiu, "Jing-gao qing-nian" (An Appeal to the Youth), *Xin-qing-nian* (New Youth), vol. 1, no. 1 (September 15, 1916): p. 5.

5. *Ibid.;* an English translation of Ch'en's article may be found in Ssu-yu Teng and John K. Fairbank, *China's Response to the West: A Documentary Survey, 1839-1923* (Cambridge, Mass.: Harvard University Press, 1954), pp. 240-45.

6. See Ch'en Duxiu, "Dong-si min-zu gen-ben si-xiang zhi cha-yi" (Differences of Basic Thought between the Eastern and Western Peoples), *New Youth*, vol. 1, no. 4 (December 15, 1915): pp. 1-4; also see Chow, *op. cit.*, pp. 294-95.

7. See Ch'en Duxiu, "Di-kang-li" (The Force of Resistance), *New Youth*, vol. 1, no. 3 (November 15, 1915): p. 4.

8. For more information on Ch'en Duxiu, see Benjamin I. Schwartz, *Chinese Communism and the Rise of Mao* (Cambridge, Mass.: Harvard University Press, 1951), chaps. 1-3; Howard L. Boorman, *Biographical Dictionary of Republican China* (New York: Columbia University Press, 1967), vol. 1, pp. 240-48; Feigon Lee, *Chen Duxiu: Founder of the Chinese Communist Party* (Princeton, N.J.: Princeton University Press, 1983), chaps. 1, 4; and Wen-shun Chi, *Ideological Conflicts in Democracy and Authoritarianism* (New Brunswick, N.J.: Transaction Books, 1986), chap. 8.

9. For more information on Li Dazhao, see Schwartz, *op. cit.*, pp. 10-18, 21, 23-26; and Meisner, *op. cit.*

10. On Hu Shi, see Grieder, *op. cit.;* Wing-tsit Chan, "Trends in Philosophy," in *China,* ed. Harley F. MacNair (Berkeley, Calif.: University of California Press, 1951), pp. 314-16; and Immanuel C. Y. Hsu, *The Rise of Modern China* (Oxford: Oxford University Press, 1983), pp. 507-98.

11. See "Jue-wu-she de xuan-yan" (Manifesto of the Awakening Society), in *Wu-si de she-tuan* (Student Societies of the May Fourth Period) 4 vols. (Beijing, 1979), vol. 2, pp. 302-3.

12. Hsu, *Zhou Enlai,* p. 22.

13. *Ibid.,* p. 24.

14. See Li Dazhao, "Wo-di Ma-ge-si zhu-yi-quan" (My Views on Marxism), *New Youth,* vol. 6, no. 5 (May 1919): Part 1, pp. 521-37; and vol. 6, no. 6 (November 1919): Part 2, pp. 612-24.

15. *Ibid.,* pt. 1, p. 537.

16. *Ibid.*

17. Li Dazhao, "Bolshevism di sheng-li" (The Victory of Bolshevism), *New Youth,* vol. 5, no. 5 (October 18, 1918): pp. 442-48, esp. pp. 443-47.

18. See Hu Shi, "Study More Problems, Talk Less of 'Ism,'" *HSWC,* vol. 2, pp. 147-53, esp. p. 151.

19. See, for example, Hu Shi, "The Meaning of the New Thought," in Teng and Fairbank, *op. cit.,* p. 255; also see Meisner, *op. cit.,* p. 107.

20. Fei Fei (Zhou Enlai), "Ping Hu Shi di 'Nu-li'" (Comments on Hu Shi's [article in the] "Endeavor"), *Shao-nian* (Youth) in *ZELWJ-1,* pp. 255, 256, 257, 258-59. *Nu-li-zhou-bao* (Endeavor Weekly) published its first issue in Beijing on May 7, 1922; for Hu's article, see "Wo-men-di zheng-zhi zhu-zhang" (Our Political Proposals), *Endeavor,* no. 2 (May 14, 1922).

21. *ZELWJ-1,* pp. 255, 256.

22. See Wilson, *op. cit.,* p. 47.

23. Zhou Enlai, "Hei-an-shi-li" (The Forces of Darkness, August 6, 1919), *PELZ,* p. 158; also see Wilson, *op. cit.,* p. 47.

24. Zhou Enlai, "The Forces of Darkness," *op. cit.,* p. 158.

25. Wilson, *op. cit.,* p. 47.

26. Hsu, *Chou En-lai,* p. 24.

27. Hu, *Young Comrade Zhou Enlai,* p. 75.

28. Edgar Snow, *Red Star over China,* rev. ed. (New York: Bantam, 1971), p. 73; also see Wilson, *op. cit.,* p. 48.

29. See, for example, *ZELWJ-1,* p. 234; *ZELWJ-2,* pp. 8-9; and Hsu, *Chou En-lai,* p. 212.

30. See MacNair and Lach, *op. cit.,* pp. 213 ff. Also see Harold R. Isaacs, *The Tragedy of the Chinese Revolution* (Stanford, Calif.: Stanford University Press, 1951), pp. 60-61.

31. *Ibid.,* p. 61.

32. See, for example, Schwartz, *op. cit.,* pp. 13-15, 16.

33. Zhou Enlai, "Zai Lun-dun zhi-biao-xiong Chen Shi-zhou" (From London, [a letter] Addressed to Cousin Chen Shi-zhou, January 30, 1921), *ZELWJ-2,* pp. 71-73.

34. *Ibid.,* pp. 71, 72.

35. *Ibid.,* p. 71.

36. *Ibid.*
37. *Ibid.*
38. *Ibid.*
39. *Ibid.*
40. *Ibid.*
41. *Ibid.*
42. *Ibid.*
43. *Ibid.*
44. *Ibid.*
45. *Ibid.*, p. 72.
46. Zhou Enlai, "Xi-ou-di 'chi'-kuang" (The 'Red' Situation in Western Europe), *Jue-you* (The Mail for the Awakening Society), no. 2 (April 15, 1923), *ZELWJ-1*, p. 275.
47. Zhou Enlai, "Zai Lun-dun zhi-biao-xiong Chen Shi-zhou" (From London, [a letter] Addressed to Cousin Chen Shi-zhou, February 23, 1921), *ZELWJ-2*, p. 74.
48. Zhou Enlai, "'Red' Situation in Western Europe," p. 274.
49. *Ibid.*, p. 275.
50. *Ibid.*
51. For more information on Marx and Marxism, see Peter H. Vigor, *A Guide to Marxism* (New York: Humanities Press, 1966); David McLellan, *Karl Marx: Selected Readings* (London: Oxford University Press, 1977); Robert C. Tucker, ed., *The Marx-Engels Reader* (New York: W. W. Norton, 1978), pts. 1-3; and Jon Elster, ed., *Karl Marx: A Reader* (London: Cambridge University Press, 1986).
52. On Marx's concept of history, see Karl Marx and Friedrich Engels, *The Communist Manifesto*, authorized English translation (New York: International Publishers, 1932), pp. 8-9, 21, 29, 44.
53. As quoted by Lenin in his article "What Is to Be Done? April 1, 1902," *Selected Works*, 3 vols. (New York: International Publishers, 1967), vol. 1, p. 518; hereafter cited as *SW*.
54. Karl Marx, "Theses on Feuerbach, Spring 1945," in Tucker, *op. cit.*, p. 144.
55. *Ibid.*
56. See Schwartz, *op. cit.*, p. 15; also see Meisner, *op. cit.*, p. 100.
57. V. I. Lenin, "Imperialism: The Highest Stage of Capitalism," *SW*, vol. 1, pp. 673-777.
58. *Ibid.*, p. 745.
59. V. I. Lenin, "Two Tactics of Social Democracy in the Democratic Revolution, 1905," *SW*, vol. 1, p. 518.

60. V. I. Lenin, "Left-wing Communism: An Infantile Disorder," *SW,* vol. 3, pp. 400-401.

61. *Ibid.,* p. 380.

62. Lenin, "What Is to Be Done?" *op. cit.,* p. 117.

63. *Ibid.,* p. 141.

64. See Wu Hao (Zhou Enlai), "Gong-chan zhu-yi yu Zhong-guo" (Communism and China), *Youth,* no. 2 (September 1, 1922), in *ZELWJ-1,* pp. 236, 237; "Zong-jiao jing-shen yu Gong-chan zhu-yi" (The Spirit of Religion and Communism"), *Youth,* no. 2 (August 1922), *ZELWJ-1,* pp. 242, 243.

65. Zhou Enlai, "Communism and China," pp. 233, 234, 235, 237, 238.

66. Zhou Enlai, "From London [a letter] Addressed to Cousin Chen Shi-zhou, January 30, 1921," pp. 71, 72.

67. Zhou Enlai, "Communism and China," pp. 233, 236-37.

68. Zhou Enlai, "Spirit of Religion and Communism," pp. 242, 243.

69. Zhou Enlai, "'Red' Situation in Western Europe," p. 274.

70. *Ibid.*

71. *Ibid.*

72. *Ibid.,* p. 275.

73. Wu Hao (Zhou Enlai), "Wu-chan-jei-ji ge-ming di E-luo-si" (The Proletarian Revolution of Russia"), *Youth,* no. 2 (December 1, 1922), *ZELWJ-2,* pp. 50-57, esp. pp. 55-56; Wu Hao (Zhou Enlai), "E-guo-ge-ming shi shi-bai liao-mo?" ("Was the Russian Revolution a Failure?"), *Youth,* no. 6 (n.d.), in *ZELWJ-1,* pp. 262, 263.

74. Zhou Enlai, "Comments on Hu Shi's [article in the] 'Endeavor,'" p. 257; Fei Fei (Zhou Enlai), "Bei-yang jung-fa yu wai-jiao-xi" (The Northern Warlords and the Diplomatic Clique), *Chi-quang* (Red Light), no. 8 (May 15, 1924), *ZELWJ-2,* p. 27; Wu Hao (Zhou Enlai), "Jung-fa tong-zhi di Zhong-guo" (China under the Warlords' Control), *Red Light,* no. 1 (February 1, 1924), *ZELWJ-2,* p. 3.

75. "Chi-kuang di xuan-yan" (The Manifesto of the *Red Light*), *Red Light,* no. 1 (February 1, 1924), *ZELWJ-2,* p. 2; Wu Hao (Zhou Enlai), "Ge-ming jiu-guo-lun" (On Saving the Country [China] through the Revolution), *Red Light,* no. 2 (February 15, 1924), *ZELWJ-2,* pp. 8, 9.

76. Zhou Enlai, "'Red' Situation in Western Europe," p. 275.

77. Lenin, "What Is to Be Done?" pp. 136, 138.

78. Zhou Enlai, "Di-guo chu-yi yu Xian-chou tiao-yue" (Imperialism and the Treaty of 1900 [published in 1924]), as quoted in Hsu, *Chou En-lai,* p. 211.

79. *Ibid.,* pp. 211-12.

80. *Ibid.,* p. 212.

81. Lenin, "Imperialism, the Highest Stage of Capitalism," p. 770.

82. V. I. Lenin, "Report to the Seventh Congress of the Russian Communist Party, March 7, 1918," *Selected Works,* vol. 3 (New York: International Publishers, 1943): p. 288.

83. V. I. Lenin, "Reports to the Central Committee of the Russian Communist Party (Bolsheviks) at the Eighth Congress, March 18, 1919," *ibid.,* vol. 8, p. 33.

84. *Ibid.*

85. V. I. Lenin, "Speech to Moscow Party Nuclei Secretaries, November 26, 1920," *ibid.,* p. 297.

86. V. I. Lenin, "Report to the Ninth All-Russian Congress of Soviets, December 23, 1921"; quoted in David J. Dallin, *Soviet Foreign Policy after Stalin* (Philadelphia: J. B. Lippincott, 1961), p. 15.

87. Quoted in Masao Onoe, "Some Factors in the Communist View of Neutrality," in *New Nations in a Divided World,* ed. Kurt London (New York: Frederick A. Praeger, 1965), p. 92.

88. *Ibid.*

89. J. V. Stalin, *Works* (Moscow: Foreign Languages Publishing House, 1955), vol. 10, p. 294.

90. See Stalin, "Marxism and Linguistics," in *The Essential Stalin: Major Theoretical Writings, 1905-1952,* ed. Bruce Franklin (New York: Doubleday, 1972), p. 443.

91. Shao-shan (Zhou Enlai), "Shao-shan bao-gao-san zhong-quan-hui cai-liao di-jiu-hao" (Shao-shan Report-Reference Item No. 9 of the Third Plenum), September 1, 1930; mimeographed. For the full Chinese text of the Shao-shan Report, see Tso-liang Hsiao, *Power Relations within the Chinese Communist Movement, 1930-1934: A Study of Documents* (Seattle: University of Washington Press, 1961), pp. 139-64. An English translation of certain parts of the Shao-shan Report may be found in *A Documentary History of Chinese Communism* ed. Conrad Brandt, Benjamin I. Schwartz, and John K. Fairbank (Cambridge, Mass.: Harvard University Press, 1958), pp. 200-202.

92. Hsiao, *op. cit.,* p. 145.

93. *Ibid.*

94. *Ibid.*

95. *Ibid.*

96. *Ibid.*

97. *Ibid.*

98. *Ibid.*

99. *Ibid.*

100. *Ibid.;* also see V. I. Lenin, "Preliminary Draft Theses on National and Colonial Questions, June 5, 1920," *SW,* vol. 3, pp. 422-27; and V. I. Lenin, "Report

on the Commission on National and Colonial Questions, July 26, 1920," *SW,*
pp. 457-58.

101. Zhou Enlai, "Shao-shan Report," in Hsaio, *op. cit.,* p. 145.

102. *Ibid.;* for the full text of "Left-wing Communism: An Infantile Disorder," see
Lenin, *SW,* vol. 3, pp. 333-420.

Chapter 4

1. For background on the origins of the first united front between the CCP and
the GMD from 1923 to 1927, see Benjamin I. Schwartz, *Chinese Communism
and the Rise of Mao* (Cambridge, Mass.: Harvard University Press, 1951),
chaps. 3-4; Lyman P. Van Slyke, *Enemies and Friends: The United Front in
Chinese Communist History* (Stanford, Calif.: Stanford University Press, 1967),
chaps. 1-2.

2. See V. I. Lenin, "Preliminary Draft Theses on National and Colonial Questions," *SW,* pp. 426-27.

3. For Zhou's elaboration of the united front strategy, see his article "Zai lun
Zhong-guo Gong-chan-chu-yi-zhe zhi jia-ru Guo-min-dang wen-ti" (More
Discussion on the Question of Chinese Communists Joining the GMD, June
1, 1924), *Red Light,* no. 9, *PELZ,* pp. 469, 470, 471, 473; "Xian-shi zheng-zhi
dou-zheng zhi wo-men" (The Chinese Communist Party [CCP] in the Present
Political Struggle, December 11, 1926), *SWZEL-1,* p. 14.

4. Zhou Enlai, "Lun tong-yi-zhan-xian" (On the United Front, April 30, 1945),
SWZEL-1, p. 239.

5. *Ibid.,* pp. 231-40.

6. Zhou Enlai, "More Discussion on the Question of Chinese Communists
Joining the GMD," pp. 470, 471.

7. Zhou Enlai, "CCP in the Present Political Struggle," p. 14.

8. Zhou Enlai, "More Discussion on the Question of Chinese Communists
Joining the GMD," pp. 470, 471.

9. Dick Wilson, *Zhou Enlai: A Biography* (New York: Viking Penguin, 1984),
pp. 73, 75, 76; Hsu, *op. cit.,* pp. 47-49.

10. Zhou Enlai, "More Discussion on the Question of Chinese Communists
Joining the GMD," p. 470.

11. See Zhou Enlai, "CCP in the Present Political Struggle," pp. 13-15.

12. For an English text of the "First Manifesto of the CCP on the Current
Situation, June 10, 1922," see Brandt *et al., Documentary History of Chinese
Communists,* pp. 54-63.

13. *Ibid.*, p. 63; also see Ch'en Kung-po, *The Communist Movement in China*, Columbia University East Asian Institute Series, no. 1 (New York: Columbia University, 1960), p. 120.

14. *Ibid.*, pp. 65-72; Schwartz, pp. 44-45; and Van Slyke, *op. cit.*, pp. 19-20.

15. For more information on Michael Borodin's role in Canton, see Dan N. Jacobs, *Borodin: Stalin's Man in China* (Cambridge, Mass.: Harvard University Press, 1981), chaps. 9-11; and Allen S. Whiting, *Soviet Policies in China, 1917-1924* (New York: Columbia University Press, 1954), pp. 244-47.

16. Jacobs, *op. cit.*, p. 141.

17. *Ibid.*, pp. 118-19.

18. See *Guo-fu quan-ji* (The Complete Works of Sun Yat-sen) (Taipei: Ron-min yin-shua-chang, 1954), vol. 2, pp. 258-59.

19. *Ibid.*, p. 262.

20. Hsu, *Chou En-lai*, p. 68.

21. Li Rui, *Mao Zedong tong-zhi di zao-qi ge-ming huo-dong* (The Early Revolutionary Activities of Comrade Mao Zedong) (Beijing: Zhong-guo qing-nian chu-ban-she, 1957), p. 237.

22. Hsu, *op. cit.*, p. 69.

23. See, for example, Zhou Enlai, "More Discussion on the Question of Chinese Communists Joining the GMD," pp. 470, 471; "CCP in the Present Political Struggle," p. 14.

24. *Ibid.*

25. See Wilson, *op. cit.*, pp. 73, 76.

26. Zhou Enlai, "More Discussion on the Question of Chinese Communists Joining the GMD," pp. 470, 471.

27. *Ibid.;* and Hsu, *op. cit.*, p. 50.

28. *Ibid.;* and Zhou Enlai, "CCP in the Present Political Struggle," pp. 14, 15.

29. *Ibid.*, p. 14.

30. See Zhou Enlai, "Comments on Hu Shi's [article in the] 'Endeavor,'" p. 257; "More Discussion on the Question of Chinese Communists Joining the GMD," pp. 470-71; and "CCP in the Present Political Struggle," p. 14.

31. Zhou Enlai, "Communism and China," p. 237.

32. Zhou Enlai, "More Discussion on the Question of Chinese Communists Joining the GMD," p. 470; and "CCP in the Present Political Struggle," pp. 13, 15, 16, 17.

33. *Ibid.*, p. 14.

34. *Ibid.*

35. *Ibid.*, p. 16.

36. *Ibid.*

37. *Ibid.*, p. 15.

38. *Ibid.*, p. 13.
39. *Ibid.*, p. 15.
40. See Hsu, *op. cit.,* p. 46.
41. Wu Hao (Zhou Enlai), "Quang-zhou zheng-xiang" (The Political Situation in Canton, October 30, 1924), *Shanghai xiang-dao zhou-bao* (Weekly Guide of Shanghai), no. 92 (1924), *Zhou Enlai xuan-ji* (The Selected Works of Zhou Enlai), 3 vols. (Hong Kong: Yi-shan-tu-shu-gong-si, 1976), vol. 3, pp. 401-2.
42. Zhou Enlai, "CCP in the Present Political Struggle," pp. 13, 14.
43. Zhou Enlai, "Political Situation in Canton," p. 401.
44. *Ibid.*
45. *Ibid.*, pp. 401-2.
46. Zhou Enlai, "CCP in the Present Political Struggle," p. 14.
47. Wilson, *op. cit.,* p. 81.
48. Hsu, *op. cit.,* pp. 57-58.
49. Zhou Enlai, "CCP in the Present Political Struggle," p. 14.
50. *Ibid.*
51. *Ibid.*
52. Zhou Enlai, "On Taking Prompt Punitive Action against Jiang Jie-shi, April 1927," *SWZEL-1,* p. 18.
53. *Ibid.*, p. 19.
54. Zhou Enlai, "On the Relations between the CCP and the GMD from 1924 to 1026, Spring 1943," *SWZEL-1,* pp. 130-31.
55. *Ibid.*, p. 135.
56. *Ibid.*, p. 137.
57. Zhou Enlai, "On the Sixth Congress of the Party, March 3 and 4, 1944," *SWZEL-1,* p. 179.
58. *Ibid.*
59. *Ibid.*
60. *Ibid.*
61. Zhou Enlai, "On Taking Prompt Punitive Action against Jiang Jie-shi," p. 18.
62. See Hsu, *Chou Enlai,* pp. 54-55.
63. The Eight-Point Proposal may be found in Luo Rui-qing, Lu Zheng-cao, and Wang Bing-nan, *Xian-shi-bian yu Zhou Enlai* (The Xi'an Incident and Zhou Enlai) (Beijing: Ren-min chu-ban-she, 1978), p. 95. For more information on the Xi'an Incident of 1936, see Edgar Snow, *Red Star over China* (New York: Random House Press, 1938), pp. 9, 11, 17; Van Slyke, *op. cit.,* pp. 75-91; Edgar Snow, *Random Notes on Red China (1936-1945)* (Cambridge, Mass.: Harvard University Press, 1957), pp. 1-14; Chiang Kai-shek (Jiang Jie-shi), *Soviet Policy in China: A Summing Up at Seventy* (New York: Farrar, 1957), pp. 72-79; Charles McLane, *Soviet Policy and the Chinese Communists, 1931-*

1946 (New York: Columbia University Press, 1958), pp. 79-90; and Clubb, *op. cit.,* pp. 202-10.

64. For background on Zhou's negotiations with Generals Zhang and Yang, see Chang Kuo-t'ao, *The Rise of the Chinese Communist Party 1928-1938,* 2 vols. (Lawrence: University of Kansas, 1972), vol. 2, pp. 481-87; and Luo *et al., op. cit.,* pp. 67-69.

65. Hsu, *op. cit.,* p. 135.

66. Zhou sought to convince Yang that more explicit concessions were not necessary and that Yang should not oppose Jiang's release. For information on this issue, see Snow, *Random Notes on Red China,* pp. 12-13.

67. Hsu, *op. cit.,* p. 135.

68. For the full text on the Six-Point proposal, see Zhou Enlai, "Yu Song Zi-wen tan-pan qing-kuang" ("The Negotiations with Song Zi-wen, December 23, 1936"), *SWZEL-1,* pp. 86-87.

69. *Ibid.,* p. 87.

70. *Ibid.,* p. 88.

71. Chang Kuo-t'ao, *op. cit.,* p. 488.

72. Zhou Enlai, "The Results of the Negotiations with Song Zi-wen and Song Mei-ling, December 25, 1956," *SWZEL-1,* p. 88.

73. *Ibid.,* pp. 88-89.

74. *Ibid.,* p. 89.

75. Zhou Enlai, "The Situation and Our Policy after the Peaceful Settlement of the Xi'an Incident, December 29, 1936," *SWZEL-1,* p. 90.

76. *Ibid.,* p. 91.

77. *Ibid.*

78. *Ibid.*

79. *Ibid.*

80. *Ibid.*

81. *Ibid.*

82. *Ibid.*

83. *Ibid.*

84. *Ibid.,* p. 92.

85. *Ibid.*

86. *Ibid.*

87. Zhou Enlai, "The Results of the Negotiations with Song Zi-wen and Song Mei-ling," p. 90.

88. Snow, *Random Notes on Red China,* p. 3.

89. *Ibid.,* preface.

90. For more information on Moscow's telegram dated December 13, 1936, and Yenan's reaction to this telegram, see Chang, *op. cit.,* p. 483.

91. On the terms of the new united front after the Xi'an negotiations, see Isaacs, *op. cit.*, p. 306.
92. See Chiang (Jiang), *Soviet Policy in China*, pp. 72-79.
93. Zhou Enlai, "On the United Front," *op. cit.*, p. 215.
94. *Ibid.*
95. On the issue of the second united front between the CCP and the GMD, see James C. Thomson Jr., "The Communist Party and the United Front in China, 1935-1936," *Papers on China*, photocopy, Harvard University, no. 11 (1957), pp. 99-148; Tetsuya Kataoka, *Resistance and Revolution in China: The Communists and the Second United Front* (Berkeley: University of California Press, 1974); Van Slyke, *op. cit.*, chap. 6; and John W. Garver, "The Origins of the Second United Front: The Comintern and the Chinese Communist Party," *CQ*, no. 113 (March 1988), pp. 29-59.
96. Zhou Enlai, "On the United Front," pp. 216-30.
97. Snow, *Random Notes on Red China*, p. 56.
98. *Ibid.*
99. *Ibid.*
100. *Ibid.*
101. Nym Wales, *Inside Red China* (New York: Doubleday, Doran and Company, 1939), p. 209.
102. *Ibid.*, p. 210.
103. *Ibid.*, p. 209.
104. Quoted in Li, *Chou En-lai*, p. 240.
105. *Ibid.*
106. Israel Epstein *et al.*, *Mao Tse-tung in Chungking* (Shanghai: Ho Chung Publishing Co., 1945), pp. 2-3; and Li Rui, *op. cit.*, pp. 240, 249 ff.
107. T. A. Bisson, *Yenan in June 1937: Talks with the Communist Leaders* (Berkeley: Center for China Studies, University of California, 1973), p. 47.
108. *Ibid.*
109. *Ibid.*, p. 48.
110. On Zhou's official capacities in the second united front between the CCP and the GMD, see Department of State, *United States Relations with China* (Washington, D.C.: Government Printing Office, 1949), p. 52; hereafter cited as *U.S. Relations with China*.
111. On Zhou's strategy in the second united front, see Hsu, *op. cit.*, p. 146, 157.
112. For a careful analysis of the CCP's united front with the GMD, see Van Slyke, *op. cit.*, chap. 6.
113. See Hsu, *op. cit.*, p. 156.
114. Bisson, *op. cit.*, p. 47.
115. *Ibid.*

116. *Ibid.*
117. *Ibid.*
118. *Ibid.*, p. 48.
119. *Ibid.*
120. *Ibid.*
121. *Ibid.*
122. For the full text of the CCP's four concessions, see "Announcement of GMD-Communist Cooperation by the Central Committee of the CCP, July 15, 1937," *SWZEL-1*, p. 94.
123. Zhou Enlai, "The Present Crisis in the War of Resistance and the Tasks to Be Undertaken in Pursuing the War in North China, November 16, 1937", *SWZEL-1*, p. 100.
124. *Ibid.*, p. 106.
125. See Van Slyke, *op. cit.*, p. 94; for Jiang's views on GMD's priorities in the war of resistance against Japan in 1938, see Kataoka, *op. cit.*, p. 155.
126. Quoted in Li, *Chou En-lai*, p. 240.
127. Zhou Enlai, "On the United Front," *op. cit.*, p. 235.
128. *Ibid.*
129. *Ibid.*
130. *Ibid.*, p. 236.
131. *Ibid.*
132. *Ibid.*
133. *Ibid.*
134. *Ibid.*
135. *Ibid.*, p. 242.
136. *Ibid.*
137. *Ibid.*, p. 241.
138. For the full text, see Zhou Enlai, "On the United Front Strategy," pp. 213-44.
139. For full texts, see Zhou Enlai "Speech at a Meeting of Welcome in Yenan, August 2, 1943") *SWZEL-1*, pp. 151-59; and "On the Sixth Congress of the Party," pp. 177-210.
140. See, for example, Mao Zedong, "Mu-qian kang-Ri tong-yi zhan-xian-zhong di ce-lue wen-ti" (Current Tactical Problems in the Anti-Japanese United Front, March 11, 1940), *Mao Ze-dong-xuan-ji* (Selected Works of Mao Zedong), 4 vols. (Beijing: Ren-min-chu-ban-she, 1951-1960), vol. 2, p. 720; hereafter cited as *MZDXJ*; and "Zhong-guo Gong-chan-dang zai min-zu zhan-zhong de di-wei" (The Role of the CCP in the National War, October 1938), *MZDXJ*, vol. 2, p. 496. For a careful elaboration of Mao's view on the domestic united front, see Van Slyke, *op. cit.*, pp. 105-6, 142-45; and J. D.

Simmonds, *China's World: The Foreign Policy of a Developing State* (New York: Columbia University Press, 1970-1971), pp. 192-94.

141. Zhou Enlai, "On the United Front," p. 238.
142. *Ibid.*
143. *Ibid.*
144. *Ibid.*
145. *Ibid.*
146. *Ibid.*, pp. 232-33.
147. *Ibid.*, p. 233.
148. *Ibid.*
149. *Ibid.*
150. *Ibid.*
151. *Ibid.*, p. 239.
152. *Ibid.*, p. 234. For a careful analysis of the CCP's strategy in winning over the middle elements, see Van Slyke, *op. cit.*, pp. 108-10, 114.
153. Zhou Enlai, "On the United Front," p. 234.
154. *Ibid.*
155. *Ibid.*, p. 238.
156. *Ibid.*, p. 234.
157. *Ibid.*
158. *Ibid.*
159. *Ibid.*, p. 239.
160. *Ibid.*
161. *Ibid.*
162. *Ibid.*, p. 231.
163. *Ibid.*, p. 232.
164. *Ibid.*
165. *Ibid.*

Chapter 5

1. Zhou Enlai, "On the United Front," *SWZEL-1*, p. 220.
2. *Ibid.*
3. *Ibid.*, p. 221.
4. *Ibid.*
5. *Ibid.*
6. *Ibid.*
7. *Ibid.*, p. 217.
8. *Ibid.*

9. Zhou Enlai, "Speech at a Meeting of Welcome in Yenan," *SWZEL-1*, p. 159.
10. *Ibid.*
11. Zhou Enlai, "On Chinese Fascism-the New Autocracy, August 16, 1943," *SWZEL-1*, p. 173.
12. Zhou Enlai, "On the United Front," p. 227.
13. *Ibid.*
14. *Ibid.*, p. 228.
15. See *U.S. Relations with China*, pp. 71, 73. For more information on Hurley's personal assessment that Jiang was the leader best qualified to carry out a policy of Sino-American cooperation, see Michael Schaller, *The U.S. Crusade in China, 1938-1945* (New York: Columbia University Press, 1978), pp. 173-74.
16. For the text of the five-point draft agreement (November 1, 1944), see *U.S. Relations with China*, pp. 74-75; or Hurley's telegram to the secretary of state, January 31, 1945 (Senate Committee on Armed Services and Committee on Foreign Relations, Hearing on *Military Situation in the Far East*, 82d Congress, 1st sess. [1951]), p. 3671; hereafter cited as *Military Situation in the Far East*.
17. *Military Situation in the Far East*, p. 3671.
18. For the text of the three-point counterproposal, see *U.S. Relations with China*, p. 75; or "Telegram, Hurley to the Secretary of State, January 31, 1945," *op. cit.*, pp. 3669-70.
19. *Ibid.*, p. 3672; and Schaller, *op. cit.*, p. 207.
20. On Hurley's initiative and the progressive breakdown of his program, see James Reardon-Anderson, *Yenan and the Great Powers: The Origins of Chinese Communist Foreign Policy, 1944-1946* (New York: Columbia University Press, 1980), pp. 51-57; and Tang Tsou, *American Failure in China 1941-1950* (Chicago: University of Chicago Press, 1963), chap. 8. Also see Harry S. Truman, *Memoirs: Years of Trial and Hope* (Garden City, N.Y.: Doubleday, 1956), vol. 2, pp. 64-66.
21. *U.S. Relations with China*, p. 76.
22. *Ibid.;* also see Reardon-Anderson, *op. cit.*, pp. 56-57.
23. *U.S. Relations with China*, p. 76.
24. *Ibid.*
25. *Ibid.*, pp. 76-77.
26. *Ibid.*, p. 77.
27. Zhou Enlai, "On the United Front," p. 229.
28. *Ibid.*
29. *U.S. Relations with China*, p. 80.
30. *Ibid.*
31. *U.S. Relations with China*, p. 82.
32. *Ibid.*, p. 83.

33. Zhou Enlai, "Past Year's Negotiations and Their Prospects, December 18, 1946," *SWZEL-1*, p. 283.
34. *Ibid.;* also see *U.S. Relations with China*, p. 579.
35. *Ibid.*, p. 580
36. Zhou Enlai, "Past Year's Negotiations and Their Prospects," p. 288.
37. *Ibid.*
38. *U.S. Relations with China*, p. 605; for the full text of "President Truman to the Special Representative of the President to China [Marshall], December 15, 1945," see *ibid.*, pp. 605-6. On Marshall's mission to China, also see Truman, *Memoirs*, pp. 66-72.
39. *U.S. Relations with China*, p. 608; for the full text of "Statement by President Truman on United States Policy toward China, December 15, 1945," *ibid.*, pp. 607-9.
40. *Ibid.*, p. 608.
41. George C. Marshall, "Memorandum for the War Department, December 9, 1945," U.S. Department of State, *Foreign Relations of the United States: Diplomatic Papers, 1945*, vol. 7 *The Far East* (Washington, D.C.: Government Printing Office, 1969), p. 761.
42. "Notes on General Marshall's First Conference with Mr. Chou En-lai, December 23, 1945," *ibid.*, p. 800.
43. *Ibid.*
44. *U.S. Relations with China*, p. 137.
45. *Ibid.*
46. *Ibid.*, p. 610.
47. For the minutes of the sixth meeting of the Committee of Three, see Lyman P. Van Slyke, intro., *Marshall's Mission to China, December 1945-January 1947: The Report and Appended Documents*, 2 vols. (Arlington, Va.: University Publications of America, 1976), vol. 1, pp. 26-65, 68-125. On the creation of the cease-fire machinery and Zhou's enhanced position within the CCP, see Reardon-Anderson, *op. cit.*, p. 136; and Donald W. Klein, "The Management of Foreign Affairs in Communist China," in *China: Management of a Revolutionary Society*, ed. John M. H. Lindbeck (Seattle: University of Washington Press, 1971), pp. 307-10.
48. Zhou Enlai, "On the Second Plenary Session of the Sixth Central Executive Committee of the GMD, March 18, 1946," *SWZEL-1*, p. 255.
49. *Ibid.*, p. 250.
50. *Ibid.*, p. 254.
51. *Ibid.*, pp. 254-55.
52. *Ibid.*, p. 255.
53. *Ibid.*

54. *Ibid.*, p. 251.
55. *Ibid.*, p. 257.
56. Quoted in Hsu, *Chou En-lai*, p. 174.
57. *U.S. Relations with China*, p. 151.
58. *Ibid.*, pp. 151-52.
59. *Ibid.*, p. 152.
60. *Ibid.*, p. 153.
61. *Ibid.*
62. *Ibid.*, pp. 154-55
63. *Ibid.*, p. 155.
64. *Ibid.*, p. 156, 158.
65. *Ibid.*, p. 158.
66. *Ibid.*, p. 160.
67. *Ibid.*
68. *Ibid.*
69. *Ibid.*, p. 161.
70. *Ibid.;* on Marshall's view of the GMD commanders' attitudes toward the significance of the fifteen-day truce, see John R. Beal, *Marshall in China* (Garden City, N.J.: Doubleday, 1970), pp. 83, 84.
71. *U.S. Relations with China*, p. 161.
72. *Ibid.*, p. 163.
73. *Ibid.;* on Marshall's plan for reorganizing the Chinese armies and Zhou's comments on the problem of military integration in China, see Forrest C. Pogue, *George Marshall: Statesman 1945-1959* (New York: Viking Penguin, 1987), pp. 91-94.
74. *U.S. Relations with China*, p. 164.
75. *Ibid.*
76. *Ibid.*, p. 165.
77. *Ibid.*
78. *Ibid.*
79. *Ibid.*, p. 164.
80. See, for instance, *ibid.*, pp. 161, 174.
81. *U.S. Relations with China*, p. 176.
82. *Ibid.*, p. 197; on Jiang's strategy, also see Tsou, *op. cit.*, pp. 353-54.
83. Quoted in Hsu, *Chou En-lai*, p. 176.
84. *Ibid.;* also see Zhou Enlai, "Speech at the Shanghai Meeting to Commemorate the Tenth Anniversary of the Death of Lu Xun, October 19, 1940," *SWZEL-1*, p. 267.
85. Quoted in Hsu, *op. cit.*, p. 176.
86. *Ibid.*

87. *U.S. Relations with China*, pp. 175-76; according to Marshall, the joint statement was Stuart's idea; see Beal, *op. cit.,* p. 162. For the full text of the Marshall-Stuart Joint Statement, see *U.S. Relations with China*, pp. 648-49.
88. *Ibid.,* 649-51.
89. *Ibid.,* p. 175.
90. *Ibid.,* p. 184; for the full text, see pp. 654-56.
91. *Ibid.,* p. 654.
92. *Ibid.*
93. *Ibid.,* p. 656; also see Pogue, *op. cit.,* p. 125.
94. *U.S. Relations with China*, p. 657; for the full text, see pp. 656-57.
95. *Ibid.,* p. 657.
96. *Ibid.;* for the full text, see pp. 657-59.
97. *Ibid.,* p. 657.
98. *Ibid.,* p. 658.
99. *Ibid.*
100. *Ibid.*
101. *Ibid.,* pp. 658-59.
102. *Ibid.,* p. 659.
103. Zhou Enlai, "The Past Year's Negotiations and Their Prospects," p. 289.
104. *U.S. Relations with China*, p. 659.
105. *Ibid.*
106. *Ibid.,* p. 668; for the full text, see pp. 667-69.
107. Quoted in Hsu, *Chou En-lai*, p. 182.
108. *U.S. Relations with China, op. cit.,* p. 662.
109. *Ibid.*
110. *Ibid.*
111. *Ibid.,* p. 663.
112. *Ibid.,* p. 664.
113. *U.S. Relations with China, op. cit.,* p. 194.
114. *Ibid.;* for the full text, see *ibid.,* pp. 667-69.
115. *Ibid.,* p. 195.
116. *Ibid.,* p. 668.
117. *Ibid.,* p. 274-75.
118. *Ibid.,* p. 200.
119. *Ibid.,* p. 201.
120. *Ibid.*
121. *Ibid.,* pp. 675-76; on Stuart's assessment of the third-party people's role, see Beal, *op. cit.,* p. 253.
122. *U.S. Relations with China, op. cit.,* pp. 674-675.
123. *Ibid.,* p. 204.

124. Zhou Enlai, "The past year's negotiations and their prospects," *op. cit.,* p. 289.
125. *U.S. Relations with China, op. cit.,* p. 679.
126. *Ibid.*
127. *Ibid.,* p. 206.
128. *Ibid.,* p. 207.
129. *Ibid.*
130. Zhou Enlai, "Statement on the GMD's Convening of a 'National Assembly,' November 10, 1946," *SWZEL-1,* p. 269.
131. *Ibid.,* p. 270.
132. *Ibid.,* p. 271.
133. *Ibid.*
134. *U.S. Relations with China,* p. 208.
135. *Ibid.;* also see Pogue, *op. cit.,* pp. 131-32.
136. *U.S. Relations with China,* p. 211; also see Beal, *op. cit.,* p. 313; and Pogue, *op. cit.,* pp. 132-33.
137. *U.S. Relations with China,* p. 211.
138. *Ibid.,* pp, 211-12.
139. *Ibid.,* p. 212.
140. *Ibid.,* p. 686.
141. *Ibid.,* p. 688; for the full text of Marshall's statement, January 8, 1947, see pp. 686-89.
142. *Ibid.,* p. 688.
143. *Ibid.,* p. 686; on President Truman's assessment of Marshall's mission to China, see his book *Memoirs,* vol. 2, pp. 74-75. For further analysis of the failure of Marshall's mission, see Pogue, *op. cit.,* pp. 141-43.
144. See, for instance, Zhou Enlai, "On Marshall's Statement on Leaving China, January 10, 1947," *SWZEL-1,* pp. 293-99, esp. pp. 294, 296-97.

Chapter 6

1. For more information on foreign policymaking as a focus of political and administrative processes, see Richard C. Snyder, H. W. Bruck, and Burton Sapin, *Decision-Making as an Approach to the Study of International Politics* (Princeton, N.J.: Princeton University Press, 1954), pp. 1-37; Richard C. Snyder, "A Decision-Making Approach to the Study of Political Phenomena," in *Approaches to the Study of Politics,* ed. Roland Young (Evanston, Ill.: Northwestern University Press, 1958), pp. 3-38; and Joseph Frankel, "Towards a Decision-Making Model in Foreign Policy," *Political Studies,* vol. 7, no. 1 (February 1959): pp. 1-11.

2. On the issue of China's foreign policymaking process, see R. G. Boyd, *Communist Chinese Foreign Policy* (New York: Frederick A. Praeger, 1962), chap. 2; A. Doak Barnett, *Bureaucracy and Political Power in Communist China* (New York: Columbia University Press, 1967), p. 429; A. Doak Barnett, *The Making of Foreign Policy in China: Structure and Process* (Boulder: Westview Press, 1985), pp. 8-9, 51-54; Allen S. Whiting, "Foreign Policy of Communist China," in *Foreign Policy in World Politics,* ed. Roy C. Macridis (Englewood Cliffs, N.J.: Prentice-Hall, 1962), pp. 282-86; and June T. Dreyer, *China's Political System: Modernization and Tradition* (New York: Paragon House, 1993), pp. 396-98.

3. For information on the role of the CCP in China's foreign policymaking process, see Edgar Snow, *Other Side of the River* (New York: Random House, 1962), pp. 321, 325; and A. Doak Barnett, *Uncertain Passage: China's Transition to the Post Mao Era* (Washington, D.C.: Brookings Institution, 1974), pp. 204-11.

4. On the principle of "democratic centralism," see John Lewis Wilson, *Leadership in Communist China* (Ithaca, N.Y.: Cornell University Press, 1963), pp. 189-90; Theodore H. E. Chen, *The Chinese Communist Regime: Documents and Commentary* (New York: Frederick A. Praeger, 1967), pp. 130-31, 136; and Harold Hinton, "China," in *Major Governments of Asia,* ed. George McT. Kahin (Ithaca, N.Y.: Cornell University Press, 1963), p. 74.

5. Hinton, "China," pp. 126, 127; James R. Townsend, *Political Participation in Communist China* (Berkeley: University of California Press, 1968), pp. 70-72; Franz Schurmann, *Ideology and Organization in Communist China* (Berkeley: University of California Press, 1966), pp. 146-147; Parris H. Chang, *Power and Policy in China* (University Park: Pennsylvania State University Press, 1975), pp. 31-32, 181-85; Alan P. L. Liu, *How China Is Ruled* (Englewood Cliffs, N.J.: Prentice-Hall, 1986), pp. 65-67; and Kenneth Lieberthal and Michel Oksenberg, *Policymaking in China: Leaders, Structure and Processes* (Princeton, N.J.: Princeton University Press, 1988), pp. 35-36, 70-72.

6. Dong Biwu, "Lun jia-jiang ren-min dai-biao-hui-yi de gong-zuo" (On Strengthening the Work Connected with the People's Representative Conference, September 23, 1951), *Ren-min ri-bao* (People's Daily), January 30, 1952, p. 3; hereafter cited as *RMRB.*

7. Deng Xiaoping, "Guan-yu xiu-gai dang-de zhang-cheng de bao-gao, zai Zhong-guo Gong-chan-dang di-ba-ci quan-guo dai-biao-da-hui-shang" (Report on Revision of the Party Constitution Delivered to the CCP's Eighth National Congress, September 16, 1956), *RMRB,* September 18, 1956, p. 3.

8. *Ibid.,* p. 2; and Zhou Enlai, "Zheng-fu gong-zuo bao-gao, zai di-yi-jie quan-guo ren-min dai-biao-da-hui di-san-ci hui-yi-shang" (Report on the Work of

the Government Made at the First Session of the Fourth NPC, June 26, 1957), *RMRB*, June 27, 1957, p. 4. For the English translation of Zhou's report, see the supplement to *People's China*, no. 14 (July 16, 1957), pp. 3-39.

9. Deng, *op. cit.*, p. 3; and Lewis, *op. cit.*, pp. 126-27. For the English text of the constitution of the CCP adopted by the Eighth National Party Congress on September 26, 1956, see Chen, *op. cit.*, pp. 127-48.

10. See A. Doak Barnett, *China after Mao* (Princeton, N.J.: Princeton University Press, 1967), p. 78; and Frederick C. Teiwes, *Leadership, Legitimacy, and Conflict in China* (New York: M. E. Sharpe, 1984), chap. 1.

11. Edgar Snow, *Red Star over China* (New York: Random House, 1938), p. 332; and Chang, *op. cit.*, pp. 171-74, 188-89.

12. For a general survey of Liu Shaoqi at the Eighth CCP National Congress held in September 1956, see Li Tien-min, *Liu Shao-ch'i* (Taipei: Institute of International Relations, 1975), pp. 103-4.

13. Schumann, *op. cit.*, p 55; and Barnett, *Uncertain Passage*, pp. 211-26.

14. For further information on the CCP's inner decision making process and Mao's political style prior to the Party's rise to national power in China, see Chang, *The Rise of the Chinese Communist Party*, vol. 2, pp. 536, 538, 539.

15. On the functions of the Politburo and the relationship between Mao and his colleagues at the Politburo level, see Schumann, *op. cit.*, pp. 55-56, 146-47; Wilson, *Leadership in Communist China*, pp. 31-34; Barnett, *China after Mao*, pp. 73, 78; Edgar Snow, *Other Side of the River* (New York: Random House, 1962), pp. 148, 154-55; and Michel C. Oksenberg, "Policy-Making under Mao, 1949-68: An Overview," in *China: Management of a Revolutionary Society*, ed. John M. H. Lindbeck (Seattle: University of Washington Press, 1971, pp. 79-83, 91-92, 102-4. For the CCP's handling of external relations during the Yenan period, see Klein, "Management of Foreign Affairs in Communist China," pp. 307-10; and Reardon-Anderson, *op. cit.*, pp. 1-3, 7.

16. On the important role of the Politburo's Standing Committee and collective leadership, see Hinton, *op. cit.*, pp. 76, 77.

17. See Ross Terrill, *A Biography of Mao* (New York: Harper and Row, 1980), pp. 333 ff.

18. From October 1949 to September 1954 the PRC utilized "the Common Program of the Chinese People's Political Consultative Conference (CPPCC)" and "The Organic Law of the Central People's Government." For English texts of these two documents, see Foreign Languages Press, comp., *The Important Documents of the First Plenary Session of the Chinese People's Political Consultative Conference* (Peking: Foreign Languages Press, 1949), pp. 1-20, 29-38.

19. For more information on the State Council, see D. J. Waller, *The Government and Politics of Communist China* (London: Hutchinson University Library, 1970), pp. 98-99.

20. Article 47 of the Constitution of the CCP adopted on September 20, 1945, by the First NPC. See *RMRB*, September 21, 1954, p. 3.

21. Zhou Enlai, "Report on the work of the government, June 26, 1957," p. 4.

22. *Ibid.*

23. On the diplomatic power of the State Council, see Franklin W. Houn, "Communist China's New Constitution," *Western Political Quarterly*, vol. 8 (June 1955): pp. 209, 217-19, 222; Barnett, *Making of Foreign Policy in China*, pp. 51-73; and Schurman, pp. 180-210.

24. See Waller, *op. cit.*, pp. 55-56.

25. For more information on the Ministry of Foreign Affairs, see Donald W. Klein, "Peking's Evolving Ministry of Foreign Affairs," *CQ*, no. 4 (October-December 1960): pp. 29-35; Klein, "Management of Foreign Affairs in Communist China," *op. cit.*, pp. 311-22, 328-30, 336-38; George P. Jan, "The Ministry of Foreign Affairs in China since the Cultural Revolution," *Asian Survey*, vol. 17, no. 61 (June 1977): pp. 514-16, 523, 529; and Barnett, *Making of Foreign Policy in China*, pp. 87-88.

26. For more information on the powers of the CCP's Politburo and its Standing Committee, see Articles 36 and 37 of the Constitution of the CCP, in Chen, *op. cit.*, pp. 140-41.

27. For Articles 47-52 of the PRC's 1954 Constitution, see *RMRB*, September 21, 1952, p. 3; also see Chen, *op. cit.*, pp. 84-85. For careful analysis of the functions of state in China, see Waller, *op. cit.*, pp. 96-100; and David Bachman, *Bureaucracy, Economy and Leadership in China* (Cambridge: Cambridge University Press, 1991), chap. 3.

28. Chang Kuo-t'ao, *op. cit.*, p. 497; also see Reardon-Anderson, *op. cit.*, pp. 33-34. For a general survey of the Mao-Zhou partnership in the early 1970s, see Terrill, *op. cit.*, pp. 366-67, 380-81, 386.

29. See Zhou Enlai, "Learn from Mao Zedong, May 7, 1949," *SWZEL-1*, pp. 371, 375, 389-92.

30. See, for example, Mao Zedong, "Zai Zhong-guo Gong-chan-dang di qi-jie Zhong-yang-wei-yuan-hui di-er-ci quan-ti hui-yi-shang di boa-gao" (Report to the Second Plenary Session of the Seventh Central Committee of the CCP, March 5, 1949), *MZDXJ*, vol. 4, p. 144; and "Zai Zhong-guo Gong-chan-dang di-qi-jie Zhong-yang-wei-yuan-hui di-san-ci quan-ti hui-yi-shang di bao-gao" (Report to the Third Plenary Session of the Seventh Central Committee of the CCP, June 6, 1950), *Zheng-fu gong-zuo bao-gao hui-bian* (Collection of the Reports on Government Work) (Beijing: Ren-min-chu-ban-she, 1950), p. 5.

31. For more information on Mao's decision to step down in favor of Liu Shaoqi in 1958-59, see Richard H. Solomon, *Mao's Revolution and the Chinese Political Culture* (Berkeley: University of California Press, 1971), pp. 374-75; Snow, *Other Side of the River,* pp. 118-19; P. H. Chang, *op. cit.,* p. 190; and "Communiqué of the Sixth Plenum Session of the CCP's Eighth Central Committee, December 17, 1958," in *Communist China, 1955-1959: Policy Documents with Analysis,* ed. Robert R. Bowie and John K. Fairbank (Cambridge, Mass.: Harvard University Press, 1962), p. 484.

32. The text of the Communiqué of the CCP's Central Committee may be found in *NCNA,* December 17, 1958.

33. For an account of Peng's criticism of Mao's economic measures and the nature of the Mao-Peng confrontation at Lushan in 1959, see David A. Charles, "The Dismissal of Marshal P'eng Teh-huai," *CQ,* no. 8 (October-December, 1961): pp. 63-76; and Stanley Karnow, *Mao and China: From Revolution to Revolution* (New York: Viking, 1972), pp. 395, 400.

34. For further reference to Liu's increasing political influence and his style of leadership, see Lowell Dittmer, *Liu Shao-ch'i and the Chinese Cultural Revolution* (Berkeley: University of California Press, 1975), chaps. 2-4. On Liu's support of North Vietnam regardless of the nature and extent of U.S. involvement and escalation, see Liu Shao-ch'i, "Chairman Liu Shao-chi's Replies to President Ho Chi-minh, January 30, 1966," *Peking Review,* vol. 9, no. 6 (February 4, 1966): pp. 5-6 (hereafter cited as *PR*); and Tien-min Li, *Liu Shao-chi* (Taipei: Institute of International Relations, 1975), chaps. 7-8.

35. See Solomon, *op. cit.,* pp. 419-20 ff; also see Zhou Enlai, "Zhong-fu gong-zhuo bao-gao, zai di-san-jie quan-guo ren-min-dai-biao-da-hui di-yi-ci hui-yi-shang" (Report of the Work of the Government Addressed to the First Session of the Third NPC, December 21-22, 1964), *RMRB,* December 31, 1964, p. 3. For an English translation of Zhou's report, see *PR,* vol. 8, no. 1 (January 1, 1965): pp. 6-20, esp. p. 15.

36. For more information on foreign policy debate within the CCP hierarchy in the mid-1960s, see Uri Ra'anan, "Peking's Foreign Policy 'Debate,' 1965-1966," in *China in Crisis: China's Policy in Asia and America's Alternatives,* ed. Rang Tsou, 2 vols. (Chicago: University of Chicago Press, 1968), vol. 2, pp. 23-71, esp. pp. 64-71; Donald Zagoria, "The Strategic Debate in Peking," *ibid.,* pp. 239-40; P. H. Chang, *op. cit.,* pp. 165-66; and Thomas M. Gottlieb, *Chinese Foreign Policy: Factionalism and the Origins of the Strategic Triangle,* Doc. no. P. 1902-NA, November (Santa Monica, Calif.: Rand Corporation, 1977), pp. 17-20.

37. On Zhou's role and his alliance with Mao and Lin during the Cultural Revolution, see Hsu, *Chou En-lai,* pp. 225-27; Wilson, *Zhou Enlai,* pp. 242, 246-49, 252-53;

Thomas W. Robinson, "Chou Enlai's Political Style: Comparisons with Mao Tse-tung and Lin Piao," *Asian Survey*, vol. 10, no. 12 (December 1970): pp. 1101-16; Thomas Robinson, "Zhou Enlai and the Cultural Revolution in China," in *The Cultural Revolution in China*, ed. Thomas Robinson (Berkeley: University of California Press, 1971), pp. 165-313; Richard C. Thorton, *China: The Struggle for Power, 1917-1972* (Bloomington: Indiana University Press, 1973), pp. 325-37; and Keith, *op. cit.*, pp. 152-153. Also see Donald Klein, "The State Council and the Cultural Revolution," *CQ*, no. 35 (July-September 1968): pp. 93-94; Melvin Gurtov, "The Foreign Ministry and Foreign Affairs during the Cultural Revolution," *CQ*, no. 40 (October-December 1969), pp. 86-90; Teiwes, *op. cit.*, pp. 72-74, 109-12; Lowell Dittmer, "Bases of Power in Chinese Politics: A Theory and Analysis of the Fall of the 'Gang of Four,'" *World Politics*, vol. 31, no. 1 (October 1978): pp. 28-40; and Backman, *op. cit.*, pp. 32-48.

38. On the issue of power and ideological conflicts within the CCP leadership, see Tang Tsou, "The Cultural Revolution and the Chinese Political System," *CQ*, no. 38 (April-June 1969): pp. 63-91; and Philip Bridgham, "Mao's Cultural Revolution: The Struggle to Seize Power," *CQ*, no. 41 (January-March 1979): pp. 1-25.

39. See Ra'anan, *op. cit.*, p. 38; and Chang, *Power and Policy in China*, pp. 194-95.

40. See, for example, *PR*, vol. 11, no. 34, Supplement (August 23, 1968): p. iv; *PR*, vol. 11, no. 40 (October 4, 1968), p. 15: and *PR*, vol. 12, no. 40 (October 3, 1969): p. 18.

41. For more information on the rise and fall of Lin and the Mao-Zhou coalition, see Ralph L. Powell, "The Increasing Power of Lin Piao and the Party-Soldiers, 1959-1966," *CQ*, no. 55 (July-September 1973): pp. 450-77; Martin Ebon, *Lin Piao: The Life and Writings of China's Leader* (New York: Stein and Day, 1970), chaps. 5, 9, 16; Ellis Joffe, "The Chinese Army after the Cultural Revolution: The Effects of Intervention," *CQ*, no. 55 (July-September 1973): pp. 450-77; and Richard Wich, "The Tenth Party Congress: The Power Structure and the Succession Question," *CQ*, no. 58 (April-June 1974): pp. 231-48; also see Terrill, *op. cit.*, pp. 334-37, 340-41, 344-45.

42. "Communiqué of the Second Session of the Ninth Central Committee of the CCP, September 6, 1970," *PR*, no. 37 (September 11, 1970): p. 6.

43. Wilson, *op. cit.*, p. 298.

44. *Ibid.*, p. 302.

Chapter 7

1. Zhou Enlai, "Zai Zhong-guo ren-min zheng-zhi xie-shang hui-yi di-yi-jie quan-guo wei-yuan-hui di-san-ci hui-yi-shang di zheng-zhi bao-gao" (Political

Report Delivered at the Third Session of the First National Committee of the Chinese People's Consultative Conference, October 23, 1951), *RMRB*, November 3, 1951, p. 1; and "Zai Zhong-guo ren-min zheng-zhi xie-shang hui-yi di-yi-jie quan-guo wei-yuan-hui di-si-ci hui-yi-shang di bao-gao" (Report to the Fourth Session of the First National Committee of the Chinese People's Consultative Conference, February 4, 1953), *RMRB*, February 5, 1953, p. 1.

2. Zhou Enlai, "Political Report, October 23, 1951," *op. cit.,* p. 1; and "Wo-men di wai-jiao fang-zhen huo ren-wu" (Our Diplomatic Strategies and Missions, April 30, 1952), *Zhou Enlai xuan-ji* (Selected Works of Zhou Enlai), vol. 2, (Beijing: Ren-min-chu-ban-she, 1984), pp. 86, 99; hereafter cited at *ZELXJ-2*.

3. Zhou Enlai, "Report on Problems Concerning the Peace Talks, April 17, 1949," pp. 360, 361; and "Our Diplomatic Strategies and Missions," pp. 86, 87.

4. Zhou Enlai, "Report on Problems Concerning the Peace Talks," p. 360.

5. Zhou Enlai, "Political Report, October 23, 1951," p. 1; and "Report, February 4, 1953," p. 1.

6. "Report, February 4, 1953," *Ibid.*

7. Article 5 of the Sino-Soviet Treaty of Friendship, Alliance, and Mutual Assistance, signed on February 14, 1950. The full text of the treaty was published in *RMRB*, February 15, 1950, p. 2; the English translation of the treaty can be found in *People's China*, vol. 1, no. 5 (March 1, 1950): pp. 25-26; hereafter cited as *PC.*

8. Article 1 of the treaty; see *RMRB*, February 15, 1950, p. 2.

9. *Ibid.*

10. Article 3.

11. Articles 1, 2, and 3 of the Agreement between the Central People's Government of the PRC and the Government of Soviet Socialist Republic Concerning the Granting of Credit to the PRC; the full text of the agreement was published in *RMRB*, February 15, 1950, p. 2. The English translation of the agreement can be found in *PC*, vol. 1, no. 5 (March 1, 1950): p. 28.

12. On the issues of the Chinese Changchun Railway, Port Arthur (or Lushun), and Dairen (or Dalian), see Articles 1, 2, and 3 of the Agreement on the Chinese Changchun Railway, Port Arthur, and Dairen, respectively. The full text of the agreement was published in *RMRB*, February 15, 1950, p. 2. The English translation of the agreement can be found in *PC*, vol. 1, no. 5 (March 1, 1950): pp. 25-27.

13. See Allen S. Whiting, *China Crosses the Yalu* (New York: Macmillan, 1960), p. vii.

14. See Article 1 of the treaty. For Zhou's emphasis on equality and mutual benefit between the two countries, see Wu Xiuquan, *Zai wai-jiao-bu ba-nian de jing-li*

(Eight-Year Experience in the Ministry of Foreign Affairs) (Beijing: Shi-jie zhi-shi chu-ban-she, 1983), pp. 11-12.

15. See Articles 1 and 5 of the treaty. For more information on the Sino-Soviet Treaty of Alliance, see Sergei N. Goncharov, John W. Lewis, and Xue Litai, *Uncertain Partners: Stalin, Mao, and the Korean War* (Stanford, Calif.: Stanford University Press, 1993), chaps. 3, 4, esp. pp. 104-9; and Max Beloff, *Soviet Policy in the Far East, 1944-1951* (London: Oxford University Press, 1953), p. 73.

16. Edward Crankshaw, *Khrushchev Remembers* (Boston: Little, Brown, 1970), p. 371.

17. *Ibid.*

18. *Ibid.*

19. *Ibid.*, p. 372.

20. *Ibid.*, p. 371-72.

21. See Royal Institute of International Affairs, *Survey of International Affairs, 1952* (London: Oxford University Press, 1955), p. 354; also see "Text of Soviet-Chinese Announcements," *New York Times*, September 16, 1952, p. 4; hereafter cited as *NYT*.

22. See "Text of Soviet-Chinese Communiqué of Seven Accords, October 11, 1954," *NYT*, October 12, 1954, p. 8.

23. See "Textual Excerpts from Speech by Molotov Outlining Soviet Union Foreign Policy," *NYT*, February 9, 1955, p. 6.

24. *New China News Agency*, January 18, 1957, p. 152; hereafter cited as *NCNA*.

25. See *ibid.*, January 16, 17, 18, 19, 1957.

26. "Zhong-Po lian-huo sheng-ming" (Sino-Polish Joint Communiqué, January 16, 1957), *RMRB*, January 17, 1957, p. 1.

27. *Ibid.*

28. *Ibid.*

29. See *Xinhau*, January 17, 1957.

30. See "Zhong-Su lian-huo sheng-ming" (Sino-Soviet Joint Communiqué, Signed by Zhou and Bulganin on January 18, 1957), *RMRB*, January 20, 1957, pp. 1, 4; for an English translation of the joint communiqué, see *NYT*, January 19, 1957, p. 2.

31. *RMRB*, January 20, 1957, p. 4.

32. *Ibid.*

33. *RMRB*, January 20, 1957, p. 4.

34. *Ibid.;* for an illuminating discussion of China's official position on the relationship between the Soviet Union and the Eastern European countries, see Donald S. Zagoria, *The Sino-Soviet Conflict, 1956-1961* (Princeton, N.J.: Princeton University Press, 1962), pp. 61-62.

35. Zhou Enlai, "Report on the Work of the Government, June 26, 1957," p. 5.

36. See, for example, "Zhong-Xiong lian-huo sheng-ming" (Sino-Hungarian Joint Communiqué, January 17, 1957), *RMRB,* January 18, 1957, p. 1.

37. See "Sino-Soviet Joint Communiqué, January 18, 1957," p. 4; and "Zhou Enlai zong-li di jiang-hua" (Premier Zhou Enlai's Speech, January 18, 1957), *RMRB,* January 19, 1957, p. 1.

38. See Sino-Hungarian Joint Communiqué," p. 1; and "Sino-Soviet Joint Communiqué," p. 4.

39. "Zhou Enlai zong-li zai huan-song yan-hui-shang di jiang-hua" (Premier Zhou Enlai's Speech at a Farewell Banquet, January 19, 1957), *RMRB,* January 20, 1957, p. 4.

40. For more information on this issue, see Lung-chu Chen and Harold D. Laswell, *Formosa, China, and the United Nations: Formosa in the World Community* (New York: St. Martin's Press, 1957), p. 1.

41. See "Pravda Cautions U.S. over Taiwan," *NYT,* August 31, 1958, p. 1.

42. See John Thomas, "The Limits of Alliance: The Quemoy Crisis of 1958," in *Sino-Soviet Military Relations,* ed. Raymond L. Garthoff (New York: Praeger, 1966), p. 142; also see A. Doak Barnett, *China and the Major Powers in East Asia* (Washington D.C.: Brookings Institution, 1977), p. 344 n. 38.

43. See Hsu, *Chou En-lai,* p. 194; and Terrill, *op. cit.,* p. 282.

44. For the full text of Zhou's speech delivered at the Twenty-First Congress of the CPSU, January 28, 1958, see *PR,* vol. 2, no. 5 (February 3, 1958): pp. 6-8.

45. Snow, *Other Side of the River,* p. 98.

46. *Ibid.*

47. *Ibid.*

48. *Ibid.*

49. On Khrushchev's motives behind his attack on Albania, see Zagoria, *op. cit.,* pp. 374-76.

50. Zhou Enlai, "Speech at the Twenty-Second Congress of the CPSU, October 19, 1961," *PR,* vol. 4, no. 43 (October 27, 1961): p. 9.

51. *Ibid.*

52. *Ibid.*

53. *Ibid.*

54. For more information on the Sino-Soviet boundary disputes, see Dennis J. Doolin, *Territorial Claims in the Sino-Soviet Conflict: Documents and Analysis* (Stanford, Calif.: Stanford University Press, 1965); and Thomas W. Robinson, "The Sino-Soviet Border Dispute: Background, Development, and the March 1969 Clashes," *American Political Science Review,* vol. 66, no. 4 (December 1972): pp. 1175-1202.

55. Zhou Enlai, "Zheng-fu gong-zuo bao-gao, zai di-san-jie quan-guo ren-min dai-biao da-hui di-yi-jie hui-yi-shang" (Report on the Work of the Government, Delivered at the First Session of the Third NPC, December 21-22, 1964), *RMRB*, December 31, 1964, p. 3.
56. *Ibid.*
57. See "Chou Discloses Soviet Accord for Border Talk, February 2, 1964," *NYT*, February 3, 1964, p. 3.
58. See "He-lu-xiao-fu shi zen-yang xie-tai-de" (Why the Downfall of Khrushchev?), *RMRB*, November 21, 1964, p. 1.
59. See "Chinese Party and Government Delegation Headed by Comrade Chou En-lai Visits Rumania and His Speech, June 17, 1966," *PR*, vol. 9, no. 26 (June 24, 1966): p. 9.
60. Zhou Enlai, "Speech at Rumania's National Day Reception, August 23, 1968," *PR*, supplement to no. 34 (August 23, 1968), pp. 3, 4; this speech was also published in *RMRB*, August 24, 1968, p. 1.
61. *Ibid.*
62. *Ibid.*
63. The Brezhnev doctrine was an attempt to legitimize Soviet military intervention in Czechoslovakia and elsewhere in Eastern Europe. On November 12, 1968, Brezhnev indicated at the Fifth Polish Party Congress that a threat to the security of the people of one socialist country was a shared problem and the concern of all socialist countries. For more information on the Brezhnev doctrine and its implications, see "Speech by Comrade L. I. Brezhnev," *Pravda* and *Izvestia*, both on November 13, 1969, pp. 1-2; reprinted as "Brezhnev Discusses Czechoslovakia at Polish Congress," *Current Digest of the Soviet Press*, no. 20 (December 4, 1968): pp. 3-5; Sergei Kouvalov, "Sovereignty and the International Duties of Socialist Countries," *Pravda*, September 26, 1968, in *Problems of Communism*, vol. 17, no. 6 (November-December 1968), p. 25; and Robin Edmonds, *Soviet Foreign Policy, 1963-1973: The Paradox of Superpower* (London: Oxford University Press, 1975), p. 74.
64. On the official Chinese view, see Neville Maxwell, "The Chinese Account of the 1969 Fighting at Chen Pao," *CQ*, no. 56 (October-December 1973), pp. 730-39.
65. See *NYT*, September 9, p. 3; "Kosygin and Chou Confer in Peking in Surprise Move, September 11, 1969," *NYT*, September 12, 1969, pp. 1-2; and "China-Soviet Talk Startles Envoys," *NYT*, September 13, 1969, pp. 1, 4.
66. See "Statement of the Government of the PRC, November 7, 1969," *PR*, vol. 12, no. 41 (October 10, 1969): pp. 3, 4.
67. For more information about the Zhou-Kosygin meeting, see Edgar Snow, "Talks with Chou En-lai: The Open Door," *New Republic*, March 29, 1971,

p. 23; and Andrey Topping, "Chou at a Dinner, Describes Birth of Rift with Soviet, May 5, 1971," *NYT,* May 21, 1971, p. 10.

68. "Statement of the Government of the PRC, October 7, 1969," p. 4.
69. *Ibid.,* p. 3.
70. See, for example, Lin Biao, "Report to the Ninth National Congress of the CCP, April 1, 1969," *PR,* vol. 12, no. 18 (April 30, 1969): p. 33; and "A Program for Anti-Imperialist Struggle," *PR,* vol. 14, no. 21 (May 21, 1971): p. 5.
71. Edgar Snow, *The Long Revolution* (London: Hutchinson, 1973), p. 10.
72. *Ibid.*
73. Zhou Enlai, "Zai Zhong-guo Gong-chang-dang di-shi-ci quan-guo dai-biao da-hui-shang di bao-gao" (Report to the Tenth Session of the National Congress of the CCP, August 24, 1973), *RMRB,* September 1, 1973, p. 3; for an English translation of Zhou's report, see *PR,* vol. 16, Nos. 35-36 (September 7, 1973), pp. 17-25.
74. See "Chinese Ask Russian for a Nonaggression Meeting," *NYT,* November 8, 1974, p. 2.
75. Zhou Enlai, "Zai Zhong-hua-ren-min gong-he-guo di-si-jie quan-guo ren-min dai-biao da-hui di-er-ci hui-yi-shang di zheng-fu gong-zuo bao-gao" (Report on the Work of the Government, Delivered at the First Session of the Fourth NPC, January 13, 1975), *RMRB,* January 25, 1975, p. 2.
76. *Ibid.;* for an English translation of Zhou's report, see *PR,* vol. 18, no. 4 (January 24, 1975): pp. 21-25.

Chapter 8

1. *U.S. Relations with China,* p. 280.
2. *Ibid.*
3. *Ibid.*
4. *Ibid.,* p. 281.
5. Secretary Dean Acheson, "An Address Delivered before the Commonwealth of California, March 27, 1950," *Department of State Bulletin,* vol. 22, no. 560 (March 27, 1950): p. 469; hereafter cited as *DSB.*
6. See Zhou Enlai's "Statement on Acheson's Speech," *PC,* vol. 2, no. 7 (April 1, 1950): p. 5; also see *RMRB,* March 19, 1950, p. 1.
7. *Ibid.*
8. *Ibid.*
9. See "President Truman's Statement on Korea," *NYT,* June 28, 1950, p. 1; or *DSB,* vol. 23, no. 574 (July 3, 1950): p. 5.

10. Zhou Enlai, "Speech at the Central People's Government, June 28, 1950," *PC,* vol. 1, no. 2 (July 16, 1950): p. 4.

11. *Ibid.*

12. *Ibid.*

13. *Ibid.*

14. *Ibid.*

15. *Ibid.*

16. *Ibid.*

17. "Zhou-wai-zhang dian Ma-li-ke he Lai-yi" (Foreign Minister Zhou Cables Malik and Lie, August 20, 1950), *RMRB,* August 21, 1950, p. 5.

18. *Ibid.*

19. "Zhou-wai-zhang zhi-dian Lai-yi" (Foreign Minister Zhou Sends Cable to Lie, September 24, 1950), *RMRB,* September 25, 1950, p. 1.

20. *Ibid.*

21. *Ibid.*

22. Zhou Enlai, "Wei gong-gu ren-min di sheng-li er fen-dou" (Fight for the Consolidation and Development of the Chinese People's Victory), *RMRB,* October 1, 1950, p. 1; or *PC,* vol. 2, no. 8 (October 16, 1950): p. 7.

23. K. M. Panikkar, *In Two Chinas* (London: Allen and Unwin, 1955), p. 110.

24. *Ibid.*

25. See Peter Colvocoressi, *Survey of International Affairs, 1949-1950* (London: Oxford University Press, 1953), p. 351.

26. Truman, *op. cit.,* p. 362.

27. *Ibid.*

28. *Ibid.,* pp. 365, 366; also see Joseph Gouldon, *Korea: The Untold Story of War* (New York: Times Books, 1982), p. 282; and Hao Yi-fan and Zhai Zhihai, "China's Decision to Enter the Korean War: History Revisited," *CQ,* no. 121 (March 1990), p. 103.

29. See Zhou Enlai, "Kang-Mei yuan-Chao, bao-wei he-ping, zai Zhong-guo ren-min zheng-zhi xie-shang hui-yi di-yi-jie quan-guo wei-yuan-hui shang di bao-gao" (Oppose U.S., Support Korea, and Defend Peace, Report Delivered at the Eighteenth Session of the Standing Committee of the First National Committee of the CPPCC, October 24, 1950), *ZELWJ-2,* p. 52; Tsou, *op. cit.,* pp. 576-77; and Hao and Zhai, *op. cit.,* pp. 99-103.

30. *Ibid.,* pp. 101-2; and Tsou, *op. cit.,* pp. 572-73, 575-76, 580.

31. United Nations Security, *Official Records,* November 16, 1950, p. 30.

32. *Ibid.*

33. Zhou Enlai's telegram, January 17, 1951; U.S. Department of State, *The Record of Korean Unification* (Washington, D.C.: Government Printing Office, 1960), pp. 114-16.

34. Tsou, *op. cit.*, p. 579.
35. Quoted in Mark G. Toulouse, *The Transformation of John Foster Dulles* (Macon: Mercier University Press, 1985), p. 243; also see "Dulles Says West Skirts No. 1 Task, May 12, 1952," *NYT*, May 13, 1952, p. 8.
36. See "Text of Eisenhower's State of the Union Message on New Domestic and Foreign Policies, February 2, 1953," *NYT*, February 3, 1953, p. 14.
37. P. V. Curl, ed., *Documents on American Relations, 1953* (New York: Harper and Row, 1954), p. 31.
38. See "Text of Secretary Dulles' Address to U.S. Newspaper Editors, April 28, 1953," *NYT*, April 19, 1953, p. 84.
39. Roscoe Drummond and Gaston Coblentz, *Duel at the Brink: John Foster Dulles' Command of American Power* (London: Widenfeld and Nicolson, 1961), p. 113.
40. See "Text of the Dulles Address to the American Legion Convention, September 2, 1953," *NYT*, September 3, 1953, p. 4.
41. See "Text of Dulles' Statement on Foreign Policy of Eisenhower Administration, January 12, 1954," *NYT*, January 13, 1954, p. 2.
42. *Ibid.*
43. *Ibid.*
44. *Ibid.*
45. *Ibid.*
46. See "Eisenhower Limits U.S. Participation in Indo-China War, February 10, 1954," *NYT*, February 11, 1954, p. 1.
47. *NYT*, April 1, 1954.
48. Dwight D. Eisenhower, *Mandate for Change, 1953-1956* (Garden City, N.Y.: Doubleday, 1963), p. 347.
49. *Ibid.*, p. 362.
50. *Ibid.*
51. See Alice L. Hsieh, *Communist Strategy in the Nuclear Era* (Englewood Cliffs, N.J.: Prentice-Hall, 1962), pp. 15, 16.
52. Secretary Dulles declared on September 2, 1953, that there was the risk that, as in Korea, the PRC might send its own army into Indochina. According to Dulles, direct Chinese Communist intervention in Indochina "could not occur without grave consequences which might not be confined to Indo-China" (see *NYT*, September 3, 1953, p. 4). On June 11, 1954, Dulles made another speech, in which he plainly stated that a clash between China and the United States was possible if there were any "open military aggression by the Chinese Communist regime" (see *NYT*, June 12, 1954, p. 2). The full text of Dulles's speech may be found in *DSB*, vol. 30, no. 783 (June 28, 1954): pp. 971-73.

324 Kuo-kang Shao

53. The full text of Zhou Enlai's six-point proposal issued on May 27, 1954, may be found in *RMRB*, May 29, 1954, p. 1.
54. *Ibid.*
55. *Ibid.*
56. For the full text of the Final Declaration of the Geneva Conference, signed on July 21, 1954, see *Further Documents Relating to the Discussion of Indo-China at the Geneva Conference, June 16-July 21, 1954* (New York: Greenwood Press, 1968), pp. 9-11. The full text of the Final Declaration was also published in *RMRB*, July 22, 1954, p. 1.
57. Zhou Enlai, "Wai-jiao bao-gao, zai Zhong-yang-ren-min cheng-fu wei-yuan-hui di-san-shi-san-ci hui-yi-shang" (Report on Foreign Relations, Delivered at the Thirty-Third Session of the Central People's Government Council, August 11, 1954), *RMRB*, August 14, 1954, p. 1.
58. *Ibid.*
59. *Ibid.*
60. *Ibid.*
61. *Ibid.*
62. *Ibid.;* for an English translation of Zhou's report, see supplement to *PC* (September 1, 1954): pp. 3-11.
63. Zhou Enlai, "Zai di-yi-jie quan-guo ren-min dai-biao da-hui di-yi-ci hui-yi-shang di zheng-fu gong-zuo bao-gao" (Report on the Work of the Government, Given at the First Session of the First NPC, September 23, 1954), *RMRB*, September 24, 1954, p. 3.
64. *Ibid.*
65. *Ibid.;* for an English translation of Zhou's report, see *NCNA*, September 24, 1954, pp. 4-12.
66. See "Wai-jiao-bu-chang Zhou Enlai guan-yu Mei-Jiang 'gong-tong-fang-wei-tiao-yue' di sheng-ming" (Foreign Minister Zhou Enlai's Statement on U.S.-Jiang [Jie-shi] "Treaty of Common Defense," December 8, 1954), *RMRB*, December 9, 1954, p. 1.
67. *Ibid.*
68. *Ibid.;* the English translation of Zhou's statement may be found in *PC* (December 16, 1954): pp. 3-5.
69. Zhou Enlai, "Speech Delivered to the Political Committee of the Asian-African Countries at Bandung, April 23, 1955," *NYT*, April 25, 1955, p. 7; also see Zhou Enlai, "Mu-qian guo-ji xing-shi he wo-guo wai-jiao zheng-ce, zai di-yi-jie quan-guo ren-min dai-biao di er-ci hui-yi-shang di fa-yan" (On the Present International Situation and China's Foreign Policy, Made at the Second Session of the First NPC, July 30, 1955), *RMRB*, July 31, 1955, p. 2.
70. Zhou Enlai, "Speech, August 23, 1955," p. 7.

71. Zhou Enlai, "On the Present International Situation and China's Foreign Policy, July 30, 1955," p. 2.

72. *Ibid.*

73. *Ibid.*

74. *Ibid.*

75. *Ibid.*

76. See, for example, "Dulles' News Conference Remarks on Red China, August 2, 1955," *NYT*, August 3, 1955, p. 4; "Talks with Communist China at Geneva, August 2, 1955," *DSB*, vol. 23, no. 842 (August 15, 1955): p. 260; and Snow, *Other Side of the River*, p. 91.

77. "Talks with Communist China at Geneva, August 2, 1955," p. 260; and Roderick MacFarquhar, *Sino-American Relations, 1949-71* (New York: Praeger, 1972), p. 126.

78. Zhou Enlai, "Zai Zhong-guo ren-min zheng-zhi xie-shang hui-yi di-er-ci quan-ti hui-yi-shang di zheng-zhi bao-gao" (Political Report Delivered at the Second Session of the Second National Committee of the CPPCC, January 30, 1956), *RMRB*, January 31, 1956, p. 2.

79. *Ibid.*

80. *Ibid.*

81. Zhou Enlai, "Guan-yu mu-qian guo-yi xing-shi, wo-guo wai-jiao zheng-ci he jie-fang Tai-wan wen-ti, zai di-yi-jie quan-guo ren-min dai-biao da-hui di-san-ci hui-yi-shang di fa-yan" (On the Present International Situation, China's Foreign Policy, and the Liberation of Taiwan, Delivered to the Third Session of the First NPC, June 28, 1956), *RMRB*, June 29, 1956, p. 2.

82. *Ibid.;* for an English translation of this report, see supplement to *PC* (July 16, 1956), pp. 3-14.

83. Kenneth T. Young, *Negotiating with the Chinese Communists: The United States Experience, 1953-1967* (New York: McGraw-Hill, 1958), p. 5. For more information on Sino-U.S. ambassadorial talks, see Wang Bingnan, *Zhong-Mei hui-tan jiu-nian hui-gu* (Recollections of the Nine-Year Sino-American Talks) (Beijing: Shi-jie zhi-shi chu-ban-she, 1985); U. Alexis Johnson, *The Right Hand of Power* (Englewood Cliffs, N.J.: Prentice-Hall, 1984). Also see Max Frankel, "U.S. and China Want More Talks; Both See Continuing Value in Meetings in Warsaw," *NYT*, April 22, 1964, p. 3.

84. Young, *op. cit.,* p. 5.

85. Zhou Enlai, "On the Present International Relations, China's Foreign Policy, and the Liberation of Taiwan, June 28, 1956," p. 2.

86. Young, *op. cit.,* p. 114.

87. Zhou Enlai, "Guan-yu Ya-Fei hui-yi di bao-gao, zai chang-wu-wei-yuan-hui di-shi-wu-ce hui-yi kuo-dai-hui-yi" (Report on the Asian-African Conference

Delivered at the Fifteenth Session of the Enlarged Conference of the Standing
Committee of the NPC, May 13, 1955), *RMRB,* May 17, 1955, p. 1.

88. *Ibid.*

89. Zhou Enlai, "Mu-qian guo-ji xing-shi he wo-guo wai-jiao zheng-ci, zai di-yi-jie
quan-guo ren-min dai-biao da-hui di-wu-ci hui-yi-shang di fa-yan" (On the
Present International Situation and China's Foreign Policy, Delivered at the
Fifth Session of the First NPC, February 10, 1958), *RMRB,* February 11,
1958, p. 2.

90. *Ibid.*

91. *Ibid.*

92. *Ibid.*

93. *Ibid.*

94. "Chinese Government's Statement on Sino-American Ambassadorial Talks,
June 30, 1958," *PR,* vol. 1, no. 19 (July 8, 1958): p. 21.

95. See "State Department Transcript of Remarks Made by Dulles at His News
Conference, July 1, 1958," *NYT,* July 2, 1958, p. 8; or *DSB,* vol. 39, no. 995
(July 21, 1958): p. 107.

96. *NCNA,* July 16, 1958.

97. Zhou Enlai, "Statement, September 6, 1958," *PR,* vol. 1, no. 33 (October 14,
1958): p. 9.

98. Snow, *Other Side of the River,* p. 91.

99. *Ibid.,* p. 92.

100. *Ibid.,* p. 93.

101. *Ibid.,* p. 91.

102. *Ibid.,* p. 87.

103. *Ibid.,* p. 91.

104. *Ibid.*

105. Zhou Enlai, "Report on the Work of the Government, Delivered at the First
Session of the Third NPC, December 21-22, 1964," p. 3.

106. *Ibid.*

107. *Ibid.;* for the English translation of Zhou's report, see *PR,* vol. 8, no. 1 (January
1, 1965): pp. 6-20.

108. See Morton H. Halpern, *China and the Bomb* (New York: Praeger, 1965),
p. 92; also see "Zhou Enlai zong-li zhi-dian shi-jie ge-guo zheng-fu shou-lao"
(Premier Zhou Cables Government Heads of the World, October 17, 1964),
RMRB, October 21, 1964, p. 1; for the English translation of Zhou's cable,
see *PR,* vol. 7, no. 43 (October 23, 1964): p. 6.

109. See *PR,* vol. 8, no. 2 (February 12, 1965): pp. 6-7.

110. G. W. Choudhury, *Chinese Perceptions of the World* (Washington, D.C.:
University Press of America, 1971), p. 12.

111. See "Premier Chou's Four-Point Statement on China's Policy toward the U.S.," *PR,* vol. 9, no. 20 (May 13, 1966): p. 5. The statement was also published in *RMRB,* May 10, 1966, p. 1.

112. See, for example, Zhou Enlai, "Report, December 21-22, 1964," p. 3; "Premier Chou Cables Government Heads of the World, October 17, 1964," *PR,* vol. 7, no. 13 (October 23, 1964): p. 6; and *PR,* vol. 12, no. 4 (October 3, 1969): p. 18.

113. See "Speech at the Reception Celebrating the Nineteenth Anniversary of the Founding of the PRC, October 1, 1968," *PR,* vol. 11, no. 40 (October 4, 1968): p. 15.

114. *Ibid.*

115. *Ibid.*

116. Young, *op. cit.,* pp. 268-69.

117. See Richard M. Nixon, "Asia after Viet Nam," *Foreign Affairs,* vol. 45, no. 1 (October 1967): p. 115.

118. Marvin Kalb and Bernard Kalb, *Kissinger* (Boston: Little, Brown, 1974), pp. 222-25, 233-38.

119. See William Rogers, "Vietnam in the Perspective of East Asia, April 21, 1969," *DSB,* vol. 60, no. 1559 (May 12, 1969): p. 398.

120. See *DSB,* vol. 60, no. 1564 (June 16, 1969): p. 505.

121. For a transcript of Nixon's Quam press conference, see Richard Nixon, *Public Papers of the Presidents of the United States, 1969,* no. 279, "Informal Remarks in Quam with Newsmen," July 25, 1969 (Washington, D.C.: Government Printing Office, 1971), pp. 544-56.

122. See Henry A. Kissinger, *White House Years* (Boston: Little, Brown, 1979), p. 728; and Kalb and Kalb, *op. cit.,* p. 216 ff.

123. Kissinger, *op. cit.,* p. 170.

124. *United States Foreign Policy, 1969-1970: A Report of the Secretary of State* (Washington, D.C.: Department of State, 1971), pp. 400-1.

125. See Nixon, "Asia after Viet Nam," pp. 111-25. For background on Nixon's new approach to the PRC, see Gordon Chang, *Friends and Enemies: The United States, China, and the Soviet Union, 1948-1972* (Stanford, Calif.: Stanford University Press, 1990), pp. 282-84, 288-90.

126. Richard M. Nixon, *U.S. Foreign Policy for the 1970s: A New Strategy for Peace* (Washington, D.C.: Government Printing, 1970), p. 141.

127. *Ibid.*

128. *Ibid.,* p. 142.

129. *Ibid.*

130. *Ibid.,* pp. 141-142.

131. Kissinger, *op. cit.,* p. 701.

132. See "Text of Zhou Enlai's Conversation with American Reporter Snow," *Zhan-wang* (Look Fortnightly) (Hong Kong), no. 214 (January 1, 1971), pp. 7-8.

133. Kissinger, *op. cit.*, p. 702; and Kalb and Kalb, *op. cit.*, p. 237.

134. See "Premier Tells U.S. Team 'Friendship' Begins Anew," *NYT*, April 15, 1971, p. 1.

135. *DSB*, vol. 64, no. 1663 (May 10, 1971): p. 595.

136. Kissinger, *op. cit.*, p. 749.

137. *Ibid.*, p. 778; also see, p. 1056.

138. *Ibid.*, p. 781; and Richard Nixon, *The Memoirs of Richard Nixon* (New York: Grosset and Dunlop, 1978), p. 565.

139. Wilson, *Zhou Enlai*, p. 275; also see Kissinger, *op. cit.*, pp. 746-47.

140. *Ibid.*, pp. 781-82.

141. See *ZELXJ-2*, p. 476.

142. *Ibid.*

143. *Ibid.*

144. *Ibid.*

145. *Ibid.*, p. 475.

146. See "President Nixon's Visit to the PRC," *Current Background*, no. 952 (March 27, 1972): p. 15; see also Kissinger, *op. cit.*, pp. 746-47.

147. Kissinger, *op. cit.*, pp. 792-93.

148. *Ibid.*, p. 1049.

149. *Ibid.*

150. *Ibid.*

151. *Ibid.*

152. *Ibid.*, p. 1063.

153. *Ibid.*

154. *Ibid.*, p. 1069.

155. *Ibid.*, pp. 1073-74.

156. *Ibid.*, p. 1087.

157. Nixon, *Memoirs of Richard Nixon*, p. 566.

158. Kissinger, *op. cit.*, p. 1074.

159. *Ibid.*

160. Henry Kissinger, *Years of Upheaval* (Boston: Little, Brown, 1982), p. 50.

161. *Ibid.*

162. *Ibid.*

163. *Ibid.*, p. 67; also see Kissinger, *White House Years*, p. 1088.

164. *Ibid.*, p. 781.

165. "[Shanghai] lian-he gong bao" ([Shanghai] Joint Communiqué), *RMRB*, February 28, 1972, p. 1.

166. *Ibid.*
167. *Ibid.*
168. *Ibid.*
169. *Ibid.*
170. *Ibid.*
171. *Ibid.;* for the full English text of the Shanghai joint communiqué signed on February 27, 1972, see *DSB*, vol. 66, no. 1708 (March 20, 1972): pp. 435-538; or *PR*, vol. 15, no. 9 (March 3, 1972): pp. 4-5.
172. *DSB*, March 19, 1973, p. 313.
173. Zhou Enlai, "Report on the Work of the Government, January 13, 1975," p. 2.
174. *Ibid.*
175. Kissinger's speech delivered at Webster College, Webster Groves, Missouri, in *Sino-American Normalization and Its Policy Implications,* eds. Gene T. Hsiao and Michael Witunski (New York: Praeger, 1983), p. xxviii; for further illuminating thoughts on the Sino-American rapprochement, see Harry Harding, *A Fragile Relationship: The United States and China since 1972* (Washington, D.C.: The Brookings Institution, 1972), pp. 34-37; and Keith, *op. cit.,* pp. 196-204.

Chapter 9

1. See Zhou Enlai, "Zai Zhong-guo ren-min zheng-zhi xie-shang hui-yi di-yi-jie quan-guo wei-yuan-hui di-si-ci hui-yi-shang di bao-gao" (Report Delivered at the Fourth Session of the First National Committee of the CPPCC, February 4, 1953), *RMRB*, February 5, 1953, p. 2; "Zai Zhong-guo ren-min zheng-zhi xie-shang hui-yi di-er-ci quan-ti hui-yi-shang di zheng-zhi bao-gao" (Political Report Delivered at the Second Session of the Second National Committee of the CPPCC, January 30, 1956) *RMRB*, February 31, 1956, p. 2; and "On the Present International Situation, China's Foreign Policy, and the Liberation of Taiwan, June 28, 1956," p. 2.
2. Zhou Enlai, "Report on Foreign Relations, August 11, 1954," p. 1; "Report on the Work of the Government, September 23, 1954," p. 3; "Zai zheng-xie quan-guo wei-yuan-hui-shang di zheng-zhi bao-gao" (Political Report Delivered at the National Committee of the CPPCC, December 21, 1954), *RMRB*, December 27, 1954, p. 1; "On the Present International Situation and China's Foreign Policy, July 10, 1955," p. 1; and "On the Present International Situation, China's Foreign Policy, and the Liberation of Taiwan, June 28, 1956," p. 2.

3. Zhou Enlai, "Political Report, January 30, 1956," p. 2; for an English translation of this report, see *NCNA,* January 30, 1956.

4. See Zhou Enlai, "Report on Foreign Relations, August 11, 1954," p. 1; "On the Present International Situation and China's Foreign Policy, July 30, 1955," p. 1; "Political Report, January 30, 1956," p. 2; "On the Present International Situation, China's Foreign Policy, and the Liberation of Taiwan, June 28, 1956," p. 2; and "Guan-yu fan-wen Ya-zhou he Ou-zhou shi-yi-guo di bao-gao, zai quan-guo ren-min zheng-zhi xie-shang hui-yi di-er-ci quan-guo wei-yuan-hui di-san-ci quan-ti hui-yi-shang" (Report on Visits to Eleven Countries in Asia and Europe to the Third Plenary Session of the Second National Committee of the CPPCC, March 5, 1957), *RMRB,* March 6, 1957, p. 1.

5. Zhou Enlai, "Report on the Work of the Government, September 23, 1954," p. 3.

6. Liu Shaoqi, "Zai Ya-zhou Ao-zhou gong-hui hui-yi-shang di jiang-ci" (Speech Delivered to the Congress of the Asian-Australian Labor Unions, November 19, 1949), *RMRB,* November 22, 1949, p. 1.

7. *NCNA,* October 8, 1953; also see *NYT,* October 9, 1953; and Zhou Enlai, "Report on Foreign Relations, August 11, 1954," p. 1.

8. On Mao's approach to the "neutral forces," see his article "Lun ren-min min-chu zhuan-zheng" (On the People's Democratic Dictatorship, June 30, 1949), *MZDXJ,* vol. 4, p. 1478.

9. For the full text of the Sino-Indian agreement on trade and intercourse between the Tibet region of China and India, signed in Beijing on April 29, 1954, see *Zhong-hua-ren-min-gong-he-guo dui-wai-quan-xi wen-jian-ji* (Documents on Foreign Relations of the PRC) (Beijing: Shi-jie zhi-shi chu-ban-she, 1958), vol. 3 (1954-55), pp. 10-14; or *White Papers: Notes, Memoranda and Letters Exchanged between the Governments of India and China,* 8 vols. (New Delhi: Government of India, 1959-63), vol. 1, pp. 98-101.

10. See Zhou Enlai, "Report on Foreign Relations, August 11, 1954," p. 1; "Political Report, December 21, 1954," p. 1; and "On the Present International Situation and China's Foreign Policy, July 30, 1956," p. 2.

11. See, for example, Zhou Enlai, "Report on Visits to Eleven Countries in Asia and Europe, March 5, 1957," p. 3.

12. *Ibid.,* p. 1; "On the Present International Situation and China's Foreign Policy, February 10, 1958," p. 2; and "Zheng-fu gong-zuo bao-gao, zai di-er-jie quan-guo ren-min dai-biao da-hui di-yi-ci hui-yi-shang" (Report on the Work of the Government Made at the First Session of the Second NPC, April 18, 1959), *RMRB,* April 19, 1959, p. 4.

13. Cyril E. Black *et al.*, *Neutralization and World Politics* (Princeton, N.J.: Princeton University Press, 1968), p. xi.

14. See Peter Lyon, *Neutralism* (Leicester, England: Leicester University Press, 1963), chaps. 1-3; A. M. Halpern, "The Communist Line on Neutralism," *CQ*, no. 5 (January-March 1961), pp. 90-115; and Kuo-kang Shao, "Chou En-lai's Diplomatic Approach to Non-Aligned States in Asia, 1953-1960," *CQ*, no. 78 (June 1979): pp. 324-38.

15. See Kuo-kang Shao, "Zhou Enlai's Diplomacy and the Neutralization of Indo-China," *CQ*, no. 107 (September 1986): pp. 483-504.

16. Zhou Enlai, "Report on Foreign Relations, August 11, 1954," p. 1; "Report on the Work of the Government, September 23, 1954," p. 3; and "On the Present International Situation and China's Foreign Policy, July 30, 1955," p. 1.

17. Zhou Enlai, "Zai Ri-nei-wa hui-yi-shang di fa-yan" (Speech at the Geneva Conference, April 28, 1954), *RMRB*, April 30, 1954, p. 1.

18. Zhou Enlai, "Zai Ri-nei-wa hui-yi-shang guan-yu Yin-du-zhi-na wen-ti di fa-yan" (Speech Concerning Indochina at the Geneva Conference, May 12, 1954), *RMRB*, May 14, 1954, p. 1.

19. The full text of Zhou Enlai's six-point proposal, issued on May 27, 1954, can be found in *RMRB*, May 29, 1954, p. 1.

20. *NYT*, June 24, 1954, p. 1.

21. "Zhong-Yin liang-guo Zong-li lian-huo sheng-ming" (Premiers Zhou Enlai-Nehru Joint Statement, June 28, 1954), *RMRB*, June 29, 1954, p. 1.

22. "Zhong-Mien liang-guo Zong-li lian-huo sheng-ming" (Premiers Zhou-U Nu Joint Statement, June 29, 1954"), *RMRB*, June 30, 1954, p. 1.

23. Zhou Enlai, "Zai Ri-nei-wai hui-yi-shang di fa-yan" (Speech at the Geneva Conference, July 21, 1954), *RMRB*, July 22, 1954, p. 1.

24. Zhou Enlai, "Report on Foreign Relations, August 11, 1954," p. 1.

25. *Ibid.*

26. *Ibid.*

27. *Ibid.*

28. *Ibid.*

29. Zhou Enlai, "Report on the Work of the Government, September 23, 1954," p. 3.

30. *Ibid.*

31. *Ibid.*

32. *Ibid.*

33. *Ibid.*

34. See Margaret W. Fisher and Joan U. Bondurant, *Indian Views of Sino-Indian Relations* (Berkeley: University of California Press, 1956), p. 10.

35. *Ibid.*

36. *Ibid.*

37. Supplement to *PC* (January 1, 1955): p. 3.

38. *Ibid.*

39. See, for example, Zhou Enlai, "Zai Ya-Fei hui-yi quan-ti hui-yi-shang di fa-yan" (Speech to the Full Conference of Asian-African Countries, April 19, 1955), *RMRB,* April 20, 1955, p. 1; "Zai Ya-Fei hui-yi quan-ti hui-yi-shang di bu-chong fa-yan" (Supplementary Speech to the Full Conference of Asian-African Countries, April 19, 1955), *RMRB,* April 20, 1955, p. 1; for an English translation of Zhou's supplementary speech, see supplement to *PC* (May 16, 1955): pp. 11-13. For more information on the Asian-African (or Bandung) Conference, see George McT. Kahin, *The Asian-African Conference, Bandung, Indonesia* (Ithaca, N.Y.: Cornell University Press, 1956); A. Doak Barnett, "Chou En-lai at Bandung," *American University Field Staff Reports,* no. ADB-1955-4 (May 4, 1955), pp. 1-15; and Joseph Camilleri, *Chinese Foreign Policy: The Maoist Era and Its Aftermath* (Seattle: University of Washington Press, 1980), pp. 79-80.

40. Zhou Enlai, "Political Report, January 30 1956," p. 2.

41. Zhou Enlai, "Speech to the Full Conference of Asian-African Countries, April 19, 1955," p. 1.

42. *Ibid.;* for an English translation of Zhou's speech, see supplement to *PC* (May 16, 1955): pp. 7-10.

43. Zhou Enlai, "Speech Delivered to the Political Committee of the Asian-African Countries at Bandung, April 23, 1955," *NYT,* April 25, 1955, p. 7.

44. Zhou Enlai, "Report on the Asian-African Conference, May 13, 1955," p. 4.

45. Zhou Enlai, "On the Present International Situation and China's Foreign Policy, Reported to the Second Session of the First NPC, July 30, 1955," p. 1.

46. *Ibid.*

47. *Ibid.*

48. *Ibid.*

49. Zhou Enlai, "Political Report, January 30, 1956," p. 2.

50. *Ibid.*

51. *Ibid.*

52. *Ibid.*

53. *Ibid.*

54. *Ibid.*

55. *Ibid.*

56. Zhou Enlai, "On the Present International Situation, China's Foreign Policy, and the Liberation of Taiwan, June 28, 1956," p. 1.

57. *Ibid.*

58. *Ibid.*, p. 2.
59. *Ibid.*
60. *Ibid.*
61. Zhou Enlai, "Report on Visits to Eleven Countries in Asian and Europe, March 5, 1956," p. 1.
62. *Ibid.*
63. *Ibid.*, p. 3.
64. See, for example, Zhou Enlai, "Report on Foreign Relations, August 11, 1954," p. 1; and "Supplementary Speech to the Full Conference of Asian-African Countries, April 10, 1955," p. 1.
65. *Ibid.;* "Speech to the Full Conference of Asian-African Countries, April 19, 1955," p. 1; also see "Report on Foreign Relations, August 11, 1954," p. 1.
66. Zhou Enlai, "Speech to the Full Conference of Asian-African Countries, April 19, 1955," p. 1; "Supplementary Speech to the Full Conference of Asian-African Countries, April 10, 1955," p. 1; "On the Present International Situation and China's Foreign Policy, July 30, 1955," p. 1; and "Political Report, January 30, 1956," p. 2.
67. Zhou Enlai, "Speech to the Full Conference of Asian-African Countries, April 19, 1955," p. 1; and "Supplementary Speech to the Full Conference of Asian-African Countries, April 10, 1955," p. 1.
68. Zhou Enlai, "Report on Visits to Eleven Countries in Asia and Europe, March 5, 1957," p. 1.
69. Zhou Enlai, "Fei-zhou di da-hao ge-ming xing-shi" (Revolutionary Prospects in Africa Excellent! February 3, 1964), *RMRB,* February 6, 1964, p. 1. For an English translation of Zhou's speech, see *PR,* vol. 7, no. 71 (February 14, 1964): pp. 5-8. For more information on Zhou's African tour, see A. C. Adie, "Chou En-lai on Safari," *CQ,* no. 18 (April-June 1964): pp. 174-94; and Camilleri, pp. 99-100.
70. See *PR,* vol. 7, no. 1 (January 3, 1964): p. 37.
71. "Zhou's Press Conference in Algiers, December 26, 1963," *PR,* vol. 7, no. 1 (January 3, 1964): p. 37.
72. *Ibid.*
73. See *PR,* vol. 7, no. 1 (January 3, 1964): p. 35.
74. *Ibid.*
75. *Ibid.*, p. 34.
76. *Ibid.;* for the full text of Zhou's speech, see pp. 34-38.
77. Zhou Enlai, "Zai A-ke-la gao-bie yan-hui-shang di jiang-hua" (Speech at the Farewell Banquet in Accra, January 15, 1964), *RMRB,* January 17, 1964, p. 4; for an English translation of Zhou's speech, see *PR,* vol. 7, no. 4 (January 24, 1964): p. 14.

78. Zhou Enlai, "Revolutionary Prospects in Africa Excellent!" p. 1.
79. *Ibid.*
80. Zhou Enlai, "Speech at the Farewell Banquet in Accra, January 15, 1964," p. 4.
81. See "Zhong-guo he So-dan lian-huo gong-bao" (China-Sudan Joint Communiqué, January 30, 1964), *RMRB,* January 31, 1964, p. 1.
82. *Ibid.*
83. *Ibid.*
84. *Ibid.;* for the English text of the joint communiqué, see *PR,* vol. 7, no. 6 (February 7, 1964): p. 31.
85. See "Premier Chou En-lai's Press Conference [in Algiers], December 26, 1963," *PR,* vol. 7, no. 1 (January 3, 1964): pp. 37-38.
86. *Ibid.,* p. 38.
87. See, for example, *RMRB,* February 26, 1964, p. 1.
88. See "Premier Chou En-lai on the Growing Friendship between Chinese and African Peoples," *PR,* vol. 7, no. 1 (January 3, 1964): p. 39. The text of China's foreign aid program under the Eight Principles was published in *RMRB,* January 18, 1964, p. 4.
89. *Ibid.*
90. *Ibid.*
91. *Ibid.*
92. *Ibid.*
93. *Ibid.*
94. *Ibid.*
95. *Ibid.*
96. *Ibid.*
97. *Ibid.;* for an English translation of China's foreign aid program under the Eight Principles, see Sino-Mali joint communiqué, January 21, 1964," *PR,* vol. 7, no. 4 (January 24, 1964): p. 16.
98. See "Premier Chou Enlai's Report on His Visit to Fourteen Countries Addressed to the Joint Session of the Standing Committee of the NPC and the Plenary Meeting of the State Council, March 24, 1964," *PR,* vol. 7, no. 18 (May 1, 1964): p. 10.
99. *Ibid.*
100. *Ibid.,* p. 7.
101. *Ibid.,* pp. 7-8.
102. *Ibid.,* p. 8.
103. Zhou Enlai, "Report on the Work of the Government, December 21-22, 1964," p. 3.
104. *Ibid.*

105. *Ibid.*

106. See "Premier Chou Answers Questions of the Middle East News Agency," *PR,* vol. 8, no. 15 (April 19, 1965): p. 9.

107. *Ibid.*

108. *Ibid.,* pp. 9-10.

109. See Peter Van Ness, *Revolution and Chinese Foreign Policy: Peking's Support for Wars of National Liberation* (Berkeley: University of California Press, 1970), pp. 78-79.

110. See "Premier Chou on China's Stand on . . . Africa-Asian Conference, September 8, 1965," *PR,* vol. 8, no. 38 (September 17, 1965): p. 9.

111. *Ibid.;* on China's futile efforts to help organize a second Asian-African conference in 1965 in Algiers, see Charles Neuhauser, *Third World Politics* (Cambridge, Mass.: Harvard University, East Asian Research Center, 1968), pp. 49-60.

112. Zhou Enlai, "Political Report, August 24, 1973," p. 3.

113. *Ibid.*

114. "Zhou Enlai zong-li di tan-hua" (Premier Zhou Enlai's Speech, May 28, 1971), *RMRB,* May 29, 1971, p. 2.

115. *Ibid.*

116. *Ibid.*

117. *Ibid.;* for the English translation of Zhou's speech, see *PR,* vol. 7, no. 23 (June 7, 1971): p. 9.

118. Zhou Enlai, "Political Report, August 24, 1973," p. 3.

119. Zhou Enlai, "Report on the Work of the Government, January 13, 1975," p. 2.

Chapter 10

1. See Alice L. Hsieh, "Communist China and Nuclear Force," in *The Dispersion of Nuclear Weapons: Strategy and Politics,* ed. R. N. Rosecrance (New York: Praeger, 1964), p. 177.

2. Zhou Enlai, "Report on the Work of the Government, April 18, 1959," p. 4.

3. Edgar Snow, *Other Side of the River* (New York: Random House, 1962), p. 645.

. 4. "Zhou Enlai Zong-li zhi-dian shi-jie-ge-guo-zheng-fu shou-lao" (Premier Zhou Enlai Cables Government Heads of the World, October 17, 1964,), *RMRB,* October 21, 1964, p. 1. For the English translation of Zhou's cable, see *PR,* vol. 7, no. 43 (October 23, 1964): p. 6.

5. See, for example, Zhou Enlai, "Jin-yi-bu ti-gao jun-dui-di zheng-zhi-su-yang" (To Promote One Step Further the Fine Political Quality of the Military, Speech at the Meeting of Officers of Army, Navy and Air Force in Shanghai, December 24, 1957), *ZELXJ-2*, p. 274.

6. "Zhong-guo zheng-fu fa-yan-ren sheng-ming—ping Su-zheng-fu ba-yue-san-ri de sheng-ming" (Statement by the Spokesman of the Chinese government—"A Comment on the Soviet Government's Statement of August 3," August 15, 1963), *RMRB*, August 15, 1963, p. 2. For the English translation of this statement, see *PR*, vol. 6, no. 33 (August 16, 1963): pp. 7-15.

7. *Fei-qing nian-bao* (Yearbook on Chinese Communism) (Taipei: Institute for the Study of Chinese Communist Problems, 1967), pp. 647-48.

8. John Wilson Lewis and Xue Litai, "Strategic Weapons and Chinese Power: The Formative Years," *CQ*, no. 1121 (December 1987): pp. 541-42.

9. *Ibid.*, p. 548.

10. *Ibid.*, p. 545.

11. *Ibid.*, p. 542.

12. Field Marshal Bernard Montgomery, "China on the Move," *Sunday Times* (London, October 15, 1961).

13. Hsieh, "Communist China and the Nuclear Force," p. 159.

14. Quoted in Suyin Han, *Eldest Son: Zhou Enlai and the Making of Modern China, 1898-1976* (New York: Hill and Wang, 1994), p. 295.

15. *Ibid.*

16. *Ibid.*

17. "Zhong-guo zheng-fu sheng-ming" (Statement by the Chinese Government, July 31, 1963), *RMRB*, July 31, 1963, p. 1. For the English translation of this statement, see *PR*, vol. 6, no. 31 (August 2, 1963): pp. 7-8.

18. "Zhong-hua-ren-min gong-he-guo zheng-fu-sheng-ming" (Statement of the Government of the PRC, October 16, 1964), *RMRB*, October 17, 1964, p. 1.

19. *Ibid.*

20. *Ibid.*

21. *Ibid.* For the English translation of this statement, see *PR*, vol. 7, no. 42 (October 16, 1964): pp. i-iv.

22. "Premier Zhou Cables Government Heads of the World, October 17, 1964," p. 1.

23. *Ibid.*

24. See *NYT*, October 22, 1964, pp. 1, 3.

25. *Ibid.*, p. 3.

26. *Ibid.*

27. Quoted in Lewis and Xue, *op. cit.*, p. 545.

28. Zhou Enlai, "Speech to the Third NPC, December 30, 1964"; quoted in William L. Ryan and Sam Summerlin, *The China Cloud: America's Tragic Blunder and China's Rise to Nuclear Power* (Boston: Little, Brown, 1967), p. 191.

29. "Zhou Zong-li guan-yu Zhong-guo dui Mei-guo zheng-ce di si-ju-hua" (Premier Zhou's Four-Point Statement on China's Policy toward the United States, April 10, 1966), *RMRB*, May 10, 1966, p. 1. For the English translation of Zhou's statement, see *PR*, vol. 9, no. 20 (May 13, 1966): p. 5.

30. Nie Rongzhen, *Nie Rongzhen hui-yi-lu* (Memoirs of Nie Rongzhen) (Beijing: Jie-fan-jun chu-ban-she, 1984), p. 810.

31. See "Statement by the Spokesman of the Chinese Government, August 15, 1963," p. 2.

32. Rosecrance, *Dispersion of Nuclear Weapons*, p. 302.

33. *Ibid.*, p. 314.

34. *Strategic Survey, 1970* (London: Institute for Strategic Studies, 1971), pp. 32-34.

35. "Official Transcript of the Wide-Ranging Interview with Premier Chou Enlai, August 9, 1971," *NYT*, August 10, 1971, p. 15.

36. *Ibid.*

37. *Ibid.*

38. *Ibid.*

39. Henry A. Kissinger, *Nuclear Weapons and Foreign Policy* (New York: Harper Brothers, 1957), p. 424.

40. *Ibid.*

41. UN General Assembly, *Document* A/123, November 21, 1949, p. 3.

42. For the full text of Zhou's cable, see *Collected Documents on the Foreign Affairs of the PRC*, vol. 1, pp. 90-91.

43. "Zhou Enlai wai-chang zhi-dian lian-huo-guo da-hui di jiu-jie hui-yi" (Foreign Minister Zhou Enlai Sends Cable to the Ninth Session of the UN General Assembly, October 10, 1954), *RMRB*, October 11, 1954, p. 1. For the English translation of Zhou's cable, see *PC*, no. 21 (November 1, 1954): pp. 3-6.

44. "Foreign Minister Chou Enlai's Statement on U.S.-Jiang 'Treaty of Common Defense,' December 8, 1954," p. 1.

45. "Transcript of President Eisenhower's Press on Foreign and Home Affairs, January 19, 1955," *NYT*, January 20, 1955, p. 12.

46. Zhou Enlai Zong-li jian wai-chang kuan-yu Mei-guo cheng-fu gan-she Zhong-guo ren-min jie-fang Tai-wan di sheng-ming" (Premier and Foreign Minister Zhou Enlai's Statement on U.S. Intervention in Liberation of Taiwan, January 24, 1955), *RMRB*, January 25, 1955, p. 1. For the English translation of Zhou's statement, see *PC*, no. 4 (February 16, 1955), supp.

47. "Zhou En-lai Zong-li fu-dian Lian-huo-guo mi-shu-chang" (Premier Zhou Enlai Sends Cable Replying to UN Secretary-General, February 3, 1955), *RMRB,* February 4, 1955, p. 1.
48. *Ibid.* For the English translation of Zhou's cable, see People's Institute of Foreign Affairs, *Oppose U.S. Occupation of Taiwan and "Two Chinas" Plot* (Peking: Foreign Languages Press, 1958), pp. 31-34.
49. Zhou Enlai, "On the Present International Situation and China's Foreign Policy, February 10, 1958," p. 2.
50. For the full text of this statement, see *Survey of Mainland Press (SCMP),* no. 2648 (December 28, 1961): pp. 34-36.
51. See George Modelski, *International Conference on the Settlement of the Laotian Question, 1961-1962* (Canberra: Australian National University, 1962); and Arthur Lull, *How Communist China Negotiates* (New York: Columbia University Press, 1958), chap. 6.
52. Zhou Enlai, "United Nations Must Be Thoroughly Reorganized, January 24, 1965," *PR,* vol. 8, no. 5 (January 29, 1965): p. 6.
53. *Ibid.*
54. Edgar Snow, *The Long Revolution* (New York: Vintage Books, 1973), p. 159.
55. "Chou Ties U.N. Seat to Taipei's Ouster," *NYT,* July 1, 1971, p. 1.
56. *Ibid.,* p. 32.
57. *Ibid.*
58. "Official Transcript of the Wide-Ranging Interview with Premier Chou Enlai, August 9, 1971," p. 14.
59. *Ibid.*
60. *Ibid.*
61. Steven FitzGerald, "Impressions of China's New Diplomacy: The Australian Experience," *CQ,* no. 481 (October-December, 1971), p. 674.
62. "Excerpts from text of Chou's Interview with Tokyo Editor, October 28, 1971," *NYT,* November 9, 1971, p. 16.
63. *Ibid.*
64. *Ibid.*
65. *Ibid.*
66. *Ibid.*
67. Quoted in Keith, *Diplomacy of Zhou Enlai,* p. 184.

Chapter 11

1. Zhou Enlai, "Political Report, October 23, 1951," *RMRB,* November 3, 1951, p. 1; and "Our Diplomatic Strategies and Missions," *ZELXJ-2,* pp. 85, 87, 88.

2. *Ibid.*, pp. 88, 91.

3. Zhou Enlai, "Report on Problems Concerning Peace Talks, April 17, 1949," *SWZEL-1,* p. 360.

4. Zhou Enlai, "Our Diplomatic Strategies and Missions," p. 86.

5. See Zhou Enlai, "The Strategy of Western Europe toward Russia and Germany, May 24, 1921," *ZELWJ-1,* pp. 26, 27; "Anglo-French Military Strategies at the Washington Conference, January 22, 1922," *ibid.,* p. 174; and "Recent Confusing Situation in Upper Silesia, July 14, 1921," *ibid.,* p. 58.

6. Zhou Enlai, "Political Report, October 23, 1951," p. 1; and "Political Report, February 4, 1953," *RMRB,* February 5, 1954, p. 1.

7. Zhou Enlai, "Our Diplomatic Strategies and Missions," p. 86; "Report on the Work of the Government, September 23, 1954," *RMRB,* September 24, 1954, p. 3; and "On the Present International Situation and China's Foreign Policy, July 30, 1955," *RMRB,* July 31, 1955, p. 1.

8. See Ronald C. Keith, *The Diplomacy of Zhou Enlai* (New York: St. Martin's Press, 1989), pp. 5-8; and Lucian Pye, "On Chinese Pragmatism in the 1980s," *CQ,* no. 16 (June 1986): pp. 212-14, 220, 226.

9. Zhou Enlai, "Political Report, October 23, 1951," p. 1; "Our Diplomatic Strategies and Missions," pp. 87, 92; "Report on Foreign Relations, August 11, 1954," *RMRB,* August 14, 1954, p. 1; and "On the Work of the Government, September 23, 1954," p. 3.

10. For Article 1 of the Sino-Soviet Treaty of Friendship, Alliance, and Mutual Assistance signed on February 14, 1950, see *RMRB,* February 15, 1950, p. 2.

11. Zhou Enlai, "Report to the Tenth Party Congress, August 24, 1973," *RMRB,* September 1, 1973, p. 3; and "Report on the Work of the Government, January 13, 1975," *RMRB,* January 25, 1975, p. 2.

12. See, for example, Zhou Enlai, "Report on the Work of the Government, September 23, 1954," p. 3.

13. Zhou Enlai, "Our Diplomatic Strategies and Missions," pp. 88, 91.

14. Zhou Enlai, "Political Report, October 23, 1951," p. 1; "Political Report, February 4, 1953," *RMRB,* February 5, 1953, p. 1; "Report on the Work of the Government, September 23, 1954," p. 3; "Speech Delivered to the Full Conference of Asian-African Countries, April 19, 1955," *RMRB,* April 20, 1955, p. 1.

15. Zhou Enlai, "Political Report, October 23, 1951," p. 1; "Political Report, February 4, 1953," p. 1; and "Report on the Work of the Government, September 23, 1954," p. 3.

16. See Zhou Enlai, "Political Report, February 4, 1953, p. 2.

17. Zhou Enlai, "Report on Problems Concerning the Peace Talks," p. 360.

18. *Ibid.*

340

Kuo-kang Shao

19. *Ibid.*
20. *Ibid.*
21. See, for instance, "Political Report, October 23, 1951," p. 1; and "Report, February 4, 1953," p. 1.
22. See Richard Lowenthal, "Communist China's Foreign Policy," in *China in Crisis: China's Policy in Asia and America's Alternatives,* ed. Tang Tsou, vol. 2, (Chicago: University of Chicago Press, 1968), pp. 11-12; and Keith, *op. cit.,* pp. 43, 151, chap. 8.
23. For Article 5 of the 1950 Sino-Soviet Treaty of Alliance, see *RMRB,* February 15, 1950, p. 2.
24. See, for example, Zhou Enlai, "Report to the Tenth Party Congress," p. 3; and "Report on the Work of the Government, January 13, 1975," p. 2.
25. See Shao, "Chou En-lai's Diplomatic Approach to Non-Aligned States in Asia, 1953-60," p. 325.
26. Zhou Enlai, "On the Present International Situation and China's Foreign Policy, July 30, 1955," *RMRB,* July 31, 1955, p. 1; "On the Present International Situation, China's Foreign Policy, and the Liberation of Taiwan, June 28, 1956," *RMRB,* June 29, 1956, p. 2; and "On the International Situation and China's Foreign Policy, February 10, 1958," *RMRB,* February 11, 1958, p. 2.
27. Zhou Enlai, "Report on Foreign Relations, August 11, 1954," p. 1; "Report on the Work of the Government, September 23, 1954," p. 3; and "On the Present International Situation and China's Foreign Policy, July 30, 1955," p. 1.
28. Zhou Enlai, "Report on the Work of the Government, September 23, 1954," p. 3.
29. Zhou Enlai, "On the Present International Situation, China's Foreign Policy, and the Liberation of Taiwan, June 28, 1956," *RMRB,* June 29, 1956, p. 2.
30. For the basic documents of China's first Five-Year Plan, see *Zhong-hua ren-min gong-he-guo fa-chan guo-min-jing-ji di-yi-wu-nian ji-hua* (First Five-Year Plan for the Development of the National Economy of the PRC) (Beijing: Ren-min-chu-ban-she, 1955); and T. J. Hughes and D. E. T. Luard, *The Economic Development of Communist China, 1949-1960* (London: Oxford University Press, 1959), chap. 5.
31. Zhou Enlai, "Report on the Work of the Government, September 23, 1954," p. 3.
32. See, for example, Zhou Enlai, "Report on Foreign Relations, August 11, 1954," p. 1; "Report on the Work of the Government, September 23, 1954," p. 3; and "Speech to the Full Conference of Asian-African Countries, April 19, 1955," p. 1.

33. Zhou Enlai, "Political Report, February 4, 1953," p. 2.

34. Zhou Enlai, "He-ping gong-chu wu-xiang yuan-ze" (The Five Principles of Peaceful Coexistence, December 31, 1953), *ZELWJ-2*, p. 118.

35. See *White Papers, Notes, Memoranda and Letters Exchanged between the Governments of India and China* (New Delhi: Government of India, 1959), vol. 1, pp. 98-101.

36. Zhou Enlai, "Speech Concerning the Question of Indo-China, May 12, 1954," *RMRB*, May 14, 1954, p. 1.

37. *Ibid.*

38. Zhou Enlai, "Report on the Work of the Government, September 23, 1954," p. 3.

39. See "Soviet-Chinese Communiqué, October 11, 1954," *NYT*, October 12, 1954, p. 8.

40. Zhou Enlai, "Speech to the Full Conference of Asian-African Countries, April 19, 1955," p. 1.

41. See chapter 3; for a careful analysis of the Chinese approach to foreign affairs, see Steven I. Levine, "Perception and Ideology in Chinese Foreign Policy," in *Chinese Foreign Policy: Theory and Practice*, ed. Thomas W. Robinson and David Shambaugh (Oxford: Clarendon Press, 1994), pp. 30-46.

42. Zhou Enlai, "Political Report, January 30, 1956," *RMRB*, January 31, 1956, p. 2.

43. *Ibid.*

44. Zhou Enlai, "On the Present Situation, China's Foreign Policy, and the Liberation of Taiwan, June 28, 1956," *RMRB*, June 29, 1956, p. 1.

45. Zhou Enlai, "Speech to the Full Conference of Asian-African Countries, April 19, 1955," *RMRB*, April 20, 1955, p. 1; "Supplementary Speech to the Full Conference of Asian-African Countries, April 19, 1955," p. 1; and "Report on the Asian-African Conference, May 13, 1955," p. 1.

46. Zhou Enlai, "Supplementary Speech to the Full Conference of Asian-African Countries, April 19, 1955," p. 1; "On the Present International Situation, China's Foreign Policy, and the Liberation of Taiwan, June 28, 1956," p. 2; "Political Report, January 30, 1956," *RMRB*, January 31, 1956, p. 2; "Report on the Work of the Government, April 18, 1959," *RMRB*, April 19, 1959, p. 4; "Report on the Work of the Government, December 21-22, 1964," *RMRB*, December 31, 1964, p. 3; and "Report on the Work of the Government, January 13, 1975," p. 2.

47. See Percy Fang and Nancy Fang, *Zhou Enlai: A Profile* (Beijing: Foreign Languages Press, 1986), p. 100; also see Zhou Enlai, "Our Diplomatic Strategies and Missions, April 30, 1952," pp. 88, 89.

48. *Ibid.*, p. 90; and Fang and Fang, pp. 100-1.

49. Zhou Enlai, "Report on the Work of the Government, April 18, 1959," p. 4; and "Report on the Work of the Government, December 21-22, 1964," p. 3.
50. *Ibid.*
51. Zhou Enlai, "On the Work of the Government, January 13, 1975," p. 2.
52. *Ibid.;* on the united front doctrine as a major influence on the formulation and conduct of China's foreign policy, see J. D. Armstrong, *Revolutionary Diplomacy* (Berkeley: University of California Press, 1977), chap. 2.
53. Zhou Enlai, "Report to the Tenth Party Congress, August 24, 1973," p. 3.
54. *Ibid.*
55. *Ibid.*
56. *Ibid.*
57. Zhou Enlai, "Political Report, January 30, 1956," p. 2; and "Report on the Work of the Government, January 13, 1975," p. 2.
58. *Ibid.*
59. *Ibid.;* on the issue of China's triangular relationship with the two superpowers, see John Gittings, "The Great Power Triangle and Chinese Foreign Policy," *CQ,* no. 39 (July-September 1969), pp. 41-54; Camilleri, pp. 113-14, 141, 173; Kenneth Lieberthal, *Sino-Soviet Conflict in the 1970s: Its Evaluation and Implications for the Strategic Triangle* (Santa Monica, Calif.: Rand Corporation, July 1978); Gottlieb, *op. cit.,* pp. 17-20; and John W. Garver, *China's Decision for Rapprochement with the United States, 1968-1971* (Boulder, Colo.: Westview Press, 1982).
60. Quoted by Fox Butterfield in "The Intriguing Matter of Mao's Successor," *NYT Magazine,* August 1, 1976, p. 12; also see Li Zhisui, "Zhou Enlai's Farewell to the Chairman," *U.S. News and World Report,* October 10, 1994, p. 90.

SELECTED BIBLIOGRAPHY

Primary Chinese Sources

Deng, Xiaoping. "Guan yu xiu-gai dang-de zhang-cheng de bao-gao" (Report on Revision of the Party Constitution, September 16, 1956). *RMRB,* September 18, 1956.

Dong, Biwu. "Lun jia-jiang ren-min-dai-biao-hui-yi de gong-zuo" (On Strengthening the Work Connected with the People's Representative Conference, September 23, 1951). *RMRB,* January 30, 1952.

Guo-fu quan-ji (The Complete Works of Sun Yat-sen). Vol. 2. Taipei: Ron-min-yin-shua-chang, 1954.

Hu Shi wen-cun (Collected Essays of Hu Shi). 4 vols. Shanghai: Ya-dung-shu-quan, 1926.

Huai En, ed. *Zhou-Zong-li qing-shao-nian shi-dai shi-wen-shu-xin-ji (Poems, Essays and Letters Composed and Written by Premier Zhou at a Young Age). Chengdu: Sichuan-ren-min-chu-ban-she, 1979.*

Liu, Shaoqi. "Zai Ya-zhou Ao-zhou gong-hui hui-yi-shang di jiang-ci" (Speech Delivered to the Congress of the Asian-Australian Labor Unions, November 19, 1949). *RMRB,* November 22, 1949.

Mao Zedong xuan-ji (Selected Works of Mao Zedong). 4 vols. Beijing: Ren-min-chu-ban-she, 1951-60.

"[Shanghai] lian-he gong-bao" ([Shanghai] Joint Communiqué, February 27, 1972). *RMRB,* February 28, 1972.

"Wai-jiao-bu-chang Zhou Enlai guan-yu Mei-Jiang 'gong-tong-fang-wei-tiao-yue' di sheng-ming" (Foreign Minister Zhou Enlai's Statement on U.S.-Jiang [Jie-shi] "Treaty of Common Defense," December 8, 1954), *RMRB,* December 9, 1954.

Zheng-fu gong-zuo bao-gao hui-bian (Collection of the Reports on Government Work). Beijing: Ren-min-chu-ban-she, 1950.

"Zhong-guo he Su-dan lian-huo gong-bao" (China-Sudan Joint Communiqué, January 30, 1964). *RMRB,* January 31, 1964.

"Zhong-guo zheng-fu fa-yan-ren sheng-ming—ping Su-zheng-fu ba-yue-san-ri de sheng-ming" (Statement of the Spokesman of the Chinese government—"A Comment on the Soviet Government's Statement of August 3," August 15, 1963). *RMRB*, August 15, 1963.

"Zhong-guo zheng-fu sheng-ming" (Statement by the Chinese Government, July 31, 1963). *RMRB*, July 31, 1963.

Zhong-hua ren-min gong-he-guo dui-wai quan-xi wen-jian-ji (Collected Documents on the Foreign Affairs of the PRC). 10 vols. Beijing: Shi-jie zhi-shi chu-ban-she, 1957-65.

Zhong-hua ren-min gong-he-guo fa-chan guo-min-jing-ji di-yi-wu-nian ji-hua (First Five-Year Plan for the Development of the National Economy of the PRC). Beijing: Ren-min-chu-ban-she, 1955.

"Zhong-hua ren-min gong-he-guo zheng-fu sheng-ming" (Statement of the Government of the PRC, October 16, 1964). *RMRB*, October 17, 1964.

"Zhong-Mien liang-guo zong-li lian-huo sheng-ming" (Premiers Zhou Enlai-U Nu Joint Statement, June 29, 1954). *RMRB*, June 30, 1954.

"Zhong-Po lian-huo sheng-ming" (Sino-Polish Joint Statement, January 16, 1957). *RMRB*, January 17, 1957.

"Zhong-Su lian-huo sheng-ming" (Sino-Soviet Joint Communiqué, January 18, 1957). *RMRB*, January 20, 1957.

"Zhong-Su you-hao tong-meng hu-zhu tiao-yue" (The Sino-Soviet Treaty of Friendship, Alliance, and Mutual Assistance, February 14, 1950). *RMRB*, February 15, 1950.

"Zhong-Xiong lian-huo sheng-ming" (Sino-Hungarian Joint Statement, January 17, 1957). *RMRB*, January 18, 1957.

"Zhong-Yin liang-guo zong-li lian-ho sheng-ming" (Premiers Zhou Enlai-Nehru Joint Statement, June 28, 1954). *RMRB*, June 29, 1954.

Zhou Enlai. "Fei-zhou di da-hao ge-ming xing-shi!" (Revolutionary Prospects in Africa Excellent! February 3, 1965). *RMRB*, February 6, 1964.

———. "Guan-yu fan-wen Ya-zhou he Ou-zhou shi-yi-guo di bao-gao" (Report on Visits to Eleven Countries in Asia and Europe, March 5, 1957). *RMRB*, March 6, 1957.

———. "Guan-yu mu-qian guo-ji xing-shi, wo-guo wai-jiao zheng-ce he jie-fang Tai-wan wen-ti" (On the Present International Situation, China's Foreign Policy, and the Liberation of Taiwan, June 28, 1956). *RMRB*, June 29, 1956.

———. "Guan-yu Ya-Fei hui-yi di bao-gao" (Report on the Asian-African Conference, May 13, 1955), *RMRB*, May 17, 1955.

———. "Jin-yi-bu ti-gao jun-dui-di zheng-zhi-su-yang" (To Promote One Step Further the Fine Political Quality of the Military, December 24, 1957), *ZELXJ-2.*

———. "Mu-qian guo-ji xing-shi he wo-guo wai-jiao zheng-ce" (On the Present International Situation and China's Foreign Policy, July 30, 1955). *RMRB,* July 31, 1955.

———. "Mu-qian guo-ji xing-shi he wo-guo wai-jiao zheng-ce" (On the Present International Situation and China's Foreign Policy, February 10, 1958). *RMRB,* February 11, 1958.

———. "Wai-jiao bao-gao" (Report on Foreign Relations, August 11, 1954). *RMRB,* August 14, 1954.

———. "Wei gong-gu ren-min di sheng-li er fen-dou" (Fight for the Consolidation and Development of the Chinese People's Victory, September 30, 1950). *RMRB,* October 1, 1950.

———. "Zai A-ke-la gao-bie yan-hui-shang di jiang-hua" (Speech at the Farewell Banquet in Accra, January 15, 1964). *RMRB,* January 17, 1964.

———. "Zai Ri-nei-wa hui-yi-shang di fa-yan" (Speech at the Geneva Conference, April 28, 1954). *RMRB,* April 30, 1954.

———. "Zai Ri-nei-wa hui-yi-shang di fa-yan" (Speech at the Geneva Conference, July 21, 1954). *RMRB,* July 22, 1954.

———. "Zai Ri-nei-wa hui-yi-shang guan-yu Yin-du-zhi-na wen-ti di fa-yan" (Speech Concerning Indochina at the Geneva Conference, May 12, 1954). *RMRB,* May 14, 1954.

———. "Zai Zhong-guo Gong-chan-dang quan-guo dai-biao da-hui-shang di bao-gao" (Report to the National Congress of the CCP, August 24, 1973). *RMRB,* September 1, 1973.

———. "Zai Zhong-guo ren-min zheng-zhi xie-shang hui-yi di bao-gao" (Report at the Chinese People's Political Consultative Conference [CPPCC], February 4, 1953). *RMRB,* February 5, 1953.

———. "Zai Ya-Fei hui-yi quan-ti hui-yi-shang di bu-chong fa-yan" (Supplementary Speech to the Full Conference of Asian-African Conference, April 19, 1955). *RMRB,* April 20, 1955.

———. "Zheng-fu gong-zuo bao-gao" (Report on the Work of the Government, September 23, 1954). *RMRB,* September 24, 1954.

———. "Zheng-fu gong-zuo bao-gao" (Report on the Work of the Government, June 26, 1957). *RMRB,* June 27, 1957.

———. "Zheng-fu gong-zuo bao-gao" (Report on the Work of the Government, April 18, 1959). *RMRB,* April 19, 1959.

———. "Zheng-fu gong-zuo bao-gao" (Report on the Work of the Government, December 21-22, 1964). *RMRB,* December 31, 1964.

———. "Zheng-fu gong-zuo bao-gao" (Report on the Work of the Government, January 13, 1975). *RMRB,* January 25, 1975.

———. "Zheng-zhi bao-gao" (Political Report, December 21, 1954), *RMRB*, December 27, 1954.

———. "Zheng-zhi bao-gao" (Political Report, January 30, 1956). *RMRB*, January 31, 1956.

"Zhou Enlai di 'liu-dian jian-yi'" (Zhou Enlai's "Six-Point Proposal" [at the Geneva Conference], May 27, 1954). *RMRB*, May 29, 1954.

Zhou Enlai, Deng Yingchao zui-jin yan-lun (Recent Remarks of Zhou Enlai and Deng Yingchao). Guangzhou: Li-sao chu-ban-she, 1938.

Zhou Enlai nian-pu (Chronicle of Zhou Enlai's Important Events). Beijing: Ren-min-chu-ban-she, 1989.

Zhou Enlai shu-xin xuan-ji (A Selection of Zhou Enlai's Letters). Beijing: Zhong-yang wen-xian, 1988.

Zhou Enlai tong-yi zhan-xian wen-xuan (A Selection of Zhou Enlai's Works on the United Front). Beijing: Ren-min-chu-ban-she, 1984.

Zhou Enlai tong-zhi lu Ou wen-ji (The European Correspondence of Comrade Zhou Enlai). 2 vols. Beijing: Wen-wu-chu-ban-she, 1979-82.

Zhou Enlai xuan-ji (Selected Works of Zhou Enlai). 2 vols. Beijing: Ren-min-chu-ban-she, 1980-84.

Zhou Enlai xuan-ji (Selected Works of Zhou Enlai). 3 vols. Hong Kong: Yi-shan tu-shu-gong-si, 1976.

"Zhou Enlai wai-chang zhi-dian Lian-huo-guo da-hui di-jiu-jie hui-yi" (Foreign Minister Zhou Enlai Sends Cable to the Ninth Session of the U.N. General Assembly, October 10, 1954). *RMRB*, October 11, 1954.

"Zhou Enlai Zong-li di tan-hua" (Premier Zhou Enlai's Speech, May 28, 1971). *RMRB*, May 29, 1971.

"Zhou Enlai Zong-li fu-dian Lian-huo-guo mi-shu-chang" (Premier Zhou Enlai Sends Cable Replying U.N. Secretary-General, February 3, 1955). *RMRB*, February 4, 1955.

"Zhou Enlai Zong-li jian wai-chang kuan-yu Mei-guo-cheng-fu gan-she Zhong-guo ren-min jie-fang Tai-wan di sheng-ming" (Premier and Foreign Minister Zhou Enlai's Statement on U.S. Intervention in Liberation of Taiwan, January 24, 1995). *RMRB*, January 25, 1955.

"Zhou Enlai Zong-li zhi-dian shi-jie ge-guo zheng-fu shou-lao"(Premier Zhou Cables Government Heads of the World, October 17, 1964). *RMRB*, December 21, 1964.

"Zhou-wai-zhang dian Lai-yi" (Foreign Minister Zhou Sends Cable to Lie, September 24, 1950). *RMRB*, September 25, 1950.

"Zhou-wai-zhang dian Ma-li-ke he Lai-yi" (Foreign Minister Zhou Cables Malik and Lie, August 20, 1950). *RMRB*, August 21, 1950.

"Zhou Zong-li quan-yu Zhong-guo dui Mei-guo zheng-ce di si-ju-hua" (Premier Zhou's Four-Point Statement on China's Policy Toward the United States, April 10, 1966). *RMRB,* May 10, 1966.

Primary English Sources

Bowie, Richard R., and John K. Fairbank, eds. *Communist China, 1955-1959: Policy Documents with Analysis. Cambridge, Mass.: Harvard University Press, 1962.*

Brandt, Conrad, Benjamin I. Schwartz, and John K. Fairbank, eds. *A Documentary History of Chinese Communism.* Cambridge, Mass.: Harvard University Press, 1958.

"Chou Ties U.N. Seat to Taiwan's Ouster." *NYT,* July 1, 1971.

Curl, P. V., ed. *Documents on American Relations, 1953.* New York: Harper and Row, 1954.

Darwin, Charles. *On the Origin of Species.* Cambridge, Mass.: Harvard University Press, 1966.

Dewey, John. *Human Nature and Conduct.* New York: Henry Holt and Co., 1944.

———. *The Quest for Certainty.* New York: G. P. Putnam's Sons, 1960.

———. *Reconstruction in Philosophy.* New York: New American Library, 1950.

Documents on the Sino-Indian Boundary Question. Beijing: Foreign Languages Press, 1960.

Eisenhower, Dwight D. *Mandate for Change, 1953-1956.* Garden City, N.Y.: Doubleday, 1963.

"Excerpts from Text of Chou's Interview with Tokyo Editor, October 28, 1971." *NYT,* November 9, 1971.

Franklin, Bruce, ed. *The Essential Stalin: Major Theoretical Writings, 1905-1952.* Garden City, N.Y.: Doubleday, 1972.

Further Documents Relating to the Discussion of Indo-China at the Geneva Conference, June 16-July 21, 1954. New York: Greenwood Press, 1968.

Hsiao, Tso-liang, comp. *Power Relations within the Chinese Communist Movement, 1930-1934. Vol. 2: The Chinese Documents.* Seattle: University of Washington Press, 1967.

The Important Documents of the First Plenary Session of the CPPCC. Peking: Foreign Languages Press, 1949.

In Quest—Poems of Zhou Enlai. Translated by Nancy T. Lin. Hong Kong: Joint Publishing Company, 1979.

Kissinger, Henry A. *White House Years.* Boston: Little, Brown, 1979.

———. *Years of Upheaval.* Boston: Little, Brown, 1982.

Legge, James, trans. *The Chinese Classics: Confucian Analects, the Great Learning, the Doctrine of the Mean.* Hong Kong: Hong Kong University, 1968.

Lenin, V.I. *Selected Works.* New York: International Publishers, 1943.

———. *Selected Works.* 3 vols. New York: International Publishers, 1967.

Mao, Zedong. *Selected Works of Mao Tse-tung.* 5 vols. Beijing: Foreign Languages Press, 1965-77.

Marx, Karl, and Friedrich Engels. *The Communist Manifesto.* New York: International Publishers, 1932.

National People's Congress. *Documents of the First Session of the First National People's Congress of the PRC.* Beijing: Foreign Languages Press, 1955.

Nixon, Richard M. "Asia after Viet Nam." *Foreign Affairs,* vol. 45, no. 1 (October 1967).

———. *Public Papers of the President of the United States, 1969.* Washington, D.C.: Government Printing Office, 1971.

———. *The Memoirs of Richard Nixon.* New York: Grosset and Dunlop, 1978.

———. *U.S. Foreign Policy for the 1970s: A New Strategy for Peace.* Washington, D.C.: Government Printing Office, 1970.

"Official Transcript of the Wide-Ranging Interview with Premier Chou Enlai, August 9, 1971." *NYT,* August 10, 1971.

"Premier Chou Answers Questions of the Middle East News Agency." *PR,* vol. 8, no. 15 (April 19, 1965).

"Premier Chou on China's Stand on African-Asian Conference, September 8, 1965." *PR,* vol. 8, no. 38 (September 17, 1965).

"Premier Chou's Four-Point Statement on China's Policy toward the U.S." *PR,* vol. 9, no. 20 (May 13, 1966).

"Premier Chou Enlai on the Growing Friendship between Chinese and African Peoples." *PR,* vol. 7, no. 1 (January 3, 1964).

"Premier Chou En-lai's Report on His Visit to Fourteen Countries, March 24, 1964." *PR,* vol. 7, no. 18 (May 1, 1964).

"[Shanghai] Joint Communiqué, February 27, 1972." *DSB,* vol. 66, no. 1708 (March 20, 1972).

"Sino-Algerian Joint Communiqué, December 27, 1963." *PR,* vol. 7, no. 1 (January 3, 1964).

"Sino-Mali Joint Communiqué, January 21, 1964." *PR,* vol. 7, no. 5 (January 31, 1964).

Stalin, J. V. *Works.* Moscow: Foreign Languages Publishing House, 1955.

"Transcript of President Eisenhower's Press on Foreign and Home Affairs, January 19, 1955." *NYT,* January 20, 1955.

Truman, Harry S. *Memoirs: Years of Trial and Hope.* Vol. 2. Garden City, N.Y.: Doubleday, 1956.

UN General Assembly. *Document* A/123, November 21, 1949.

U.S. Congress. Senate. Committee on Foreign Relations and Committee on Armed Services. *Joint Hearings, Military Situation in the Far East.* 82d Cong., 1st sess., 1951.

U.S. Department of State. *The China White Paper.* Introduction by Lyman P. Van Slyke. 2 vols. Stanford, Calif.: Stanford University Press, 1967.

————. *Foreign Relations of the United States: Diplomatic Papers, 1944. Vol. 6:* China. Washington, D.C.: Government Printing Office, 1967.

————. *Foreign Relations of the United States: Diplomatic Papers, 1945.* Vol. 7: The Far East: China. Washington, D.C.: Government Printing Office, 1969.

————. *Foreign Relations of the United States, 1951.* Vol. 7, pt. 1. Washington, D.C.: Government Printing Office, 1983.

————. *Foreign Relations of the United States, 1952-1954.* Vol. 16: *The Geneva Conference.* Washington, D.C.: Government Printing Office, 1981.

————. *Foreign Relations of the United States, 1955-1957.* Vol. 3: *China.* Washington, D.C.: Government Printing Office, 1986.

U.S. Department of State. *United States Relations with China.* Washington, D.C.: Government Printing Office, 1949.

Van Slyke, Lyman P., intro. *Marshall's Mission to China,* December 1945-January 1947. 2 vols. Arlington, Va.: University Publications of America, 1976.

White Papers: Notes, Memoranda and Letters Exchanged between the Governments of India and China. 8 vols. New Delhi: Government of India, 1959-63.

Zhou Enlai. *China and the Asian-African Conference.* Beijing: Foreign Languages Press, 1955.

————. *The First Year of People's China.* Bombay: People's Publishing House, 1950.

————. *A Great Decade.* Beijing: Foreign Languages Press, 1959.

————. *On the Present International Situation, China's Foreign Policy and the Liberation of Taiwan.* Beijing: Foreign Languages Press, 1956.

————. *Report on the Work of Government.* Beijing: Foreign Languages Press, 1959.

————. *Selected Works of Zhou Enlai.* Vol. 1. Beijing: Foreign Languages Press, 1981.

———. "Speech at the Central People's Government, June 28, 1950." *People's China*, vol. 2, no. 2 (July 16, 1950).

———. "Speech at Rumania's National Day Reception, August 23, 1968." *PR*, supplement to no. 34 (August 23, 1968). The speech was first published in *RMRB*, July 20, 1968.

———. "Speech Delivered at the 21st Congress of the CPSU, January 28, 1958." *PR*, vol. 2, no. 5 (February 3, 1958).

———. "Speech Delivered to the Political Committee of the Asian-African Conference at Bandung, April 23, 1965." *NYT*, April 15, 1955.

Secondary English and Chinese Sources

Acheson, Dean G. *The Pattern of Responsibility*. Edited by McGeorge Bundy. Boston: Houghton Mifflin, 1951.

———. *Present at the Creation: My Years in the State Department*. New York: W. W. Norton, 1969.

Adie, A. C. "Chou En-lai on Safari." *CQ*, no. 18 (April-June 1964).

Archer, Jules. *Chou En-lai*. New York: Hawthorn Books, 1973.

Armstrong, J. D. *Revolutionary Diplomacy*. Berkeley: University of California Press, 1977.

Backman, David. *Bureaucracy, Economy and Leadership in China*. Cambridge: Cambridge University Press, 1991.

Balazs, Etienne. *Political Theory and Administrative Reality in Traditional China*. London: School of Oriental and African Studies, University of London, 1965.

Barnett, A. Doak. *Bureaucracy and Political Power in Communist China*. New York: Columbia University Press, 1967.

———. *China after Mao*. Princeton, N.J.: Princeton University Press, 1967.

———. *China and the Major Powers in East Asia*. New York: Brookings Institution, 1977.

———. "Chou En-lai at Bandung." *American University Field Staff Reports*, no. ADB-1955-4 (May 4, 1955).

———. *The Making of Foreign Policy in China: Structure and Process*. Boulder, Colo.: Westview Press, 1985.

———. *Uncertain Passage: China's Transition to the Post-Mao Era*. Washington, D.C.: Brookings Institution, 1974.

Baskin, Wade, ed. *Classics in Chinese Philosophy*. New York: Philosophical Library, 1972.

Beal, John Robinson. *Marshall in China*. Garden City, N.Y.: Doubleday, 1970.

Beloff, Max. *Soviet Policy in the Far East, 1944-1951*. London: Oxford University Press, 1953.

Bianco, Lucian. *Origins of the Chinese Revolution, 1915-1949*. Stanford, Calif.: Stanford University Press, 1971.

Bisson, T. A. *Yenan in June 1937: Talks with Communist Leaders*. Berkeley, Calif.: Center for China Studies, 1973.

Black, Cyril E., Richard A. Falk, Klaus Knorr, and Oran R. Young. *Neutralization and World Politics*. Princeton, N.J.: Princeton University Press, 1968.

Boorman, Howard L., ed. *Biographical Dictionary of Republican China*. New York: Columbia University Press, 1967.

Bourne, Kenneth. *The Foreign Policy of Victorian England, 1830-1902*. Oxford: Clarendon Press, 1970.

Boyd, R. G. *Communist Chinese Foreign Policy*. New York: Praeger, 1962.

Braun, Otto. *A Communist Agent in China, 1932-1939*. Stanford, Calif.: Stanford University Press, 1982.

Bridgham, Phillip. "The Fall of Lin Piao." *CQ*, no. 55 (July-September 1973).

———. "Mao's Cultural Revolution: The Struggle to Seize Power." *CQ*, no. 41 (January-March 1979).

Brzezinski, Zbigniew. *The Soviet Bloc*. Rev. ed. Cambridge, Mass.: Harvard University Press, 1976.

Buhite, Russell D. *Patrick J. Hurley and American Foreign Policy*. Ithaca, N.Y.: Cornell University Press, 1973.

Calvocoress, Peter. *Survey of International Affairs, 1949-50*. London: Oxford University Press for Royal Institute of International Affairs, 1954.

Camilleri, Joseph. *Chinese Foreign Policy: The Maoist Era and Its Aftermath*. Seattle: University of Washington Press, 1980.

Ch'an, Wing-tsit. *A Source Book in Chinese Philosophy*. Princeton, N.J.: Princeton University Press, 1963.

Chang, David W. *Zhou Enlai and Deng Xiaoping in the Chinese Leadership Succession Crisis*. Lanhan, Md.: University Press of America, 1984.

Chang, Kuo-t'ao. *The Rise of Chinese Communist Party, 1928-1938*. 2 vols. Lawrence: University of Kansas Press, 1972.

Chang, Parris H. *Power and Policy in China*. University Park: Pennsylvania State University Press, 1975.

Charles, David A. "The Dismissal of Marshall P'eng Teh-huai." *CQ*, no. 8 (October-December 1961).

Chavan, R. S. *Chinese Foreign Policy: The Chou Enlai Era*. New Delhi: Sterling Publishers, 1974.

352 Kuo-kang Shao

Ch'en, Jerome. *Mao and the Chinese Revolution.* New York: Oxford University Press, 1965.

Chen, King. *Vietnam and China 1938-1954.* Princeton, N.J.: Princeton University Press, 1969.

Ch'en Kung-po. *The Communist Movement in China.* East Asian Institute Series no. 1. New York: Columbia University, 1960.

Chen, Lung-chu, and Harold D. Lasswell. *Formosa, China, and the United Nations: Formosa in the World Community.* New York: St. Martin's Press, 1967.

Chen, Theodore H. E. *The Chinese Communist Regime: Documents and Commentary.* New York: Praeger, 1967.

Chern, Kenneth S. *Dilemma in China: America's Policy Debate, 1945.* Hamden, Conn.: Shoe String Press, 1980.

Ch'i, Hsi-sheng. *Warlord Politics in China, 1916-1928.* Stanford, Calif.: Stanford University Press, 1976.

Chi, Madeleine. *China Diplomacy, 1914-1918.* Cambridge, Mass.: Harvard University, East Asian Research Center, 1970.

Chi, Wen-shun. *Ideological Conflicts in Democracy and Authoritarianism.* New Brunswick, N.J.: Transaction Books, 1986.

Chiang, Kai-shek. *Soviet Policy in China: A Summing Up at Seventy.* New York: Farrar, 1957.

Choudhury, G. W. *Chinese Perceptions of the World.* Washington, D.C.: University Press of America, 1971.

Chow, Ts'e-tsung. *The May Fourth Movement: Intellectual Revolution in Modern China.* Cambridge, Mass.: Harvard University Press, 1960.

Clubb, O. Edmund. *Twentieth Century China.* New York: Columbia University Press, 1964.

Cohen, Jerome, and Hungdah Chu, eds. *People's China and International Law.* Princeton, N.J.: Princeton University Press, 1974.

Cohen, Warren I. *America's Response to China: An Interpretative History of Sino-American Relations.* New York: John Wiley and Sons, 1971.

Crankshaw, Edward. *Khrushchev Remembers.* Boston: Little, Brown, 1970.

Dallin, David J. *Soviet Foreign Policy after Stalin.* Philadelphia: J. B. Lippincott, 1961.

de Bary, Wm. Theodore. *Neo-Confucian Orthodoxy and the Learning of Mind-and-Heart.* New York: Columbia University Press, 1981.

———. *The Unfolding of Neo-Confucianism.* New York: Columbia University Press, 1970.

de Bary, Wm. Theodore, and Irene Bloom, eds. *Principle and Practicality: Essays in Neo-Confucianism and Practical Learning*. New York: Columbia University Press, 1979.

Devillers, Phillipe, and J. Lacouture. *End of a War*. New York: Praeger, 1969.

Dittmer, Lowell. "Bases of Power in Chinese Politics: A Theory and Analysis of the Fall of the 'Gang of Four.'" *World Politics*, vol. 31, no. 1 (October 1978).

———. *Liu Shao-ch'i and the Chinese Cultural Revolution*. Berkeley: University of California Press, 1975.

Doolin, Dennis J. *Territorial Claims in the Sino-Soviet Conflict: Documents and Analysis*. Stanford, Calif.: Stanford University Press, 1965.

Dreyer, June T. *China's Political System: Modernization and Tradition*. New York: Paragon House, 1993.

Drummond, Roscoe, and Gaston Coblentz. *Duel at the Brink: John Foster Dulles' Command of American Power*. London: Widenfeld and Nicolson, 1961.

Dulles, Foster Rhea. *China and America: The Story of Their Relations since 1784*. Princeton, N.J.: Princeton University Press, 1964.

Ebon, Martin. *Lin Piao: The Life and Writings of China's Leader*. New York: Stein and Day, 1970.

Edmonds, Robin. *Soviet Foreign Policy, 1963-1973: The Paradox of Superpowers*. London: Oxford University Press, 1975.

Elster, Jon, ed. *Karl Marx: A Reader*. London: Cambridge University Press, 1986.

Fairbank, John K. *China Perceived: Images and Policies in Chinese-American Relations*. New York: Alfred A. Knopf, 1974.

Fang, Percy, and Lucy Fang. *Zhou Enlai—A Profile*. Beijing: Foreign Languages Press, 1986.

Feis, Herbert. *The China Tangle: The American Effort in China from Pearl Harbor to the Marshall Mission*. Princeton, N.J.: Princeton University Press, 1953.

Ferrel, Robert H. *George C. Marshall*. New York: Cooper Square Publishers, 1967.

Fisher, Donald. "Chou En-lai, A Life Style Analysis Based on Aldevian Psychological Theory." Ph.D. diss., United States International University, San Diego, 1981.

Fisher, Margaret W., and Joan U. Bondurant. *Indian Views of Sino-Indian Relations*. Berkeley: University of California Press, 1956.

FitzGerald, Steven. "Impression of China's New Diplomacy: The Australian Experience." *CQ*, no. 481 (October-December 1971).

Frankel, Joseph. "Towards a Decision-Making Model in Foreign Policy." *Political Studies,* vol. 7, no. 1 (February 1959).

Fung, Yu-lan. *A History of Chinese Philosophy.* Vol. 2. Translated by Derk Bodde. Princeton, N.J.: Princeton University Press, 1953.

Gardner, John. *Chinese Politics and the Succession to Mao.* London: Macmillan, 1982.

Garthoff, Raymond L., ed. *Sino-Soviet Military Relations.* New York: Praeger, 1966.

Garver, John W. *China's Decision for Rapprochement with the United States, 1968-1971.* Boulder, Colo.: Westview Press, 1982.

————. "The Origins of the Second United Front: The Comintern and the Chinese Communist Party." *CQ,* no. 113 (March 1958).

Gittings, John. *Survey of the Sino-Soviet Dispute: A Commentary and Extracts from the Recent Polemics, 1963-1967.* New York: Oxford University Press, 1968.

Goldstein, Steven. "Zhou Enlai and China's Revolution: A Selective View." *CQ,* no. 96 (December 1983).

Goncharov, Sergei N., John W. Lewis, and Xue Litai. *Uncertain Partners: Stalin, Mao and the Korean War.* Stanford, Calif.: Stanford University Press, 1993.

Gottlieb, Thomas M. *Chinese Foreign Policy: Factionalism and the Origins of the Strategic Triangle.* Santa Barbara, Calif.: Rand Corporation, 1977.

Gray, Colins. *The Geopolitics of Superpower.* Lexington: University of Kentucky Press, 1988.

Grieder, Jerome B. *Hu Shih and the Chinese Renaissance. Cambridge, Mass.: Harvard University Press, 1970.*

Griffith, William. *Sino-Soviet Relations, 1964-1965.* Cambridge, Mass.: MIT Press, 1967.

Gross, Feliks. *Foreign Policy Analysis.* New York: Philosophical Library, 1954.

Guhin, Michael A. *John Foster Dulles: A Statesman and His Times.* New York: Columbia University Press, 1972.

Gurtov, Melvin. "The Foreign Ministry and Foreign Affairs during the Cultural Revolution." *CQ,* no. 40 (October-December 1969).

Gurtov, Melvin, and Byong-Moo Hwang. *China under Threat: The Politics of Strategy and Diplomacy.* Baltimore: John's Hopkins University Press, 1980.

Halpern, A. M. "The Communist Line on Neutralism." *CQ,* no. 5 (January-March 1961).

Halpern, Morton H. *China and the Bomb.* New York: Praeger, 1965.

Han, Suyin. *Eldest Son: Zhou Enlai and the Making of ModernChina, 1898-1976.* New York: Hill and Wang, 1994.

Hao, Yu-fan, and Zhai Zhiha. "China's Decision to Enter the Korean War: History Revisited." *CQ,* no. 121 (March 1990).

Harding, Harry. *A Fragile Relationship: The United States and China since 1972.* Washington, D.C.: Brookings Institution, 1972.

Hinton, Harold. *The Bear at the Gate.* Stanford, Calif.: Hoover Institution of War, Peace, and Revolution, 1971.

Hsiao, Gene T., ed. *Sino-American Debate and Its Policy Implications.* New York: Praeger, 1974.

Hsiao, Gene T., and Michael Witunski, eds. *Sino-American Normalization and Its Policy Implications.* New York: Praeger, 1983.

Hsieh, Alice L. *Communist Strategy in the Nuclear Era.* Englewood Cliffs, N.J.: Prentice-Hall, 1962.

Hsu, Immanuel C. Y. *The Rise of Modern China.* Oxford: Oxford University Press, 1983.

Hsu, Kai-yu. "Chou En-lai." In *Revolutionary Leaders of Modern China.* Edited by Chun-tu Hsueh. New York: Oxford University Press, 1971.

———. *Chou En-lai: China's Gray Eminence.* Garden City,N.Y.: Doubleday, 1968.

———. "Chou En-lai: The Indispensable Man of Compromise." *New Republic,* vol. 156, no. 14 (8 April 1967).

Houn, Franklin W. "Communist China's New Constitution." *The Western Political Quarterly,* vol. 8 (June 1955).

Hu, Hua. *The Early Life of Zhou Enlai.* Beijing: Foreign Languages Press, 1980.

———. *The Story of Premier Zhou's Childhood.* Shengyang: Liaoning People's Press, 1979.

———. *The Young Comrade Zhou Enlai.* Beijing: China Youth Press, 1977.

Huai, En. *The Youth of Zhou Enlai.* Chongqing: Sicuan People's Press, 1980.

Hughes, T. J., and D. E. T. Luard. *The Economic Development of Communist China, 1949-1960.* London: Oxford University Press, 1959.

Huxley, T. H., and Julian Huxley. *Evolution of Ethics, 1893-1943.* London: Pilot Press, 1947.

Iriye, Akira. *The Cold War in Asia: A Historical Introduction.* Englewood Cliffs, N.J.: Prentice-Hall, 1974.

Isaacs, Harold R. *The Tragedy of the Chinese Revolution.* Stanford, Calif.: Stanford University Press, 1951.

Jacobs, Dan N. *Borodin: Stalin's Man in China.* Cambridge, Mass.: Harvard University Press, 1981.

Jain, R. K., ed. *China-South Asian Relations, 1949-1980. Vol. 1.* New Delhi: Radiant Publishers, 1981.

Jan, George P. "The Ministry of Foreign Affairs in China since the Cultural Revolution." *Asian Survey,* vol. 17, no. 6 (June 1977).

Jin Chongji, ed. *Zhou Enlai zhuan, 1898-1949* (Biography of Zhou Enlai, 1898-1949). Beijing: Ren-min-chu-ban-she, 1989.

Joff, Ellis. "The Chinese Army after the Cultural Revolution: the Effects of Intervention." *CQ,* no. 55 (July-September 1973).

Johnson, U. Alexis. *The Right Hand of Power.* Englewood Cliffs, N.J.: Prentice-Hall, 1984.

Kahin, George McT. *The Asian-African Conference, Bandung, Indonesia.* Ithaca, N.Y.: Cornell University Press, 1956.

———, ed. *Major Governments of Asia.* Ithaca, N.Y.: Cornell University Press, 1963.

Kalb, Marvin, and Bernard Kalb. *Kissinger.* Boston: Little, Brown, 1974.

Kalick, J. H. *The Pattern of Sino-American Crises: Political and Military Interactions in the 1950s.* Cambridge: Cambridge University Press, 1975.

Keith, Ronald C. *The Diplomacy of Zhou Enlai.* New York: St. Martin's Press, 1989.

———. "The Origins and Strategic Implications of China's Independent Foreign Policy." *International Journal,* vol. 41, no. 1 (Winter 1985-86).

Kennan, George F. *Memoirs (1925-1950).* Boston: Little, Brown, 1967.

Kissinger, Henry A. *Nuclear Weapons and Foreign Policy.* New York: Harper Brothers, 1957.

Klein, Donald. "The Management of Foreign Affairs in Communist China." In *China: Management of a Revolutionary Society.* Edited by John Lindbeck. Seattle: University of Washington Press, 1971.

———. "The State Council and the Cultural Revolution." *CQ,* no. 35 (July-September 1968).

Klein, Donald W. "Peking's Evolving Ministry of Foreign Affairs." *CQ,* no. 4 (October-December 1960).

Klein, Donald W., and Anne B. Clark, eds. *Biographic Dictionary of Chinese Communism, 1921-1965. 2 vols.* Cambridge, Mass.: Harvard University Press, 1971.

Larkin, Bruce D. *China and Africa, 1949-1970: The Foreign Policy of the People's Republic of China.* Berkeley: University of California Press, 1971.

Lasater, Martin. *The Taiwan Issue in Sino-American Strategic Relations. Boulder,* Colo.: Westview Press, 1984.

Lee, Chae-jin. *Zhou Enlai: The Early Years*. Stanford, Calif.: Stanford University Press, 1994.

Lee, Feigon. *Chen Duxiu: Founder of the Chinese Communist Party*. Princeton, N.J.: Princeton University Press, 1983.

Levine, Steven I. "Perception and Ideology in Chinese Foreign Policy." In *Chinese Foreign Policy: Theory and Practice*. Edited by Thomas W. Robinson and David Shambaugh. Oxford: Clarendon Press, 1994.

Lewis, John Wilson, and Xue Li-tai. "Strategic Weapons and Chinese Power: The Formative Years." *CQ*, no. 1121 (December 1987).

Li, Rui. *Mao Zedong tong-zhi di zao-qi qe-ming huo-dong* (The Early Revolutionary Activities of Comrade Mao Zedong). Beijing: Zhong-guo qing-nian chu-ban-she, 1957.

Li, Tien-min. *Chou En-lai*. Taipei: Institute of International Relations, 1970.

———. *Liu Shaoch'i*. Taipei: Institute of International Relations, 1975.

———. "A Review of the Selected Writings of Chou En-lai." *Issues and Studies*, vol. 17, no. 5 (May 1981).

Liang, Ch'i-chao. *Intellectual Trends in the Ch'ing Period*. Translated by Immanuel C. Y. Hsu. Cambridge, Mass.: Harvard University Press, 1959.

Lieberthal, Kenneth. *Sino-Soviet Conflict in the 1970s: Its Evaluation and Implication for the Strategic Triangle*. Santa Monica, Calif.: Rand Corporation, 1978.

Lieberthal, Kenneth, and Michel Oksenberg. *Policymaking in China: Leaders, Structure, and Processes*. Princeton, N.J.: Princeton University Press, 1988.

Lindbeck, John M. H., ed. *China: Management of a Revolutionary Society*. Seattle: University of Washington Press, 1971.

Liu, Alan P. L. *How China Is Ruled*. Englewood Cliffs, N.J.: Prentice-Hall, 1986.

Liu Xiao. *Chu-shi Su-lian ban-nian* (Eight Years as Ambassador to the Soviet Union). Beijing: Zong-gong dang-shi zi-liao chu-ban-she, 1986.

Lo Ruiqing, Lu Zheng-cao, and Wang Bing-nan. *Xi'an shi-bian he* Zhou Enlai tong-zhi (The Xi'an Incident and Comrade Zhou Enlai). Beijing: Ren-min-chu-ban-she, 1978. London, Kurt. *New Nations in a Divided World*. New York: Praeger, 1965.

Lu, David John. *Sources of Japanese History*. 2 vols. New York: McGraw-Hill, 1973.

Luhbeck, Don. *Patrick J. Hurley*. Chicago: Henry Regnery, 1956.

Lull, Arthur. *How Communist China Negotiates*. New York: Columbia University Press, 1958.

Lyon, Peter. *Neutralism*. Leicester, Eng.: Leicester University Press, 1963.

MacFarquhar, Roderick. *The Origins of the Cultural Revolution. Vol. 1*. New York: Columbia University Press, 1974.

———. *Sino-American Relations, 1949-71*. New York: Praeger,1972.

MacNair, Harley F., and Donald F. Lach. *Modern Far Eastern International Relations*. New York: Octagon Books, 1975.

Maxwell, Neville. "The Chinese Account of the 1969 Fighting at Chen Pao." *CQ*, no. 56 (October-December 1973).

McLane, Charles B. *Soviet Policy and the Chinese Communists, 1931-1946*. New York: Columbia University Press, 1958.

McLellan, David. *Karl Marx: Selected Readings*. London: Oxford University Press, 1977.

McMorran, Ian. "Wang Fu-chih and the Neo-Confucian Tradition." In *The Unfolding of Neo-Confucianism*, Edited by Wm. Theodore de Bary. New York: Columbia University Press, 1970.

Medvedev, Roy. *China and the Superpowers*. Oxford: Basil Blackwell, 1986.

Meisner, Maurice. *Li Ta-chao and the Origins of Chinese Communism*. Cambridge, Mass.: Harvard University Press, 1967.

Melby, John F. *The Mandate of Heaven: Record of a Civil War China, 1945-1949*. Toronto: University of Toronto Press, 1968.

Modelski, George. *International Conference on the Laotian Question, 1961-1962*. Canberra: Australian National University, 1962.

Montgomery, Bernard. "China on the Move." *Sunday Times* (London), October 15, 1961.

Morgenthau, Hans J. *In Defense of the National Interest: A Critical Examination of American Foreign Policy*. New York: Alfred A. Knopf, 1951.

Mui, Loncoln Ying-tso. "Chou En-lai: A Study of Political Leadership Behaviour." Ph.D. diss., University of Notre Dame, 1977.

Ness, Peter Van. *Revolution and Chinese Foreign Policy: Peking's Support for Wars of National Liberation. Berkeley: University of California Press, 1970*.

Neuhauser, Charles. *Third World Politics*. Cambridge, Mass.: Harvard University, East Asian Research Center, 1968.

Nicolson, Harold. *Diplomacy*. London: Oxford University Press, 1937.

Nie Rongzhen. *Nie Rongzhen hui-yi-lu* (Memoirs of Nie Rongzhen). Beijing: Jie-fan chu-ban-she, 1984.

Nishikawa, Takashi. *The Path of Zhou Enlai*. Tokyo: Tokuma shoten, 1976.

Ojha, Ishwer. *Chinese Foreign Policy in an Age of Transition: The Diplomacy of Cultural Despair. Boston: Beacon Press, 1972*.

Oksenberg, Michael C. "Policy-Making under Mao, 1949-1968: An Overview." In *China: Management of a Revolutionary Society*. Edited by John M. H. Lindbeck. Seattle: University of Washington Press, 1971.

Oksenberg, Michel, and Robert B. Oxnam. *China and America: Past and Future.* New York: Foreign Policy Association, 1977.

Oppose U.S. Occupation of Taiwan and "Two Chinas" Plot. Peking: Foreign Languages Press, 1958.

Panikkar, K. M. *In Two Chinas.* London: Allen and Unwin, 1955.

Pogue, Forrest C. *George Marshall: Statesman 1945-1959.* New York: Viking Penguin, 1987.

Powell, Ralph L. "The Increasing Power of Lian Piao and the Party-Soldiers, 1959-1966." *CQ,* no. 34 (April-June 1968).

Pusey, Reeve. *China and Charles Darwin.* Cambridge, Mass.: Council on East Asian Studies, Harvard University Press, 1966.

Pye, Lucian. "On Chinese Pragmatism in the 1980s." *CQ,* no. 16 (June 1986).

———. *Warlord Politics: Conflict and Coalition in the Modernization of Republican China.* New York: Praeger, 1971.

Ra'anan, Uri. "Peking's Foreign Policy 'Debate,' 1965-1966." In *China in Crisis: China's Policy in Asia and America's Alternatives.* Vol. 2. Edited by Tang Tsou. Chicago: University of Chicago Press, 1968.

Reardon-Anderson, James. *Yenan and the Great Powers: The Origins of Chinese Communist Foreign Policy, 1944-1946.* New York: Columbia University Press, 1980.

Robinson, Thomas W. "Chou Enlai's Political Style: Comparisons with Mao Tse-tung and Lin Piao." *Asian Survey,* vol. 10, no. 12 (December 1970).

———, ed. *The Cultural Revolution in China.* Berkeley: University of California Press, 1971.

———. "The Sino-Soviet Border Dispute: Background, Development, and the March 1969 Clashes." *American Political Science Review,* vol. 66, no. 4 (December 1972).

Robinson, Thomas W., and David Shambaugh, eds. *Chinese Foreign Policy: Theory and Practice.* Oxford: Clarendon Press, 1994.

Roots, John McCook. *Chou: An Informal Biography of China's Legendary Chou En-lai.* Garden City, N.Y.: Doubleday, 1978.

Rosecrance, R. N., ed. *The Dispersion of Nuclear Weapons: Strategy and Politics.* New York: Praeger, 1964.

Royal Institute of International Affairs. *Documents on International Affairs: 1951.* London: Oxford University Press, 1954.

———. *Documents on International Affairs: 1955.* London: Oxford University Press, 1958.

————. *Survey of International Affairs: 1952.* London: Oxford University Press, 1955.

Ryan, William L., and Sam Summerlin. *The China Cloud: America's Tragic Blunder and China's Rise to Nuclear Power.* Boston: Little, Brown, 1967.

Satow, Sir Ernest. *A Guide to Diplomatic Practice.* London: Longman's Green, 1957.

Scalapino, Robert. *On the Trail of Chou En-lai in Africa.* Santa Monica, Calif.: Rand Corporation, 1964.

Schaller, Michael. *The U.S. Crusade in China, 1938-1945.* New York: Columbia University Press, 1978.

Schram, Stuart R. *The Political Thought of Mao Tse-tung.* Revised and enlarged ed. New York: Praeger, 1969.

Schurmann, Franz. *Ideology and Organization in Communist China.* Berkeley: University of California Press, 1966.

Schwarcz, Vera. *The Chinese Enlightenment: Intellectuals and Legacy of the May Fourth Movement of 1919.* Berkeley: University of California Press, 1986.

Schwartz, Benjamin. *In Search of Wealth and Power and the West.* Cambridge, Mass.: Harvard University Press, 1964.

————. *Chinese Communism and the Rise of Mao.* Cambridge, Mass.: Harvard University Press, 1951.

Shao, Hsi-ping. "From the Twenty-one Demands to the Sino-Japanese Agreement, 1915-1918: Ambivalent Relations." In *China and Japan: Search for Balance Since World War I.* Edited by Alvin D. Coox and Hilary Conroy. Santa Barbara, Calif.: Clio Books, 1978.

————. "Tuan Chi-jui, 1912-1918: A Case Study of the Military Influence on the Chinese Political Development." Ph.D. diss., University of Pennsylvania, 1976.

Shao, Kuo-kang. "Chou En-lai's Diplomatic Approach to Non-Aligned States in Asia, 1953-1960." *CQ,* no. 78 (June 1979).

————. "Communist China's Foreign Policy toward the Non-Aligned States with Special Reference to India and Burma, 1949-1962." Ph.D. diss., University of Pennsylvania, 1972.

————. "Zhou Enlai's Diplomacy and the Neutralization of Indo-China, 1954-55." *CQ,* no. 107 (September 1986).

Sheridan, James E. *Chinese Warlord: The Career of feng Yu-hsiang.* Stanford, Calif.: Stanford University Press, 1966.

Simmons, Robert. *Strained Alliance: Peking, Pyongyang, Moscow and the Politics of Korean Civil War.* New York: Free Press, 1975.

Snow, Edgar. *The Long Revolution.* London: Hutchinson, 1973.

———. *The Other Side of the River.* New York: Random House, 1962.

———. *Random Notes on Red China, 1936-1945.* Cambridge, Mass.: Harvard University Press, 1974.

———. *Red Star over China.* New York: Random House, 1938. Snyder, Richard C., and Burton Sapin. *Decision-Making as an Approach to the Study of International Politics.* Princeton, N.J.: Princeton University Press, 1954.

Solomon, Richard H. *Mao's Revolution and the Chinese Political Culture. Berkeley: University of California Press, 1971.*

Steiner, H. Arthur. "Constitutionalism in Communist China." *The American Political Science Review, vol. 49, no. 1 (March 1955).*

Strategic Survey, 1970. London: Institute for Strategic Studies, 1971.

Talbott, Strobe, ed. *Khrushchev Remembers.* Boston: Little, Brown, 1970.

Tang, Peter S. H. *The Twenty-Second Congress of the Communist Party of the Soviet Union and Moscow-Tirana-Peking Relations. Washington, D.C.: Research Institute on the Sino-Soviet Bloc, 1962.*

Teiwes, Frederick C. *Leadership, Legitimacy, and Conflict in China.* New York: M. E. Sharpe, 1984.

Teng, Ssu-yu. "Wang Fu-chih's Views on History and Historical Writing." *Journal of Asian Studies,* vol. 28, no. 1 (November 1968).

Ten, Ssu, and John K. Fairbank. *China's Response to the West: A Documentary Survey, 1839-1923.* Cambridge, Mass.: Harvard University Press, 1954.

Terrill, Ross. *A Biography of Mao.* New York: Harper and Row, 1980.

Thomas, John. "The Limits of Alliance: The Quemoy Crisis of 1958." In *Sino-Soviet Military Relations.* Edited by Raymond L. Garthoff. New York: Praeger, 1966.

Thomson, James C., Jr. "The Communist Party and the United Front in China, 1935-1936." *Papers on China.* Photocopy. Harvard University, 1957.

Thompson, Kenneth W., and Roy C. Macridis. "The Comparative Study of Foreign Policy." In *Foreign Policy in Modern Politics.* Edited by Roy C. Macridis. Englewood Cliffs, N.J.: Prentice-Hall, 1958.

Thorton, Richard C. *China: The Struggle for Power, 1917-1972.* Bloomington: Indiana University Press, 1973.

Townsend, James R. *Political Participation in Communist China.* Berkeley: University of California Press, 1968.

Tsou, Tang. *American Failure in China 1941-1950.* Chicago: University of Chicago Press, 1963.

————. ed. *China in Crisis: China's Policy in Asia and America's Alternatives.* 2 vols. Chicago: University of Chicago Press, 1968.

————. "The Cultural Revolution and the Chinese Political System. " *CQ,* no. 38 (April-June 1969).

Tucker, Robert C. *The Marx-Engels Reader.* New York: W. W. Norton, 1978.

Van Slyke, Lyman P. *Enemies and Friends: The United Front in Chinese Communist History.* Stanford, Calif.: Stanford University Press, 1967.

Vigor, Peter H. *A Guide to Marxism.* New York: Humanities Press, 1966.

Wales, Nym. *Inside Red China.* New York: Doubleday, Doran and Company, 1939.

Waller, D. J. *The Government and Politics of Communist China.* London: Hutchinson University Library, 1970.

Wang, Bingnan. *Zhong-Mei hui-tan jiu-nian hui-gu* (Recollections of the Nine-Year Sino-American Talks). Beijing: Shi-jie-zhi-shi chu-ban-she, 1985.

Weidenbaum, Rhoda. "Chou En-lai, Creative Revolutionary." Ph.D. diss., University of Connecticut, 1981.

Whiting, Allen S. *China Crosses the Yalu.* New York: Macmillan, 1960.

————. *The Chinese Calculus of Deterrence.* Ann Arbor: University of Michigan Press, 1975.

————. *Soviet Policies in China, 1917-1924.* New York: Columbia University Press, 1954.

Wich, Richard. "The Tenth Party Congress: The Power Structure and Succession Question." *CQ,* no. 58 (April-June 1974).

Wilson, Dick. *Zhou Enlai: A Biography.* New York: Viking Penguin, 1984.

Wilson, John Lewis. *Leadership in Communist China.* Ithaca, N.Y.: Cornell University Press, 1963.

Wu, Xiuquan. *Zai-wai-jiao-bu ba-nian de jing-li* (Eight-Year Experience in the Ministry of Foreign Affairs). Beijing: Shie-jie zhi-shi chu-ban-she, 1983.

Wusi shi-qi-de she-tuan (Student Societies of the May Fourth Period). 4 vols. Beijing: Zhong-guo she-hui-ke-xue chu-ban-she, 1979.

Yahuda, Michael B. *China's Role in World Affairs.* New York: St. Martin's Press, 1978.

Yan Fu. *Tian-yan-lun* (The Theory of Evolution). Taipei: Shang-wu Publishing Co., 1967.

Yang Rong-guo, *et al. Jian-ming Zhong-guo zhe-xue-shi* (Brief History of Chinese Philosophy). Beijing: Ren-min-chu-ban-she, 1973.

Yen, Ching-wen. *Zhou Enlai ping-zhuan* (Biography of Zhou Enlai). Hong Kong: Po Wen Books, 1974.

Young, Kenneth T. *Negotiating with the Chinese Communists: The United Experience, 1953-1967.* New York: McGraw-Hill, 1958.

Zagoria, Donald S. *The Sino-Soviet Conflict, 1956-1961.* Princeton, N.J.: Princeton University Press, 1962.

Zhang, Shu-guang. *Deterrence and Strategic Culture: Chinese-American Confrontations, 1949-1958.* Ithaca, N.Y.: Cornell University Press, 1992.

Zhou Enlai zhuan, 1898-1949 (Biography of Zhou Enlai, 1898-1949). Beijing: Ren-min and zhong-yang wen-xian, 1989.

INDEX